I AM GOD YOUR SAVIOUR

A FORM-CRITICAL STUDY OF THE MAIN GENRES
IN IS. XL-LV

SUPPLEMENTS

TO

VETUS TESTAMENTUM

EDITED BY

THE BOARD OF THE QUARTERLY

VOLUME XXIV

LEIDEN
E. J. BRILL
1973

I AM GOD YOUR SAVIOUR

A FORM-CRITICAL STUDY OF THE MAIN GENRES
IN IS. XL-LV

BY

ANTOON SCHOORS

LEIDEN
E. J. BRILL
1973

ISBN 90 04 03729 2

PRINTED IN BELGIUM

WITH GRATITUDE TO MY PARENTS

TABLE OF CONTENTS

PREFACE

Since H. GUNKEL laid the basis of the form-critical method, Deutero-Isaiah has received particular attention from form-critical scholars, who have devoted some very important studies to the subject. These works are summarized in the first chapter of the present study. Nevertheless, this method has rarely been applied to an understanding of the message of the prophet. The authors have mostly confined themselves to a short study of the structures of each genre, without paying any great attention to the contents. Until recently, there was no single commentary composed according to the form-critical method.

The original intention of this book was to present a complete form-critical commentary of all the pericopes in Is. xl-lv. But the realisation of this intention has often been interrupted by excessive teaching charges and administrative work. Meanwhile the excellent commentary by C. WESTERMANN appeared in *Das Alte Testament Deutsch*, and it has fulfilled to a large degree my wishes. But I am convinced that a second work according to the same method is not yet superfluous, the more so as I have some objections against several interpretations of the German scholar. In order not to delay the publication indefinitely, I decided to confine myself in this work to the two main genres of our prophet, viz. the words of salvation and the polemical genres, by which I understand the trial speeches and the disputations.

I must admit that, this way, several much debated pericopes, such as the so-called Servant Songs, remain undiscussed. But I am convinced that these pericopes do not have the importance they are generally given by the scholars, since originally they are about the prophet himself. They describe his designation and mission. Only chapter liii offers more difficult problems concerning authenticity and interpretation, but, in my opinion, their solution should follow the lines proposed by H.M. ORLINSKY in *Supplements to Vetus Testamentum* XIV. An analysis of the two genres mentioned above, permits us to grasp some very important components of Dt.-Isaiah's message in their mutual connection.

I express my gratitude to all my teachers who introduced me in the world of the Bible and the Ancient Near East and helped me in acquiring a sound method of scientific research in this field. They are the professors of the Faculty of Theology and the Oriental Institute at

Louvain as well as those of the Pontifical Biblical Institute in Rome. Among them I single out Prof. J. COPPENS, who directed the beginnings of this work, and the late Prof. R. DE LANGHE, who was my first professor of biblical languages. I thank also the Council of the Oriental Institute at Louvain (KUL) for accepting the present work as a doctoral dissertation. To Prof. C. BREKELMANS, the director of this dissertation, I express my sincere gratitude for his help and important corrections. Prof. E. LIPIŃSKI and Prof. L. DEQUEKER read the manuscript and made many valuable suggestions. I am also very much indebted to the Editorial Board of *Vetus Testamentum*, and in particular to Prof. P.A.H. DE BOER, for permitting the publication of this work in the *Supplements to Vetus Testamentum* and making some important remarks. In this connection Prof. E. NIELSEN also should be mentioned. My thanks are due the students M. FITZPATRICK, M. CASEY and A. DROMEY, who improved my English considerably. Finally, I am most grateful to my wife for her continuous encouragement and invaluable help in preparing the manuscript, in proofreading and in composing the indexes.

April, 1972 Antoon SCHOORS

CHAPTER ONE

FORM-CRITICAL STUDIES ON DEUTERO-ISAIAH

In his short history of the literature of Israel, published in 1906, H. Gunkel stressed the necessity of examining the literary genres or types, their proper character and, if possible, their history.[1] Especially concerning the prophets, he indicated the importance of an exact delimitation of the small units. Furthermore, he listed a series of the genres which can be found in the prophetical books, and he posed the problem of the distinction between the genuine and non genuine prophetic forms in these writings.[2] The first one to examine chapters xl-lv of the book of Isaiah according to this method was H. Gressmann.[3] For the first time, he broke through the current conception of Dt.-Is. as one structuralized book by appealing to purely literary considerations. The structural unity of at least part of Dt.-Is., varying from chs. xl-xlviii to xl-lxvi, had thus far almost not been questioned.

Apart from the Jewish commentator Ibn Ezra (12th century) the literary unity of the book of Isaiah was rejected for the first time in the 18th century by J. C. Döderlein (1775) and J. G. Eichhorn (1783).[4] Little by little one started to think of Is. xl-lxvi as the work of an exilic prophet, whose name is unknown to us. This view conquered the whole exegetical world. For a long time catholic scholars felt some hesitation,[5] owing to, among other factors, the decree of the

---

[1] H. Gunkel, "Die israelitische Literatur", *Die orientalischen Literaturen*, Leipzig 1906, p. 52: "So folgt, dass die Literaturgeschichte zunächst die Aufgabe hat, die Gattungen, ihre Eigenart und womöglich auch ihre Geschichte zu erforschen ...".

[2] H. Gunkel, *o.c.*, pp. 82-87.

[3] H. Gressmann, "Die literarische Analyse Deuterojesajas", *ZAW* XXXIV 1914, pp. 254-297.

[4] Cf. M. Friedlander, *The Commentary of Ibn Ezra on Isaiah*, I, London 1873, pp. 170-171; III 1877, p. 64; J. C. Döderlein, *Esaias ex recensione textus hebraei ad fidem codicum manuscriptorum et versionum antiquarum latine vertit notasque varii argumenti subjecit*, Altdorf 1755; 2nd edition, Neurenberg 1789. Neither of these editions was at my disposition. — J. G. Eichhorn, *Einleitung ins alte Testament*, III, Leipzig 1783; 3d edition 1803, pp. 67-84.

[5] Cf. i.a. J. Knabenbauer, *Commentarius in Isaiam prophetam*, II Parisiis 1887, pp. 5-27; F. Vigouroux, *Les Livres Saints et la critique rationaliste*, V, Paris 1891,

Biblical Commission of June 29, 1908 [1]. Even in 1962 S. M. Gozzo defended the traditional image of one Isaiah, author of all 66 chapters.[2] But one can also find defenders of the unity of Isaiah among other Christian and Jewish scholars.[3]

After this important step the critics did not immediately proceed to a further desintegration of the book. It was held to be self-evident that Is. xl-lxvi was the work of one unknown prophet. In his commentary published in 1892 B. DUHM presented for the first time the thesis of a third Isaiah. In his view, Dt.-Is. was limited to chs. xl-lv, in which later additions, especially of the so-called Servant Songs, were to be found. He considered Is. lvi-lxvi as the work of one author who wrote in the time of Ezra.[4] As a matter of fact B. STADE, though

---

pp. 107-125; e.g. pp. 124-125: "Tous les efforts de l'incrédulité pour arracher à Isaïe le plus beau fleuron de sa couronne prophétique sont donc vains et impuissants". — A. VAN HOONACKER, *Het boek Isaias*, Brugge 1932, p. 14, note 1. F. FELDMANN and J. FISCHER hesitate, although we clearly feel their preference to the critical view. Likewise A. FEUILLET does not make clear his standpoint. Cf. F. FELDMANN, *Das Buch Isaias*, II, Münster 1926, pp. 2-14; J. FISCHER, *Das Buch Isaias*, II, Bonn 1939, pp. 2-5 and p. 25; L. DENNEFELD, *Isaïe etc.*, Paris 1947, pp. 147-148; A. FEUILLET, "Isaïe", *DBS*. IV, Paris 1949, col. 690-698.

1 Especially *Dubium V*: "Utrum solida prostent argumenta, etiam cumulative sumpta, ad evincendum Isaiae librum non ipsi soli Isaiae, sed duobus, imo pluribus auctoribus esse tribuendum ? — Resp.: Negative. " Cf. *Dub.* III and IV; *Enchiridion Biblicum*, Romae 1961, n. 278-280.

2 S. M. GOZZO, *La dottrina teologica del libro di Isaia*, Roma 1962, pp. VIII-XVI. Cf. ID., "De catholicorum sententia circa authenticitatem Is. 40-66 inde ab anno 1908", *Antonianum*, XXXII 1957, pp. 369-410; F. SPADAFORA, "Gli esuli del 597 e la seconda parte d'Isaia", *Divinitas*, III 1959, pp. 438-450.

3 E.g. A. RUTGERS, *De echtheid van het tweede gedeelte van Jesaia*, Leiden 1866; C. W. NÄGELSBACH, *Der Prophet Jesaia*, Bielefeld 1877, pp. XXI-XXXII; M. LÖHR, *Zur Frage über die Echtheid von Jesaia 40-66*, Berlin 1878-1879; W. C. COBB, "On Integrating the Book of Isaiah", *JBL*. XX 1901, pp. 77-100; J. RIDDERBOS, *Jesaja*, Kampen 1932, esp, pp. 250-254; J. SCHELHAAS, *De lijdende Knecht des Heeren*, Groningen 1933, pp. 23-32; O. T. ALLIS, *The Unity of Isaiah*, Philadelphia 1950; P. I. BRATSIOTIS, *Ὁ προφήτης Ἡσαΐας*, I, Athens 1956, pp. 8-12; A. KAMINKA, *Le prophète Isaïe*, Paris 1925; R. MARGALIOTH, *The Indivisible Isaiah. Evidence for the Single Authorship of the Prophetic Book*, New York 1964. — At the 5th World Congress of Jewish Studies in Jerusalem (1969), Y. RADDAY read a paper on *Statistical Linguistics and the Problem of the Unity of the Book of Isaiah*, in which he demonstrated how he came to accept the Deutero-Isaiah theory on the ground of his computer analysis.

4 B. DUHM, *Das Buch Jesaja*, 2nd ed., Göttingen 1902, p. XIII; cf. also pp. XVII-XIX. I was not able to consult the first edition. DUHM had already insisted on the distinct literary character of the Servant Songs, over against the remainder of Dt.-Is., in his *Die Theologie der Propheten*, Bonn 1875. pp. 288-289.

accepting *grosso modo* the unity of Is. xl-lxvi, had previously come close to DUHM's hypothesis. He ascribed Is. lvi 9-lvii, 13a; lviii 13-lix 21 to another author; he also raised objections to the authenticity of ch. lxii and, finally, he contended that Is. lxiii-lxvi in its present form cannot come from Dt.-Is.[1]

The hypothesis of a Trito-Isaiah drew adherents very quickly. Some scholars who hesitate to accept two distinct authors for Is. xl-lv and lvi-lxvi, nevertheless admit a literary division between these parts.[2] In 1961 J. MORGENSTERN formulated the thesis that not only Is. lvi-lxvi, but even xxxiv-xxxv and xlix-lv belong to Trito-Is., the latter name indicating not one but a series of prophets who were active between 520 and the middle of the 4th century B.C. He thus reduced Dt.-Is. to Is. xl-xlviii, with the exclusion of a number of verses, which are trito-Isaian too.[3] Others had already defended this opinion before him.[4]

Most of the critics envisaged Dt.-Is. as a somewhat structuralized whole. A great number of them treated Is. xl-xlviii as a first part of the structure.[5] It is just such a view that the *Gattungsgeschichte* fundamentally breaks through. While it is true, that a large number of small units had been recognized before, this had been done mostly on archaeological, historical or thematic grounds, and never on the ground of the literary form of the pericopes. Thus C. J. BREDENKAMP

---

[1] B. STADE, *Geschichte des Volkes Israel*, II, Berlin 1888, p. 70, note 1.

[2] J. FISCHER (1916), F. FELDMANN (1926), A. FEUILLET (1949), V. DE LEEUW (1956).

[3] J. MORGENSTERN, *The Message of Deutero-Isaiah*, Cincinnati 1961, pp. 2-3: "... the whole of Deutero-Isaiah is to be found in Isa. 40-48". Cf. also pp. 19-20. The unity of Trito-Isaiah had already been denied by T. K. CHEYNE (1895), W. H. KOSTERS (1896), K. CRAMER (1905), K. BUDDE (1906), L. E. BROWNE (1920; with nuances), J. MARTY (1924), R. ABRAMOWSKY (1925). It was defended by E. LITTMANN (1899), K. MARTI (1900), E. SELLIN (1901), A. ZILLESEN (1906), M. HALLER (1914), K. ELLIGER (1928). — Cf. K. ELLIGER, *Die Einheit des Tritojesaja*, Stuttgart 1928.

[4] Cf. A. KUENEN, *De profetische Boeken des Ouden Verbonds*, Leiden 1889; W. H. KOSTERS, "Deutero- en Trito-Jezaja", *Theologisch Tijdschrift*, XXX 1896, pp. 586-587; 603-604; T. K. CHEYNE, *The Book of the Prophet Isaiah*, London 1898, p. 131; W. STAERK, *Die Ebed-Yahwe-Lieder in Jes. 40ff.*, Leipzig 1913, pp. 68-102.

[5] So A. KNOBEL (1843), R. RÜETSCHI (1854), T. K. CHEYNE (1886), A. KUENEN (1889), F. DELITZSCH (1889), A. DILLMANN (1890), G. A. SMITH (1890), S. R. DRIVER (1891), R. SMEND (1893), G. WILDEBOER (1895), C. H. CORNILL (1896), E. KÖNIG (1898), W. W. BAUDISSIN (1901), E. SELLIN (1901), B. DUHM (1902), A. ZILLESEN (1904), A. CONDAMIN (1905), L. GAUTIER (1906); H. STRACK (1906), A. VAN HOONACKER (1909), W. STAERK (1909), J. FISCHER (1916), E. TOBAC (1924), R. LEVY (1925), P. VOLZ (1932), A. FEUILLET (1949), P. SAYDON (1953); S. C. THEXTON (1959).

suggested that the division xl-xlviii / xlix-lvii / lviii-lxvi was based on external rather than on internal evidence. He discovered in the collection various pre-exilic units, which would have originated from Isaian circles (Is. xlii 1-7; lii 13-liii 12; lvi 9-lvii 11; lix; lxv 3ff).[1] As early as 1498 ISAAC ABARBANEL wrote in his commentary on Is. liii, that the prophecies in this book are put together without any connection, as may be seen by the contents.[2] In the opinion of some scholars the splintering of the book into small units is connected with the fact that the pericopes belong to different historical periods and are even written by different authors. Thus L. BERTHOLDT finds in Is. xl-lxvi different authors on the ground of stylistic peculiarities (*Colorit*, *Darstellungsmanier*), and he maintains that these authors wrote at different times, both before and after the exile. Is. xl-lxvi would then be a fortuitous collection of units without chronological order.[3] According to G.A. SMITH, Is. xl-lxvi consists of a number of pieces from different authors and different periods, arranged afterwards according to chronology and contents.[4] In the *Schweich Lectures* of 1909, R. H. KENNETT dealt with the composition of the book of Isaiah in the light of archaeology and history. He concluded that it is a mosaic of pieces, whose dates range from Isaiah's time until the second century B.C.[5] The first to reject the literary unity of Dt.-Is. on form-critical grounds was H. GRESSMANN, whose views I shall now expose.

---

[1] C. J. BREDENKAMP, *Der Prophet Jesaia*, Erlangen 1887, pp. 226-228.

[2] Quoted by T. K. CHEYNE, "Critical Problems of the Second Part of Isaiah", *JQR*. III 1891, p. 591.

[3] L. BERTHOLDT, *Einleitung in die Schriften des Alten und Neuen Testamentes, IV*, Erlangen 1814, pp. 1375; 1390; 1407-1408.

[4] G. A. SMITH, *The Book of Isaiah*, II, London 1890, pp. 20-21.

[5] R. H. KENNETT, *The Composition of the Book of Isaiah in the Light of History and Archaeology*, London 1910, p. 31: "... these subjects are treated in fragments, undated and anonymous, which moreover are arranged in no discoverable order, and with them are combined other passages, apparently much later". — Cf. pp. 84-85. Some of his datations: Cyrus's time: xiii; xiv 1-27; xxi; xl; xli 1-7, 21-29; xliii; xliv 9-20, 24-28; xlv 1-13; xlvi-xlvii; xlviii 12-15, 20-21; between Nabuchadnezzar and Alexander the Great: xv; xvi 1-12; xxxvi-xxxix; time of Alexander the Great: xxiii 1-14; second century B.C.: xli 8-20; xlii; xliv 1-8, 21-23; xlv 14-25; xlviii 1-11, 16-19, 22; xlix-lxvi.

§1. H. GRESSMANN, DIE LITERARISCHE ANALYSE DEUTEROJESAJAS [1]

In a first section, titled *Der gegenwärtige Stand*, GRESSMANN illustrates his new methodological starting-point : in the study of the prophets we must give up the "book" as a basic unit, because the prophetical "books" consist of short utterances, rarely longer than one chapter.[2] This principle, which he borrows from H. GUNKEL,[3] GRESSMANN seeks to demonstrate concretely in Is. xl-lv.

The first task consists in delimiting the literary units. Although external characteristics often suffice to mark out a pericope, the ultimate norm to be taken into account must be the logic of the text. First of all, we have the introductory and final formulas. Where they occur, there can be no doubt about the delimitation. But they are often missing, sometimes because of the negligence of the copyists; in other instances they have been added by glossators at the wrong place (e.g. in Is. lii 4-6). In this connection, GRESSMANN warns against dangerous generalizations : each case needs proper examination.

At the end of this paragraph the German scholar concludes that Dt.-Is. embraces a large number of units: 49 independent utterances, which have nothing to do with one another, apart from the fact that they come from the same prophet. These units have the same average length as in Amos, Hosea, Isaiah and Jeremiah.

Although he received much praise, GRESSMANN was also criticized for this part of his work. E. KÖNIG, when pointing to the danger of splintering the biblical works, criticized especially the idea that the text was divided into small units by means of introductory and final formulas. The frequent occurrence of these formulas should be ascribed to the typical Hebrew pleonastic style. On this point E. KÖNIG has been followed by J. SCHELHAAS.[4] Even L. KÖHLER, whom we have to

---

1 H. GRESSMANN, "Die literarische Analyse Deuterojesajas", *ZAW*. XXXIV 1914, pp. 254-297.

2 H. GRESSMANN, *ZAW*. XXXIV 1914, p. 258: "Das πρῶτον ψεῦδος der bisherigen Literarkritik ist, dass sie zu sehr am *Begriff der Bucheinheit* haften bleibt".

3 Cf. H. GUNKEL, *RGG*. IV, Tübingen 1913, col. 1878.

4 E. KÖNIG, *Hermeneutik des alten Testaments*, Bonn 1916, pp. 51-61; — J. SCHELHAAS, *De lijdende Knecht des Heeren*, p. 20: "Het moet wel als gekunsteld en mechanisch worden aangevoeld, wanneer zulke herhalingen worden benut als middel van begrenzing en afscheiding".

deal with in the next paragraph, raises the objection that GRESSMANN was not aware of Dt.-Isaiah's tendency to use such formulas more freely.[1] The same criticism has been expressed by S. SMITH,[2] who remarks that GRESSMANN has been induced to find small units, misled as he was by a false analogy with the earlier prophecies, which "fell into short utterances of types that could be labelled".[3] But S. SMITH is in fact inconsistent, as a few pages further on he writes : "The chapters were, too, what they appear to be, not a book, but a series of prophetic utterances ...".[4] SMITH also says : "If logic is the final resort, it cannot be replaced, even partly, by an argument from formulae. If the formulae alone decide, then logic is not the final resort".[5] Such exclusivism is not the best quality of the literary critic. We must admit that GRESSMANN does not always avoid a too mechanical use of the principle of formulas and therefore is inclined to break the text into units which are too short. But in his defense we may call attention to his own warning against generalizations. His fundamental view, however, is sound and it will prove very useful throughout our inquiry.

Now GRESSMANN comes to the study of the different types, divided into prophetical and non-prophetical ones (*fremde Gattungen*). Among the prophetical types he treats of the oracles which break up into threats (*Drohungen*) and promises (*Verheissungen*). Typical of Dt.-Is., when compared to his predecessors, is the absence of threats against Israel. On the other hand, promises are quite numerous, for Dt.-Is. is a prophet of salvation. GRESSMANN counts 43 of them within a total of 49 oracles. Themes which are constantly found in this group, are: the destruction of the enemies, the accomplishment of former predictions about the capture of Babylon by Cyrus, the liberation from exile and the journey through the desert, the glorification of

---

1 L. KÖHLER, *Deuterojesaja stilkritisch untersucht*, Giessen 1923, p. 104: "Dtjes verwendet, wie das Folgende zeigt, mit Vorliebe die einzelnen Formbestandteile des Botenspruches: Einleitungen, Weiterleitungen, Ausleitungen; und diese meist aus künstlerischer Absicht und nicht mehr mit der sachlichen Strenge, mit der es die früheren Propheten tun. Dies hat GRESSMANN (S. 261-265) vielleicht nicht ganz genügend beachtet".

2 S. SMITH, *Isaiah Chapters XL-LV*, London 1944, p. 92, note 46; cf. K. ELLIGER, *Deuterojesaja in seinem Verhältnis zu Tritojesaja*, Stuttgart 1933, p. 142.

3 S. SMITH, *o.c.*, pp. 7-9.

4 S. SMITH, *o.c.*, p. 22.

5 S. SMITH, *o.c.*, p. 7.

Zion and the subjection and conversion of all nations. The motif of Zion's glory occurs nine times in Is. xlix-lv, as against twice in xl-xlv (i.e. xl 9-11; xlii 18-xliii 7). Hence the author concludes: 1. one cannot divide Is. xl-lv into two clearly distinct parts; 2. the book of Dt.-Is. has not been built up according to a definite plan, and no chronological conclusions can be drawn from the position of the oracles. Finally, GRESSMANN points out that the promises have mostly been combined with other types to form larger compositions.

With the pre-exilic prophets the rebuke (*Scheltrede*) mostly occurs in connection with a threat, to which it forms the motivation (*Begründung*). In Dt.-Is., however, where there is a complete absence of threats, we find some five rebukes, united with a promise (Is. xlv 9-13; xlii 18-25; xliii 22-28; xlviii 1-11; l 1-2a). The rebukes are not presented strictly as a word from Yahwe but as a saying of the prophet. Among the pericopes listed immediately above, however, three are pronounced by Yahwe. As I see it, this means that GRESSMANN's labeling these pericopes as one type is inadequate. The final remark of Gressmann is that "the nature and the contents of the genre have changed": 1. the rebuke has become milder; 2. Deutero-Isaiah's rebukes are intended to teach and to convince; 3. historical considerations often furnish the evidence therefore: the dt-Isaian rebuke is directed more against the past sins than against the present ones. One may question whether the author grasps the outlines of a really distinct genre in this instance. We shall see in the third chapter that the pericopes, he refers to, belong to two different types, and that they go together with other units, a fact which GRESSMANN overlooks.

Next to the promises the words of comfort (*Trostworte*) are the most typical genre in Dt.-Is. But they never had an independent existence so that we can hardly call them a distinct type. They are very close to admonitions, and they are mostly united to promises, sometimes to hymns. The words of comfort are properly a reply to a lamentation of the people, which in some cases is quoted explicitly (e.g. Is. xl 27; xlix 14, 24).[1] This point has been developed by J. BEGRICH and his followers, so as to give it its full form-critical bearing. My impression is that promises and words of comfort must be taken together as one type or as two sub-types of one larger genre. GRESS-

---

[1] Instances of this form: Is. xl 1-2a, 27-31; xlvi 12-13; xlix 15-17; li 7-8, 12-13; liv 1-6; lv 1-3.

MANN himself admits further on that they often become merged into one another.[1]

The trial speeches (*Gerichtsworte*) can be recognized commonly by the introduction ("Let us draw near for judgment ...") or by technical terms, such as "witness" or "prove" (Is. xli 1-13, 21-29; xliii 8-13; xliv 6-20; xlv 20-21; xlviii 12-16). Dt.-Is. gave a completely new tenor to this genre. Instead of trial against Israel because of its sins, the action here is against the pagan gods about the question whether Yahwe really has foretold Cyrus's activities and especially the capture of Babylon. In the present study most of the trial speeches, alleged by GRESSMANN, will be retained as such, but he did not mention all of them, nor did he make clear the relations between this form and the so-called rebukes.

Among the non-prophetic types, the most important form, because it is most characteristic of this prophet, it the hymn.[2] First the author deals with hymnic motifs, then with independent hymns. A first form of a hymnic motif is the enlargement of the prophetic introductory formulas. In Dt.-Is. the phrase "Thus says Yahwe" is often enlarged with distinctly hymnic motifs (creation of the universe, the Exodus wonders), which are formulated in participial phrases (e.g. Is. xlii 5; xliii 16).

Two theophany formulas provide a typical introduction of an oracle in Dt.-Is., viz. "I am Yahwe" and "Fear not". Both occur abundantly in these prophecies and always at an important point of the oracle.[3] This kind of introductory formula can be enlarged with hymnic motifs too (e.g. Is. xliv 24-26a). In GRESSMANN's opinion, such a *Selbstprädikation der Gottheit*, which in the prophetic literature appears only in Dt.-Is., must be explained by Babylonian influence.[4] L. KÖHLER raises the objection that here the author did not quote

[1] H. GRESSMANN, *a.c.*, p. 295. In chapter II, I deal with this genre as "salvation word".

[2] H. GRESSMANN, *a.c.*, p. 284: "... für keinen Prophet sind die Hymnen so charakteristisch wie gerade für Deuterojesaja".

[3] The first formula cf. Is. xli 4, 10, 13, 17; xlii 6, 8-9; xliii 3, 11, 13, 15; xliv 24; xlv 3, 5, 6-7, 18-19, 21; xlviii 17; li 12, 15; the second one: Is. xli 10, 13, 14; xliii 1, 5; xliv 2, 8; li 12.

[4] Dt.-Is. has an impressive number of these so-called *Selbstprädikationen*: Is. xli 4, 10, 13, 17; xlii 8-9; xliii 11-13; xliv 6; xlv 3-5, 12, 18-19, 21; xlvi 9; xlviii 11-13, 17; xlix 26; l 2-3; li 15-16. Cf. *a.c.*, p. 290. More recently cf. H. M. DION, "Le genre littéraire sumérien de l'"hymne à soi-même' et quelques passages du Deutéro-Isaïe", *RB.* LXXIV, 1967, pp. 215-234.

all the important instances, nor did he distinguish properly between different uses of the same formula. Furthermore, dependence on Babylonian parallels has not been proven.[1] This criticism may be too severe, but GRESSMANN surely did not grasp the exact form-critical function of these formulas, as we shall see in the second chapter of the present study.

In Is. xlviii 12-16, where the oracle proper does not exceed the length of one verse (vs. 14b),[2] set between *Selbstprädikationen*, one can see to what degree the dt.-Isaian oracle can be overloaden with hymnic motifs. Hymnic formulas also often supplanted the prophetic final word *n^e'um yhwh*. At times the oracle ends with a complete, although very short, hymn (e.g. Is. xlv 8, 15-17; xlviii 20-21; xlix 13; l 2b-3; li 3; lii 9-10). Two longer hymns can be found in Is. xl 12-16 and xlii 10-13, both of which are intended to be an introduction to an oracle. H. GRESSMANN concludes his survey by stating that the hymns, however much characteristic of our prophet, are not for all that the main constituent of his book; they act only as an accompaniment to his preaching. To have pointed out the importance of the hymnic style in Dt.-Is. is one of GRESSMANN'S merits in this article.[3] And J. BEGRICH is wrong when objecting that the hymnic form is not so frequently attested, as may be induced from GRESSMANN'S statements[4].

As a general conclusion GRESSMANN states that with Dt.-Is. the dissolution of the prophetic types begins.[5] The borderlines of the genres are not very neat (e.g. promises and words of comfort) and hymnic elements penetrate into almost every oracle. Although this makes the literary analysis of the book very difficult, GRESSMANN remains optimistic as to the possibility of distinguishing the literary units.

As GRESSMANN'S analysis is the first of its kind, it is open to some criticism. Maybe he was wrong to start with this prophetic book before the form-critical study of the earlier prophets had been grappled

---

1 L. KÖHLER, "Die Offenbarungsformel 'Fürchte dich nicht' im Alten Testament", *Schweizerische Theologische Zeitschrift*, XXXVI 1919, pp. 38-39.

2 H. GRESSMANN reads the suffixes in the first person; cf. *a.c.*, p. 291, note 3.

3 So L. KÖHLER, *Deuterojesaja*, p. 121.

4 J. BEGRICH, *Studien zu Deuterojesaja*, München 1963, p. 67.

5 H. GRESSMANN, *a.c.*, p. 295: "Will man Deuterojesaja in die Literaturgeschichte der israelitischen Prophetie einreihen, so darf man als charackteristisch bezeichnen, dass bei ihm die *Auflösung der prophetischen Gattungen* beginnt".

with.[1] But his general views on the method seem to be sound, and a number of his observations are still useful.

§2. L. Köhler, Deuterojesaja stilkritisch untersucht

At first H. Gressmann's analysis seems to have passed without being perceived. Not before 1923 L. Köhler asserts that this study, next to the works of J. C. Döderlein (1775) and B. Duhm (1875 and 1892) means the only important progress in the exegesis of Deutero-Isaiah.[2] His own work is more than a purely form-critical study, but anyhow, it is the first important step in this field after Gressmann. In the first place he presents an amended text and translation, metrically arranged and divided into pericopes. His division constitutes a regression, as compared to Gressman's, because it is not grounded on literary indications, but exclusively on the meaning of the text. As a matter of fact his division often coincides with Gressmann's, but he clearly shows a tendency towards smaller units and he thus has a larger number of pericopes. But we have the impression that this division does not deal with independent units but only renders the articulation of a structuralized text,[3] which may be seen e.g. from the fact that he breaks up the taunt song of Is. xlvii into five parts.

When dealing with the syntactical characteristics of our prophet, Köhler holds that the prophetic style has been changed into a rhetorical one.[4] If this proves to be true, a form-critical analysis has to take it into account. The rhetorical character of our prophet may have induced him to change the style of a certain type, as to put a step forward in the evolution of that type. But before accepting that, Köhler's assertion should be tested thoroughly. He appeals only to the analysis of one example, which he overdoes a good deal (Is. xl 1-2).

---

[1] L. Köhler, *Schweiz. Theol. Zeitschr.* XXXVI 1919, p. 33: "... auch wenn man fragen mag, ob die Behandlung gerade dieser spätern Schrift und Entwicklungsform tunlich gewesen sei, ehe noch die ältern und einfachern Formen genügend untersucht sind".

[2] L. Köhler, *Deuterojesaja*, p. 1.

[3] L. Köhler, *o.c.*, p. 2: "Ich lege ihn (= den Text), in Sinnabschnitte zerlegt, deren Abtrennung aber bei den fliessenden, springenden Gedankengang unseres Schriftstellers problematisch bleibt...".

[4] L. Köhler, *o.c.*, p. 85.

In a very superficial manner the parallelism, which is so typical of all poetic texts in the Bible, is taken for a rhetorical *Zerdehnung*.[1]

We are most interested in the chapter which is entitled *Formen und Stoffe*.[2] Therein KÖHLER treats the so called *Botenspruch*. That is the name he gives to the stereotyped phrase, which introduces a message, indicating the sender and nearly always the addressee.[3] We find an example in Gen. xxxii 5: "Thus you shall say to my lord Esau: Thus says your servant Jacob: ..." KÖHLER examines Is. xl 1-2 and finds the *Botenspruch* to be quite modified. In his opinion, Dt.-Is. uses the formula no longer functionally but rather artificially. He does not speak as a prophet but like a prophet, i.e. the formula has been dissociated from its prophetical *Sitz im Leben* and is used in a merely literary way.[4] This important statement needs further examination. The fact is that we should ascertain whether this so-called process of literarization can be proven with respect to other formulas and types also. Further on, KÖHLER uses the term *Botenspruch* to designate the whole of the message.[5] The conclusion of his examination is that Dt.-Is. uses the formulas of the *Botenspruch* more freely than the earlier prophets.[6] We must agree with R. RENDTORFF's remark that KÖHLER's analysis is very insufficient, as he confines it to the formulas without giving any attention to the structure, the style and other features of the genre. A similar criticism may be found in C. WESTER-

---

[1] For another criticism in this connection cf. S. SMITH, *Isaiah chs. XL-LV*, p. 12: "Oddly enough, this supposed verbosity does not prevent Professor KÖHLER from considering the prophet a great stylist".

[2] L. KÖHLER, *o.c.*, pp. 102-142.

[3] With *Botenspruch* L. KÖHLER really means here this introductory formula. C. WESTERMANN, on the contrary, calls *Botenspruch* the proper message, while indicating the introductory phrase with *Botenformel*; cf. C. WESTERMANN, *Grundformen prophetischer Rede*, München 1960, p. 72.

[4] L. KÖHLER, *o.c.*, p. 104.

[5] L. KÖHLER, *o.c.*, p. 106: "Das sind die dreizehn Botensprüche Dtjes's, die durch eine Einleitung als solche von vornherein gekennzeichnet sind". In *Kleine Lichter*, Zürich 1945, pp. 15-16, he clearly determines the Botenspruch as the complete unit, which is introduced by a *Botenformel*: "Mit dieser Einsicht in Wesen und Zweck der Formel ist auch der Name gegeben, den wir als den sachlich treffenden der Satzgruppe oder Einheit beilegen, welche mit dieser Formel eingeleitet wird. Wir heissen sie Botenspruch".

[6] L. KÖHLER, *o.c.*, p. 109: "Unverkennbar ist die Verwendung dieser Formeln bei Dtjes eine freiere als bei den ältern Propheten".

MANN's study of the basic forms of prophetical speech.[1] But a complete rejection of KÖHLER's *Botenspruch*, such as made by J. BEGRICH, is out of place. WESTERMANN's above-mentioned work has proven that KÖHLER, in spite of his defective analysis, discovered here a highly important prophetic type together with its antecedents and origin, i.e. its *Sitz im Leben*.[2]

Next, KÖHLER tackles the study of the disputation (*Streitgespräch*), which is rooted in the Israelite administration of justice. After a short description of the lawsuit in Israel, he presents a list of the disputations in Dt.-Is. and of the constituent parts of the genre. According to KÖHLER, our prophet often uses these constituent parts in other genres too, which means that Dt.-Is. mixes the genres. Passim the author indicates quite a number of technical terms of the genre, such as *rîb*, *dîn*, etc. When summing up the main themes of the dt.-Isaian disputations KÖHLER points out that the whole of the book is dominated by a double dispute. On the one hand, Yahwe goes to law with the gods, on the other, he is at law with Israel. In the last case Yahwe defends himself against the accusation of having abandoned Israel. In our third chapter we shall see that KÖHLER's so-called *Streitgespräch* needs further specification and that it comprises two distinct genres.

By *Prädikation* the author understands all kinds of sayings that express the essence, the proper activity, the power of the deity. The speech is either in the first person, when the deity himself acts in a theophany (*Selbstprädikation*), or in the second or third person, when the worshipper in his prayer wants to reach precisely this and no other deity and to obtain his favour (*Fremdprädikation*). The latter form is hymnic and therefore to be considered non-prophetic. Both forms occur frequently and in all kinds of genres. In this respect, KÖHLER stresses again the mingling of genres as characteristic of Dt.-Is.[3] My investigation will point out some intances of such a

---

[1] R. RENTDORFF, "Botenformel und Botenspruch", *ZAW*. LXXIV 1962, p. 165; C. WESTERMANN, *Grundformen prophetischer Rede*, p. 26.

[2] J. BEGRICH, *Studien zu Deuterojesaja*, p. 67: "Gegen Köhlers Botenspruch müssen wir uns im ganzen ablehnend verhalten. Was dafür angeführt wird, reicht nicht aus, eine Gattung sicherzustellen". Cf. also C. WESTERMANN, "Sprache und Struktur der Prophetie Deuterojesajas", *Forschung am A.T.*, München 1964, p. 95: "Er führt aber über GRESSMANN darin hinaus, dass er die Vorgeschichte und Herkunft des Botenspruches entdeckt und damit seinen 'Sitz im Leben' bestimmt".

[3] Cf. also L. KÖHLER, *o.c.*, p. 124.

mingling, but the main picture will be that of well shaped types with regard to the structure as well as to the contents.

Finally, KÖHLER deals with all kinds of themes and forms, borrowed from the theophany descriptions. From a form-critical point of view he does not tell us much about it. In his opinion, a kind of large world theophany, accomplished through Yahwe's salvific activity, is the central theme of Is. xl-lv. Hence the frequent use of the theophany formula: "Fear not".[1] My form-critical evaluation of this formula will be quite different. I may make mine the criticism of WESTERMANN: KÖHLER saw the importance of the oracles of salvation (he calls them theophanies), but he did not find the proper type or genre in which these so-called theophanic materials have been worked up. And this failure induced him to contradict himself : sections which he formerly put forward as *Botensprüche*, he now advances as forms of a theophany, although the messenger's speech is quite different from that of a seer.[2]

§3. S. MOWINCKEL, K. ELLIGER AND W. CASPARI

In the article *Jesaja* in the second edition of *Die Religion in Geschichte und Gegenwart*, E. BALLA takes the form-critical study of Dt.-Is. for granted. In the literary section of his article, he gives an almost exhaustive enumeration of the genres occurring in Is. xl-lv. His conclusion is that Dt.-Is. was not only a prophet but also a poet, which appears from the hymns and from the hymnic style of the other genres.[3] An article in an encyclopaedia must confine itself to a simple enumeration, without thorough justification. At times, the appellations of the genres sound rather new and prudent : e.g. *Ichhymnen in Form von Gerichtsreden, Verkündigungsauftrag*. But it is not clear to me why E. BALLA distinguishes between promises and oracles of salvation, Is. lii 7-12 being the only sample of the latter.

More important is S. MOWINCKEL's article on the composition of Dt.-Is.[4] Loud in praise of the studies of H. GRESSMANN and L. KÖHLER,

---

1 L. KÖHLER, *o.c.*, p. 124; cf. also ID., *Schweiz. Theol. Zeitschr.* XXXVI 1919, pp. 38-39.

2 C. WESTERMANN, *a.c.*, *Forschung am A.T.*, p. 97.

3 E. BALLA, "Jesaja", *RGG.* III, Tübingen 1929, col. 100.

4 S. MOWINCKEL, "Die Komposition des deuterojesajanischen Buches", *ZAW.* XLIX 1931, pp. 87-112; 242-260. MOWINCKEL resumes his principal positions in "Neuere Forschungen zu Deuterojesaja, Tritojesaja und dem 'Äbäd-Jahwe-Problem", in *Act Or.* XVI 1937, esp. pp. 11-12; 38-39.

he explicitly presupposes them and he considers his own work as an extension of theirs. Dt.-Is. would be a collection of short, originally independent units. It does not necessarily follow that the units have been collected without any design. The compiler may have followed a design or certain principles of composition in the arrangement of his material. MOWINCKEL intends precisely to detect the principles according to which the units have been arranged (*Anreihungsprinzip*).

In the second part of his article, MOWINCKEL analyzes the 41 pericopes of the book[1]. In each case he examines what reason may explain the insertion of a given pericope: thematic affinity, catchwords, assonances, similar introductory formulas. Meanwhile he regularly makes judicious remarks, either in the text or in the extensive footnotes, on the literary type of the pericope under consideration. In the footnotes he also defines the metrical and strophic structure of each pericope and he often justifies his delimitation of the literary units. In this respect he more than once enters into discussion with L. KÖHLER, who goes farther in the division of some units. S. MOWINCKEL thus accepts a smaller number of them in agreement with H. GRESSMANN.

From his examination S. MOWINCKEL infers that any planned composition, even the simple binary structure of the book (xl-xlviii; xlix-lv), must be rejected.[2] Former scholars had pointed out certain differences between the two so-called main parts. In MOWINCKEL's opinion, these differences are but an accidental consequence of the arrangement of the units according to affinity of form and contents. There is thus no plan. Also chronological conclusions, such as e.g. that Is. xl-xlviii was written before the deliverance of the exiles and the other part after it, cannot be drawn from the alleged differences.[3] Finally, it is hard to accept that the compiler would have been the prophet himself. Indeed, the most important principle of arrangement, viz. that of catchwords, is not a working principle of an original author. In other words, the catchwords may have induced a compiler to join existing pericopes, but they cannot explain the creation of the units themselves.

Most of the criticism that has been affered against MOWINCKEL's article concerns the principle of catchwords, especially the exaggerated

---

1 In a postscript, he divides Is. xlviii 12-19 into two separate units: vss. 12-16 and 17-19. Thus he finally obtains 42 pericopes. Cf. *a.c.*, pp. 257-260.

2 See p. 3.

3 Against e.g. C. H. CORNILL, *Einleitung in das A.T.*, Tübingen 1918, p. 168.

and mechanical application of it.[1] C. WESTERMANN, however, states that, once the division of Is. xl-lv into a large number of small units is accepted, MOWINCKEL's thesis of a mechanical arrangement cannot be avoided.[2] Of course, we should avoid easy generalizations; each case must be tested carefully. As my main interest is in the relation between form and contents in the small units, I shall not deal with this question at great length. I must admit that it is hard to find a large scale design in Is. xl-lv and that every attempt to find one suffers a great deal of subjectivism. I shall show in the present analysis that some larger compositions in Is. xl-lv are original, but on the whole MOWINCKEL is right.

As appears from the title of his book[3], K. ELLIGER's intention is not directly form-critical either. He wants to examine whether Trito-Isaiah,—in his opinion the only author of Is. lvi-lxvi,[4] — also has a hand in Is. xl-lv, i.e. whether in Dt.-Is. some additions from Trito-Isaiah may be found, and whether or not the latter is the compiler of the dt.-Isaian book. For this purpose he appeals to the vocabulary and expressions, stylistic properties, literary genre and contents. He thus uses the form-critical method in the course of his investigation. In this respect he has some valuable considerations on the delimitation of the pericopes as well as on the definition of their literary type. Thus, e.g. from the fact that Is. l 1-3 is a rebuke which does not end in a promise (cf. GRESSMANN), he infers that this pericope cannot belong to Dt.-Is. Elsewhere he holds, against nearly all his predecessors, that Is. liv and lv are both complete literary units which one should not break up. In the chapter dealing with the adaptation of some dt.-Isaian pieces by Trito-Is.,[5] form-critical considerations are very scanty.

---

1 P. VOLZ, *Jesaia II*, Leipzig 1932, p. XXXV; J. SCHELHAAS, *De lijdende Knecht des Heeren*, p. 22; K. ELLIGER, *Deuterojesaja in seinem Verhältnis zu Tritojesaja*, Stuttgart 1933, pp. 223-224; O. EISSFELDT, *Der Gottesknecht bei Deuterojesaja*, Halle 1933, p. 10; S. SMITH, *Isaiah chs. XL-LV*, p. 21; J. LINDBLOM, *The Servant Songs in Deutero-Isaiah*, Lund 1951, p. 9.

2 C. WESTERMANN, *Forschung*, p. 105: "Zunächst muss zugegeben werden, dass sich aus einer konsequenten Aufteilung von Jes. 40-55 in sehr viele (40-50) kleine Einheiten eine These wie die Mowinckels zur Komposition des Ganzen eigentlich notwendig ergibt".

3 K. ELLIGER, *Deuterojesaja in seinem Verhältnis zu Tritojesaja*, Stuttgart 1933.

4 Cf. K. ELLIGER, *Die Einheit des Tritojesaja*, Stuttgart 1928.

5 K. ELLIGER, *Deuterojesaja*, pp. 167-219: "Bearbeitung deuterojesajanischer Stücke durch Tritojesaja".

In his last chapter, the author presents his conclusions concerning the composition of Is. xl-lv. The compiler and first redactor of Is. xl-lv would be Trito-Is. himself. According to which principle did he accomplish this task? Here ELLIGER repeats, in agreement with GRESSMANN, KÖHLER and MOWINCKEL, that we must replace the idea of a « book » with that of a « collection ».[1] Has this collection, then, been made without any plan or arrangement? After having rejected MOWINCKEL's criteria as too external, he proceeds to his own examination. This section of ELLIGER's work is the most interesting for us. It presents the delimitation of all the units, in each case discussing the divisions which have been proposed formerly. ELLIGER leans especially on the rhythm, but he also takes account of the introductory formulas and the contents. He rarely determines the genre of the pericopes under consideration. In this respect, "hymn" is about the only appellation to be found here. The final conclusion of his study is: 1. Trito-Is. is the compilor; 2. some units had been combined into small compositions before him; 3. the collection has been made according to the contents (against MOWINCKEL); 4. it does not form one whole, however, but consists of larger sections, which have not been joined to one another (xl 1-11; xl 12-xlii 9; xlii 10-xliv 23; xliv 24-xlvii 15; xlviii 1-lii 12).[2]

ELLIGER's work generally met with a favorable reception.[3] The main criticism was made against his word statistics. As J. BEGRICH rightly remarked, the results of this method must be tested by those of the form-critical study, viz. lexicographic affinity between a pericope in Is. xl-lv and another in Is. lvi-lxvi, does not necessarily point to the same author. This similarity may be due to the similarity of genre.[4] At any rate the lexicographical method does not apply to the problem ELLIGER wanted to solve, because there is not a sufficient

---

[1] K. ELLIGER, *o.c.*, p. 222: "Die literarische Analyse im Sinne der Gattungsforschung ergibt Einwandfrei, dass die vermeintlich geschlossene Komposition in ein paar Dutzend selbständig nebeneinanderstehender Einheiten aufzulösen ist und dass nur von einer 'Sammlung' die Rede sein kann".

[2] K. ELLIGER, *o.c.*, p. 268.

[3] Recensions by W. STAERK, *Theologische Blätter*, XIII 1934, pp. 58-59; N. PETERS, *TGl.* XXVI 1934, pp. 495-496; W. RUDOLPH, *DLZ.* V 1934, pp. 2353-2357; J. COPPENS, *ETL.* XII 1935, pp. 80-82; A. WENDEL, *TLZ.* LX 1935, pp. 243-245; B. CELADA, *Ci Tom.* XXVI 1934, pp. 218-219. A less favorable judgment was emitted by J. REIDER, *JQR.* XXVI 1935-1936, pp. 194-195; P. VOLZ, *OLZ.* XXXVIII 1935, pp. 228-231.

[4] J. BEGRICH, *Studien*, pp. 66-67.

bulk of material for it in Is. xl-lv.[1] Neither did he make clear according to what criteria the work of a compiler can be distinguished from that of an original author.[2] From a form-critical point of view, I object against ELLIGER that he determines the genre of the pericopes too exclusively on the basis of the contents. He does not apply form-critical rules to do it. Thus he calls the whole of chapter liv a promise of salvation, whereas on the basis of the form he might have found several distinct promises.

With the foregoing studies by S. MOWINCKEL and K. ELLIGER we may class the one by W. CASPARI, as it also pays particular attention to the *Redaktionsgeschichte*.[3] Together with this it contains important considerations in the domain of form criticism. He distinguishes two principal genres in the collection. In the course of his investigation he calls them "divine utterances" (*Gottessprüche*) and "*Zusatz-Reden*". The latter are distinguished from the former by only one characteristic: they are utterances about God or to him. One recognizes the division into oracles and songs.

His basic principle is that of the loose collection. The first task of the interpreter is thus to look for the smallest sections by tracing borders, seams and major themes. With much care and nuance W. CASPARI traces the borderlines between the units. Seldom does he pay attention to the literary type of the units obtained in this way. He regularly admits that certain verses may belong to the preceding pericope as well as to the following one (e.g. Is. xliv 23). Moreover, he supposes that certain sections, which now form a unit, have been composed of originally smaller elements, the latter ones possibly being transformed. Therefore it is impossible to fix the exact number of the units. In his opinion, the separate units, frequently used as they were, underwent changes independently of their insertion in the deutero-Isaian collection. We must reckon not only with strictly outlined oracles, but with mixed types. These remarks are evidently very important. But my analysis shows that in Dt.-Is. the units generally are pure, although some adaptations, made by later redactors,

---

[1] Cf. S. SMITH, *Isaiah chs. XL-LV*, p. 15: "Hebrew of the sixth century is not so well known that it is possible to distinguish the rare use by an author of a common word from a distinctive use peculiar to an individual".

[2] Cf. C. WESTERMANN, *Forschung*, p. 104.

[3] W. CASPARI, *Lieder und Gottessprüche der Rückwanderer* (*Jesaja 40-55*) (*BZAW*. 65), Giessen 1934.

appear, especially in the immediate context of the so-called Servant Songs.

In his ninth paragraph, CASPARI analyzes conceptions and formulas borrowed from the administration of justice.[1] First he lists several images and expressions, belonging to this sphere: e.g. the idea of God as a judge and as a pleader, different categories from marriage law, hereditary law, redemption, etc. Many of these elements are commonly listed under a collective noun "disputation" (*Streitgespräch*). This genre, though having an established existence in the prophetical writings, cannot have arisen from the prophetical action as such; it has its origin, at least partly, in the actual administration of justice. Although he considers the disputes not to be so numerous in Dt.-Is. as his predecessors claim, nevertheless he finds some samples of it in our prophet. The disputation now has become a form of the oracle (e.g. Is. xliii 8-13; xlix 14-21). As to the major themes of this genre, he holds with L. KÖHLER, pointing out Yahwe's double dispute in Is. xl-lv.

Although this part of CASPARI's work met with a favorable reception,[2] we shall see, however, that he missed the point by not making clear that the class of the so-called *Streitgespräch* or *-rede* really consists of two types, quite distinct from one another as to form and content, viz. the trial speech and the disputation.

The next paragraph bears the heading *Vorstellungen und Formeln aus dem Kult.* CASPARI remarks that oracles may have a hymnic introduction, so that they are a product of cult. He finds also in Dt.-Is. a frequent use of cultic formulas (e.g. Is. lii 7), hymnic elements and expressions that are borrowed from confessions of guilt and lamentations (e.g. Is. xli 17). The author devotes a long explanation to curses and benedictions, which would be very numerous in Dt.-Is.[3] He insists on the importance of the *parallelismus membrorum* to add force to these formulas.[4] By joining together two binary phrases a

[1] W. CASPARI, *o.c.*, pp. 112-129: "Vorstellungen und Formeln des Rechtslebens".

[2] Cf. L. ROST, *DLZ.* LVI 1935, p. 795; R. VAN DE WYNCKEL, *ETL.* XII 1935, pp. 360-363; J. ZIEGLER, *TR.* XXXIV 1935, p. 325.

[3] Curses: Is. xl 17; xli 2b, 11, 16a, 24, 29; xlii 17; xlv 16; xlvii 1-5, 9, 11, 14-15; l 9b, 11; li 8, 23; liii 8b-9; benedictions: xl 31; xliii 2; xliv 4; xlv 8, 17, 25; xlviii 19b, 21; xlix 9b-10, 18b, 23; li 7, 8b, 12; lii 12; liii 10b-11; liv 1, 3, 10.

[4] W. CASPARI, *o.c.*, p. 166: "Die Kraft der Segen und Flüche hangt nicht zuletzt von deren voller Sprache ab ... Zweckmässig ist daher für sie der synthetische Parallelismus, nächst ihm der antithetische".

three- or fourfold parallelism may arise. The latter must not be ascribed to the rhetorical style of our prophet (against L. KÖHLER). In this respect I ask why not ascribe it simply to the general use of such parallelism in Hebrew poetry. Furthermore, CASPARI highly exaggerates the number of curses, not seeing the form-critical function of the alleged phrases in their context. Nor did he grasp the role of his so-called "benedictions". He tried to determine the difference between an oracle of salvation and a benediction. The only distinction would be in the way they affect a person: a benediction affects both things and persons completely and in a lasting manner, whereas an oracle only affects persons and not necessarily in their total existence[1]. We may ask whether this distinction is relevant to a form-critical study of Dt.-Is. CASPARI here fails to delineate Dt.-Isaiah's most important genre, viz. the cultic oracle of salvation, although he was very close to it when pointing to the cult as the setting of the oracle. Anyhow, he has rightly stressed the importance of cultic and hymnic elements in Dt.-Is., in agreement with H. GRESSMANN. In CASPARI's opinion the so-called secularization of the genre — above I called this "dissolution", when dealing with GRESSMANN — has been overestimated. We can find antecedents of all the alleged phenomena in the Old Testament (e.g. the insertion of the introductory formula in the oracle proper).

The alternation of *Ich-* and *Du*-sections in the oracles results from the original form of the private oracle, which somebody received in his prayer. Dt.-Is. imitates such forms, e.g. in oracles supposedly directed to Cyrus, but as a matter of fact intended for the exiles. Thus in Dt.-Is. the private oracle ultimately is only a purely literary fiction. We shall see that this remark should be fully elaborated in the study of two types of the salvation oracle.

In his final chapter [2] the author assails the idea of a personal Dt.-Is., in other words, he does not accept that the pericopes of Is. xl-lv emanate from one author. Is. xl-lv is a somewhat arranged collection of anonymous songs and oracles, which originated in Babylon about the end of the exile.[3] In this historical setting the march song would be the

---

[1] W. CASPARI, *o.c.*, p. 176.

[2] W. CASPARI, *o.c.*, pp. 190-244: "Die durch Zusammensetzung und Zweck bedingte Einheit von Jes 40-55 (Dekomposition)".

[3] W. CASPARI, *o.c.*, p. 244: "Der persönliche Dtjes. war eine Zimmerpflanze auf dem Gelehrten-Schreibtische. Ranke und Ableger, welche den Bestand des Buches ausmachen, stammen schlechtweg von dem Baume der alttestamentlichen Religion und gedeihen

most obvious type. Without neat borderlines, pilgrim songs, festive songs and home songs have been added. These pieces have a meaning only in the mouth of a collectivity. They have been inserted in the book as a kind of responsories to utterances of an individual, seemingly a prophet. As C. WESTERMANN rightly remarked, this dissolution into different kinds of songs has been made without any serious investigation of these alleged types.[1] As to CASPARI's principal thesis, it has not been proven, and, as yet, nobody has adopted it.[2] Finally I may mention that most of the critics rightly reproached CASPARI for his almost unreadable style,[3] which, at times, makes it hard to grasp what he means exactly.

§4. J. BEGRICH, H. E. VON WALDOW AND C. WESTERMANN

A very important contribution to the form-critical analysis of Dt.-Is. we owe to J. BEGRICH in the first chapter of his study on this prophetical book.[4] In his introduction he underlines the necessity of marking out the literary units. But this operation is insufficient, if not at the same time the literary character of those units is determined. This way the form-critical problem is clearly formulated. Neither task has as yet been satisfactorily accomplished, as appears from the great divergences of opinion among the critics. After having listed the literary units and enumerated the literary types of our prophet, J. BEGRICH proceeds to a detailed analysis. He distinguishes 70 units, thus greatly exceeding the number attained by GRESSMANN.

The type most frequently attested is the oracle of salvation or oracle of grant, such as it was given in the cult after the lament and before the assertion of confidence. In the next chapter we shall deal at length with BEGRICH's analysis of this genre. He asserts that typical features

auf dem Boden der Frömmigkeit, wie ihre Erforschung im Erdboden der Geschichtlichen Tatsachen wurzelt".

[1] C. WESTERMANN, *Forschung*, p. 101.

[2] Cf. S. MOWINCKEL, *Act Or.* XVI 1937, pp. 13-15; S. SMITH, *Isaiah chs. XL-LV*, pp. 14-15; C. WESTERMANN, *l.c.*

[3] J. HEMPEL, *ZAW.* LII 1934, p. 142; L. ROST, *DLZ.* LVI 1935, p. 795; R. VAN DE WYNCKEL, *ETL.* XII 1935, p. 363; P. VOLZ, *OLZ.* XXXIX 1936, p. 96; S. MOWINCKEL, *l.c.*

[4] J. BEGRICH, *Studien zu Deuterojesaja* (*BWANT.* IV, 25), Stuttgart 1938; this has been republished by W. ZIMMERLI, *Theologische Bücherei*, XX, München 1963. In the present work this second edition is always quoted.

of the dt.-Isaian oracle of salvation in general are the absence of the vocative (*namentliche Anrede*), of the exhortation "Fear not" and of the nominal phrases, the subject of which is Yahwe, corresponding to the motif of confidence in a lament. It is hard to understand how BEGRICH did not grasp the importance of these very elements, which are truly present in six pericopes, for the determination of a clearly distinct type, as we shall see further on.[1] At the end of this paragraph, the author calls attention to the fact that in Dt.-Is. the introductory formula is often elaborated with participles and relative clauses, which does not properly belong to the genre.

Next to the oracle of salvation, BEGRICH studies the trial speech (*Gerichtsrede*). In a brief outline of an Israelite lawsuit,[2] BEGRICH gives the different trial speeches their place in this setting and he concludes that the great variety of actions leads to a greater mobility in the use of the motifs. Nevertheless, it is possible to indicate some general *topoi*, proper to each sub-type, e.g. in the defence of the accused, one finds the question about the "why" of the accusation. Among the pleadings, Is. xliii 22-28 gets special treatment, because Yahwe does not defend himself against an accusation, but against a claim, which Israel wants to invoke against him. But the pericopes xli 1-5; l 1-2; xliv 6-8; xli 21-29; xliii 8-13 are also analyzed. All the elements of these texts are situated by BEGRICH as moments of a lawsuit. Peculiar to the "prophetic" judicial genres is the fact that Yahwe is sometimes both judge and party (cf. Ps. lxxxii 2-7; Is. xli 21-29). BEGRICH believes that identity of judge and party was possible in the actual administration of justice in Israel (cf. Sir. viii 14).[3] It seems to the

---

1 Contrast his paper: J. BEGRICH, "Das priesterliche Heilsorakel", *ZAW*. LII 1934, p. 85.

2 In this respect he refers to L. KÖHLER, "Die hebräische Rechtsgemeinde", *Jahresbericht der Universität Zürich*, 1930-1931, reprinted in L. KÖHLER, *Der hebräische Mensch*, Tübingen 1953, pp. 143-171.

3 He quotes L. KÖHLER, *a.c.*, *Der hebräische Mensch*, p. 152. But the latter only asserts the possible identity of judge and witness. The text from Sir. does not prove the thesis. BEGRICH wrongly translates: "Prozessiere nicht mit einem Richter. Denn nach seinem Gutbefinden wird er urteilen". (Cf. J. BEGRICH, *Studien*, p. 44). The Greek phrase runs as follows: ... *κατὰ γὰρ τὴν δόξαν αὐτοῦ κρινοῦσιν αὐτῷ*. Thus the judge is judged by others (cf. BEGRICH's note 147). BEGRICH reads the Hebrew text thus: *kî kirᵉṣônô yišpōṭ*. He does not remark that *yš(pṭ)* is conjectural and may be read as a niphal or as a plural. A doublet of the phrase occurs after IV, 27, but there it runs: *krṣwnw tšpwṭ ʿmw* (remark the *scriptio plena* and the second person). Cf. R. SMEND, *Die Weisheit des Jesus Sirach*, Berlin 1906, p. 8.

present writer that BEGRICH exaggerates the importance of the different moments of a lawsuit for the exegesis of Dt.-Isaiah's *Gerichtsreden*. On the other hand, he does not analyze the form or style of the genre sufficiently.

The third paragraph deals with the disputations (*Disputationsworte*), which, though akin to the *Gerichtsreden*, are nevertheless to be clearly distinguished from them. The aim of a disputation consists in convincing somebody and in invalidating his objections. This genre, as well as the foregoing one, is a prophetic imitation of living forms of speech taken from daily life. The disputations show between them a certain similarity of setting, aim and form, but the contents may vary to a notable degree. Typical of Dt.-Is. is a frequent use of hymnic motifs and forms in the disputations. But for all that we are not allowed to call them hymns. The hymnic elements are due to the particular contents of the dt.-Isaian disputations as we shall see in the third chapter of the present work.

In the next section of his book, BEGRICH tackles the study of the lyrical genres in Dt.-Is. He finds two hymns (Is. xlii 10-13; xliv 23), a collective song of thanksgiving (xlix 13), two individual laments (l 4-9; li 9-16), an individual song of thanksgiving (xlix 1-6), a royal enthronement song (lii 7-10) and a taunt song (xlvii). When analyzing these types, the author continually follows H. GUNKEL's introduction to the psalms, which has been completed by BEGRICH himself.[1]

In his conclusions, J. BEGRICH thinks that, in more than one respect, he dissents from H. GRESSMANN and L. KÖHLER. In opposition to the former he denies the existence of threats, promises, rebukes and songs of victory in Is. xl-lv. Furthermore he considers that GRESSMANN exaggerated the number of hymns. In contrast with KÖHLER, he rejects the *Botenspruch* as a genre. But he especially stresses the striking fact that Dt.-Is. chiefly uses non-prophetical genres.[2] This certainly is a very important conclusion,[3] but it must be considered to be an overstatement. Finally we note that BEGRICH presents our

---

1 H. GUNKEL - J. BEGRICH, *Einleitung in die Psalmen*, Göttingen 1933, § 2, 2. 3. 23. 28. 51; § 3, 2.4.9. 11d; § 6,6. 8. 11. 19. 21. 23; § 7, 4. 8; § 8, 32. 35. 39; § 12,5.

2 J. BEGRICH, *Studien*, p. 67: "... die auffällige Tatsache, welche alle Aufmerksamkeit verdient, dass Deuterojesaja sich vorwiegend in Gattungen nichtprophetischen Ursprunges bewegt und dass typisch prophetische Redeformen auffallend gering vertreten sind".

3 Cf. F. BLOME, *TGl.* XXXII 1940, p. 45.

prophet as a writer. It is true, he builds up his oracles as oral utterances, but nevertheless, they are only written imitations of oral types.[1]

BEGRICH's work met with a very favorable reception and, from a form-critical point of view, he undoubtedly surpasses all his predecessors.[2] But we may ask whether he is right in presenting Dt.-Is. as a writer only, in other words in stressing the character of imitation, which would affect all his genres. We also may assert that he did not completely grasp all the typical features of the important genres, and thus the subject needs further investigation.

In 1953, H. E. VON WALDOW graduated with a thesis on the setting of Dt.-Isaiah's preaching. More exactly, he investigates in his work whether this preaching has any relation to the cult. To him there is only one valuable starting-point for such a study, viz. a form-critical analysis. In this respect he refers to BEGRICH's work, which would have made fairly certain three conclusions: 1. Is. xl-lv is a collection of rather small independent units. 2. It is usually possible to come to an exact delimitation of the units. 3. The type most frequently used is the priestly oracle of salvation. But he is aware of the above-mentioned deficiencies of BEGRICH's work, and for this reason he opens his dissertation with a chapter on the genres in Dt.-Is.[3], out of which we notify only the new views.

From the purity of form, characteristic of the dt.-Isaian oracles of salvation, as well as from their very close literary contact with the lamentations, VON WALDOW deduces that these oracles were pronounced in their original liturgical setting. They are thus not at all literary imitations (against BEGRICH).

In the disputations also, the simple structure suggests an original setting: there is no literary imitation.[4] In the discussion of the *Gerichtsreden* the author goes his own way.[5] According to BEGRICH these pericopes are imitations of words pronounced in an actual profane lawsuit. But VON WALDOW distinguishes between a cultic and a more secularized type (*profanisiert*; the latter e.g. in Jer. ii 4-13, 29-32;

---

1 J. BEGRICH, *o.c.*, p. 97.

2 Cf. J. ZIEGLER, *TR.* XXXIX 1940, p. 51; L. ROST, *TGegw.* XXXIII 1939, p. 93: "Es is wohl die seit Jahren bedeutendste Erscheinung zur Dt-Jes-Frage".

3 H. E. VON WALDOW, *Anlass und Hintergrund der Verkündigung des Deuterojesaja*, Diss. Bonn 1953, pp. 11-61: "Die Gattungen bei Dtjes."

4 H. E. VON WALDOW, *o.c.*, pp. 35-36.

5 H. E. VON WALDOW, *o.c.*, pp. 37-47.

Mich. vi 1ff), because, as we shall see in chapter III, the prophets imitate a cultic lawsuit situation, but sometimes develop this form to resemble more the profane lawsuit. The manifest identity of judge and accuser points to a very close connection between these pericopes and cult. The Convenant Festival, however, is out of the question, since Yahwe does not direct his pleading against Israel but against the nations and their gods. The cultic background is probably a cosmic eschatological Enthronement Festival.[1] Thus, Dt.-Is. would have enlarged the prophetical *Gerichtsrede* in a universalist sense.

In the conclusion to his first chapter, VON WALDOW points out that 60 % of the dt.-Isaian material consists of the oracles of salvation, the disputations and the trial speeches, viz. genres which occur rarely or not at all in other prophetic books. They are typical of this prophet as against the other ones. This statement, it seems to me, is rather exaggerated. The three main genres would still reflect their original setting and are not to be considered as imitations.

H. E. VON WALDOW's investigation goes farther than BEGRICH's, for he tries to determine as precisely as possible the actual setting of the dt.-Isaian oracles. After having formulated as neatly as possible the nexus between Dt.-Is. and cult,[2] he studies the cultic setting of the oracle of salvation in general. The setting of such an oracle is either a private cultic act, when the oracle is a reply to the supplication of an individual, or a public liturgy of lament (e.g. 2 Chron. xx). In such circumstances, however, the oracle is pronounced not by a priest but by a cult prophet. In VON WALDOW's opinion, it would be preferable not to call it a priestly oracle of salvation but a prophetic cult oracle.[3] The oracles of Dt.-Is. certainly do not belong to a private cult, as they are directed at the whole community. But the prophet pronounced them at collective liturgies of lamentation among the exiles.[4] In other words, Dt.-Is. is a cult prophet; he belongs to the circles of nebiism. This explains the exceeding importance of the oracle of salvation in

---

[1] H. E. VON WALDOW, *o.c.*, p. 45: "Wahrscheinlich ist der kultische Hintergrund dieser Gerichtsreden ein kosmisch-eschatologisches Thronbesteigungsfest Jahve's, das in dem Zukunftsbild des Dtjes. eine grosse Rolle spielt".

[2] H. E. VON WALDOW, *o.c.*, pp. 63-71: "Das kultische Problem bei Deuterojesaja".

[3] H. E. VON WALDOW, *o.c.*, pp. 73-90. Against J. BEGRICH, "Das priesterliche Heilsorakel", *ZAW*. LII 1934, pp. 81-92.

[4] H. E. VON WALDOW, *o.c.*, pp. 91-123: "Der 'Sitz im Leben' des prophetischen Kultorakels bei Deuterojesaja". Cf. ID., "*... denn Ich erlöse dich*". *Eine Auslegung von Jesaja 43*, Neukirchen 1960, pp. 56-59.

his collection. Certain typical themes, such as the destruction of the enemy and the election and honor of Israel, would also get their full meaning from this setting.

H. E. VON WALDOW devotes his last chapter to the setting of disputations and trial speeches in Dt.-Is.[1] The people's faith has been deeply shaken by the catastrophe that fell on them. Therefore the prophet was obliged to defend his message of salvation in these genres. They thus have some connection with the cultic oracles of salvation. But they do not belong to the cult themselves. Dt.-Is. would have been not only a cult nabi, but a pastor as well.

The thorough studies of BEGRICH and VON WALDOW have been substantially improved by C. WESTERMANN, who also wrote the first commentary which is consistently based on a form-critical analysis.[2] All through the present work, the reader will be able to see how much I am indebted to these outstanding studies. I generally agree with his positions, although I shall have more than one occasion to enter into discussion with him and, as I hope, to improve on some of them.

In the first part of his article,[3] WESTERMANN already exhibits some pessimism about the possibility of dividing Is. xl-lv into small units in the manner suggested by the foregoing form critics. He asserts that the composition of Dt.-Is. out of independent units is only one side of the picture; the units are, in contrast with what happens in the pre-exilic prophetical books, set in a larger organized whole[4]. He quotes with approval J. MUILENBURG, according to whom "the poems are developed literary compositions".[5] MUILENBURG accepts

---

[1] H. E. VON WALDOW, *Anlass und Hintergrund*, pp. 135-155: "Anlass und Hintergrund der Disputationsworte und Gerichtsreden".

[2] C. WESTERMANN, "Sprache und Struktur der Prophetie Deuterojesajas", *Forschung am Alten Testament* (*Theologische Bücherei*, 24), München 1964, pp. 92-170; ID., *Das Buch Jesaja. Kap. 40-66* (*ATD*, 19), Göttingen 1966. A more popular commentary which takes into account the results of form criticism is G. FOHRER, *Das Buch Jesaja*, III, Zürich 1964. According to this commentary, the most important genres in Dt.-Is. are the salvation oracle, the hymn and the disputation.

[3] C. WESTERMANN, *Forschung*, pp. 92-117: "Der Stand der Diskussion".

[4] C. WESTERMANN, *a.c.*, p. 106: "Jeder, der die Kapitel des Dtjes.-buches unbefangen liest, hat das Empfinden, dass es hier anders ist als bei Kapiteln vorexilischer Prophetenbücher, in denen kurze Prophetenworte aneinandergereiht sind. Dafür klingt die Sprache Dtjes.' einfach zu fliessend". Cf. S. SMITH, *Isaiah chs. XL-LV*, pp. 7-9.

[5] J. MUILENBURG, *The Book of Isaiah, Chapters 40-66*, *The Interpreter's Bible*, V, New York 1956, p. 391.

that the prophet used certain "literary forms and types", such as the critics of the *Gattungsforschung* identified. But, in his opinion, we should recognize an evolution toward Dt.-Is., where "we often have a fusion of literary types, a combination of several forms to make a whole".[1] He sees "a remarkable persistence of major motifs all the way through". Nobody will deny this, but, as I see it, this is no argument against the presence of independent units. The developed character of Dt.-Isaiah's units is not so self-evident, and, anyhow, it remains fruitful to analyze for themselves the basic types used by our prophet.

Analogous attempts to find larger compositions have been made by E. KISSANE and M. HARAN. The former opposes a "collection theory" and proposes a certain form of "book unity". He accords to certain pericopes, which he calls tail-pieces, a proper literary function. This way he considers three songs of thanksgiving (Is. xlii 10-12; xliv 23; xlix 13), three summaries of the prophetic message (xlviii 20-21; lii 9-11; lxii 10-12) and three oracles summarizing the preceding poem (xlvi 12-13; lvi 1-2; lix 20-21). With the help of these he divides Is. xl-lxvi into ten sections, each one showing a certain thematic unity. On the basis of introductory formulas, changes of contents and strophic structures, he discovers in each section three poems, "which are often as distinct from each other as the different psalms in the Psalter".[2] As for M. HARAN, he finds some recurrent cycles of the same motifs, each cycle having its own inner unity.[3]

When dealing with the oracles of salvation, WESTERMANN provides an important form-critical contribution by distinguishing between two types, which he calls oracle or promise of salvation and proclamation of salvation. We shall deal with this in the next chapter. He describes the structure of both types, which does not coincide exactly with that proposed by BEGRICH and VON WALDOW.

---

[1] J. MUILENBURG, *o.c.*, p. 385.

[2] E. KISSANE, *The Book of Isaiah*, II, Dublin 1943, pp. XXI-XXXIII. His division on pp. XXXII-XXXIII: three poems + tail-piece in each section: xl 1-11 / 12-31 / xli-xlii 9 // xlii 10-12 /// 13-xliii 13 / 14-xliv 5 / 6-22 // 23 /// 24-xlv 13 / 14-25 / xlvi 1-11 // 12-13 /// xlvii / xlviii 1-11 / 12-19 // 20-21 /// xlix 1-7 / 14-23 / 24 + l 1-3 + xlix 8-12 // 13 /// l 4-11 / li 1-8 / 9-lii 10 // 11-12 /// lii 13-liii / liv / lv // lvi 1-2 (8) /// etc.

[3] M. HARAN, בין ראשונות לחדשות, Jerusalem 1963, pp. 11-23. His cycles are: xl / xli 1-20 / 21-xlii 17 / 18-xliii 10 / 11-xliv 5 / 6-28 / xlv / xlvi 1-11 / (xlvii) / xlviii 1-16. In English cf. M. HARAN, "The Literary Structure and chronological Framework of the Prophecies in Is., XL-XLVIII", *SVT*. IX, Leiden 1963, pp. 127-155.

The disputation has a very loose structure, and we had perhaps better call it "contestation" (*Bestreitung*), rather than "disputation", since we only hear the voice of one party, whereas in a real disputation both of them should be heard. It is especially in connection with this genre that WESTERMANN underlines the presence of larger compositions in Dt.-Is. As to the *Gerichtsreden*, in agreement with L. KÖHLER, he distinguishes the double contest in Dt.-Is.: between Yahwe and the nations and, on the other side, between Yahwe and Israel. This distinction will draw our attention in the third chapter. We shall see that the double point of this genre involves a double line of evolution with regard to the traditional prophetic trial speech. WESTERMANN concedes that it is hard to find a setting for this genre, which, moreover, is characterized by a strongly abstracting stylization.[1] Further on WESTERMANN pays attention to the Cyrus oracle (xliv 24-xlv 7), the form-critical and redactional structure of chapters xlvi and xlviii, and the hymns of praise in Dt.-Is. The latter are responsories to the announcement of God's deed of redemption (Is. xl 9-11; xlii 10-13; xliv 23; xlv 8; xlviii 20-21; xlix 13; lii 9-10; liv 1-2). Most of them act as a conclusion, so that they appear very important for the study of the structure of the whole book. In his final summary, he presents this structure, such as he conceives it.[2] Once again he stresses the importance of this structure for the understanding of the message; one should take into account both the meaning of the units, according to their type, and the general structure, in which the units are inserted.[3] According to its aim, the present study is limited to the first task. As to the second one, the writer is not convinced of the presence of large thematic compositions in Is. xl-lv, such as presented by WESTERMANN, although some smaller original compositions may show up in a form-critical analysis. Even WESTERMANN must admit that at least in Is. xl-xlv, the units mostly stand for themselves, whereas from chapter xlvi on the units would be joined to form larger compositions.[4]

---

[1] C. WESTERMANN, *a.c.*, p. 135: "Von einem 'Sitz im Leben' dieser Gerichtsreden wird man kaum sprechen können".

[2] C. WESTERMANN, *a.c.*, pp. 164-165: four larger compositions: xl-xliv / xlv-xlviii / xlix-liii / liv-lv.

[3] C. WESTERMANN, *a.c.*, p. 167: "Beides muss gleich sorgfältig und als gleich bedeutsam berücksichtigt werden: die je von ihrer Gattung her zu verstehenden einzelnen Teile und die Zusammenhänge, in die gefügt sie uns vorliegen".

[4] C. WESTERMANN, *a.c.*, p. 164; *Jesaja 40-66*, p. 13.

Summary

Let us now sum up the results of our survey. First of all, it must be stated that the form-critical method is now generally accepted for the study of prophetical texts. More and more, scholars realize that a valuable interpretation is impossible without a precise knowledge of the genre proper to the text under consideration.[1] In respect to the prophetical books, the opinion is gaining ground, that they consist of separate units, the type of which must first be determined, whereas their eventual mutual connection in the arrangement of the book as a whole must be proved.[2] It thus is very important for the interpretation of Dt.-Is. to mark out the original literary units and to make clear to which type they belong[3]. In this respect one should endeavour to apply standards which are as objective as possible. In the Servant problem also, there is no prospect of a solution if one does not go into the form-critical aspects of these pericopes, although here the question of authenticity remains important too.[4]

---

[1] Cf. O. Eissfeldt, *Einleitung in das AT*, Tübingen 1964, pp. 10-13; W. Oesterley-Th. Robinson, *An Introduction to the Books of the Old Testament*, London 1934, p. 272; B. Balscheit, *Der Gottesbund. Einführung in das Alte Testament*, Zürich 1943, p. 173; A. Bentzen, *Introduction to the Old Testament*, I, Copenhagen 1948, pp. 183-202; A. Weiser, *Einleitung in das AT*, Göttingen 1963, p. 29; R. H. Pfeiffer, *Introduction to the OT*, London 1953, p. 452; C. Kuhl, *Die Entstehung des Alten Testamentes*, Bern 1953, p. 193; T. W. Manson - H. H. Rowley, *A Companion to the Bible*, Edinburgh 1963, pp. 130-131; A. Robert - A. Feuillet, *Introduction à la Bible*, I, Paris 1957, pp. 479-482; *De Wereld van de Bijbel*, Utrecht 1964, pp. 342-377.

[2] Cf. H. Van den Bussche, *De profetie in Israel*, s.l., 1959, p. 20; G. Fohrer, *TRu.* XIX 1951, pp. 299-300.

[3] O. Eissfeldt, *o.c.*, pp. 455-457; R. Augé, *Isaïas II*, Montserrat 1936, pp. 26-27; M. Garcia Cordero, *Libros Proféticos*, Madrid 1961, pp. 59-61: "... una 'colección' de oràculos tenidos en diversas épocas, agrupados sin orden cronológico en su mayor parte".; P. Volz, *Jesaja II*, Leipzig 1932, p. XXXV: "Es ist unter allen Umständen festzuhalten, dass *die einzelnen Lieder* (oder Liedkompositionen) für sich ständen und für sich ausgelegt werden müssen". Other concrete examples of the use of form criticism in the interpretation of Dt.-Is. are: K. Elliger, "Der Begriff 'Geschichte' bei Deuterojesaja", *Fs. O. Schmitz*, Witten 1953, pp. 26-36; B. J. van der Merwe, *Pentateuchtradisies in die Prediking van Deuterojesaja*, Groningen 1955; R. Rendtorff, "Die theologische Stellung des Schöpfungsglaubens bei Deuterojesaja", *ZTK.* LI 1954, pp. 3-15; E. Jenni, "Die Rolle des Kyros bei Deuterojesaja", in *TZ.* X 1954, pp. 241-256.

[4] Cf. E. Sellin, "Die Lösung des deuterojesajanischen Gottesknechträtsels", *ZAW.* LV 1937, pp. 181-183; J. Coppens, *Nieuw licht over de Ebed-Jahweh-liederen*, Leuven 1950, p. 5; J. Lindblom; *The Servant Songs in Deutero-Isaiah*, Lund 1951, pp. 12-51: "The Literary Character of the Ebed-Yahweh Songs"; V. de Leeuw, *De Ebed Jahweh-profetieën*, Assen 1956; pp. 114-116 and 124-134; O. Kaiser, *Der königliche Knecht* (*FRLANT.* 70), Göttingen 1959.

As to Dt.-Is., it is a fact that he uses mainly four prophetical types: the oracle of salvation and the proclamation of salvation, the trial speech and the disputation. Besides these he often has hymns and, in the properly prophetic genres, hymnic features are very frequent.

What may we then conclude from these data with respect to the prophet's message? To answer this question, one must investigate which is the original setting of these genres and whether they are still rooted in that original setting. In other words, does the prophet imitate certain types which are normally attached to another setting, or was he really in that situation (BEGRICH, VON WALDOW)? Thus, the attempts of form criticism to define the setting of the texts from Dt.-Is. must be on two levels: 1) the real and to Dt.-Is. himself existing *Sitz im Leben*; 2) the *Sitz im Leben* which originally forms the background of the genres used by him. Both may coincide but they do not necessarily do so.

Since the studies of BEGRICH, VON WALDOW and WESTERMANN, there is no longer much doubt about the laws of the chief genres in Dt.-Is. But the question of whether the prophet himself, especially in cases of literary imitation, did not combine some of these literary units in compositions of his own (e.g. a prophetical liturgy) remains to be investigated. This is important, not only for the interpretation of the text, but also for making clear the place of our prophet in the literary evolution of prophetism. Is it true that with him the dissolution of the prophetic types begins (H. GRESSMANN)? That he continually mixes the genres (L. KÖHLER)? That in chs. xlvi-lv, he builds the classical types into larger poems (C. WESTERMANN)? If such shows to be true, the fact is almost necessarily connected with the setting and the nature of his message. How can we clarify this connection?

It will appear from the present analysis that the original units, when inserted into the collection, have not been altered very much (against W. CASPARI). But the collection itself is a problem. It seems indeed impossible to demonstrate that Is. xl-lv has been composed according to a certain design. It is also hard to decide whether the prophet himself or a disciple or anybody else has collected the oracles (MOWINCKEL, ELLIGER, CASPARI). This may be of no importance at all for the interpretation of the text; but, if the final redactor appears to have worked according to a plan, it certainly will be of importance. In that case, after having described the message of the original oracles, one could enquire into the theology of the last redactor. But to do such surpasses our design, which is to investigate the message of the original prophecies.

Table I

Delimitation of the Units according to Form Critics

Gressmann	Köhler	Mowinckel	Elliger	Begrich	Westermann
xl 1-2	xl 1-2	xl 1-2	xl 1-2	xl 1-8	xl 1-11
3-5	3-5	3-5	3-5		
6-8	6-8	6-8	6-8		
9-11	9-11	9-11	9-11	9-11	
12-31	12-16	12-19a.xli 6-7.xl 19b-31	12-17	12-17	12-18.21-31
	17-19a.xli 6-7.xl 19b-20		(18-20)	18-20.xli 6-7.xl 25-26	
	21-26		21-26	21-24	
	27-31		27-31	27-31	
xli1-13	xli 1-5	xli 1-4.8-13	xli 1-5	xli 1-5	xli 1-5
			(6-7)	(6-7)	xl 19-20.xli 6-7
	8-10		8-10	8-13	8-13
	11-13		11-13		
14-20	14-16	14-16	14-16	14-16	14-16
	17-20	17-20	17-20	17-20	17-20
21-29	21-24	21-29	21-29	21-29	21-29
	25-29				
xlii 1-4	xlii 1-4	xlii 1-4	xlii 1-4	xlii 1-4	xlii 1-4
5-9	5-9	5-9	5-9	5-9	5-9
10-17	10-13	10-17	10-13	10-13	10-13
	14-17		14-17	14-17	14-17
18-xliii 7	18-25	18-xliii 7	18-xliii 7	18-25(?)	18-25
	xliii 1-7			xliii 1-7	xliii 1-7
8-13	8-13	8-13	8-13	8-13	8-15
14-15	14-15	14	14-15	14-15	
16-21	16-21	15-xliv 5	16-21	16-21	16-21
22-xliv 5	22-28		22-xliv 5	22-28	22-28
	xliv 1-5			xliv 1-5	xliv 1-5
6-20	6-8	6-9.21-22	6-8	6-8	6-8.21-22
	(9-20)	(10-20)	(9-20)	9-20	(9-20)
21-23	21-22	21-22	21-22	21-22	
	23	23-28	23	23	23
24-28	24-28		24-28	24-28	24-xlv 1-7
xlv 1-8	xlv 1-7	xlv 1-8	xlv 1-7	xlv 1-7	
	8		8	8	8
9-13	9-10	9-13	(9-10)	9-13	9-13
	11-13		11-13		
14-17	14-17	14-17	14-17	14-17	14
					15
					16-17
18-25	18-25	18-25	18-25	18-25	18-19
					20-25

Gressmann	Köhler	Mowinckel	Elliger	Begrich	Westermann
xlvi 1-13	xlvi 1-2	xlvi 1-2	xlvi 1-4	xlvi 1-2	xlvi 1-4
	3-4	3-13		3-4	
	(5-8)		(5-8)	5-11	(5-8)
	9-13		9-11		9-13
			(12-13)	12-13	
xlvii 1-15	xlvii 1-4	xlvii 1-15	(xlvii 1-15)	xlvii 1-15	xlvii 1-15
	5-7				
	8-10a				
	10b-12				
	13-15				
xlviii 1-11	xlviii 1-11	xlviii 1-11	xlviii 1-11	xlviii 1-11	xlviii 1-11
12-16	12-16	12-16	12-15	12-15	12-17
			16	16	
17-21	17-19	17-19	(17-19)	17-19	18-19
	20-21	20-21	20-21	20-21	20-21
xlix 1-6	xlix 1-6	xlix 1-6	xlix 1-6	xlix 1-6	xlix 1-6
7	7-13	7-13	7-12	7	7-12
8-13			13	8-13	13
14-21	14-21	14-21	14-21	14-21	14-26
22-26	22-23	22-23	(22-26)	22-23	
	24-26	24-26		24-26	
l 1-3	l 1-3	l 1-3	l (1-3)	l 1-3	l 1-3
4-10(11)	4-9	4-11	4-11	4-9	4-9
	10(11)			10-11	
li 1-3	li 1-8	li 1-8	li 1-3(4-5).6-8	li 1-3	li 1-2.4-8(+10-11)
4-8				4-5	
				6-8	3
9-16	9-10	9-10(11)12-14	9-10	9-16	9-lii 3
	12-16	(15-16)	(11-16)		
17-23	17-23	17-23	17(18)19-23	17-23	
lii 1-3	lii 1-2	lii 1-2(3-6)7-10	lii 1-2	lii 1-2	
(4-6)	(3-6)		(3-6)	3-6	(4-6)
7-12	7-12		7-12	7-10	7-10
		11-12		11-12	11-12
13-liii 12	13-liii 12	13-liii 12	(13-liii 12)	13-liii 12	13-liii 12
liv 1-3	liv 1-6	liv 1-10	(liv 1-17)	liv 1-3	liv 1-10
4-8				4-6	
9-10	7-10			7-10	
11-17	11-14a	11-17		11-17	11-17
	14b-17				
lv 1-5	lv 1-5	lv 1-5	(lv 1-13)	lv 1-5	lv 1-5
6-7	6-7	6-13		6-7	6-11
8-13	8-13			8-13	12-13

CHAPTER TWO

THE WORDS OF SALVATION

§1. Definition of the genre

As the salvation word is Dt.-Isaiah's most common genre, it is normal to open the present study with an analysis of this genre which is so characteristic of our prophet. The term "salvation oracle" (*Heilsorakel*) has been used for the first time by J. Begrich, who devoted a short paper to the type in *Zeitschrift für die alttestamentliche Wissenschaft.* He elaborated his article in his *Studien zu Deuterojesaja.*[1] Most of the pericopes, classified by him in this genre, were formerly reckoned by H. Gunkel and his disciples among the promises (*Verheissung*). With this name, the form critics indicated the oracles in which the prophet promised salvation, whilst they called threat (*Drohung*) the prophecies of disaster.[2] Gunkel analyzed rather superficially the characteristics of these genres.[3] In *Der Messias,* H. Gressmann devoted a chapter to the promises, which he opens with a paragraph on the introduction formulas. In his opinion, the promises do not have proper introductions. Some formulas, however, may have their origin in that genre, since they are mainly used there. Among these are quoted *bayyôm hāhû'*, *bayyāmîm hāhēm*, *bā'ēt hāhî'*, *hinnēh yāmîm bā'îm*, *be'aḥărît hayyāmîm.* Gressmann defends their eschatological nature. Let us remark from the outset that none of these expressions occurs in Dt.-Is.,[4] nor are they typical of an oracle of salvation. The fact that in pre-exilic prophecy they occur more often in promises than in threats is, from a literary standpoint, accidental.

---

1 J. Begrich, "Das priesterliche Heilsorakel", *ZAW.* LII 1934, pp. 81-92; *Studien zu Deuterojesaja,* pp. 14-26.

2 H. Gunkel, "Die Propheten als Schriftsteller und Dichter", in H. Schmidt, *Die grossen Propheten,* Göttingen 1915, p. il; H. Gressmann, *Der Messias,* Göttingen 1929, p. 69.

3 Cf. A. Schoors, "Methode van de vormkritische analyse der profeten", *Bijdragen,* XXXII 1971, p. 273.

4 One finds ביום ההוא in Is. lii 6, but Is. lii 3-6 is not authentic. I exposed my arguments in my article "Arrière-fond historique et critique d'authenticité des textes deutéro-isaïens", *Orientalia Lovaniensia Periodica,* II 1971, pp. 125-127.

After a short digression on the arrangement of oracles in collections, GRESSMANN deals with the structure of the genre. In this respect he points out that it does not have a typical structure. He spends the remainder of the paragraph on the so-called conditional promise, which includes an admonition. The latter developed into a distinct genre for the first time with Isaiah. As to the contents, GRESSMANN distinguishes in the promises of salvation between political motifs (royal power, world-dominion), natural motifs (fertility, a rich harvest, etc.) and ethic-religious motifs (purity of Yahwism, social justice, etc.).[1] Our analysis will make out in what sense these motifs occur in Dt.-Is. We may say that, from a form-critical point of view, we did not learn much from GRESSMANN's study. In this chapter, BEGRICH, VON WALDOW and WESTERMANN will be our most important guides.

1. *Sitz im Leben*

The so-called words of salvation in Dt.-Is. cannot be recognized merely by the fact that they contain a promise of bliss. They also have a definite structure, which has to be distinguished from the many promises of salvation in other prophetic writings. In order to typify the genre we must refer to the cultic *Sitz im Leben*, which for the dt.-Isaian oracles is unquestionable.

At the end of the psalms of lamentation we sometimes find a reversal of mood, whereby the supplication changes into thanksgiving or praise (e.g. Pss. vii 18; xxvi 12b). Critics of the psalms have called this motif "promise of thanksgiving" (*vorgreifende Danksagung*) or even "certainty of granting" (*Gewissheit der Erhöhrung*).[2] The phenomenon is currently explained as follows: the Israelite is convinced of his duty to proclaim Yahwe's salvific intervention. Therefore, in his distress, he promises explicitly that he will give thanks to Yahwe in the liturgy of thanksgiving if he may experience his help. A more plausible explanation ascribes the reversal to an oracle of salvation, in which, in the name of God, the petition of the prayer is granted.

The first to develop this was F. KÜCHLER, in a paper on the cultic

---

[1] H. GRESSMANN, *o.c.*, pp. 82-83: "Die Verheissungen".

[2] Cf. H. GUNKEL - J. BEGRICH, *Einleitung in die Psalmen*, pp. 243-245; H. J. KRAUS, *Psalmen*, Neukirchen 1966, p. xlvi; P. DRIJVERS, *Over de Psalmen*, Utrecht 1964, pp. 104-105.

oracle published in the *Baudissin Festschrift*.[1] H. Gunkel had already expressed a similar view as a hypothesis,[2] and in his later form-critical studies he developed the subject.[3] To S. Mowinckel is due the merit of having elaborated the idea in his *Psalmenstudien*, to the point of eliminating its hypothetical character. In the first volume, dealing with the individual psalms of lament, he pays attention to the oracles of granting, in which the divine reply to a supplication or lamentation is given, and in the third volume he deals more fully with the subject.[4]

The close connection between the collective lament and a certain type of oracle can no longer be questioned. According to Jud. xx 23, 27, it was customary "to inquire of the Lord" at a liturgy of lamentation and the text tells us about the oracle following the enquiry (vss. 23 and 28). In Jos. vii 7-15 we read something similar. In Chronicles, king Jehoshaphat, attacked by Moabites and Ammonites, proclaims a fast and he himself pronounces the lamentation, after which a temple servant replies in the spirit of Yahwe, promising the divine help (2 Chron. xx 3-17). Likewise Yahwe answers Hezekiah's prayer with an oracle by the prophet Isaiah (2 Kings xix 14-34 = Is. xxxvii 14-35), although in this case the prophet does not only promise bliss. On the occasion of the public fast, proclaimed by Jehoiakim, Jeremiah has his oracles read by Baruch (Jer. xxxvi) but here an organic connection between the liturgy and the giving of oracles is not clear. One rather has the impression that the prophet chose the occasion because it provided him with an important audience. According to Dan. ix, the man of God said a prayer on behalf of his people, until an angel appeared to reassure him of the destiny of his countrymen.

The Israelite usage corresponds with what we know about Assyro-Babylonian practices.[5] There, too, the oracle of salvation is added

[1] F. Küchler, "Das priesterliche Orakel in Israel und Juda", *Festschrift W. W. Baudissin*, Giessen 1918, pp. 299-301.

[2] H. Gunkel, "Psalmen", *RGG*. Tübingen 1909-1913, IV, col. 1935: "Man darf sich demnach vielleicht vorstellen, dass bei den ältesten Klagefeiern zunächst das Gebet gesprochen worden ist worauf dann der Priester die Antwort im Namen des Gottes verkündet hat".

[3] E.g. in H. Gunkel - J. Begrich, *Einleitung in die Psalmen*, pp. 133, 136-138, 177-178, 409-411.

[4] S. Mowinckel, *Psalmstudien I. Awän und die individuellen Psalmen*, Kristiania 1921, pp. 145-146; III. *Kultprophetie und prophetische Psalmen*, Kristiania 1923.

[5] An article that expressly deals with these parallels is P. B. Harner, "The Sal-

to the prayer of the king. Such appears e.g. from this fragment of a longer prayer by Assurbanipal to Nebo:[1]

> [*Ich, Assurbanipal,* habe] deinen Ruhm verkündet, Nabu, unter der Gesamtheit der Grossen Götter;
> möge durch meine [*Neider alle Zusammen*] mir nicht immer wieder ans Leben gegangen werden!
> [*Im Ezida-Tempel von*] Nineveh wende ich mich immer wieder an dich, du Kriegerischster unter seinen (!) Brüdern;
> [bist du doch die] Hilfe Assurbanipals für die Zukunft, ja für immer!
> [*Ich, dein ....Knecht*], legte mich nieder zu den Füssen Nabus,
> [dass] Nabu [mich *tröste*] unter allen meinen Neidern.
>
> Ich habe dich [*eingesetzt*], Assurbanipal, ich, Nabu, (noch) für fernste Tage,
> dass deine Füsse nicht immer wieder lahm werden, deine Hände nicht erzittern!
> Diese deine Lippen sollen nicht müde werden, sich immer wieder an mich zu wenden,
> dass deine Zunge nicht immer wieder durcheinandergebracht werde *in* deinen Lippen!
> Ich, der ich dir immer wieder gute Rede schenke,
> werde dein Haupt erheben,[2] deine Gestalt *aufheben* lassen im Tempel von Emaschmasch.

Other instances can be found in the collections published by H. ZIMMERN and FALKENSTEIN-VON SODEN, as well as in GRESSMANN's article, which I analyzed in the first chapter.[3] All of them belong to a period dating from the middle of the 9th to the middle of the 7th centuries. That the custom was known also in the West-Semitic area appears among other sources from the famous stele of *Zkr*, found at Afis. In this inscription the king of Hamath and La'aš describes how he prayed to Baalshamen when menaced by a hostile coalition and how Baalshamen granted his prayer:[4]

---

vation Oracle in Second Isaiah", *JBL.* LXXXVIII 1969, pp. 418-434. I came to study these parallels independently from this paper.

[1] Translation in A. FALKENSTEIN - W. VON SODEN, *Sumerische und Akkadische Hymnen und Gebete,* Zürich 1953, p. 292. An older English translation in D. D. LUCKENBILL, *Ancient Records of Assyria and Babylonia,* II, Chicago 1927, par. 1122-1123. Text in J. A. CRAIG, *Assyrian and Babylonian Religious Texts,* I, Leipzig 1895, pp. 5-6. Cf. H. ZIMMERN, *Babylonische Hymnen und Gebete,* II, Leipzig 1911, pp. 20-21; M. JASTROW, *Die Religion Babyloniens und Assyriens,* I, Giessen 1905, pp. 442-443.

[2] Cf. מרים ראשי as a title of Yahwe in Ps. iii 4.

[3] H. ZIMMERN, *o.c.,* I, Leipzig 1905, p. 8; *Das Babylonische Neujahrfest,* Leipzig 1926, p. 12; H. GRESSMANN, *ZAW.* XXXIV 1914, p. 289; A. FALKENSTEIN - W. VON SODEN, *o.c.,* pp. 105-109, 199, 263, 286.

[4] Text and translation in H. DONNER - W. RÖLLIG, *KAI.* 202. The translation quoted here is taken from *ANET,* p. 655. Cf. H. J. ZOBEL, *VT.* XXI 1971, pp. 91-99.

But I lifted up my hand to Beʿelshamayn, and Beʿelshamayn heard me.[1] Beʿelshamayn [spoke] to me through seers and through *diviners*[2]. Beʿelshamayn [said to me]: Do not fear, for I made you king, and I shall stand by you and deliver you from all [these kings who] set up a siege against you... [3]

We find traces of the connection between lamentation and oracle of salvation in the so-called prophetic liturgies, to which GUNKEL paid a particular attention. He dealt particularly with Mic. vii 7-20 and Is. xxxiii. He considers these pericopes as prophetic imitations of the alternation of prayer and oracle of salvation.[4] In the conclusion of Micah's book he sees a liturgy of lamentation, actually celebrated on days of mourning for the fallen and not yet restored Jerusalem.[5] The structure of this composition runs as follows:

A { I. Lamentation of Zion (vss. 7-10)
  II. answered with an oracle (vss. 11-13)
B { III. Lamentation of Israel (vss. 14-17)
  IV. continued with a hymn, expressing the certainty of the coming salvation (vss. 18-20).

The prophetic liturgy in Is. xxxiii also consists of a double sequence of lament and oracle:

A { I. Collective lamentation (vs. 2)
  II. Oracle of salvation (vss. 3-6)
B { III. Lamentation (vss. 7-9)
  IV. Oracle (vss. 10-13) [6]

Also Joel i-ii is a liturgy of humiliation and prayer, organized on the occasion of a locust plague and ending in an oracle of salvation. In the book of Habacuc again we find the pattern of such a liturgy of lamentation. It begins with a psalm, in which we recognize the complaint (i 2), the description of the distress (i 3-4) with the quotation of an

---

[1] The technical term we find in the psalms: ויענני.

[2] Aramaic: עדד; ביד חזין וביד עדדן should be synonymous or at least parallel with חזי; cf. Arab. *ʿadda*, "to count" (also used in connection with oracle sticks, omina, etc.); cf. H. DONNER - W. RÖLLIG, *KAI*, II, p. 208. According to H. L. GINSBERG, the root עדד means "to send" (he refers to Ug. *ʿdd*); cf. *DISO*, p. 204. The meaning of Ug. *ʿdd*, however, is uncertain. C. H. GORDON, *UT*, § 19.1819, does not pronounce on it, whereas J. AISTLEITNER, *Wörterbuch der ugaritischen Sprache*, Berlin 1963, nr. 2003, has "erzählen", referring also to Arab. *ʿadda*.

[3] Further on the text is very damaged.

[4] H. GUNKEL - J. BEGRICH, *Einleitung*, p. 409.

[5] H. GUNKEL, "Der Micha-Schluss", *ZS*. II 1923, pp. 145-178.

[6] H. GUNKEL, "Jesaia 33, eine prophetische Liturgie", *ZAW*. XLII 1924, pp. 177-208.

oracle of doom (i 5-11), and the motif of the honor (i 12-13). Between the latter and the certainty of being heard (ii 5-20) the divine answer is transmitted.[1]

H. GUNKEL enumerates all the places in the prophetical books in which we can find a collective lamentation and an oracle linked together: Is. xxvi 8-14a + 14b-15; 16-18 + 19-21; xxxiii 2 + 3-6; 7-9 + 10-13; xlix 14 + 15ff.; 24 + 25-26; lix 9-15a + 15b-20; lxiii 7-lxiv 11 + lxv; Jer. iii 22b-25 + iv 1-2; xiv 2-9 + 10; 19-22 + xv 22; xxxi 18-19 + 20; li 34-35 + 36-49; Hos. vi 1-3 + 4-6; xiv 3-4 + 5-9; Hab. i-ii (cf. *supra*); Joel i 5-ii 11 + 12-14; 15-17 + 18-20 (cf. *supra*); Bar. iv 9-29 + 30-v 9; Mic. vii 7-10 + 11-13; 14-17 + 18-20.[2] Naturally, a few texts are open to discussion, and the oracle does not always contain a promise of salvation, especially with Jeremiah. But this presents no real difficulty. When the oracle of doom is pronounced precisely where an oracle of salvation is expected, the effect is striking: Yahwe refuses to hear the prayer.

Finally, the psalms show that the liturgy of humiliation and prayer included such an oracle. We find some short samples in Pss. xii 6; xx 9-13; lx 8-10; lxxxv 9-14; cviii 8-10; cxv 12-16. The royal psalm xx consists of a blessing prayer on the king and a replying oracle, a composition which we find in a somewhat more complicated form in Ps. cxxxii. In Ps. lx, which must be placed after a military set-back, the oracle (vss. 8-10) is set within lamentations.[3] Also in Ps. Sal. xvii the collective supplication for a Messiah (vss. 21-25) changes without a clear cesura into a divine prediction of the Messiah's coming.[4] In Ps. xii we even see how the supplicant reacts to the oracle with a grateful utterance of confidence, in which he expresses his certainty that his prayer has been heard. A number of psalms, in which the oracle of granting is no longer transmitted, still conserve this utterance of confidence or a song of thanksgiving as a conclusion.[5]

---

[1] Cf. S. MOWINCKEL, *Psalmenstudien III*, p. 27.

[2] H. GUNKEL, *ZS.* II 1923, pp. 161-162; ID., *Die grossen Propheten*, p. lxii, note 5; H. GUNKEL - J. BEGRICH, *Einleitung*, pp. 137-138.

[3] H. J. KRAUS, *Psalmen*, p. 427.

[4] Cf. R. HARRIS - A. MINGANA, *The Odes and Psalms of Solomon*, Manchester 1916. Syriac text in vol. I, pp. 105-107; translation in vol. II, pp. 430-432.

[5] E.g. Pss. vi 9-10; vii 18; x 16-18; xxvi 12; xxviii 6-7; xxxi 20-25; liv 6-9; lvi 11-14; lvii 6-12; lxiv 8-11; lxix 33-34; lxxxvi 12-13; cix 30-31; cxl 13-14; cxv 17-18; xciv 12-15, 22-23.

J. Begrich summarizes the setting of the cultic oracle as follows: when somebody had pronounced the lamentation and supplication in the sanctuary, a priest addressed to him an oracle, probably on the grounds of a sacrificial omen. He promised him that his prayer would be granted, describing God's intervention with reference to the prayer itself. Comforted by this oracle the supplicant expressed his certainty of being heard and concluded with a vow.[1] R. G. Castellino criticized this position, but his criticism is superficial and does not really touch any of Begrich's arguments.[2]

According to Begrich the oracles of Dt.Is. were not actually pronounced in a cultic situation. They are but poetical imitations of real priestly oracles.[3] Besides, he limits the *Sitz* of the oracle of salvation to the individual liturgy of lamentation. But among the above-quoted examples, more than one hints at the same usage within the framework of a collective liturgy. In the first chapter I mentioned von Waldow's thesis, according to which Dt.-Isaiah's oracles of salvation are real cultic oracles, pronounced on the occasion of collective liturgies of lamentation, in which the catastrophe of 587 was commemorated[4]. Whether we have to agree with Begrich or with von Waldow will only appear after our analysis of the texts.

2. *Form and contents*

In this analysis the ideas of Begrich and von Waldow will be our starting point. Suggestions from other scholars will be indicated as such.

The oracle of salvation is always a word of Yahwe,[5] directed to an individual, usually a man. That is why the receiver of the oracle is addressed in masculine singular. I think, however, that this should not be exaggerated, because the oracle of salvation does not exclusively belong to the individual liturgy. Further on we shall return to this question in more detail.

---

[1] J. Begrich, *ZAW*. LI 1934, p. 82. Cf. G. Widengren, *The Accadian and Hebrew Psalms of Lamentation*, Uppsala 1936, p. 28.

[2] R. G. Castellino, *Le lamentazioni individuali e gli inni in Babilonia e in Israele*, Torino 1939, pp. 139-140.

[3] J. Begrich, *Studien*, p. 97; *ZAW*. LII 1934, p. 91.

[4] Cf. supra p. 24. To the same effect H. W. Wolff, *EvTh*. XV 1955, pp. 461-462; J. Lindblom, *Prophecy in Ancient Israel*, p. 270.

[5] Is. xli 8ff., 14ff.; xliii 1; xliv 2; xlviii 17; xlix 7, 15; li 12; liv 8; Jer. xxx 10-11 = xlvi 27-28; Lam. iii 57; cf. Ps. xxxv 3.

a. Structure

The introduction very often consists of the formula of reassurance: "Fear not".[1] According to H. GRESSMANN, the formula comes from the theophany, where it belongs to the word of self-revelation (cf. Gen. xv 1; xxvi 24). A divine apparition overawes the seer and therefore the deity reassures him and reveals himself: "I am X". As the examples are few in the O.T., GRESSMANN supposes Dt.-Is. does not depend on an Israelite tradition but rather imitates Babylonian parallels.[2] *Lā tapallaḫ* is indeed a frequent formula in Assyro-Babylonian oracles, such as this oracle directed to Esarhaddon : "I, Ishtar of Arbela, will go before you and behind you: fear not!"[3] This connection between the formula and the self-revelation proper to the theophany has been overstressed by GRESSMANN, since hardly any of the parallels in the O.T. are caused by an immediate divine self-revelation. W. ZIMMERLI has shown that, in cult as well as in prophecy, the formula got differentiated functions, that are to be distinguished carefully.[4] The most important of these is to act as an introduction of an oracle of granting, as clearly appears from biblical [5] and extra-biblical parallels.[6] I just quote another eloquent example:

Kniend sitzt auf seinen Unterschenkeln Assurbanipal,
wendet sich immer wieder an seinen Herrn Nabu:
Ich habe dich lieb gewonnen, Nabu, verlass mich doch nicht!...

Fürchte dich nicht, Assurbanipal!
Ich werde dir ein langes Leben schenken... [7]

Closer than the theophany-formulas are some "Fear not"-formulas, directed to Israel in the holy war (e.g. Jos. viii 1; x 8; Num. xxi 34;

---

[1] Is. xli 10, 13, 14; xliii 1, 5; xliv 2; li 7; liv 4; Jer. xxx 10-11 = xlvi 27-28.

[2] H. GRESSMANN, *ZAW*. XXXIV 1914, pp. 287-289.

[3] M. JASTROW, *Die Religion Babyloniens und Assyriens*, II, pp. 155-163; F. STUMMER, "Einige keilschriftliche Parallelen zu Jes. 40-66", *JBL*. XLV 1926, p. 177; I borrowed the translation from R. H. PFEIFFER, *ANET*, p. 450.

[4] Cf. W. ZIMMERLI, "Ich bin Jahwe", *Gottes Offenbarung*, München 1963, pp. 11-40, esp. p. 34.

[5] E.g. Gen. xxi 17; xxvi 24; xlvi 3; Lam iii 57; cf. W. ZIMMERLI, *a.c.*, pp. 25-26.

[6] E.g. the Assyrian oracle just quoted: *ANET*, pp. 449-450, 604-606; also the stele of *Zkr*: *KAI*. 202.

[7] A. FALKENSTEIN - W. VON SODEN, *Sumerische und akkadische Hymnen und Gebete*, p. 293.

Deut. i 21; Ex. xiv 13-14).[1] In Dt.-Is. the formula must be understood within the framework of the oracle of salvation, as will appear from our investigation of the texts. Possibly, the oracular "Fear not"-formula is an imitation of the formulas used by a great king when addressing his vassal, as might appear from a letter sent by the Hittite king Šuppiluliuma to Niqmadu of Ugarit.[2]

Regularly the assurance is substantiated by means of the next clause, whether or not opening with *kî*.[3] God's helpful nearness is expressed here, mostly in a nominal clause.[4] To these phrases correspond expressions of confidence in the psalms of lament, such as: "You are my God".[5] In Ps. xxxv 3, the suppliant asks for an oracle, which he epitomizes precisely by means of such a promise of God's nearness: "Say to my soul: I am your deliverance". Sometimes the assurance of intervention itself (A motif, cf. below), is directly connected by means of *kî* with the formula of reassurance, and thus acts as a substantiation (Is. xliii 1; xliv 3). Next to the "Fear not" the introduction of an oracle of salvation may have the messenger's formula: "Thus says Yahwe ..." (e.g. xliii 1, 14, 16-17; xlv 14; xlviii 17); further a *Heroldsruf*: "Hear ..." (e.g. Is. xliv 1; xlvi 12); lastly the receiver may be called by his name, either immediately after the messenger's formula (Is. xliii 1) or together with the *Heroldsruf* (xliv 1), or even together with the formula of reassurance (xli 14). When all these elements are missing, the call by name may be the only introduction (Is, liv 11). Is. xlii 14-17; li 12-15 and liv 7-10 are oracles of salvation without any introduction.

In its complete form the body of the oracle shows the following threefold structure:

A. the assurance of Yahwe's intervention;
B. the clauses, which express the consequence of the divine intervention and deal with the reversal of the situation of distress;
C. the final aims of Yahwe's intervention.[6]

---

[1] C. Westermann, *Das Buch Jesaja. Kap. 40-66*, p. 60. P. E. Dion, "The 'Fear not' Formula and Holy War", *CBQ*. XXXII 1970, pp. 565-570, gives good arguments to contest the thesis that "Fear not" is a typical formula of the holy war.

[2] Cf. *PRU*. IV, pp. 35-36: nr. 17.132, 11. 1-6 and 30-32.

[3] With כי: Is. xli 10; xliii 5; xliv 3; li 8; liv 8; Jer. xxx 10-11. Without כי: Is. xli 4.

[4] E.g. Is. xli 10: כי עמך־אני; כי־אני אלהיך; Jer. xxx 10: כי הנני מושיעך.

[5] Pss. cxl 7; xxxi 15; iii 4; xxii 4; xxv 5; xl 18; xliii 2; lxxi 3,5; lxxxvi 2; cxlii 6; cxliii 10. — Cf. H. Gunkel - J. Begrich, *Einleitung*. pp. 233-235.

[6] J. Begrich, *Studien*, pp. 15-16; H. E. von Waldow, *o.c.*, pp. 13-19.

In BEGRICH's opinion, one of these motifs often is missing, but the first one only once (Is. xlv 14-17). To this exception VON WALDOW observes that the A motif is essential and should not be wanting, so that we cannot designate this pericope as an oracle of salvation.

In the A motif, as a rule, the subject is Yahwe and the verb is in the perfect tense. We find, however, imperfect tenses also (Is. xli 17b; xlii 14) and even nominal clauses (xliii 19a; li 12a; liv 11). The pronouncement is mostly very general, but in a subjoined clause it may be explained, such as in Is. xli 14-15:

> I help you, says Yahwe;
> your Redeemer is the Holy One of Israel.
> Behold (*hinnê*), I make of you a threshing sledge,
> new, sharp and having teeth...

The particle *hinnê* is typical of this motif. It underlines the effectiveness of Yahwe's promised intervention. Lastly there may follow a motivation (*Begründung*) of Yahwe's intervention. Thus in Is. liv 7-10 the motif A is built up this way: Yahwe's intervention (vss. 7-8), explanation (v. 9), motivation (v. 10).

In the second motif the verbal form always is imperfect and new subjects appear. The change of subject and, if A is in the perfect tense, the change of tense unmistakably indicate the transition from A to B. To this sequence of perfect-imperfect corresponds a similar sequence in the lament motif called "certainty of hearing"[1]:

> Yahwe has heard the sound of my weeping,
> Yahwe has heard my supplication,
> Yahwe has accepted my prayer.[2]
> All my enemies shall be ashamed and surely troubled. (Ps. vi 9-11)

The C motif expresses the aim of Yahwe's intervention, which is generally the glory of Yahwe or the acknowledgment (*daʿat*) of Yahwe. It often comprises an imperfect form of the verb *ydʿ*, introduced with a consecutive *waw* or with the particle *lᵉmaʿan*. This motif also has its correlative in the psalms of lament, e.g. "That men may know (*yēdᵉʿû*) that God rules over Jacob" (Ps. lix 14), or "Be gracious to me, O Yahwe ... that (*lᵉmaʿan*) I may recount all thy praises" (Ps. ix 15).

---

1 J. BEGRICH, *ZAW*. LII 1934, p. 85.

2 The ipf. יקח is used in parallelism with a perf. and has the same value, as often in poetical texts. Cf. M. DAHOOD, *Psalms I*, Garden City 1966, p. 39. Thus also LXX and Vg.

Until now we analyzed the structure of the priestly oracle of salvation according to BEGRICH and VON WALDOW. Starting from this analysis C. WESTERMANN made an important step forward.[1] On the basis of Is. xli 8-13 he reformulates the same structure as follows:

1. Address (*Anrede*)
2. Assurance of salvation (*Heilszuspruch*): Fear not!
3. Substantiation: a) nominal clause (I am with you, I am your God)
(A) b) verbal clause (perf.: I help you, I strengthen you)
(B) 4. Outcome (imperf.) on behalf of the supplicant and against his enemy
(C) 5. (Final goal).

One recognizes the resemblance to the structure proposed by BEGRICH and VON WALDOW.[2] But WESTERMANN points to a strange fact: in 1934 BEGRICH found only eight priestly oracles of salvation in Dt.-Is., whereas in 1938 this number had increased to 24. In order to be able to apply his scheme to the 24 units, BEGRICH was obliged in his *Studien* to accept quite a number of exceptions and to dispose of several difficulties. It is striking that, among the former eight texts, six contain the formula "Fear not" (xli 8-13, 14-16; xliii 1-4, 5-7; xliv 1-5; liv 4-6). This formula is addressed specifically to an individual and precisely the above mentioned pericopes seem to reply to an individual lament. They thus represent the oracle of salvation or the oracle of granting proper. All of them show the same structure as does xli 8-13, though the sequence of motifs is relatively free. Only in these texts every structural element corresponds to the cultic *Sitz im Leben.*[3] The address is always direct, mostly by the name of Jacob-Israel. Here is an essential distinction of these oracles as against the other words of salvation, which I deal with below.

The substantiation of the assurance of salvation mostly consists of two parts, in which God's intervention is granted and the outcome of this intervention is indicated (BEGRICH's A and B motifs). The first motif, for which WESTERMANN reserves the name *Begründung*, is built out of a nominal clause and a verbal one. The former expresses

[1] C. WESTERMANN, "Das Heilswort bei Deuterojesaja", *EvTh.* XXIV 1964, pp. 355-373; resumed briefly in "Sprache und Struktur der Prophetie Deuterojesajas", *Theologische Bücherei*, 24, München 1964, pp. 117-124; and in *Das Buch Jesaja. Kapitel 40-66*, pp. 13-15.

[2] The letters (A), (B), (C) indicate the corresponding elements in BEGRICH's structure.

[3] C. WESTERMANN, *EvTh.* XXIV 1964, p. 359: "Nur bei solcher Begrenzung kann schlüssig und eindeutig nachgewiesen werden, dass *diese* Texte wirklich einer Form entsprechen, deren 'Sitz im Leben' jeder einzelne Teil entspricht ..."

God's turning towards those addressed, a lasting relationship between God and the recipient, while the latter speaks of his intervention. These two divisions reflect the two divisions of the prayer in the psalms of lamentation begging God to turn towards the suppliant and then to intervene.[1] The verbal element is generally put in the perfect tense, which underlines the effectiveness of Yahwe's intervention (*perfectum executionis*). It is not a proclamation of something that is to take place later on, as has been pointed out by von Waldow also.

A proclamation of that kind is to be found in the motif of outcome, which therefore has the imperfect tense. Yahwe as well as terrestrial beings may be the subject here (contra von Waldow). This motif is rather variable and of less fixed form than the former. The same applies to the conclusion motif, in which the final goal of Yahwe's intervention is expressed. It corresponds to the vow in the psalms of lamentation and it does not occur in all the oracles of salvation. Westermann rightly points out that only these texts, in which the assurance of salvation with the nominal and perfective substantiation is central, belong to the type of the oracle of salvation.[2]

The structure proposed by Westermann, although it occurs as such in the Bible only in Dt.-Is., corresponds nevertheless to a real pattern of a cultic salvation oracle. Such can be proved beyond any doubt from the extra-biblical cult oracles, which show exactly the same basic structure. P.B. Harner is the first to have tried to present an exhaustive analysis of the topic.[3] The best examples are five oracles from the sanctuary of Ishtar at Arbela, addressed to Esarhaddon.

Harner expressly states that the reassurance "Fear not" is intended to grant salvation now. It is strengthened by statements in the present tense (e.g. I am your gracious shield) and in the past tense (e.g. I have not rejected you; cf. Is. xli 9), whereas the fourth motif is in the future tense. The order of these elements may vary and more than once they are quite elaborate, but they are easily recognizable. I quote one example:

---

[1] G. Widengren, *The Accadian and Hebrew Psalms of Lamentation*, pp. 274-275.

[2] C. Westermann, *a.c.*, p. 365: "Nur diese Texte, in deren Mitte der Heilszuspruch und die nominale und perfektische Begründung enthalten sind, gehören eindeutig zur Gattung des Heilsorakels".

[3] P. B. Harner, "The Salvation Oracle in Second Isaiah", *JBL.* LXXXVIII 1969, pp. 418-423.

1. [Esarhad] don, king of the countries,
2. Fear not!
3. I am the great divine lady, I am the goddess Ishtar of Arbela...
4. I shall lie in wait for your enemies, I shall give them to you... [1]

The same pattern is to be found in several oracles to Assurbanipal[2], in the above-quoted oracle to king *Zkr* (inscription of Afis), and more or less in an oracle referred to in the text *I will praise the Lord of Wisdom.*[3]

What about the other oracles of salvation that are recognized as such by BEGRICH and VON WALDOW? They bear some affinity with the pericopes analyzed above. They are, however, clearly distinct from them. From Is. xli 17-20 WESTERMANN deduces the following structure:

I. An allusion to the *collective* lament
II. The proclamation of salvation
  1. God's turning towards Israel
  2. God's intervention (called elsewhere: the outcome; in any case concrete)
III. The end in view (final goal).

WESTERMANN calls this genre "the proclamation of salvation" (*Heilsankündigung*). It is formulated in the imperfect tense. There is thus no "assurance of salvation" with its substantiation. The same structure may be found in Is. xlii 14-17; xliii 16-21; xlv 14-17; xlix 7-12, and also in some salvation utterances that are combined with other types (e.g. Is xlix 14-26). Evidently the motif II bears a close affinity with the motif of outcome of the oracle of salvation. They belong, however, to two formally distinct types, for each of them has a proper structure and point. Whereas in the oracle of salvation the main affirmation sounds general and perfective, the proclamation of salvation has its centre of gravity in concrete salvific facts that are promised for the future. The proclamation of salvation is related to the collective lamentation, while the assurance of the oracle of salvation originally replies to an individual lamentation. Moreover, both of these relations do not have the same bearing. The proclamation of salvation presupposes such a lamentation; but it is of too loose a form to be a really cultic reply. Hence WESTERMANN concludes with regard to the *Sitz im Leben* that, whereas the oracle of salvation reflects a cultic

---

[1] Cf. *ANET*, pp. 449-450.
[2] Cf. *AOT*, p. 266; *ANET*, pp. 450-451.
[3] Cf. *ANET*, pp. 434-437; esp. p. 436.

function (a priest or cultic prophet), the proclamation, on the contrary, belongs in its historical concreteness to a purely prophetic function. J. BEGRICH thus rightly explained the oracle of salvation as a reply to an individual lamentation, but he assigned too large a number of pericopes to this type.

WESTERMANN's structural analysis improves to a large extent the result obtained by BEGRICH and VON WALDOW. His distinction between oracle and proclamation of salvation does more justice to the various texts of Dt.-Is. In the next paragraphs (§2 and 3) I shall go along with this distinction. Furthermore, he defines better the point of both types. In his view the formula "Fear not" (assurance of salvation, reassurance according to VON WALDOW) is the centre of the oracle of salvation, while VON WALDOW reckoned it to be the introduction.

b. Terminology and Phraseology

To prove the connection between the lament and the oracle or proclamation of salvation, we can appeal to the so-called *Stoff*, the common expressions and formulas. Here follows a general survey; we shall go into details when studying the different pericopes properly:

— "I am thy servant" (Pss. cxliii 12; xix 12; xxvii 9; xxxi 17; lxix 18; lxxxvi 2, 4, 16; cix 28) — "You my servant" (Is. xli 8, 9; xliv 1; Jer. xxx 10);
— worm (תולעה) Ps. xxii 7 - Is. xli 14;
— despised by the people (בזוי עם) (Ps. xxii 7) — deeply despised, abhorred by the nations (בזוי נפש,[1] מתעב גוי) (Is. xlix 7);
— poor, miserable: עני (Pss. ix 13, 19; x 12, 17; xii 6; xxxv 10; xl 18; etc.), אביון (Pss. xii 6; xxxv 10; xl 18) — עניה (Is. li 21; liv 11), העניים והאביונים (Is. xli 17);
— expressions of fear: Pss. xxxi 14; xxxviii 19; lv 3-4; lxiv 2; lxix 18; cii 3; — "Fear not" (Is., *passim*; Lam. iii 57; Jer. xxx 10-11);
— "Why hast thou forsaken me (עזב)?" (Ps. xxii 2; cf. Pss. lxxi 9, 11, 18; xxvii 9; Is. xlix 14) — "With little emotion I abandoned you" (Is. liv 7);
— hide the face (הסתיר פנים) (Pss. xiii 2; xxvii 9; xxx 8; lxix 18; lxxxviii 15; cii 3; cxliii 7) — הסתרתי פני (Is. liv 8);

---

[1] Read בְּזוּי instead of בְּזֹה in accord with IQIa.

— forget (שכח) (Pss. ix 13, 19; x 12; xiii 2; xlii 10) — Is. xlix 14-15;
— God's silence (חרש; חשה) (Pss. xxviii 1; xxxv 22; xxxix 13; lxxxiii 2; cix 1) — "For a long time I have kept still ..." (Is. xlii 14);
— scorn or slander from enemies: מכל־צררי הייתי חרפה (Ps. xxxi 12); נשאתי חרפה כסתה כלמה פני ··· וחרפות חורפיך נפלו עלי (Ps. lxix 8-10; cf. Ps. xxxix 9; xlii 11; lv 13; lxix 20-21; lxxxix 51-52; cii 9; cix 25; Jer, xv 15; xx 8; Job xvi 10) — חרפת אנוש ··· גדפתם (Is. li 7); אל־תכלמי··· חרפת אלמנותיך לא תזכרי־עוד (Is. liv 4);
— hear my prayer (ענני) (Pss. iv 2; xiii 4; xvii 6; xxvii 7; xxxviii 16; lv 3; etc.) — I hear you (them) (Is. xli 17; xlix 8);
— save me (הושיעני) (Pss. iii 8; vi 5; vii 2; xxxi 17; liv 3; lix 3; lxix 2; lxxi 2; etc.) — אני מושיעך (Is. xliii 3; Jer. xxx 10);
— help: עזרני (Ps. cix 26); היה עזר לי (Ps. xxx 11) — עזרתיך (Is. xli 10, 13, 14);
— uphold (תמך): Pss. xli 13; lxiii 9 — תמכתיך (Is. xli 10).
— redeem me (גאל) (Ps. lxix 19; Lam. iii 58); גאלי (Ps xix 15) — גאלתיך (Is. xliii 1); גאלך (Is. xli 14; xlviii 17; liv 5, 8);
— have mercy: חנני (Pss. li 3; lvi 2; lxxxvi 3, 16) — רחמתיך (Is. liv 8);
— "Contend with those who contend with me" (Ps. xxxv 1) — "I will contend with those who contend with you" (Is. xlix 25);
— not be put to shame: אל אבושה (Pss. xxv 2, 20; xxxi 2, 18; lxxi 1; Jer. xvii 18) — לא תבושי (Is. xlix 23; liv 4);
— curses against the enemies: Pss. xxv 3; xxxi 18; xxxv 4-6, 26; xl 15-16; etc. — Is. xli 11-12;
— different expressions of confidence:
  — "I am thine" (Ps. cxix 94) — "You are mine" (Is. xliii 1);
  — "Thou art my God" (Pss. xxii 11; xxv 5; xxxi 15; xliii 2; lxxxvi 2; cxl 7) — "I am your God" (Is. xli 10, 13; xliii 3);
  — "Thou art with me" (Pss. xxiii 4; xlvi 8, 12) — "I am with you" (Is. xli 10; xliii 2, 5; Jer. xxx 11).

This extensive list of terminological contacts abundantly shows that the connection between the salvation utterance and the lament is very close.

§2. The oracles of Salvation in Is. xl-lv

The structure of these oracles can be represented in this table:

Table II

The Oracles of Salvation

	Intr.	Address	Assur. of Salv.	Substantiation Nom.	Verb.	Outcome	Goal	
xli 8-13		8-9	10a	10a	10b	11-12		13
14-16		14aβ	14aα	14bβ	14bα	15-16a	±16b	
xliii 1-4	1a		1bα	1bδ	1bβγ	2-4		
5-7			5aα	5aβ		5b-6	± 7	
xliv 1-5	2a	1.2b	2bα			3-4	5	
liv 4-6			4a	5	6	4b		

I. *Is. xli 8-13*

8 But you, Israel, my servant,
Jacob, whom I have chosen,
the offspring of Abraham, my friend;
9 you whom I have seized from the ends of the earth,
whom I have called from its farthest corners,
I have said to you, "You are my servant,
I have chosen you and not cast you off";
10 Fear not, for I am with you,
be not afraid, for I am your God.
I strengthen you, truly I help you,
I uphold you with my saving right hand.
11 Behold, they shall all be ashamed and confounded
who are incensed against you;
they shall be as nothing and shall perish,
the men who go to law with you;
12 you shall seek them, and not find them,
the men who contend with you;
they shall be as nothing at all,
the men who war against you.
13 For I, Yahwe, am your God,
who holds your right hand,
saying to you, "Fear not,
I help you".

The delimitation of this oracle is simple. It is clear that vs. 13 (For I, Yahwe, am your God ...) is the final verse of an oracle, and that vs. 14 (Fear not ...) is the beginning of a new one. In the vss. 1-13 the question is not so clear. There is no doubt that 6-7 is out of place here; but should we take 1-4, 8-13 as one unit or does 8-13 make out a distinct unit? K. Elliger even considers 8-10 and 11-13 as two distinct oracles on the ground of rhythm. In view of the obvious typical structure of the salvation oracle, the second opinion is undoubtedly right. G. Fohrer also thoroughly demonstrates Is. xli 8-13 to be one independent unit, on the strength of content, strophic composition, the inclusion with the basic words *'al tîrā'* and *'ăzartîkā*, the genre and the fact that the vss. 11-13, without address are very incomplete.[1]

The oracle opens with an elaborated address (vss. 8-9). It is directed in singular to Jacob-Israel, who is determinated more precisely as the servant of Yahwe, his chosen, offspring of his friend Abraham. The prophet uses profusely the terminology of election and calling, thus stressing the relationship between Yahwe and his people.

Let us remark that the prophet, though actually speaking to Judaeans, addresses his message to the whole of Israel, the twelve tribes of Jacob. When the name "Israel" does not indicate the northern kingdom but theologically refers to the whole nation, the idea of covenant is somewhat implied. The double name "Jacob-Israel" is characteristic of Dt.-Is. (Is. xl 27; xli 8, 14; xlii 24; xliii 1, 22, 28; xliv 1, 21, 23; xlv 4; xlviii 12; xlix 6) Perhaps we should not exaggerate the significance of this phenomenon, as it may be simply ascribed to the poetic parallelism, although the frequent use may include a design. There could be a reference to the traditions of the patriarchs, more precisely to the Jacob-tradition. We are allowed to think so because further on we shall encounter more precise references to the promises given to the patriarchs. By this name the prophet thus recalls the promises to Jacob (Gen. xxviii 13-15). Further on we shall see that a crisis of faith with respect to the divine promises is one element of the exilic milieu. This will appear especially from the disputations. In this respect the double name "Jacob-Israel" refers to Yahwe's fidelity to his first promises. Thus it is a motive of confidence, supporting the oracle.[2]

The word *'ebed*, meaning "servant", expresses the relationship of the people to Yahwe under the aspect of dependence and servitude. This does not necessarily mean a relationship of slavery, for the servant

---

[1] G. Fohrer, "Zum Text von Jes. xli 8-13", *VT*. V 1955, p. 240.

[2] H. E. von Waldow, "... *denn Ich erlöse dich*". *Eine Auslegung von Jesaja 43*, Neukirchen 1960, pp. 17-24.

of the king was an important person, as is evident from the *'ebed melek*-seals.[1] In a famous inscription of Barrakib from Zinjirli (8th century) this king of Sam'al calls himself "Servant of Tiglat Pileser", thus formulating his condition of vassalage. In 2 Sam. x 19 also, *'ebed* is used to indicate vassal kings. As C. R. NORTH rightly points out, the word expresses the relation of the weaker to the stronger partner in a covenant.[2] In the Ugaritic legend of Keret, the hero has the epithet *'bd il*, besides that of "son of El".[3] V. DE LEEUW is right when he states: "The word *'ebed* connotes a certain honor and distinction, so that one may boast of this title, especially when the word is connected with the name of a highly placed person or a king".[4]

The expression "your servant", a formula of etiquette used in letters to indicate the writer, passed into the style of prayer. In this respect C. LINDHAGEN's statement is remarkable, according to which the expression occurs in the Bible only in the individual psalms of lamentation.[5] Moreover LINDHAGEN points out the important fact that in these psalms the formula is found in a context, where the suppliant appeals to his particular bond with Yahwe: his condition of *'ebed* is a reason why his prayer should be granted.[6] This throws a light on the use of the title "my servant" in the address of the oracle of salvation. Yahwe recalls his close bonds with the addressee. The word has been used to indicate all kinds of persons, who stood in a particular relationship with Yahwe: the prophets (e.g. 2 Kings xxi 10); the Israelites in general (1 Kings viii 23; 2 Kings vi 14) or the faithful in particular (2 Chron. ix 7; Ps. xxxiv 23); the patriarchs (Ex. xxxii 13; Deut. ix 27); Moses (Ex. xiv 31; Num. xii 7-8); Joshua (Jos. xiv 29; Jud. ii 8); David (2 Sam. iii 18; vii 5-8) etc. On the whole the title

---

1 C. LINDHAGEN, *The Servant Motif in the Old Testament*, Uppsala 1950, pp. 6-39: instances from the surrounding literatures. The same title occurs at Ugarit; cf. A. F. RAINEY, *The Social Structure of Ugarit* (Hebrew), Jerusalem 1967, pp. 53-54.

2 Cf. *KAI.* 216: 1-3: אנה ברכב··· מלך שמאל עבד תגלתפליסר. Cf. R. DE VAUX, "Le roi d'Israël, vassal de Yahvé", *Mélanges E. Tisserant*, I, Città del Vaticano 1964, pp. 123-124. C. R. NORTH, *The Second Isaiah*, p. 97.

3 *UT.* Krt: 153, 155, 299-300; *bn il* in 125: 10, 21, 110.

4 V. DE LEEUW, *De Ebed Jahweh-profetieën*, Assen 1956, p. 138: "Uit het woord *ebed* spreekt een zekere eer en voornaamheid, zodat men zich op deze titel kan beroemen, vooral als het woord in verbinding staat met de naam van een hooggeplaatste persoon of van een koning". At Ugarit a class of high officials is designated with *'bd*.

5 C. LINDHAGEN, *o.c.*, p. 263. Cf. V. DE LEEUW, *o.c.* p. 139; Cf. also supra p. 45.

6 C. LINDHAGEN, *o.c.*, pp. 265-275; i.a.: "... the close association of the עבד theme with the idea of the covenant".

suggests that its bearer, by means of his charge, stands in Yahwe's particular service. Thus the title is apt to indicate a task. Its use in the singular with a collective meaning goes back to the time of the exile, as it is attested for the first time in Jer. xxv 10; xlvi 27-28 and Dt.-Is. (xli 8-9; xlii 19; xliv 1-2, 21; xlv 4; xlviii 20). Moreover with Dt.-Is. the meaning of the formula receives some qualification: it no longer denotes in the first place a charge but rather an election.[1] Now it is used in connection with *bḥr*, exactly as in our text: because of the parallelism, "Servant" is tantamount to "Chosen".

Elsewhere also we find *bḥr* in close connection with "Servant of Yahwe" (1 Kings xi 13, 32-34; Pss. cv 26; cxxv 4; Hag. ii 23). Both expressions are thus complementary: the election by Yahwe constitutes one his servant. The word *bḥr* received a particular meaning as a theological *terminus technicus*, indicating the special election of Israel to be Yahwe's property (*naḥălâ*).[2] The basic meaning of the word is "to destinate, to dispose of something". In religious speech, stress is laid on grace or love as the motive of the election and there is often a connotation of "election to a task".[3] In Deut. vii 6-8, the *magna charta* of Israel's election, the complete gratuity is fairly stressed. In vss. 9-15 of the same chapter the sanction with a covenant and the ethical bearings of the election are also given much importance. The idea of a task is more explicit when individuals are elected: they are chosen for an office or mission (cf. Deut. xviii 5; xxi 5; 1 Sam. ii 28; 2 Sam. vi 21; 1 Kings viii 16). The official connotation of the title *'ebed* is related to this. According to T. C. Vriezen and G. Quell the deuteronomic theology has definitely qualified the relationship between God and Israel as a divine election, whereas formerly it was formulated only in terms of a covenant.[4] K. Koch, however, has shown that the deuteronomic vision is most probably later than the one we find in some psalms (Pss. cv 5-6, 42-43; cxxxv 4; cvi 5; xlvii 5). His main argument is based on the historical conception of both visions. According to these psalms, the patriarchs, esp. Jacob, have been

---

[1] V. de Leeuw, *o.c.*, p. 144. A very good study of the term עבד in *o.c.*, pp. 137-146; more profusely in the quoted work by C. Lindhagen.

[2] Cf. T. C. Vriezen, *Die Erwählung Israels nach dem A.T.*, Zürich 1953, p. 36; G. Quell, "Die Erwählung im A.T.", *TWNT*. IV, pp. 163-167; K. Koch, "Zur Geschichte der Erwählungsvorstellung in Israel", *ZAW*. LXVII 1955, pp. 205-226.

[3] T. C. Vriezen, *o.c.*, pp. 41-42; G. Quell, *TWNT*. IV, p. 168.

[4] Cf. the texts in T. C. Vriezen, *o.c.*, pp. 47-48; cf. also G. Quell, *TWNT*. IV, p. 163; G. Fohrer, *Jesaja III*, p. 38.

chosen, whereas in Deuteronomy the nation was elected in the liberation from Egypt. It would be hard to understand that the moment of the election has been transferred from Moses's time to that of the patriarchs, and precisely to the North-Israelite ancestor Jacob. The reversed process is more acceptable, as in the whole of the O.T. Moses's time was regarded as the basic happening in the history of salvation. So the utterances in Psalms on the election do not depend on Deuteronomy, but both come forth from a common older tradition.[1] Dt.-Is. depends on the same tradition but stands closer to its elaboration in the above-mentioned psalms than to the deuteronomic one, for he also connects the election with the names of the patriarchs Jacob and Abraham. The general close relationship between the prophet and the hymnic literature, to which I shall often have occasion to refer, points in the same direction. According to VRIEZEN, in Dt.-Is. the election is always connected with the responsibility and the mission of the people.[2] Yet here in vss. 8-9 and in xliv 2 this aspect is not explicit. One may even ask whether it is present at all. The stress seems to be laid on the alliance between Yahwe and Israel due to the election. It seems to me that VRIEZEN argues too much from the Ebed Yahwe pericopes, where the aspect of mission is indeed of paramount importance.

G. FOHRER wants to eliminate vs. 8b as a later addition, because the threefold verse 8 breaks the rhythmical movement of the surrounding verses (3 + 3), and, furthermore, the qualification of Abraham as a friend of Yahwe is post-exilic (2 Chron. xx 7).[3] This standpoint has no support in the textual tradition. Besides, this one instance from Chronicles is a very narrow basis and nothing proves that the Chronicler does not depend on Dt.-Is. Indeed, the mention of Abraham fits the context very well, as we have seen above with regard to the idea of election, and as appears from vs. 9, where "whom I have taken from the ends of the earth" refers to the call of Abraham in Haran.[4] If we want to improve the text rhythmically, it would be better to suppose a parallel stichos of vs. 8b to be dropped, rather than the latter to be

---

[1] K. KOCH, *ZAW*. LXVII 1955, pp. 216-217: "Die deuteronomische Erwählung-s anschauung ist also die spätere ... Beide gehen von einer gemeinsamen älteren Tradition aus, die verschieden umgestaltet wird".

[2] T. C. VRIEZEN, *o.c.*, p. 48.

[3] G. FOHRER, *VT*. V 1955, pp. 241-242.

[4] Cf. J. KAHMANN, "Die Heilszukunft in ihrer Beziehung zur Heilsgeschichte nach Is., 40-55", *Bib*. XXXII, 1951, p. 85; T. C. VRIEZEN, *o.c.*, p. 65.

added.[1] Israel's election to be *'ebed* is the foundation of the assurance of salvation which follows. The last word of the long address is already a transition to the oracle: "I have not cast you off". This negative wording of the election is of interest in the present context, for Yahwe actually seems to have cast off his people. It is striking that the same expression occurs also in an Assyrian oracle of salvation, addressed to Esarhaddon, where we read *lā aslî(ka)*, "I have not cast you off".[2]

The assurance of salvation is repeated in the parallel stichos with *'al-tišta'* (vs. 10). Formerly this verbal form was commonly explained as a hitpael of *š'h*, "to gaze about", while it was inferred from the context that this gazing was full of fear.[3] But we decidedly have here the qal of the root *št'*, which is the same as Ugaritic *ṯt'*, also a parallel with *yr'* (Phoenician *št'*).[4]

In the setting of the holy war also, the reassurance is substantiated with "Yahwe, your God, is with you" (Deut. xx 1; xxxi 8; Jud. vi 12). This does not definitely prove that the formula has its roots in the traditions of the holy war.[5] If this were the case, this presence of Yahwe would refer, through its setting in the holy war, to his interventions during the exodus and the conquest, which are, especially in the deuteronomic traditions, the prototype of the holy war. Indeed, also in the texts, which I just quoted with regard to the holy war, the former glorious deeds of Yahwe are referred to (Jud. vi 13; Deut. xxxi 4). The ground of the promised salvation is Yahwe's presence with his people, according to the basic meaning of *'im*, "together with". This close alliance is formulated in another way in "I am your God". The formula should be understood against the rich theological background of the vss. 8-9, as exposed above. At the same time it corresponds to the motif of confidence in the psalms of lament: "Thou art

---

1 So also B. Duhm, *Jesaja*, p. 271; S. Mowinckel, *ZAW*. XLIX 1931, p. 91, note 1.

2 Cf. F. Stummer, "Einige keilschriftliche Parallelen zu Jes. 40-66", *JBL*. XLV 1926, p. 177. The text is to be found in H. C. Rawlinson, *The Cuneiform Inscriptions of Western Asia*, IV, 2nd ed. 1891, pl. 61; translation by R. H. Pfeiffer, *ANET*, p. 450.

3 So J. Bachmann, *Praeparation und Commentar zum Deutero-Jesaja*, Berlin 1890, p. 18; still *KB*, p. 1000.

4 Thus e.g. *UT* 49 VI: 30 and 67 II: 7. Cf. C. H. Gordon, *UT* § 19.2763; Jean-Hoftijzer, *DISO*, p. 322; Zorell, p. 885. Cf. also C.R. North, *The Second Isaiah*, p. 96.

5 Contra H. E. von Waldow, "... *denn Ich erlöse dich*". *Eine Auslegung von Jesaja 43*, pp. 38-39. G. von Rad, *Der heilige Krieg im alten Israel*, Zürich 1951, does not pay any attention to this formula.

my God" (Pss. cxl 7; iii 4; xxxi 4).[1] On different occasions we shall see that the prophet hints at a lack of confidence on the part of his hearers, in his words of salvation as well as in his disputations. When, in the framework of an oracle of salvation, he resumes a well-known motif of confidence, this may be intended to inspire them with a new confidence.

According to the verbal substantiation (vs. 10b), Yahwe upholds Israel with "the right hand of his righteousness". The word *ṣedeq*, and in general all the derivatives of the root *ṣdq*, are extremely frequent in the whole of the Old Testament, and it is often hard to grasp their precise meaning. Therefore, they have stimulated an extensive literature.[2] The same statement applies to the use of the root in Dt.-Is. K. Cramer thought *ṣedeq* here indicates the just judgment with which the oppressors will be punished. Others regard it as a salvific reality for Israel, e.g. F. Zorell, who translates the passage as: dextera mea salutifera. According to C. R. North, *ṣedeq/ṣᵉdāqâ*, here and in some other places in Dt.-Is., means "victory". K. Fahlgren hesitates between "victory" and "salvation".[3]

According to H. H. Schmid, the root is used in six areas of speech: wisdom, nature and fertility, war and victory, cult and sacrifice, justice and finally kingship.[4] He devotes a thorough analysis to the complex ideology which in the ancient Near East links these areas together. I have to treat it as briefly as possible. The *trait d'union* between these areas is kingship: the king is qualified and responsible for justice, wisdom, etc. But in this function, the king is only the son or representative of the *summus deus*, who created all these areas as one world order. The pre-Israelite background of *ṣdq* is thus an idea of a general world order, expressing and realizing itself in these five or six fields, created by the highest god and guaranteed on earth by the king. Originally, there was a difference between *ṣedeq* and *ṣᵉdāqâ*,[5]

---

[1] J. Begrich, *ZAW*. LII 1934, p. 83; Gunkel-Begrich, *Einleitung*, pp. 233-235. Cf. § 1, b.

[2] Cf. H. H. Schmid, *Gerechtigkeit als Weltordnung*, Tübingen 1968, pp. 1-2, note 1, where all the important studies are listed.

[3] K. Cramer, "Der Begriff צדקה bei Tritojesaja", *ZAW*. XXVII 1907; Zorell, p. 683; C. R. North, *The Second Isaiah*, pp. 93 and 97; F. Fahlgren, *Ṣᵉdāḳā, nahestehende und entgegengesetzte Begriffe im Alten Testament*, Uppsala 1932, p. 103.

[4] H. H. Schmid, *o.c.*, pp. 14-23.

[5] Cf. already A. Jepsen, "צדק und צדקה im alten Testament", *Gottes Wort und Gottes Land. Fs. H. W. Hertzberg*, Göttingen 1965, pp. 78-89.

the former being the world order just described, the latter indicating an attitude or action conforming to that order or creating it.[1] But this distinction was not always observed, as has been pointed out by A. JEPSEN and H. H. SCHMID.

Because of the following verses (11-12) SCHMID supposes that in Is. xli 10, *ṣedeq* belongs to the sphere of war and victory. He thus joins C. R. NORTH's opinion. I do not agree, since I am convinced that the word must be explained in the framework of the oracle of salvation. Further on we shall see that even vss. 11-12 are built up of formulas taken from the psalms of lament. Now, let us first investigate if the use of *ṣedeq* in that class of psalms is able to throw some light on the present verse.[2] In the psalms, Yahwe, the *summus deus*, is often represented as the warrant of right and justice. He is the world judge (*Weltrichter*), who judges *beṣedeq*, according to the world order. Sometimes that order is supposed to consist concretely in the covenant between Israel and Yahwe. In Ps. 1 e.g., Yahwe comes to judge (*dîn*) his people (vs. 4), according to the *ṣedeq*, which *in casu* is the covenant (vs. 16; cf. also Ps. xcix 4). Within the book of Psalms the *ṣdq*-order is mentioned mostly in the psalms of individual lament. The psalmist prays for justice, he himself being for the most part the falsely accused. Yahwe should do him justice, according to his *ṣedeq*, his order, or his *ṣedāqâ*, which means "by executing his *ṣedeq*" (Ps. lxxi 1; xxxi 2). At stake is the just adjudication of life and death: the just deserves life but his enemies seek his death. We find a similar appeal to *ṣedāqâ* in Pss. v 9; xxii 32; li 16; cxliii 1, 11-12. With *ṣedāqâ* is meant not only Yahwe's activity according to his world order, but also the result of his activity, viz. the salvation operated by it. In Pss. xxiv 4-5; lxix 28, we should translate it almost as "salvation". In as much as he warrants *ṣedeq*, Yahwe is called just, *ṣaddîq* (cf. Pss. vii 10, 12; ix 5-6; xi 6-7; cxxix 4). The same ideas passed from the laments into the hymns, which in many respects may be considered to be the reverse of the laments, as they take for granted what laments ask for (cf. Pss. xcvii; lxv; xxxvi).

We thus may find in Is. xli 10 some more contacts with the lament. Besides *'zr* (cf. Ps. xix 26) and *tmk* (cf. Pss. xli 13; lxii 9), *ṣedeq* also is a technical term borrowed from that genre. Yahwe thus speaks to

---

[1] H. H. SCHMID, *o.c.*, pp. 23-69; esp. p. 67. The idea of צדק would be very close to Egyptian *mꜣ'ṭ*.

[2] For the following exposition, cf. H. H. SCHMID, *o.c.*, pp. 144-154.

Israel as if to a suppliant who appeals to his *ṣedeq* in order to obtain his help against his enemies. When Yahwe warrants his *ṣedeq*, this means that in the present circumstances he acts in accordance with his world order. According to the preceding verses, it visualizes more precisely the alliance between Yahwe and his people because of the election. From the following verses it appears that Yahwe's *ṣedeq* will be effective by prevailing over Israel's enemies. Yahwe's *ṣedeq* is thus the principle of the salvation which the prophet has to announce. This will be confirmed, when we analyze the other texts, where the divine justice is often put parallel to salvation (Is. xlv 8; xlvi 13; li 5-6) or even *šālôm* (Is. xlviii 18; liv 13-14). Rather than a victory, an effect of God's justice, the prophet refers to a divine quality, a characteristic attitude of Yahwe. If God realizes the promised salvation, he does so because of his *ṣedeq*, which is at once his justice and his salvific will, which are specified for Israel in his election. The hand of his righteousness is his hand which realizes all this.

The formerly known textual evidence did not call for any doubt about the authenticity of vss. 11-12, the motif of outcome. Some critics, however, had remarked that these verses are of little poetical value and, above all, that vs. 12b is only a repetition of 11b. K. MARTI raised objections against the image of Israel's enemies in the present verses. They would be enemies, with whom Israel is still fighting, possibly the neighbouring nations. However, Dt.-Is. never speaks of a victory, which the Israelites have to gain by force of arms. Therefore MARTI judges the piece not to be dt.-Isaian and to have in view Israel's final or eschatological enemies.[1]

G. FOHRER also brings forward the strophic pattern, viz. the inequality of both stanzas (vss. 8-10 and 11-13), but he admits that this does not prove anything. From a stylistic point of view he remarks that the connection of *'ayin* and *'epes* is typical of Dt.-Is. On the contrary the sequence *'ayin - 'bd* in one stich is very unusual in the whole of the Old Testament. Also the phrase *tᵉbaqᵉšēm wᵉlō' timṣā'ēm*, concerning annihilated enemies, would be very recent and thus open to doubt in the present context. Well then, exactly both phrases are missing in IQIa. FOHRER then investigates whether this omission is due to the copyist of the manuscript or to his *Vorlage*. A first copyist

---

1 B. DUHM, *o.c.*, p. 272; K. BUDDE, *Das Buch Jesaia Kap. 40-66* (E. KAUTZSCH, *Die Heilige Schrift des A.T.*, II), Tübingen 1922, p. 661; K. MARTI, *Das Buch Jesaja*, Tübingen 1900, p. 281.

apparently left some space, according to Fohrer, because his copy had been damaged at this place. If this space has not been filled in afterwards, it is due to the fact that either the corrector's *Vorlage* did not have another text or that he overlooked the necessary correction. The latter however is excluded, because of the extent of the open space (1 1/3 line). For the words *yihyû k*^{e}*'ayin* no space is left, so that they probably were absent from the first copyist's *Vorlage*. Now, Fohrer goes on, when certain words from MT are missing in IQIa, the latter often offers a better reading. The stylistic argument together with the textual tradition from Qumran support the opinion that the words under discussion are not original.[1] The verse would originally have run like this:

11 הן יבשו ויכלמו כל הנחרים בך
ויאבדו אנשי ריבך ואנשי מצתך
12 יהיו כאין וכאפס אנשי מלחמתך

I admit that this reconstruction is of a better poetical quality than MT, but the internal argument is very weak and IQIa is quite isolated in the textual tradition. The more elaborated parallelism of Fohrer's text, being perhaps more in accordance with our taste, certainly does not recommend itself more than the simple parallelism of MT. The fact that the first copyist left a rather large space proves that in his *Vorlage* something more was to be found than in IQIa. This has apparently been overlooked by Fohrer in his conclusion, although he started his reasoning from this gap.

In vss. 11-13, the realisation of salvation is presented under its more negative aspect: the annihilation of the enemies. Against this presentation one could object with J. Morgenstern: "Israel in Babylon could have had as enemies no nation or people whatsoever".[2] In any case it is hard to accept that Israel was at war (*milḥāmâ*) with any nation. Yet, Morgenstern accepts vss. 11-13 as authentic. In his opinion, the enemies are presented rather as individuals than as nations, as against the vss. 14-16, where they can be but the neighbouring nations which, in his hypothesis, overcame Judah in 485 and reduced it to slavery.[3] This remark deserves our attention. As a

---

[1] For more details cf. G. Fohrer, *VT*. V 1955, pp. 242-249.

[2] J. Morgenstern, *The Message of Deutero-Isaiah*, p. 148.

[3] Cf. on this so-called catastrophe J. Morgenstern, "Jerusalem 485 B.C.", *HUCA*, XXVII 1956, pp. 101-179; XXVIII 1957, pp. 15-47; XXXI 1960, pp. 1-29. I dealt

matter of fact, the enemies are called *'anšê* and not *gôyim* or anything similar. The first style *neḥěrîm* (besides only in Is. xlv 24) is a nifal of *ḥrh*, "to burn", i.e. "to be aflame with wrath". This nifal is quite unusual and therefore G. R. DRIVER proposes to read *hannōḥărîm*, a qal participle of *nḥr*, which means "to snort" (e.g. of a horse). He refers to Aramaic *nḥr* with the same meaning.[1] But the root is attested in Hebrew also with that meaning, as a verb in Jer. vi 29 and Cant. i 6 (piel), and as a noun in Job xxxix 20; Jer. viii 16 and Job xli 12 (*neḥîrayim*, "nostrils"). The proposition is thus acceptable but does not affect the meaning of the phrase: in both cases adversaries "rage" against Israel.

The following three expressions must be taken together for their parallelism. Only *milḥāmâ*, in the sense of "war", can present a problem, because at the time Israel was not at war. The term *rîb* means a legal contest (cf. Is. xli 21; l 8; li 22). *'îš rîb* is a technical term for the adversary in a lawsuit (Job xxxi 35).[2] The word *maṣṣut* is a *hapax* in the Hebrew Bible. Still we find it in Sir. xxxi 26 and in later Hebrew.[3] A biblical synonym is *maṣṣâ*, no less than *maṣṣut* deduced from the root *nṣh*, which in the nifal means "to quarrel" without including necessarily a war (cf. Ex. ii 13; xxi 22; Lev. xxiv 10; 2 Sam. xiv 6). The noun *milḥāmâ* mostly supposes a war *sensu stricto*. But according to KÖHLER-BAUMGARTNER, the basic meaning of the root *lḥm* is "to be closely packed" and hence the nifal means "to fight hand to hand". In Pss. xxxiv 1 and lv 2-3, the participle *lōḥēm* indicates the personal enemies of the just. These persons are persecutors, whose malicious intentions are described with different images, among which the word *rîb* figures. Both terms again belong to the language of the lament, where they indicate adversaries or oppressors. The whole motif of the confusion or annihilation of the enemies has its place in the supplication of the laments (cf. the former paragraph). Yahwe addresses Israel as an individual, whom he promises that he will confound his enemies.

---

with the problem in "Arrière-fond historique et critique d'authenticité des textes deutéro-isaïens", *Orientalia Lovaniensia Periodica*, II 1971, pp. 105-135; and in particular with Is. xli 11-16 on pp. 127-131.

[1] G. R. DRIVER, "Linguistic and Textual Problems: Isaiah xl-lxvi", *JTS.* XXXVI 1935, p. 398.

[2] KB, pp. 888-889; cf. L. KÖHLER, *Deuterojesaja*, pp. 110-116.

[3] Cf. ZORELL, p. 466; KB, p. 558: mhb. מצות; G. DALMAN, *Aramäisch-neuhebräisches Handwörterbuch*, Hildesheim 1967, p. 248.

In the hypothesis of an oppression of the Jews by Nabonidus,[1] the three expressions are quite acceptable, without supposing a condition of war. Within the framework of the literary type, they are a threefold indication of people, who oppress or persecute the Jewish community. This oracle of salvation can be situated in a certain discouragement of the exiles, as a result of an oppression, which had also religious aspects and created doubts about Yahwe's powerful presence to his people. The enemies under consideration are certainly the Babylonians. According to J. STEINMANN, the prophet cannot name them because of the danger.[2] The general formulation, indicating concrete oppressors, must be ascribed to the language of the genre or to the form-critical connection with the psalms of lament.

In the final verse 13 the promise is substantiated again in a sentence, that, as a matter of fact, is an oracle of salvation *in nuce*.[3] It simply resumes the assurance of salvation with the nominal and perfective substantiation.

2. *Is. xli 14-16*

14 Fear not, you worm Jacob,
you earthworm Israel!
I help you — the oracle of Yahwe, —
your Redeemer is the Holy One of Israel.
15 Behold, I make of you a threshing sledge,
sharp, new, with double edges.
You shall thresh mountains and crush them
and make hills into chaff.
16 You shall winnow them, the wind shall bear them away,
and the tempest shall scatter them.
But you shall rejoice in Yahwe,
in the Holy One of Israel you shall glory.

---

[1] J. M. WILKIE, "Nabonidus and the Later Jewish Exiles", *JTS*. n.s. II 1950-1951, p. 42: "Their despair in 2 Isaiah's time therefore, is hardly likely to have been due merely to the protraction of the exile, and seems to receive a more adequate explanation if it is linked with the harsh treatment, which they were receiving, especially as the two are closely linked in the oracles of the prophet. It is much more likely that it was this treatment, which other evidence seems to connect with Nabonidus's religious programme, which was causing many to despair of their ancestral faith, since Jahweh seemed to them to be doing nothing about their sufferings".

[2] J. STEINMANN, *Le livre de la consolation*, Paris 1960, p. 103.

[3] H. E. VON WALDOW, *o.c.*, p. 187, note 34; B. DUHM, *o.c.*, p. 272.

There is a large consensus about the literary unity of these verses, though some scholars suppose that the oracle has been digested in a larger framework.[1] IQIa treats vss. 14-16 as one pericope and the analysis will show that they make out a complete oracle of salvation.

This oracle too is directed to Jacob-Israel, who is addressed here as "worm". In this way the address again corresponds to certain expressions in the laments, where the suppliant calls himself a worm (Ps. xxii 7). The image is not an expression of affectionate compassion with human helplessness.[2] EVA HESSLER rightly points out that especially the disdain is focused, with which Israel is looked upon.[3] In Ps. xxii 7 the image is used parallel with *ḥerpâ* and *bāzûy*. Both terms belong to the terminology of Dt.- Is. (cf. Is. xlix 7; li 7; liv 4).

The second vocative is *m*ᵉ*tê yiśrā'ēl*, an old problem for interpreters and textual critics. The expression means "men of Israel", which makes good sense. But there is a problem with parallelism, the more so as vs. 14a*a* and the following verses are in the singular. On the authority of IQIa, Aquila, Theodotion and the Vulgate, one could read *mētê*, the participle of the verb *mût*, meaning "dying ones". Such a qualification the suppliant sometimes applies to himself in a lament (Pss. lxxxviii 6; cxliii 3; Lam. iii 6).[4] But it should not be disregarded that the suppliant never calls himself *mēt*. He only declares that he is counted among the dead, etc. Moreover, the problem of the plural still exists.

G. R. DRIVER conserves the consonnantal complex *mty*, the singular of which, *mt*, would correspond to the Akkadian *mutu*, "louse". In his opinion, the Peshitta somewhat attests to his explanation. In the expression *mnynh d'sr'l*, the Syriac translator probably used the word *mnînâ*, to be translated with *curculio, cynips, musca*.[5] DRIVER thus renders *mty yiśrā'ēl* as "lice of Israel".[6] With regard to the parallelism it would be better to keep to the singular. This interpretation would have the advantage of presenting a real parallel, while conserving the transmitted text. The meaning of the Akkadian

---

[1] In a larger framework: C. C. TORREY, A. BENTZEN, D. BRUNO, J. STEINMANN, Eva HESSLER.

[2] Against F. FELDMANN, *o.c.*, p. 47; J. FISCHER, *o.c.*, p. 45.

[3] E. HESSLER, "Die Struktur der Bilder bei Deuterojesaja", *EvTh.* XXV 1965, p. 354.

[4] IQIa: מיתי; Vg: qui mortui estis.

[5] C. BROCKELMANN, *Lexicon Syriacum*, Halle 1928, p. 394.

[6] C. R. DRIVER, *a.c.*, *JTS.* XXXVI 1935, p. 399. So also *BHS*.

mutu, however, is not that clear. LANDSBERGER translates the Sumerian ideogram UḪ.KÚ.E, which corresponds to it in one of the witnesses of the syllabary, published by him, as *"fressendes Ungeziefer"*. He regards *mutu* as a dialectal word for *Laus*. But he abandoned this opinion in his critical edition of the syllabary, where he put UḪ.KÚ.E = (*kal*) *mu-tu*.[1] The word *mutu* with the meaning he proposed formerly does not exist.

Certain scholars conserve MT, with the remark that *mat*, pl. *m^{e}tîm*, occurs in Hebrew mostly in a context indicating a condition of dependence or weakness.[2] So in Gen. xxxiv 30; Deut. iv 27; Jer. xliv 28, *m^{e}tê mispār* refers to a scanty and powerless group. In Job xxiv 12, the *m^{e}tîm* are the oppressed, who groan. We find the expression *m^{e}tê-'āwen* in Job xxii 15, while *m^{e}tê-šāw'* in Ps. xxvi 4 and Job xi 11 also has a pejorative meaning. In this connection it is interesting to refer to the LXX reading of the word under consideration, that is: ὀλιγοστός, "very scanty". Eva HESSLER, starting from this reading, completes *m^{e}tê* with *m^{e}'āṭ*, referring to Deut. xxvi 5 and xxviii 62, where *m^{e}tê m^{e}'āṭ* alludes to respectively the small group of Israel in Egypt, that will grow into a great nation, and the remnant that remains after Yahwe's judgment.[3] This reconstruction gives rhythmical balance to the verse, provides a convenient parallel of the first semi-colon and has in its favour, besides the LXX reading, also a good biblical background. However, the testimony of the LXX is not so clear, for ὀλιγοστός is the only adjunct and is put between "Jacob" and "Israel". So nothing corresponds here to the Hebrew *tôla'at* of the first semi-colon. Moreover, the difficulty of the plural remains unresolved. But with respect to this it may be pointed out that *m^{e}tê m^{e}'āṭ* could be felt as a singular (the opposite of a collective singular). This happens in Gen. xxxiv 30, where Jacob says: *'ănî m^{e}tê m^{e}'āṭ*, literally:

> "I am men of a small number".

The vast majority of commentators correct *m^{e}tê* to *rimmat*, which also means "worm" (constr. state).[4] This word balances *tôlē'â* in Is.

---

[1] B. LANDSBERGER, *Die Fauna des alten Mesopotamiens*, Leipzig 1934, pp. 20-21; 126; ID., *Materialien zum sumerischen Lexicon*, VIII 2, Roma 1962, p. 28.

[2] T. K. CHEYNE, *The Prophecies of Isaiah*, II, London 1889, p. 137; M. HALLER, *Das Judentum*, p. 22; J. MUILENBURG, *Isaiah 40-66*, p. 457.

[3] E. HESSLER, *l.c.*

[4] E.g. *BHK*, H. EWALD, B. DUHM, L. KÖHLER, F. FELDMANN, C. C. TORREY, P. VOLZ, A. VAN HOONACKER, J. FISCHER, D. BRUNO, U. E. SIMON, C. R. NORTH, C. WESTERMANN, P. AUVRAY - J. STEINMANN.

xiv 11 and Job xxv 6 too. This way we obtain two vocatives, which are not only parallel but also synonymous. According to C. C. TORREY, this reading urges itself because of the feminine suffixes in the following verses.[1] The argument is not conclusive, for the MT itself is not consistent (e.g. *tādûš* in vs. 15b) and the consonantal text allows one to read the whole pericope in masculine. As a matter of fact, IQIa has but masculine suffixes, for the *he* as *mater lectionis* removes any doubt. The reading *rimmat* demands only a slight graphic change *pace* J. KOENIG.[2] A definite choice is impossible. But the last correction has my preference, although it is barely attested in the ancient versions and other textual witnesses.[3] Nevertheless, it satisfies in every respect, and especially because of its singular form it surpasses all the other ones, for the address in the singular is characteristic of the cultic oracle of salvation.[4] To vs. 14aβ one sometimes adds *'al-tištᵉʿî*, borrowed from vs. 10.[5] This way a complete parallelism is given to vs. 14 and we obtain a uniform rhythm in the whole oracle (3 + 3). Though not to be excluded, the last amplification does not urge itself.

The nominal substantiation in vs. 14bβ sound thus: "The Holy One of Israel is your Redeemer". The title *qᵉdôš yiśrā'ēl* expresses the special relation between Yahwe and his people. Holiness is the nucleus of Yahwe's personality.[6] Dt.-Is. too calls Yahwe the Holy One *tout court* in xli 25, but he prefers and very often uses "Holy One of Israel" (xli 14, 16, 20; xliii 3, 14, 15; xlv 11; xlvii 4; xlviii 17; xlix 7; liv 5; lv 5). Half of these contexts have the same connection between "the Holy One of Israel" and "your Redeemer". Thus we meet here a really dt.-Isaian formula, which tells us something important about his message. The title "Holy One of Israel" itself, the prophet has borrowed from Isaiah, who uses it very frequently.[7] It is correlate to Israel's definition as Yahwe's holy nation (cf. Code of Holiness, Lev. xi 44; xix 2; xx 26). Theologically the latter goes back to the election

---

[1] C. C. TORREY, *The Second Isaiah*, New York 1928, p. 317.

[2] U. E. SIMON, *A Theology of Salvation*, London 1953, p. 247, note f: "The rule of parallelism and good sense demands this slight change". J. KOENIG, *Ugaritica VI*, p. 336.

[3] J. KOENIG, *Pléiade*, II, Paris 1961, p. 140, appeals to the Peshitta reading *mnînâ*, which he translates as *charançon*, "weevil". Cf. L. COSTAZ, *Syriac-English Dictionary*, Beyrouth 1963, p. 187.

[4] Cf. supra, p. 42.

[5] E.g. *BHK*, L. KÖHLER, C. WESTERMANN, G. FOHRER.

[6] J. J. STAMM, *Erlösen und Vergeben im Alten Testament*, Bern 1940, pp. 41-42.

[7] Outside the book of Isaiah, only in Jer. l 29; li 5; Pss. lxxi 22; lxxviii 41; lxxxix 19.

and the Sinaitic covenant (cf. Ex. xix 5-6). In the deuteronomic tradition too, the Sinaitic covenant is the background of the expression "holy nation" (Deut. vii 6; xiv 21; xxvi 17, 19). Very probably Isaiah had in view the covenantal relation, when using the expression "Holy One of Israel", correlate to "holy nation". This is confirmed by the fact that he uses the name in opposition to the unfaithful nation (Is. i 4; v 19, 24; xxix 19-20; xxx 12-13; xxxi 1), or when he predicts the conversion of that unfaithful nation (x 20-22; xvii 1-2; xxx 15). All this supposes Israel's particular alliance with Yahwe (cf. also "a people for his own possession" in Ex. xix 5; Deut. vii 6; xiv 2), an alliance from which proceed particular obligations which the people did not perform.[1] Now, Dt.-Is. has lifted the title "Holy One of Israel" out of the oracle of threat to make it a motif of the oracle of salvation. The title becomes a foundation of the promise of salvation, as it is formulated in the oracle; that's why it is used in the substantiation motif. In the trend of the dt.-Isaian theology we should also think of Yahwe's sovereign disposal of all means to realize the promised salvation (cf. Is. xl 25; xli 20; xliii 14-15; xlv 11). In that sense also holiness is the nucleus of Yahwe's personality.[2] This is connected with the strong monotheism of the prophet, which finds expression in his trial speeches and his disputations, as we shall see in the next chapter.

Yahwe is Israel's *gō'ēl*. The word *g'l* means "to lay claim to a person or a thing, to claim back from an other's authority, to redeem".[3] Dt.-Is. uses the participle *gō'ēl* very frequently (Is. xli 14; xliii 14; xliv 6, 24; xlvii 4; xlviii 17; xlix 7, 26; liv 5, 8). In the Israelitic legal usage the word is a technical term indicating the next in blood who was obliged to the *g^{e}'ullâ*, i.e. the duty of redemption in the four cases of loss of property (Lev. xxv 24-28; Jer. xxxii 7; Ruth iv 4-6), bondage (Lev. xxv 48-49), levirate (Ruth iii 13; Deut. xxv 5-10) and blood-vengeance (Num. xxxv 12, 19, 21; Deut, xix 6, 12; Jos. xx 3, 5, 9; 2 Sam. xiv 11; 1 Kings xvi 11). As against *pdh* the term *g'l* presupposes a connection between the redeemer and the redeemed.[4] Dt.-Is., who uses the term in connection with the liberation from the *gôlâ* (e.g. Is. xliii 1-7; xlviii 20-21), thus expresses the idea that Yahwe delivers

---

[1] J. KAHMANN, "Die Heilszukunft in ihrer Beziehung zur Heilsgeschichte nach Is. 40-55", *Bib.* XXXII 1951, pp. 142-144.

[2] Cf. W. EICHRODT, *Theologie des Alten Testaments*, I, Göttingen 1959, p. 184.

[3] KB, pp. 162-163.

[4] J. VAN DODEWAARD, "Verlossing", *BW*², col. 1757-1758; J. J. STAMM, *o.c.*, pp. 28-30; G. FOHRER, *Jesaja III*, p. 41.

his people as a human *gō'ēl* does in behalf of his next of kin, i.e. on the ground of an existing relationship. Such can be understood only in reference to the election, a.v. to the relation of covenant between Yahwe and his people.[1] The fact that Dt.-Is. refers to this relationship through the title of *gō'ēl* also has a historical depth. For the word *g'l* became in the tradition of the Old Testament a technical term for the deliverance from Egypt (Ex. vi 6; xv 3; Pss. lxxiv 2; lxxvii 16; lxxviii 35; cvi 10; cvii 2; Is. lxiii 9). Precisely in that deliverance, Yahwe practised for the first time his *g^e'ullâ* on behalf of Israel and, by acting so, he, as it were, founded it. So Yahwe's intervention about the end of the exile is not to be disjoined from his fundamental act in the exodus and refers to the election and the covenant, connected with it. In other pericopes this is further developed into the idea of a second exodus.

It remains for us to make a third consideration with regard to this theme: it belongs to the context of the lament and supplication. The suppliant prays for redemption (*g'l*: Pss. lxix 19; cxix 154; Lam. iii 58),[2] or a former act of redemption is to him a motive of confidence (Ps. lxxiv 2), which is expressed also in the title *gō'ēl*, given to Yahwe by the suppliant (Ps. xix 5). The title *gō'ēl* in Is. xli 14 thus is to be seen in the framework of this setting, together with the rich background of the relation of *g^e'ullâ* between Yahwe and his people, which has its roots in Yahwe's mighty deed of deliverance during the exodus.

Under the image of the threshing sledge, which makes hills into chaff (vs. 15), one generally sees a victory over enemies. Already in an inscription of Tiglath-Pileser II we find the same images: "The land of Bit-Amukkan I crushed as with a threshing sledge".[3] The Targum too supports this interpretation: "You shall slay the nations and exterminate them and you will make the kingdoms into chaff".[4]

---

[1] O. PROCKSCH, "*λύω κτλ*. Die Wortgruppe im A.T.", *TWNT*. IV, p. 331: "So verstanden, führt der Ausdruck in die Tiefe des Verhältnisses zwischen Gott und Mensch, das hier als Verwandtschaftsband erscheint, das Gott an die Lösepflicht bindet, nun freilich nicht nach dem Gesetze des Blutes, sondern der Erwählung".

[2] The verbs of this and the following verses are in a precative perfect; cf. JOÜON § 112 k. This phenomenon, which had already been dealt with by H. EWALD, was neglected by recent grammarians and commentators. Exceptions are M. BUTTENWIESER, *The Psalms Chronologically Treated with a New Translation*, Chicago 1938; M. DAHOOD, *Psalms I-III*, Garden City, 1966-1970.

[3] P. VOLZ, *Jesaia II*, p. 21.

[4] Targ: תקטיל עממיא ותשיצי ומלכוותא כמוצא תשוי.

The Old Testament has some eloquent parallels. In Mic. iv 13, the same verbs are used with respect to the *gôyim*; *tādûš* also in Hab. iii 12. Am. i 3 uses the same images as Is. xli 15 to typify a very cruel treatment of the enemies. In Is. xxi 10 Israel is the threshed one, while in Jer. li 2 the winnowing represents a merciless war. The traditional interpretation of the image as referring to a hostile treatment is thus much better founded than S. SMITH's far-fetched historical explanation. In his opinion the insignificant and oppressed Judah receives the task "to work on mountain-tops and hill-sides so that they permit the passage of troops".[1]

The problems start, when we must define the object of the action. Can mountains be a symbol for enemies and who are they? It seems impossible to give a definite answer to that question. According to J. MORGENSTERN the image of Israel as an exterminator of its enemies does not fit the message of Deutero-Isaiah, who proclaims the salvation of all mankind. But it would be settled very well in the hopes of the nationalist party, which, in his opinion, was active in Palestine about 520 B.C. and later on.[2] K. MARTI already wanted to eliminate these verses, together with 11-13. Nevertheless the authenticity of the whole oracle must be accepted on literary grounds: Is. xli 14-16 is an oracle of salvation typical of our prophet, as appears from the present analysis.[3]

When investigating what the mountains and hills mean in the other texts of Dt.-Is., we obtain a rather varied result. In xl 4 and xlix 11 mountains and hills are made low. The situation there is that of the return from Babylon. If the mountains have any symbolic bearing, they signify hindrances on Israel's way back. Mostly, however, the mountains in Is. xl-lv have a cosmic meaning, as an element of the created world, whether they jubilate together with the whole cosmos (Is. xliv 23; xlix 13; lv 12), or their dependence upon Yahwe is underlined (xl 12), or they are considered as the solid part of nature, which nevertheless will pass away in contrast with God's eternal salvific will (liv 10). The text that comes closest to Is. xli 15-16 is xlii 15: "I will waste mountains and hills ...". Here, however, mountains and hills are not a symbol but an element of nature together with plants and rivers, exactly as in the texts just mentioned. In a word, Dt.-Is. provides no valuable parallel.

---

[1] S. SMITH, *Isaiah. chs. XL-LV*, p. 69.

[2] J. MORGENSTERN, *The Message of Deutero-Isaiah*, p. 147.

[3] Cf. A. SCHOORS, *Orientalia Lovaniensia Periodica*, II 1971, p. 130.

If enemies are intended, then mountains and hills suggest the small neighbouring nations, Edom, Moab and Ammon, rather than Babylon.[1] Because of many conflicts with Israel these neighbours became the prototype of the enemy (cf. the numerous speeches of threat in the prophetical books).[2] It must be remarked that in Ez. xxxv; xxxix 2; Ob. 8-9, 19, 21; Mal. i 3, the image of the mountains applies to Edom in a context of oracles of threat (cf. 2 Chron. xx 22-23). Is. xli 15-16 thus may refer to the neighbouring nations, which during the exile plundered Judah and even lodged themselves in some parts of it (Ez. xxv 12-14; xxxv 10; xxxvi 5).[3] However, speaking about them the prophet may have in mind "the" enemies of his people. Then the promise implies that Israel will overcome every enemy who will rise against it. As to the contents, our verses may not be so different from xli 11-12. We should not exaggerate the cruel aspect of the picture. The prophet joins the traditional terminology of the prophetical threats.

Sometimes this obvious explanation is contested with the remark that Dt.-Is. could not visualize a political or military supremacy. But who can prove that? It seems to me that such an objection is founded too much on the knowledge that the restoration did not realize such a supremacy. But a victory of that kind may very well have belonged to the future, as the prophet visualized it, especially when, in certain respects, he put himself in the line of the former prophecy. Why should Dt.-Isaiah's message necessarily be completely different from the one of his predecessors? Of course the fact remains that nowhere else does our prophet announce something of the kind. C. Westermann evades this problem, as he explains the object "mountains and hills" by referring to Is. xl 4, where that image points to the obstacles blocking Israel's return. Then the promise of Is. xli 15-16 would be this: "I make of you an instrument capable of overcoming the obstacles set up by your foes, which separate you

---

[1] B. Duhm, *o.c.*, p. 272; F. Feldmann, *Das Buch Isaias*, II, p. 48. According to G. Fohrer, *Das Buch Jesaja*, III, Zürich 1964, p. 41, the mountains would represent Babylon.

[2] E.g. Is. xv; xxxiv 5-7; Jer. ix 25; xlviii; xlix 1-22; Ez. xxi 33-37; xxv 1-14; xxxv; Am. i 11-15; ii 1-3; Zeph. ii 8-11; Ob. 6-12; Ps. cxxxvii; cf. A. van den Born, *BW*³, col. 52 and 334.

[3] G. Ricciotti, *Storia d'Israele*, II, Torino 1935, p. 74; W. Zimmerli, *Ezechiel*, Neukirchen 1969, pp. 596-597; F. F. Bruce, *Israel and the Nations*, Exeter 1963, p. 92.

from your homeland".[1] In that case, the picture of "threshing and winnowing" seems to be very exaggerated. And as we can see, even this explanation cannot be dissociated from the enemies' activity.

Anyhow, Eva HESSLER's explanation is too far-fetched. Schematically it runs as follows. In the present verses threshing is an activity of Israel. Now, in Dt.-Is., Israel's activity *par excellence* is its witness of faith. The object, — the mountains —, can be but an image of the other gods, viz. what is destroyed by Israel's witness.[2] In order to justify the identification, gods = mountains, she refers to the fact that cult-places usually were on the mountains and she invokes prophetical texts, such as Is. ii 2, 5-22. To be sure, in these oracles of threat the prophets sometimes turn against the mountains and hills, which symbolize idolatry (Ez. vi; cf. Jer. iii 23). This symbolism is connected with the fact that idolatry was practized on the heights, which is profusely illustrated by the pre-exilic prophets. Nevertheless, in Ez. vi, as in the other prophetical texts, the prophet deals with the cult of Baal in a Canaanite context. This perspective is completely absent from Dt.-Is. Moreover, in the O.T. the mountains never represent the deities themselves. As to Is. ii 5-22, the mountains there obviously symbolize the human arrogance in face of Yahwe.[3] A valuable remark of the author is that in the coming events Israel only executes what Yahwe enables it to. But when she understands *rûaḥ* as Yahwe's *rûaḥ*, she again overdoes the theological bearing of vs. 16a. The verse normally follows the preceding ones as the completion of the picture they conveyed. It simply wants to underline how thorough the destruction is, by showing the wind bearing the last chaff away (cf. Dan. ii 35).

A similar hypothesis, but somewhat more acceptable, had been formulated before by E. J. HAMLIN. The mountains of vs. 15 would refer to the idolatry of the gentiles, represented by the *ziggurat* of the Babylonian cities, more especially the one of Babylon.[4] This hypothesis takes more account of Dt.-Isaiah's real situation. In order to substantiate it, HAMLIN refers to Jer. li 25, where Babylon is called a "destroying mountain", with the threat that Yahwe will make it a

---

[1] C. WESTERMANN, *Jesaja 40-66*, p. 65; here, I quote the English edition *Isaiah 40-66*, London 1969, p. 77.

[2] E. HESSLER, *EvTh.* XXV 1965, pp. 355-357.

[3] J. KOENIG, *Pléiade*, II, p. 11; H. WILDBERGER, *Jesaja*, Neukirchen 1966, p. 109.

[4] E. J. HAMLIN, "The Meaning of 'Mountains and Hills' in Isa. 41, 14-16", *JNES.* XIII 1954, pp. 185-190.

"burnt mountain". Also the tower of Babel in Gen. xi 1-9, mostly identified with the *ziggurat*, is a symbol of human rebellion against God. Furthermore, in Is. xiv 12-16 and Jer. li 53, the pride of Babylon is connected with a height (the *ziggurat*?). Thus Israel would destroy idolatry and the prophet would have in mind a destruction of the sanctuaries on the heights. Such an action of Israel's would be a renewed execution of God's order given during the exodus (Ex. xxxiv 13; Deut. xii 2-3) and a repetition of Josiah's reform (2 Kings xxiii). However, the quoted texts have another terminology and, therefore, they do not seem to me to be related to vs. 15. Although HAMLIN's hypothesis is well presented, the explanation I proposed above, recommends itself better, as it is founded upon more literal parallels.

J. KOENIG explains the whole metaphor of the oracle as follows. Israel is presented as a threshing sledge, but this image is derived from the conception of Yahwe's chariot: Israel is Yahwe's chariot. This idea is made possible by the fact that Israel is in the west, Akk. *amurru*, written ideographically MAR.TU, while MAR, provided with the index GIŠ of instruments, is the ideogram for "chariot". On the other hand, Babylon is in the east, ideographically TU_{15}KUR.RA. The latter, stripped of its secondary elements, gives KUR, the ideogram for "mountain". This explanation is not convincing at all, no more than the ones proposed by some of his predecessors in exegesis who are so reviled [1].

Verse 16b is the motif formulating the final goal of Yahwe's intervention, viz. his glory which is concretely revealed in the jubilation of the delivered Israel.

3. *Is. xliii 1-4*

1 But now: thus says Yahwe,
Your Creator, Jacob, and your Maker, Israel:
Fear not for I redeem you,
I have called you by name,
you are mine.
2 When you pass through water, I am with you, —
and through rivers, they shall not overwhelm you.
When you walk through fire, you shall not be burnt,
and the flame shall not scorch you.

---

[1] J. KOENIG, "La revanche d'Amurru sur Babel", *Ugaritica VI*, Paris 1969, pp. 333-347.

3 For I, Yahwe, am your God,
the Holy One of Israel, your Saviour.
I give Egypt as your ransom,
Cush and Seba in exchange for you.
4 Because you are precious in my eyes,
and important, and I love you.
I will give men in return for you,
nations in exchange for your life.

H. E. von Waldow was the first to split up Is. xliii 1-7 into two oracles, viz. xliii 1-3a and 5a, 3b-7. He displaces vs. 5a, for as a typical oracular introduction it must, in his view, be put at the beginning of the second oracle.[1] C. Westermann treats Is. xliii 1-7 as one pericope, built up in two parallel parts, vss. 1-4 and 5-7. But both show the characteristics of a complete oracle of salvation, so that I analyze them separately, remitting till later the investigation of their possible mutual connection. Some scholars appeal to the first word *we'attâ* in order to prove that the verses are linked up with the preceding ones. However, von Waldow rightly points out that this particle belongs to the terminology of the oracle of salvation. It indicates the reversal from the lament to the corresponding oracle (cf. Is. xliv 1; xlix 5).[2] It thus comes from the original setting and has no direct bearing on the actual context in the book.

The oracle opens with the messenger's formula, which, as usually in Dt.-Is., is enlarged in a hymnic, participial style (cf. Is. xliii 14a, 16-17; xliv 2; xlviii 17a; xlix 7; liv 8). This is not specific to his oracles of salvation, but still it gives them a particular perspective. For in these formulas Yahwe is introduced as the saving God, who wrought the great salvific events of the past. So the promise in the oracle is put in continuity with salvation history.[3] This continuity is also suggested with the double name "Jacob-Israel", as was seen in the commentary on xli 8.

In the formula of xliii 1 there is no reference to a concrete event. The prophet uses more general terms with a strong theological bearing.

---

1 H. E. von Waldow, *Anlass und Hintergrund*, pp. 180-181, note 6.

2 H. E. von Waldow, *Jesaja 43*, p. 15: "... das 'und nun' kennzeichnet die Wende von der vorgetragenen Klage zu einem antwortenden Orakel".

3 J. Kahmann, *Bib.* XXXII 1951, esp. pp. 141-152: "Die Auserwählungsmotive in den Einleitungs- und Schlussformeln der Verheissungen".

He defines God as the creator of Israel: *bōrē'* and *yōṣēr*. The last word is used in Is. xliv 2 also, together with *'ōśeh*. It is well known that Dt.-Is. uses *br'* very frequently (xl 26, 28; xli 20; xlii 5; xliii 1, 7, 15; xlv 7 (bis), 8, 12, 18 (bis); xlviii 7; liv 16 (bis)). About one third of the occurences of *br'* in the O.T. are to be found in Is. xl-lv. In the O.T. *br'* is a technical term for God's creation, since in the qal its only subject is God, and it connotes somewhat the idea of a *creatio ex nihilo*, since it is provided nowhere with any determination of the *materia ex qua.*[1] In the next chapter we shall see how, in his disputations, this prophet presents Yahwe who appeals to his universal creative power. But, as in the present oracle, the prophet often calls him Creator of Israel. Through the election (*bḥr, qr'*), to which Yahwe appeals in xli 8-9, he made Israel.[2] The use of the same term to indicate the creation of the cosmos and the formation of Israel, underlines the unity of the creating and the saving God, of the act of creation and salvation. More than once Dt.-Is. uses terminology of creation in order to display Yahwe's activity in history (xlii 9; xlviii 3, 7), just like Isaiah and Jeremiah already did before him (Is. xxii 11; xxix 16-17; Jer. xviii 1-11).[3] In Is. xliv 2, 24 creation and redemption are parallel. In xlii 6 also, with respect to Cyrus, vocation and election are tantamount to creation. In short, such enlarged messenger's formulas strongly underline the fact that Yahwe himself made his people. He will make the same creative power subservient to his will to sustain them and conduct them on the path of salvation.[4]

Such an introduction needs to be understood as a fundamental

---

[1] P. Humbert, "Emploi et portée du verbe bârâ, créer, dans l'Ancien Testament", *TZ.* III 1947, pp. 401-422, contests the presence of the idea of *creatio ex nihilo* in the O.T. As a matter of fact nobody asserts that this idea is expressed clearly and explicitly, unless in 2 Macc. vii 28. However, W. Eichrodt, *Theologie des A.T.*, II, Göttingen 1961, pp. 63-66, shows how, esp. in Gen. i, the idea of creation tends toward a *creatio ex nihilo*.

[2] J. Kahmann, *a.c.*, p. 145: "... dass der entsprechende Titel 'Schöpfer, Bildner Israels' auf eine mit der Auserwählung verbundene Tätigkeit Jahwehs hinweist". — A. Bentzen, *Jesaja 40-66*, København 1943, p. 41.

[3] Cf. C. Stuhlmueller, "The Theology of Creation in Second Isaias", *CBQ.* XXI 1959, p. 435.

[4] Cf. R. Rendtorff, "Die theologische Stellung des Schöpfungsglaubens bei Deuterojesaja", *ZTK.* LI 1954, pp. 8-12; G. von Rad, "Das theologische Problem des alttestamentlichen Schöpfungsglaubens", *Werden und Wesen des A.T.* (*BZAW* 66), Giessen 1936, pp. 138-147 = *Theologische Bücherei*, 8, München 1965, pp. 136-147; *Theologie des A.T.*, I, München 1966, pp. 150-151.

motivation of the oracle that follows. As H. REVENTLOW rightly remarks, the suppliant can be sure that his prayer is heard, only if there is a close relationship between Yahwe and himself. What Yahwe says about himself in the oracle of salvation bears upon that relationship.[1] The form of those formulas is related to the formula of self-presentation: "I am Yahwe, your God", which also expresses Yahwe's gracious turning towards his people, so that it gets the character of a *Heilsgeschichts- oder Huldformel.*[2] When in the introductions of his salvation oracles, Dt.-Is. uses a terminology of creation to express the historical relationship with his people, this is not incidental from a form-critical point of view. In the individual oracle of salvation, the relationship between God and the suppliant, on which the oracle and consequently the suppliant's confidence are based, is the relationship between the Creator and his creature. The expressions *bōra'ăkā* and *yōṣerᵉkā* have their setting in the individual oracle of salvation and refer to the personal relation "Creator-creature" between God and the recipient. H. REVENTLOW demonstrated this in a convincing manner. However, when Dt.-Is. adopts these formulas in his salvation oracles to Israel, they are necessarily invested with the salvation-historic contents, which I dealt with above.

When dealing with this creation motif, REVENTLOW discusses whether it passed from the oracle of salvation to the hymn or whether the individual oracle borrowed it from the hymn, where would be its original setting. The second position is defended by G. VON RAD and R. RENDTORFF.[3] A complete analysis of the questions involved goes beyond the limits of the present study. I think we must admit that the conception of Yahwe as the Creator of the universe is an original motif of the hymn. Very often Dt.-Is. borrows that motif from the hymnic tradition in his own hymns, in his disputations and even in his proclamations of salvation. He even kept it in the typical participial style of the hymn. In this RENDTORFF is right. But in the salvation oracle *stricto sensu*, this motif does not occur. In this type, we twice find the motif of the personal relationship between Creator and creature, expressed in a participle with suffix of the second person

---

[1] H. REVENTLOW, *Liturgie und prophetisches Ich bei Jeremia*, Gütersloh 1963, pp. 30-37.

[2] Thus K. ELLIGER, "Ich bin der Herr — euer Gott", *Festschrift K. Heim*, Hamburg 1954, p. 16.

[3] R. RENDTORFF, *a.c.*; G. VON RAD, *Theologie des A.T.*, II, München 1965, p. 252.

singular (here and in xliv 2). We find it a third time in a somewhat modified form in liv 5 (*'ōśayik*). RENDTORFF himself points out the difference of both motifs and the quite personal aspect of the second one.[1] It is not yet proven that the more "personal" motif in the oracle of salvation is a later qualification of the more general motif in the hymn. RENDTORFF thinks so, but, as I see it, it is an axiom that proceeds from our more elaborated idea of creation. Nor has the opposite view, viz. that the hymnic motif arose from a generalization of the more personal oracular motif, been proven by REVENTLOW. Anyhow, both motifs are different in form and setting. The discussion does not affect my statement that in xliii 1, Dt.-Is. keeps a typical motif of the individual oracle of salvation.

In vs. 1b follow, in very short wording, the assurance, the perfective and the nominal substantiation. The clause "I have called you by name", continues the very personal, even individual tone of the oracle. In the O.T. the expression is used only with reference to a special task, as the one which devolves upon Bezalel in Ex. xxxi 2; xxxv 30, or on Cyrus in our prophet (Is. xlv 3-4). In Is. xl 26, Yahwe calls into being the stars by calling them by name. In xliii 1, where Jacob-Israel is the object of the call, the expression must be put into the sphere of election. As it seems to me, the perfect tense *qārā'tî* expresses an anteriority with respect to *g^e'altîkā*. Because Yahwe has called, he now redeems. Thus vs. 1bγ substantiates the perfective substantiation "I redeem you" and the nominal one "you are mine" as well. The latter corresponds to the motif of confidence, "I am thine", which occurs in the psalms of lament (Ps. cxix 94).

According to xliii 2, the chosen people will be invulnerable, as a result of Yahwe's intervention: they are able to pass through water and fire. The prophet means the obstacles on the journey home from exile. The theme of the safe passage through water reminds one of the exodus, but I do not see the same connection as far as the fire is concerned.[2] In the present verse, the promise of salvation is not really made concrete but only repeated under poetical metaphors: "In any distress I shall protect you". In Ps. lxvi 12, the same metaphor is used

---

[1] R. RENDTORFF, *a.c.*, pp. 8-9: "43,1 zeigt die schon besprochene Verbindung der Partizipien mit dem Suffix der 2. Person, also die Wendung der Aussage über Jahwe den Schöpfer ins Persönliche".

[2] Thus J. STEINMANN, *Le livre de la consolation*, p. 120; J. FISCHER, "Das Problem des neuen Exodus", *Theologische Quartalschrift* CX 1929, p. 114.

to indicate a condition of distress (cf. also Pss. xxxii 6; lxix 3, 15-16; lxviii 63; lxxxviii 18; cxliv 7). According to J. Begrich, the prophet borrowed the wording from an oracle of salvation in the context of an ordeal, from which Ps. lxvi 12 also proceeds.[1] This interpretation remains purely hypothetical.

In vs. 3a another nominal substantiation is inserted in the middle of the motif of outcome. Its first member is the same as Is. xli 10; the second one calls the Holy One of Israel also its Saviour. This title derives from the root *yš'*, which means in the hifil "to help", and mostly supposes a condition of distress; hence the frequent meaning "to save". The fundamental meaning would be "to give room", thus "to help out of a scrape, to save one out of distress".[2] The participle here becomes a title of Yahwe; he is "the" saver of Israel, its Saviour.[3]

H. J. Boecker developed the thesis that *môšîa'* is a technical term in the juridical language, to indicate the one who helps when hearing a cry of murder (*Zeterruf*). When somebody gets into distress (*ṣārâ*) because of injustice and oppression, he should shout (*z'q*/*ṣ'q*: Deut. xxii 24, 27; 2 Kings viii 1-6; iv 1; vi 26; Hab. i 2): "Violence!" (2 Sam. xxii 3; Jer. xx 8; Hab. i 2; Job xix 7) and cry for help with the word *hôšî'â* (2 Sam. xiv 4; xxii 3; 2 Kings vi 26; Hab. i 2). From Deut. xxii 27 it appears that the one who helps in that circumstance is called *môšîa'*.[4] Boecker admits that in many occurrences of the same terminology in the psalms this original connection is no longer felt, but in some of them it is still recognizable (Pss. iii 8; vii 2). In the psalms of lament, Yahwe is addressed as *môšîa'* (Ps. xvii 7; Jer. xiv 8), or the suppliant recalls the title in the motif of confidence (Ps. vii 11) as well as in the song of thanksgiving (2 Sam. xxii 3). Besides, we must point out the very frequent appeal "Save me", in the psalms (Pss. iii 8; vi 5; vii 2; xxxi 17; liv 3; lix 3; lxix 2; etc.). The word thus belongs to the setting in which the oracle of salvation originated. Dt.-Is. applies the title to Yahwe in xlv 5; xlix 26, while in his disputations he denies to the pagan gods the right to call themselves *môšîa'* (xlv 21; xliii 11; cf. Hos. xiii 4). At the same time he expression,

---

1 J. Begrich, *ZAW*. LII 1934, p. 90.

2 Arabic *wasi'a*, "to be large, spacious". Cf. Zorell, p. 338; KB, p. 412.

3 P. Volz, *o.c.*, p. 37.

4 H. J. Boecker, *Redeformen der Rechtssprache im A.T.*, Neukirchen 1964, pp. 63-66; esp. p. 64: "Nach diesem Text [Deut. xxii 23-27] ist מושיע terminus technicus für den, der auf einen Zeterruf hin helfend eingreift". Cf. also G. Fohrer, "Der Stamm ישע im A.T.", *TWNT*. VII, p. 974.

exactly like *gō'ēl* and similar titles, refers to Yahwe's historical interventions, as appears from Ps. cvi 21, where it is parallel with "who had done great things in Egypt" (*'ōśeh gᵉdôlôt bᵉmiṣrāyim*). Yahwe eminently showed himself the Saviour of Israel in the deliverance from Egypt.

The motif of outcome introduces a second theme, in which the concrete action is visualized more from Yahwe's viewpoint. Yahwe will give Egypt, Cush and Seba in exchange for Israel.[1] One often understands it as if Yahwe gives these countries to Cyrus and that the prophet regards this gift as the price for the liberation of Israel.[2] In my opinion, Egypt etc. should not be understood too topographically. The point is, as appears from vs. 4b, that Yahwe gives nations in exchange for Israel. It does not matter which nations exactly are given over. That it would be a metaphor for the conversion of these nations to Israel and its God Yahwe, as supposed by U. E. SIMON,[3] is a theologoumenon, meant to bring the pericope into logical accord with xlv 14, but it forces our text. H. E. VON WALDOW grasped the theological bearing of the text much better when he found two main ideas in this picture. 1) To Yahwe the deliverance from exile is an event that will be accomplished on the scene of world history. In other words: Israel is the centre of the events and God's actions in the pagan nations always have something to do with Israel's salvation. 2) The greatness of Yahwe's love is made concrete by the immense ransom, which he is ready to pay.[4] The same scholar connects the

---

[1] Cush is Upper-Egypt or Ethiopia in almost all biblical texts, as well as in Akkadian and Egyptian. For that reason, one usually locates Seba, mentioned together with Egypt and Cush, in N.E. Africa (Already Fl. JOSEPHUS, *Ant.* II 10:2). In the table of nations (Gen. x 7) it is a son of Cush. — Cf. P. VOLZ, *o.c.*, p. 37; J. FISCHER, *o.c.*, p. 61; *BJ*, p. 352, note e. But according to Gen. x 7, Havila belongs to Cush, although on the other hand it may be located in Arabia (a land of gold; etymology in connection with חול, "sand"; mention of it in a N. Arabian context in Gen. xxv 18). The Al-'Amrān tribe gives the name Cush to the region of Zabid (Yemen). Thus it would be preferable to understand Cush as the territory on both sides of the southern part of the Red Sea. — Cf. KB, p. 429. Then a location of Seba in Arabia is not excluded. According to A. VAN DEN BORN the distinction between Seba and Sheba may be artificial (cf. *BW*², col. 1574).

[2] Cf. P. VOLZ, *o.c.*, p. 37; J. FISCHER, *o.c.*, p. 61; P. AUVRAY - J. STEINMANN, *Isaïe*, p. 179, note a.

[3] U. E. SIMON, *A Theology of Salvation*, pp. 99-100.

[4] H. E. VON WALDOW, *Jesaja 43*, p. 41: "An konkrete politische Verhältnisse wird demnach hier kaum gedacht sein".

term *kōper* with the *gō'ēl* relationship between Yahwe and Israel. Although this relationship includes that the *gō'ēl* redeems his relatives who are enslaved, yet, in the O.T. *kōper* never occurs in such a context. Nonetheless, the image of redemption undoubtedly recalls that relationship.

In vs. 4a, Yahwe's way of acting is motivated, viz. "because Israel is precious in Yahwe's eyes". This is formulated with words that are less theological than *bḥr*, *g'l*, e.a. But let us remark that in Is. xli 9, Abraham is called *'ōhăbî*, so that the verb *'hb* in xliii 4a still has something to do with the theology of election. Anyhow, the deepest fundament of the election is thus expressed: God's gratuitous love, which makes Israel something precious to him.

4. *Is. xliii 5-7*

5 Fear not, for I am with you;
I will bring your offspring from the east,
and from the west I will gather you.
6 I will say to the north: Give up,
and to the south: Do not withhold;
bring my sons from afar
and my daughters from the end of the earth,
7 every one who is called by my name,
whom for my glory I have created —
I have formed and made.

The next oracle opens, without any introduction, with the assurance of salvation and the nominal substantiation, "I am with you" (vs. 5a). The concrete salvific event now is the return from the diaspora. Sometimes the existence of a real diaspora in Dt.-Isaiah's time has been questioned, but wrongly, as it seems to me. Dt.-Is. and his fellow-exiles knew very well about a dispersion of their countrymen in foreign lands.[1] Against this background, Is. xliii 5-7 is quite understandable. Several scholars, on the contrary, induced from these verses that a certain diaspora existed already in the days of the Babylonian captivity.[2] If one wants geographical precision, we may

[1] Cf. A. Schoors, "Arrière-fond historique et critique d'authenticité des textes deutéro-isaïens", *Orientalia Lovaniensia Periodica*, II 1971, pp. 132-135.

[2] T. K. Cheyne, *The Prophecies of Isaiah*, I, p. 274; J. Knabenbauer, *Commentarius in Isaiam prophetam*, II, Parisiis 1887, p. 128; B. Duhm, *o.c.*, p. 288; J. Fischer, *Das*

say that the East is Babylon, the North Damascus and Assyria, the South Patros, Egypt and eventually Arabia, the West the Aegean world (cf. xli 1). But, even if the existence of a diaspora in Arabia or the Greek world at that time is uncertain, the consciousness of any dispersion is enough to make possible a text such as Is. xliii 5-7. The mentioning of the four parts of the world does not aim at geographical accuracy; it is but a circumscription of "the whole world". Such is explicitly said in vs. 6b: "from the end of the earth".[1] To F. FELDMANN the last expression proves that the prophet does not have in mind the diaspora of his time, but that he thinks of the messianic future.[2] As I have written elsewhere, I am sceptical about eschatology and messianism in Dt.-Is.[3] Anyhow, he could not have conceived the messianic restoration under these images, if he had no knowledge of any diaspora.

In verse 6 the tone is more individualistic. The prophet no longer speaks of the personified Israel in the singular, but stresses Yahwe's peculiar care of all the Israelites, his children. The close relationship between Yahwe and Israel is not only collective, it has an individual impact in the sense that there is a relationship like that of father and child between God and the individual Israelite. Here Dt.-Is. continues a tendency, which was already present with Jeremiah and Ezekiel. The evolution to a more individual religion and ethics has been fastened about and during the exile (e.g. Ez. xviii), as some external supports of the collective piety fell away. The personal relationship between the faithful and God receives more attention, and this is expressed by the image of the father-son relationship, which passes from the people (e.g. Ex. iv 22) to the individual.[4] However, let us remark that the individual application of the title "son of God" is already found in Deuteronomy (Deut. xiv 1-2; cf. Ps. lxxiii 15).

Buch Isaias, II, p. 62; J. STEINMANN, *Le livre de la consolation*, p. 120. According to S. D. LUZZATTO, *Il Profeta Isaia*, Padova 1867, p. 476, the prophet, although he mentions the four directions, only means the גלות בבל, since the Babylonian empire was very large.

[1] Compare the Mesopotamian royal titles, in which the kings pretend their universal leadership by calling themselves "kings of the four regions". Cf. M.-J. SEUX, *Epithètes royales akkadiennes et sumériennes*, Paris 1967, pp. 305-308.

[2] F. FELDMANN, *Das Buch Isaias*, II, p. 68.

[3] Cf. A. SCHOORS, "L'eschatologie dans les prophéties du Deutéro-Isaïe", *Recherches bibliques*, VIII 1966, pp. 107-128.

[4] W. EICHRODT, *Theologie des A.T.*, II, pp. 118-119; 168-172: "Der politische Zusammenbruch und die Neuprägung der Individualität".

And even there one joins a very old belief, which appears in the theophoric names.

Verse 7 once more stresses that personal relationship. Moreover it adds the motif of Yahwe's glory. The verse, though structurally belonging to the motif of outcome, is related, in its content, to the motif of final goal. So the oracle becomes manifestly theocentric. The salvific action, announced in the oracle, aims at Yahwe's glory. This will appear even more clearly in Is. xliv 1-5 and some proclamations of salvation having a C motif *in forma*.

P. Volz and H. E. von Waldow treat vs. 7b as a strict goal motif. They suppose the suffixes to correspond to a neuter and to refer to the preceding promise of salvation: "For my glory I create *it*..."[1] But in Hebrew, a feminine suffix would fit this meaning better. With J. Steinmann, J. Morgenstern, J. L. McKenzie, and *RSV*, I prefer to read an asyndetic relative clause parallel with *hanniqrā'*.[2] The old translations too gave a personal meaning to the suffixes.[3] There is no need to drop the *waw* before *likᵉbôdî*, as proposed by *BHK*.

It is hard to arrive at a definite conclusion concerning the original connection between Is. xliii 1-4 and 5-7. It seemed self-evident to scholars that Is. xliii 1-7 is a unit, and even most of the form-critics look at it that way. For the most part they did not go into the question and, from a form-critical point of view, the pericope certainly consists of two distinct oracles. But certain literary data provide the thesis of the original unity with a high degree of probability. The absence of a real conclusion in the first and of an introduction in the second oracle points in that direction. The messenger's formula in vs. 1 seems to concern the whole of vss. 1-7. Such is confirmed by an inclusion. Whereas in vs. 1 the prophet recalls the fact that Yahwe created and formed Israel, he says in vs. 7 that this was done for his own glory (*br'*, *yṣr*). It is true, in vs. 7b one verb seems to be superfluous and many commentators together with *BHS*, eliminate *yᵉṣartîw*. The textual tradition does not give one any support for doing so and one could drop *'ap-'ăśîtîw* as well. Moreover, without the second verb the inclusion, though less impressive, still stands. The inclusion

---

[1] P. Volz, *o.c.*, p. 38; H. E. von Waldow, *Anlass und Hintergrund*, pp. 96 and 218, note 13; otherwise in *Jesaja 43*, p. 44.

[2] J. Steinmann, *o.c.*, p. 119; J. Morgenstern, *o.c.*, pp. 123 and 132; J. L. McKenzie, *Second Isaiah*, Garden City 1968, p. 49. Cf. my translation.

[3] LXX: *κατεσκεύασα αὐτὸν*; Targ: בריתינון; Vg: creavi eum.

goes further. To the substantiation, "I called you by name" (vs. 1), corresponds the designation of the Israelites as "all who are called by my name" (*qr' b^{e}šēm*). Thus very probably Is. xliii 1-7 is an original composition that goes back to the prophet himself. The concrete description of the salvation (motif of outcome) then shows a tidy climax: protection on the journey home (vs. 2); the deliverance is an event of world dimensions (vs. 3), it is a return of the diaspora from all over the world (vss. 5-7).

5. *Is. xliv 1-5*

1 But now hear, O Jacob my servant,
Israel whom I have chosen:
2 Thus says Yahwe, your maker,
who formed you in the womb and *helps you*[a]:
Fear not, O Jacob, my servant,
Jeshurun whom I have chosen.
3 For I will pour water on the thirsty soil,
streams on the dry ground.
I will pour my spirit upon your descendants,
and my blessing on your offspring.
4 They shall sprout *like the green ben tree*[b],
like willows by the watercourses.
5 One will say, 'I belong to Yahwe',
another *will be called*[c] by the name of Jacob,
and another will write on his hand 'Yahwe's'
and *be surnamed*[c] by the name of Israel."

[a] IQIa: ועוזרכה, perhaps original reading.

[b] IQIa: כבין loco בבין; cf. LXX: *ὡσεὶ χόρτος ἀνὰ μέσον ὕδατος*; Targum: כלבלבי עסב; cf. the discussion below, p. 79, note 1.

[c] Lg. יִקָּרֵא cum Sym.; lg. יְכֻנֶּה cum Targ.: יתקרב; Pesh: ܢܬܟܢܐ. So both cola are completely parallel.

In this oracle, the messenger's formula (vs. 2a) is surrounded by a developed address (vss. 1 and 2b), which again recalls the election and the *'ebed*-situation. Only the unusual name Jeshurun needs some further explanation. Besides here it only occurs in Deut. xxxii 15; xxxiii 5, 26 and Sir. xxxvii 25 (H). In Deut. also the context is poetical (Song of Moses) and the appellation is parallel with Jacob. It is a poetic *surname* for Israel with unexplained meaning. It is mostly seen in connection with the root *yšr*, meaning "upright".[1] The rendering in Aq. Sym., Theod. (ὁ εὔθυς) and Vulgate (*rectissime*) points in the same direction. Septuagint translates it with ὁ ἀγαπημένος (here + Ἰσραηλ). The reading of Is. xliv 2 is not absolutely clear, since four manuscripts, Septuagint, Peshitta and Targum have "Israel". The masoretic reading, however, is to be preferred as the best attested and as *lectio difficilior*. The Septuagint does not witness in the opposite sense for it has a *lectio conflata*.

Also the messenger's formula itself is developed in hymnic style. From the adjunct *mibbeṭen*, WESTERMANN deduces that the expression "who formed you" does not only intend the historic beginnings of the nation, but God's creative activity, more precisely the creation of each individual Israelite.[2] Although not impossible, this interpretation is not positively favored by the text. Once again we should take into account the prophet's stylistic firmness of forms. The term *mibbeṭen*, just like *yōṣerᵉkā* and similar participles, is originally situated in the introduction of an individual oracle of salvation (cf. xliii 1) and correlatively in the expressions of confidence in the psalms of lament. When applying the style of the individual oracle to Israel, Dt.-Is. uses personification, as we stated already. So it is quite normal that he continues the personification, speaking of Israel's "being formed from the womb". He means the birth of Israel represented as an individual. Therefore *mibbeṭen* is evidently not meant in a literal way, but receives, just like *yṣr*, a historico-theological reinterpretation, and becomes a metonymy for the beginnings of Israel's history. The more so as the same expression occurs with the same meaning in Is. xliv 24. In xlviii 8 the expression "rebel from the womb" is applied to the personified Israel. In a plural context we find *minnî-beṭen* in Is. xlvi 3 but here too the reference to Israel's origin as a nation is quite probable. Finally, according to Job xxxi 18, *mibbeṭen* is parallel with *minnᵉʿûray*. Yet, "Israel's youth" is a fixed formula to indicate the beginning of its history at the time of the Exodus (Hos. ii 17; Jer. ii 2; iii 4, etc.; Ez. xvi 22; xxiii, passim).[3]

In the second member of verse 2, Yahwe is presented as the God,

---

[1] Cf. P. AUVRAY - J. STEINMANN, *Isaïe*, p. 184, note e; B. DUHM, *o.c.*, p. 296; F. FELDMANN, *o.c.*, p. 68; J. FISCHER, *o.c.*, p. 68; J. MORGENSTERN, *o.c.*, p. 145; GK § 86 g; BROWN-DRIVER-BRIGGS, p. 440.

[2] C. WESTERMANN, *o.c.*, p. 110. For מִן meaning "in" cf. M. DAHOOD, *Bib.* XLVIII 1967, p. 427.

[3] Cf. B. J. VAN DER MERWE, *Pentateuchtradisies*, pp. 128; 173.

who is continually turned towards Israel. He remains the one who gave existence to the people (participle) and continually helps it (imperfect).

The oracle is somewhat different from the former examples, since there is no nominal or perfective motivation after the assurance of salvation. The prophet directly passes to the motif of outcome, which still has the *kî* of the dropped motivation. The promise of salvation is formulated in imaginative speech, which is interpreted immediately. Yahwe will give rain on the dry land (vs. 3). This means blessing of fertility for Israel: God's nation will grow luxuriantly (vs. 4).[1] The dry land is an image of the exiled and oppressed Israel. Quite wrongly Auvray-Steinmann explain Yahwe's *rûaḥ* (vs. 3b) as the prophetical Spirit of the eschatological era (cf. Is. xi 2; Joel iii 1-2).[2] Yahwe's spirit is his vital breath, which gives life to the plants and animals (Is. xxxii 15; Ps. civ 30) and mankind (Num. xvi 22; xxvii 16; Eccl. xii 7). The blessing too must be understood as a blessing of fertility (Gen. i 22, 28).[3] It seems probable to me that this blessing of fertility is thought of in the line of that promised to the patriarchs (Gen. xii 3; xxii 17; xxvi 3-4; xxviii 14). In that sense one may agree with J. Kahmann, when he asserts that the formulas "maker" and "former of Israel" in the introduction also refer to the election of the patriarchs.[4]

---

[1] The words בבין חציר have always been a *crux*. Two good solutions have been proposed by J. M. Allegro and A. Guillaume, who emend the first *beth* to *kaph*, according to 10 mss, IQIa, LXX and Targ. Guillaume then connects בין with Arab. *bînon*, which means "a region, tract, area, a piece of land extending as far as the eye can reach". He renders the verse as follows:

They shall spring up like a field of grass
Like willows by the watercourses.

In Allegro's opinion, the first colon needs the name of a tree balancing כערבים. He finds it in בין: Arab. *bânon*, "moringa", English "ben tree"; Aram. בינא in *TB Gittin* 68b, which has been glossed by Rashi as ערבא; Syr. *bînâ*, "tamarisk"; Akk. *binu*, "tamarisk". Then חציר should be emended to חצור, "green", an adjective of the *qaṭāl* type. His rendering is:

They shall spring up as the green ben tree,
as willows by the watercourses.

Cf. J. M. Allegro, "The Meaning of בין in Isaiah XLIV, 4" *ZAW*. LXIII 1951, pp. 154-156; A. Guillaume, "A Note on the Meaning of בין", *JTS*. n.s. XIII 1962, pp. 109-110. Both solutions are very good, but Allegro's seems to be preferable because of the complete parallelism.

[2] *BJ*, pp. 1032; 1029, note k; 1000, note k.

[3] Cf. J. Fischer, *o.c.*, p. 68; P. van Imschoot, *BW*³, col. 467; C. Westermann, *o.c.*, p. 111.

[4] J. Kahmann, *Bib.* XXXII 1951, p. 145.

However, not only a physical fertility is meant. The miraculous growth of the nation certainly is part of the coming salvation, according to our prophet (cf. Is. xlviii 18-19; xlix 20-21). Verse 5 stresses that Yahwe's community will grow through the fact that many adhere to him. This verse, although structurally belonging to the promise of salvation, partly corresponds to the C motif, as far as contents are concerned. That vs. 5 has in view the conversion of pagans to Yahwe is not at all certain.[1] An opening to universalism in this context is not proved, and if it does not appear in other oracles of our prophet, it must be rejected here also. According to L. Rost and P. A. H. de Boer, there is even a restriction of the name Jacob-Israel to the Judaeans.[2] We may find here a new concept of God's people as the community of those who adhere to Yahwe. But the parallelism in the verse makes clear that adhering to Yahwe includes belonging to Israel. If there were any opening to universalism (cf. xlv 14), belief in Yahwe still passes trough the historic Israel.

E. Hessler has tried to deepen theologically the cohesion of the oracle. Vss. 3a and 4 would not merely offer an image to illustrate a salvific fact. The image also includes a creation motif, — *Yahwe gives* the rain, — which is connected with the promise of salvation. The image thus is typological of Yahwe's working. So the concrete bearing of the verse would be: Yahwe, who creates everything, e.g. also the rain, will now create his people anew (vs. 3b). The idea of creation would be the fundament of the announcement of salvation in the verse under consideration.[3] However attractive this comment may be, to me it seems overdone. If present at all, this theological background is extremely implicit.

6. *Is. liv 4-6*

4 Fear not, for you will not be ashamed;
be not confounded, for you will not be put to shame;
on the contrary, you will forget the shame of your bondage,

---

[1] Cf. C. C. Torrey, *The Second Isaiah*, p. 344. Against T. K. Cheyne, *o.c.*, pp. 282-284; J. Knabenbauer, *o.c.*, pp. 148-149; F. Delitzsch, *Commentar über das Buch Jesaia*, Leipzig 1889, p. 461; K. Marti, *o.c.*, p. 301; C. Westermann, *l.c.*

[2] L. Rost, *Israel bei den Propheten*, Stuttgart 1937, p. 92; P. A. H. de Boer, *Second-Isaiah's Message*, Leiden 1956, p. 115.

[3] E. Hessler, *EvTh.* XXV 1965, pp. 362-364: "Das 'Bild' ist ... eigentlich nicht als 'Bild' gemeint, obwohl es infolge des Characters der Motive so ausfällt, sondern es liefert das theologische Fundament für die Verkündigung".

and the dishonor of your widowhood you will remember no more.
5 For your maker is your husband,
Yahwe of hosts is his name,
and the Holy One of Israel is your redeemer,
the God of the whole earth is he called.
6 For Yahwe calls you like a wife forsaken
and grieved in spirit.
A wife of youth, will she ever be rejected?
says your God.

We recognize in Is. liv 4-6 the structure of an oracle of salvation in the strict sense. WESTERMANN points in the same direction, as he treats the vss. 1-10 as a unit in his commentary, whereas in his form-critical articles he mentions liv 4-6 with the salvation oracles, though it be between brackets.[1] It thus astonishes me that in his commentary he does not point out this oracle structure.

The oracle is directed to Jerusalem, personified as a widow, as appears from vs. 4b. The assurance of salvation "Fear not" is developed with a parallel "be not confounded" and two *kî*-phrases, which thematically express the same idea but stylistically refer to the deplaced motif of outcome. The motivations appear only in the vss. 5-6. Verse 4b does not act as a motivation, for *kî* here is an affirmative particle following a negative phrase: "not ... on the contrary".[2] The promise of salvation again clearly corresponds to a typical motif of the lament (Pss. xxv 2; xxxi 2, 18; lxix 7; lxxi 1; Jer. ix 18). K. ELLIGER thinks the image of the wife is not dt.-Isaian.[3] As a matter of fact, our prophet does not use it frequently, but it does occur in Is. l 1 and perhaps implicitly in xlix 14. It is certainly older than Dt.-Is. and well known in prophetic literature (Hos. i-iii; Jer. ii 2; iii 1, 6-12; Ez. xvi; xxiii). It evidently is related to the dt.-Isaian theme of "mother Zion".

Jerusalem is addressed as a widow. It is commonly accepted that this widowhood refers to the exilic situation.[4] Many authors think

---

[1] C. WESTERMANN, "Das Heilswort bei Deuterojesaja", *EvTh.* XXIV 1964, p. 359; "Sprache und Struktur der Prophetie Deuterojesajas", *Forschung am alten Testament*, München 1964, p. 118.

[2] KB, p. 431; ZORELL, p. 353: *kî-adversativum*; GK § 163b.

[3] K. ELLIGER, *Deuterojesaja*, p. 145. ELLIGER considers the whole of Is. liv as trito-Isaian.

[4] T. K. CHEYNE, *o.c.*, pp. 54-55; F. DELITZSCH, *o.c.*, p. 561; J. KNABENBAUER, *o.c.*, pp. 341-342; K. MARTI, *Das Buch Jesaia*, p. 354; B. DUHM, *o.c.*, p. 369; A. CONDAMIN,

the "shame of your youth" is the bondage in Egypt.[1] According to K. MARTI and B. DUHM one should add to this the oppression by Assyria. P. VOLZ extends it to all the sufferings of Israel before the exile.[2] J. KNABENBAUER thinks of the sins in the desert immediately after the establishing of the covenant, whereas K. ELLIGER and J. FISCHER refer both the shame of youth and the widowhood to the exile. That the exile is meant in one of the two terms is beyond any doubt. Jerusalem is a widow, she has been abandoned by Yahwe, her husband. Whether the shame of youth refers to an earlier situation cannot be deduced from the context. The word "youth" could be a hint in that direction (Ez. xvi 4-8).

Whereas widowhood is a shame in itself, such is not true of "youth". Indeed, the word *'ălûmîm* nowhere has a pejorative meaning (Ps. lxxxix 46; Job xx 11; xxxiii 25). This creates a problem which I tried to solve by proposing a new interpretation of *'ălûmîm*. I believe that in the present context, the word concretely means "bondage". The root *'lm* is often found in that sense in Aramaic, Ugaritic (*ǵlm*) and even a few times in Hebrew (1 Sam. xx 22; Cant. vi 8). I have gathered the evidence elsewhere.[3] So the text gets a more balanced meaning. In parallel phrases, the prophet uses the image of bondage and that of widowhood as well to indicate the exile. So we meet to some extent the interpretation already mentioned, which ELLIGER and FISCHER proposed. The latter understands *'ălûmîm* as "single life", concretely indicating widowhood, in strict parallelism to *'almenût*. However, the word nowhere has the technical sense of "single life", no more than *'almâ* includes the condition of being unmarried like *betûlâ*.[4] The further deduced meaning "widowhood" then becomes hardly defensible.

The interpretation, I just proposed, is well-founded not only from a semantic point of view but also in a literary respect. For, to the twofold promise of salvation in vs. 4b chiastically corresponds a twofold nominal motivation in vs. 5. Jerusalem must forget her widowhood because Yahwe is her husband. It is true, B. DUHM deletes vs. 5, because it would separate the *Trostgrund* (vs. 6) from the word

---

Le Livre d'Isaïe, p. 345; F. FELDMANN, *o.c.*, p. 176; A. VAN HOONACKER, *Het boek Isaias*, p. 261; K. ELLIGER, *o.c.*, p. 138; J. FISCHER, *o.c.*, p. 142.

[1] The same except KNABENBAUER, ELLIGER and FISCHER.

[2] P. VOLZ, *o.c.*, p. 133.

[3] A. SCHOORS, "Two Notes on Is. xl-lv", *VT*. XXI 1971, pp. 503-505.

[4] Cf. KB, p. 709; *DISO*, p. 214; B. VAWTER, "The Ugaritic Use of Galmat", *CBQ*. XIV 1952, pp. 319-322. — Against ZORELL, p. 603.

of comfort (vs. 4).[1] But he overlooks: 1. that the participial style of the verse is quite dt.-Isaian; 2. that the terminology is reminiscent of Dt.-Is.; 3. that vs. 5 is the most fundamental *Trostgrund* of the whole oracle. Does vs. 5 mean that Yahwe marries Zion *anew*?[2] The participle *bōʿălayik* could suggest this: "For your maker marries you". According to LXX and Targum,[3] one could read also *beʿālayik* in a nominal phrase: "Your maker is your husband".[4] In this case the prophet invokes the still existing marriage bond between Yahwe and his people. This interpretation is more probable as appears from vs. 6b and Is. 1 1.[5] In other words, the fact that Yahwe is Jerusalem's husband must be the fundament of her confidence. He does not abandon her, though as yet she seems to be abandoned. I cannot agree with C. H. Gordon, who parses *bōʿălayik* as a participle of the verb *bʿl*, a dialect form of *pʿl*, "to make", thus making it synonymous with *ʿōśayik*.[6] I do not contest the existence of such a form in Ugaritic, nor do I exclude it apriori in Hebrew. But the word does not become the present context. Gordon has been misled by a certain overestimation of the importance of Ugaritic for the understanding of Dt.-Isaiah's Hebrew and by an underestimation of the literary context as expedient for interpreting a word.

The second motive of the promise, — and this confirms my interpreation of *ʿălûmîm*, — is the *gōʾēl*-relationship between Yahwe and Jerusalem. I have already gone into the subject of this relationship. It is true, in order to remain in the symbolism of marriage, Š. Porúbčan has connected the word *gōʾēl* with the levirate (cf. Ruth iii-iv).[7] This is not acceptable. Certainly, the levirate belongs to the complex of the *geʾullâ*, but it is inconceivable that Yahwe has an obligation of *gōʾēl* to himself. Moreover, this meaning of *gōʾēl* is found

---

1 B. Duhm, *o.c.*, p. 354.

2 Š. Porúbčan, *Il patto nuovo in Is. 40-66*, Roma 1958, p. 178: "... le seconde nozze con Jahwe".

3 LXX: *κύριος*; Targ: מריך.

4 Remark the pl. בֹּעֲלַיִךְ and עֹשַׂיִךְ. This is commonly explained as a *plurale maiestatis* in analogy to אלהים; cf. Joüon, § 136 e; F. Delitzsch, *Commentar*, p. 561; K. Marti, *o.c.*, p. 354. According to C. C. Torrey, however, עשיך is a singular (*lamed-he* roots in this case do not have distinct forms for sing. and pl.) and בעליך is adapted to it by assonance.

5 So also B. Duhm, *o.c.*, p. 370.

6 C. H. Gordon, *UT* § 19.494.

7 Š. Porúbčan, *l.c.*

nowhere else in Dt.-Is. On the contrary, with our prophet, the root *g'l* is always related concretely to the deliverance from bondage in Egypt or Babylonia.

Who is this divine husband and redeemer? He is the Maker of Israel (*'ōśeh*) and its Holy One (*qᵉdôš yiśrā'ēl*). The motivation thus is the same as the one found in the introductions and other parts of the oracles we analyzed already. Besides, with the name "Yahwe of hosts" and "God of the whole earth", Yahwe's universal creation and domination are recalled (cf. Is. li 15; xlv 12-13; xliv 24; Am. iv 13; v 8; ix 6),[1] another fundament of the prophet's message of salvation, as will appear further on.

The verbal substantiation in vs. 6 only repeats the nominal one of vs. 5a. Now Yahwe calls back to him his temporarily abandoned (not repudiated) and grieving spouse. B. DUHM justly points out that not the first call is intended, but the renewed call after the exile. We are able to confirm this from a form-critical viewpoint. Taking into account the function of the perfective substantiation in the oracle of salvation, we must understand *qᵉrā'āk* as a *perfectum executionis*, expressing an actual intervention of Yahwe.

Would Yahwe ever forsake his "wife of youth" (vs. 6b)? From Mal. ii 14-15; Prov. v 18 it appears that "wife of youth" is a technical term for the legitimate wife. The particle *wᵉ...kî*, like *'ap kî* in other instances, denotes an unbelieving or unreal question,[2] a stylistic device to express an absolute certainty: Yahwe does not forsake Zion.

§3. THE PROCLAMATION OF SALVATION IN IS. XL-LV

The structure of the proclamation of salvation, which I described in the first paragraph in dependence on WESTERMANN, shows up in the following pericopes: Is. xli 17-20; xlii 14-17; xliii 16-21; xlvi 12-13; xlix 7-12; xlix 14-26; li 1-3, 6-8; li 9-14; li 17-23; liv 7-10; liv 11-17 and lv 1-5. Except for a couple of minor problems, the structure of the pericopes mentioned is easily recognizable. It is somewhat more

---

[1] Cf. W. EICHRODT, *Theologie*, I, p. 120-121; H. GRESSMANN, *Ursprung der Israelitisch-jüdischen Eschatologie*, Göttingen 1905, p. 73; P. VAN IMSCHOOT, *Théologie de l'A.T.*, I, Tournai 1954, pp. 20-22; B. N. WAMBACQ, *L'épithète divine Jahvé Sᵉba'ôt*, s.l. 1947, esp. p. 198: "En plusieurs sections où la puissance créatrice de Jahvé est décrite, on lit: Jahvé Sᵉba'ôt est son nom. Ce qui dénote une connexion entre cette conclusion et la puissance créatrice". On pp. 220-222, WAMBACQ demonstrates that in Is. liv 5, *Yahweh Ṣᵉbā'ôt* is the Creator and the Lord of the forces of nature.

[2] Cf. KB, p. 432, nr 12; ZORELL, p. 354, nr III, 3.

complicated in Is. xlvi 12-13 and li 1-3, 6-8. For the meaning of I, II and III in table III, the reader is referred to p. 44.

Table III

The Proclamations of Salvation

	Introd.	I	II		III
			1	2	
xli 17-20		17a	17b	18-19	20
xlii 14-17		14a	14b	15-16	17
xliii 16-21	16-17	18	19a	19b-20	21
xlvi 12-13	12a	12b	13	13	13bβ
xlix 7-12	7a	7ab	8a	8b-12	7cd
14-26		14	15-16	17-20(21)	
	22aα	21		22-23b	23c
	25aα	24		25-26a	26b
li 1-3, 6		1a	3a	3b-6	
7-8	7a	7b	7b	8	
9-14(16)		9-11	12-13	14	
17-23	17a, 21, 22a	17b-20	22bcα	22cβ-23	
liv 7-10		7a, 8a	7b, 8b	9-10	
11-17		11a	11b-13a	13b-17	
lv 1-5		1-3	3b-4	5a	5b

1. *Is. xli 17-20*

17 The poor and needy seek water, and there is none,
their tongue is parched with thirst.
I, Yahwe, answer them,
I, the God of Israel, forsake them not.
18 I will open rivers on bare heights,
and springs in the midst of the valleys;
I will make the wilderness a pool of water,
and the dry land a fountain.
19 I will put in the wilderness cedars,
acacias, myrtles and olives;
I will set in the desert cypresses,
planes and box trees as well,
20 that they may see and know,
may also consider and understand,
that the hand of Yahwe has done this,
the Holy One of Israel has created it.

There is a very large consensus about the delimitation of this pericope. BEGRICH, VON WALDOW and FOHRER reckon it among the salvation oracles. It is, however, the typical example of what has been called the proclamation of salvation by WESTERMANN.[1]

In the allusion to the lament (17a), the condition of distress is specified as a great drought and thirst. In motif II, 1 (vs. 17b), the hearing of the prayer is granted in words that clearly refer to the wording of the prayer: "Israel's God will not forsake them" (Pss. iii 5; iv 2; xiii 4; xvii 6; cxviii 5; also Gen. xxxv 3; 1 Sam. vii 9; viii 18; etc.).[2] Yahwe's intervention consists in giving plenty of water and wonderful vegetation in the desert. What does the oracle mean concretely? In what does the condition of distress and salvation consist?

One could imagine a real drought. But from vss. 18-19 it appears that such is not the case, for the thirst of the poor is caused by the desert. Therefore, it is obvious that many scholars understand the verses as announcing a repetition of the miraculous water episodes during the march through the desert. GRESSMANN and BEGRICH rather suppose a transformation of nature.[3] For the theme of the renewed desert march there are sufficient parallels in Dt.-Is. (Is. xliii 18-21; xlviii 21; xlix 9-11; lii 11-12; lv 13). One may invoke also Jer. ii 6, where the march out of Egypt through the desert is recalled with the same words: *midbār*, *'ereṣ ṣiyyâ* and *'ărābâ*. Finally, I refer to the expressions *'ên mayim* in Ex. xvii 1 and *ûmayim 'ayin* in Num. xx 5. It thus seems that Is. xli 17-20 recalls the exodus in poetic language after the manner of Pss. lxxviii 15-16; cv 41; cxiv 8.

However, let us remark that there is no allusion to the way or the march and that the picture is somewhat overdone, if the prophet only views Yahwe's care of his people during the journey through the

---

[1] J. BEGRICH, *Studien*, p. 14; H. E. VON WALDOW, *Anlass und Hintergrund*, p. 27; C. WESTERMANN, *EvTh.* XXIV 1964, pp. 365-366; G. FOHRER, *Das Buch Jesaja*, III, Zürich 1964, p. 43.

[2] Cf. H. E. VON WALDOW, *o.c.*, p. 106. However, I cannot agree with this scholar in explaining vs. 17a as the adress to the suppliants. In the whole oracle, there is no trace of a second person. Moreover, in that case the text should have מבקשי (so *BHK*) or המבקשים instead of מבקשים. My objection does not invalidate the suggested contact with the lamentation.

[3] H. GRESSMANN, *Der Ursprung der Israelitisch-jüdischen Eschatologie*, Göttingen 1905, p. 216; J. BEGRICH, *Studien*, p. 83; also somewhat J. L. MCKENZIE, *Second Isaiah*, p. 32.

desert.[1] Vs. 19 especially is hard to connect with that journey. Vss. 18-19 seem to take up the traditional motif of the *Naturwandlung* as a manifestation of Yahwe's might (cf. Pss. cvii 33-35; civ 27-30). But it must be interpreted according to its functional place in the whole proclamation. The interpretation of the promised salvation presupposes an exact idea of the condition of distress. We should understand the thirst in 17a as an image of such a condition. We are invited to say so by the general terms *'ānî* and *'ebyôn,* borrowed from the psalms of lament, where they indicate the suppliant or an other distressed person. Moreover, the literature of lament repeatedly uses the image of thirst (Pss. xxii 16; cxxxvii 6; Lam. iv 4), often by metonymy, to stress the absence of Yahwe and the longing for his presence (Pss. xlii 2; lxiii 2; cxliii 6). It is hard to decide what kind of distress the prophet precisely means: Yahwe's absence? a state of oppression? or the exile *tout court*? Perhaps it is distress in general and vss. 18-19 are only strong figurative language to say: "I shall turn misery into happiness".[2]

I propose the following interpretation. In the proclamation, the restoration is foretold symbolically. The prophet has in mind the journey home as well as the rebuilding of the homeland. To the former he alludes through referring to the water episodes (vs. 18). On this point I agree with most of the commentators. But the picture as a whole refers to something more. According to E. HESSLER, to the description of paradise in Gen. ii.[3] In favour of her opinion one can invoke Ez. xxxi 8-9, where *'erez* and *b^erôš* are presented as trees of paradise. Against this, B. VAN DER MERWE asserts that the prophet has in view concrete regions such as Lebanon, Carmel, Tabor and Gilead.[4] In any case, the paradisiac vegetation in the desert symbolizes the restoration of the land of Israel. One may suppose that a lament resembling to Jer. xiv 2-9; iii 21-25; xii 7-13 precedes. One should also remember the former oracles of doom, according to which Israel would become a desert (Hos. ii 5; Ez. vi 14; xii 20; xxxii 29). The value of this interpretation is illustrated by Is. li 3, where Zion's restoration

---

1 F. FELDMANN, *Das Buch Isaias,* II, p. 49: "Wer glaubt, dass dieser Vers sich einzig auf die Heimkehr aus Babel beziehe wird den ausdrücken nicht gerecht".

2 Cf. T. K. CHEYNE, *The Prophecies of Isaiah,* I, pp. 257-258; J. KNABENBAUER, *Commentarius,* II, p. 95; F. DELITZSCH, *Commentar über das Buch Jesaia,* p. 433.

3 E. HESSLER, *a.c.,* p. 360.

4 B. J. VAN DER MERWE, *Pentateuchtradisies in die Prediking van Deuterojesaja,* Groningen 1955, p. 52.

is presented as the change from a desert into a paradise. In Is. xliv 3-4, an analogous image serves to indicate an extraordinary increase of the population and of Yahwe's community.

I thus defend a concrete salvation-historical interpretation. According to H. E. von Waldow, Is. xli 18-19 does not view a concrete situation. In reply to the lament, Yahwe would only promise a complete reversal of the condition, in other words, an eschatological event. He rejects an interpretation in terms of a journey through the desert with this argument: "If this were the idea, then Yahwe should make roads in the desert instead of pools, and fruit trees instead of ornamental plants".[1] Such a reasoning betrays an astonishing lack of comprehension of poetical and symbolic speech. E. Hessler proposed a theological interpretation which is exaggerated. Yahwe would be creating because he makes possible the knowledge of God in the still "uncreated" land of the pagans (the desert) by "planting" Israel in that region. This interpretation would rest on the symbolical significance of the trees in the book of Isaiah (Is. ii 10-19; x 16-19, 33-34; v 7; lx 21; lxi 3).[2] But the first three texts present an opposite picture to Is. xli 18: the trees are destroyed. In Is. ii 10-19, the high trees symbolize human pride. Only in Is. x the cut down forest is a symbol of the punished Israel. In Is. v, Israel is presented as a vineyard planted by Yahwe, whereas, according to lx 21; lxi 3 it will be again "a planting of Yahwe" in the era of salvation. The image of the vineyard has nothing to do with Is. xli 18. The two trito-Isaian texts are the best parallel of Is. xli 18, but precisely in these texts, the image involves a promise of restoration.

In verse 20 of the present pericope, we meet for the first time a motif of goal *in forma*. It is introduced with the particle *lᵉmaʿan* and it announces the acknowledgment that Yahwe, the Holy One of Israel, has realized the salvific event. This acknowledgment is the aim of the promised salvific act and its subjects are the *'ebyônîm* (vs. 17), i.e. Israel itself. There is no reason to suppose a shift of the subject in vs. 20. Thus, one should make no mention of a universal recognition of Yahwe (against E. Hessler).

W. Zimmerli devoted an extensive monograph to the *Erkenntnis-*

[1] H. E. von Waldow, *o.c.*, pp. 91-92 and 217, note 1: "Wäre wirklich daran gedacht, hätte Jahwe in der Wüste besser Wege statt Sümpfe und mehr Fruchtbäume statt Holz- und Zierpflanzen schaffen sollen".

[2] E. Hessler, *a.c.*, pp. 360-361.

formel in Ezekiel.[1] His conclusions are important for the understanding of Dt.-Is. also. The recognition of Yahwe, expressed in the formula in question, is always caused by his acting: it is not speculative but empirico-logical. This is illustrated repeatedly by the wording. Beside "to acknowledge that I am Yahwe", we often find a more developed formula: "to acknowledge that I, Yahwe, have done so and so". We find the latter in Is. xli 20. The formula is old and we can trace it back to the period of the early monarchy, since it already shows up in J. We find it in different literary contexts, such as: the oracles of threat by Ezekiel, the pareneses of Deuteronomy, the traditions about Moses in P and J, prophetic words belonging to the holy war (1 Kings xx). The formula cannot be reduced to one *Sitz im Leben.* But in all the contexts it has the empirico-logical bearing just explained.

The formula of "knowing" (*yd'*) is originally connected with the phenomenon of the "token of proof". It occurs in human relations e.g. in the lawsuit, where after the exhibition of the evidence the answer is given (*yd'*; e.g. Gen. xlii 33-34). In a religious context, we meet an analogous situation, when people inquire of God in distress, or before a battle (e.g. 1 Sam. vi; xiv 8-10), or at any difficult problem (Gen. xxiv 12-14: who will be Isaac's wife?). Often Yahwe grants the token on his own initiative, especially in prophetic contexts. The token always has a decisive value with regard to an alternative question: Did Joseph's brothers speak the truth or not? Should Jonathan attack the Philistines or not? Is Yahwe the strongest or Pharao and his gods? In Israel, the token is thus also able to prove Yahwe's dominion or the truth of the mission of a divine messenger. The formula "You will know, they will know" thus has a strong accent of historical *Entscheidung.*

In Dt.-Is. we find the formula more than once, and not only as a conclusion of salvation words. I shall go deeper into the use of it in the disputations and trial speeches in the next chapter. There the decisive character of the phrase is very clear. When the formula occurs at the end of a salvation word, we should keep in mind the same background. The promised salvific event is thus a token: it will bring Israel (in other instances the nations) to insight. It thus has a decisive value in a dilemma. Which dilemma? The answer to this question must appear from the object of the formula of recognition.

---

[1] W. ZIMMERLI, *Erkenntnis Gottes nach dem Buche Ezechiel,* Zürich 1954; republished in ID., *Gottes Offenbarung,* München 1963, pp. 41-119.

In the oracle xli 17-20, the acknowledgment concerns the fact that Yahwe creates the promised salvation (*br'*). Ultimately, the oracle thus announces an answer to the alternative: is Yahwe able to deliver his people or not? In the next chapter, we shall see that this question dominates the disputations and trial speeches in Is. xl-lv. The proclamation of salvation, which we are analyzing, appears to be bound up with the same question. Our oracle thus is to be understood as a retort to the doubts or unbelief of the exiles with regard to Yahwe's salvific action. According to the prophet, the announced reversal of the situation will have a revealing character: Yahwe shows his salvation-historical and creative power.

2. *Is. xlii 14-17*

14 For a long time I have held my peace,
I have kept still and restrained myself.
Like a woman in travail I will cry out;
I will destroy and also devour.
15 I will lay waste mountains and hills
and dry up all their herbage;
I will turn the rivers into islands
and dry up the pools.
16 I will lead the blind in a way that they know not,
in paths that they know not I will guide them.
I will turn the darkness before them into light,
the rough places into level ground.
These are the things I do,
and I forsake them not.
17 They shall be turned back and utterly put to shame,
who trust in graven idols,
who say to molten images:
"You are our gods".

As to the contents these verses are a proclamation of salvation. Therefore, we expect to find at the beginning a reference to the lamentation, which indeed appears in vs. 14a. We can refer to complaints like: "Wilt thou be silent for ever?" (cf. Hab. i 13; Ps. xxxv 22), or better to Is. lxiv 11: "Wilt thou restrain thyself (*tit'appaq*) at these things, Yahwe? Wilt thou keep silent (*teḥěšeh*) and afflict us sorely?" God acknowledges the complaint to be well-founded: indeed, he has kept silent.

The announcement of the reversal contrasts with the complaint: Yahwe will cry loudly. In the present condition, it means that he will act, intervene. The image of the woman in travail is somewhat strange in the context. In the Bible the metaphor is often used to typify a condition of supreme distress, e.g. the eschatological distress, either as a consequence of Yahwe's judgment (Is. xiii 8) or as Israel's oppression just before Yahwe's intervention (Is. xxxvii 3). But this interpretation does not hold when the image refers to Yahwe himself. The problem itself is wrong, because Yahwe is not presented as a woman in travail. The particle k^e here means "like" and the *tertium comparationis* is not the condition of distress but the crying. We should not look for something concrete behind the image. The woman in travail is only a term of comparison to picture Yahwe's loud crying. In short, there is no metaphor but a simile. Verse 14b cannot mean anything concrete owing to its function in the whole of the oracle: it is the motif of God's turning towards the people (motif II, 1), while the announcement of a concrete intervention follows in the next verses. Verse 14b is mostly translated as "I will gasp and pant" (*RSV*). So the three verbs of vs. 14b would typify Yahwe's attitude as that of a woman in travail. The form *'eššōm* then is derived from the root *nšm*, which would mean "to breathe vehemently". But P. JOÜON justly pointed out that this verb would be *hapax legomenon* and that the nuance "vehemently" is purely conjectural. In Arabic *nšm* means "to breathe gently". He suggests that the form *'eššōm* is derived from the root *šmm*, "to destroy" in accordance with the ancient translations and with the dictionaries of W. GESENIUS and E. KÖNIG.[1] The verbs *šmm* and *š'p* are used in parallelism in Ez. xxxvi 3 also. The verb *š'p* means "to inhale, to snap", and by extension "to swallow up, to devour".[2] It is remarkable that this suggestion of JOÜON remained unnoticed, although it is pertinent. A slight problem exists with regard to the qal form of *šmm*, which usually has a stative meaning. Nevertheless, in the cited text Ez. xxxvi 3, the infin. qal *šammôt* also has a transitive meaning.[3] But nothing prevents us from reading a hifil (*'āšēm*). Together with GESENIUS and JOÜON we can

---

[1] LXX: ἐκστήσω καὶ ξηρανῶ; Vg: dissipabo et absorbebo; Targ: יצדון ויסופון כחדא; Pesh: ܐܬܒܗ ܘܐܬܘܪ ܐܟܚܕܐ. W. GESENIUS, *Thesaurus Linguae Hebraicae et Chaldaicae*, II Lipsiae 1840, p. 922. The reference to KÖNIG is wrong; cf. *Hebräisches und aramäisches Wörterbuch*, Leipzig 1910, p. 291.

[2] P. JOÜON, "Notes philologiques sur le texte hébreu", *Bib.* X 1929, pp. 195-196.

[3] On this unusual infinitive form cf. GK^{26}, § 67 r; W. ZIMMERLI, *Ezechiel*, p. 854.

translate: "Like a woman in travail I will cry; I will destroy and also devour". This way, we have in vs. 14b a transition to vs. 15, and once more it appears that the image of the woman in travail is only a simile for Yahwe's crying and has nothing to do with the other verbs.

Vss. 15-16 seem to consitute the motif II, 2. As vs. 15 offers some problems, I first explain vs. 16, which clearly relates to the new exodus. The image of the road through the desert (cf. xl 3-5) as well as the reminiscence of the pillar of fire (Ex. xiii 21) point to that sense. Furthermore, the hifil *hōlîk* is often used in connection with the exodus (Deut. viii 15; Jer. ii 6; Ps. cxxxvi 16; cf. Is. xlviii 21 and Ps. cvi 9). The Israelites are presented as blind (vs. 16a) and, according to 16b, they are in darkness. In Is. xlii 18, 19 and xliii 8, their blindness is of ethical or religious nature: it symbolizes their unbelief. In xlii 16 also it may have that sense,[1] although in the context, unbelief plays no part. It may be better to understand the blindness as a symbol of the exile. Also at other places, the exile is typified as blindness and darkness (Is. xlii 7; xlix 9).

Verse 15 has the same function as vss. 18-19 in ch. xli, which I dealt with above. When comparing both texts, we see a completely opposite picture: whereas in the former oracle plenty of water and rich vegetation were promised, here we find dryness and withering. Since the former image indicated the salvation and restoration of Israel, the latter can only mean disaster for the enemies. From vs. 17 it appears that these enemies are considered not so much a political as a religious entity: they are the worshippers of idols. I prefer this interpretation to L. KÖHLER's, according to whom vs. 15 means the clearance of obstacles on the way home: the annoying vegetation and the rivers that block the way.[2]

Verse 17 does not express formally the goal of Yahwe's intervention. Yet, through its place and contents it corresponds to the motif III. But the prophet does not use the formula of recognition. On the contrary, he borrows his expressions from the classical motif of the confusion of the enemies that belongs to the psalms of lament (Pss. xxxi 18; xxxv 4-5; xl 15-16; lxx 3-4; lxxi 13; cxix 6). Thus we have, instead of recognition of Yahwe, confusion of the idol worshippers, which is essentially the same. It is not clear at all, whether these worshippers are pagans or unfaithful Israelites; certainly the former,

---

[1] So C. WESTERMANN, *o.c.*, p. 89.

[2] L. KÖHLER, *Deutrojesaja*, p. 134; cf. G. FOHRER, *Jesaja III*, p. 56.

perhaps both.[1] Historically it is not clear whether or not apostasy had large dimensions among the exiles. In any case, Is. xlviii 5 suggests the existence of image-worship. Once again, the point at issue in the trial speeches belongs to the background of the proclamation of salvation.

3. *Is. xliii 16-21*

16 Thus says Jahwe,
who makes a way in the sea,
a path in the mighty waters,
17 who leads out chariot and horse,
army and commander as well;
they lie down, they cannot rise,
they are extinguished, quenched like a wick:
18 "Remember not the former things,
nor consider the things of old.
19 Behold, I am doing a new thing;
now it bursts forth, do you not perceive it?
Indeed, I make a way in the wilderness,
and *paths*[a] in the desert.
20 The wild beasts will honour me,
the jackals and the ostriches;
for I give water in the wilderness,
and rivers in the desert,
to give drink to my chosen people.
21 The people whom I formed for myself
will tell my praises."

[a] Cf. comments.

The present pericope certainly contains a promise of salvation, but the structure of the proclamation of salvation is not immediately recognizable. The problem is whether the oracle does have a motif I: the allusion to the lament?

The participles in the messenger's formula refer to the deliverance out of Egypt, represented in the picture of the passage through the Reed Sea (Ex. xiv 21-27) and the destruction of the Egyptians.[2]

---

[1] Cf. B. J. VAN DER MERWE, *o.c.* pp. 59-60; J. L. MCKENZIE, *o.c.*, p. 44.

[2] The word עזוז, "strong, mighty" probably indicates the commander of the army. In Ps. xxiv 8, it is in parallelism with גבור.

The prophet is so much convinced of the divine intervention in that event, that he considers even the Egyptian army as conducted by Yahwe himself to its own destruction. The prophet goes back to Yahwe's fundamental act, with which he created his people. In a free form he quotes the central articles of Israel's creed.

Vs. 18 opens God's word proper, which is dominated by the theme "the former things — the new things" (*ri'šōnôt* — *ḥădāšâ*). An exact understanding of this theme presupposes a study of the other texts where it shows up (Is. xli 22; xlii 9; xliii 9, 18-19; xlvi 9; xlviii 3-6). I have already studied this question,[1] showing that, in the present oracle, "the former things" can only mean the events of the exodus. Now Yahwe promises a new exodus, i.e. the return from Babylon to the land of promise. This interpretation is accepted almost universally.[2] I also mentioned VON WALDOW's opinion, according to whom the description of the exodus in vss. 16-17 belongs to the introduction and not to the oracle proper, which opens only in vs. 18. The word *ri'šōnôt* (vs. 18) thus would not relate to vss. 16-17, but to the lament which preceded the oracle and in which the "former things" were mentioned. The "former things" would consist in the accomplishment of the oracles of doom by the former prophets; oracles that were realized in the fall of Jerusalem and the exile.[3] My refutation was this: 1. The word *qadmōniyyôt*, parallel with *ri'šōnôt*, points to a remote past; 2. the introduction should not be separated from the oracle and its themes are functionally related to the promised salvation; 3. when, on the one side the "former things" are opposed to a "new thing", and, on the other side, the "new thing" is the second exodus, then the "former things" can only be the first exodus, described immediately before. Now, I would like to add another, stylistic argument to this refutation. But first I would make a textual emendation. In vs. 19, *nehārôt* should be replaced by *netîbôt*, in accordance with IQIa. So we have a complete parallelism between the cola of vs. 19b. The two words resemble each other graphically and the proximity of *nehārôt bîšîmôn* in vs. 20b has probably brought about the masoretic reading of vs. 19b. We now find a striking antithetic parallelism between 16 and 19b:

---

[1] A. SCHOORS, "Les choses antérieures et les choses nouvelles dans les oracles deutéro-isaïens", *ETL.* XL 1964, pp. 19-47; on Is. xliii 16-21 cf. pp. 23-25.

[2] Even S. CYRIL OF ALEXANDRIA wrote that the *priora* referred to the passage of the Reed Sea, the *nova* however to Christ; cf. *PG.* LXX, col. 905.

[3] H. E. VON WALDOW, *o.c.*, p. 240; again in "... *denn Ich erlöse dich*" p. 48.

16 בים דרך ····· במים נתיבה
19b במדבר דרך··· בישמון נתיבות

This parallelism underlines the continuity between the introduction and the oracle proper: it is the same Yahwe who realizes the first fact as well as the second. Between them are the vss. 18-19a, in which another antithetic parallelism appears, which, placed between the members of the above mentioned figure, links them together:

16 בים דרך ····· במים נתיבה
18 ראשנות··· וקדמניות
19a חדשה····· עתה
19b במדבר דרך··· בישמון נתיבות

It is beyond any doubt that the *riʾšōnôt* refer to the way through the sea, i.e. the exodus, whereas *ḥădāšâ* consists in a way through the desert, i.e. a new exodus. Even VON WALDOW was not able to back out of the logic of the text. In his commentary on Is. xliii, he admits that "the former things" refer to the exodus. But he sticks to his earlier standpoint as well. Combining both together, he concludes: "The 'former things' are the whole salvation history, which started at the exodus but which, because of the continuous infidelity of the people, ended with the destruction of Jerusalem and the exile".[1] It would have been better if he had abandoned his former opinion completely.

The first figure of speech is continued in vs. 20b, though in a less vigorous form: *bammidbār mayim — nehārôt bîšîmōn.* Instead of making a way through the waters, now Yahwe will give both a way and water in the desert. The water miracle of Meriba (Ex. xvii 1-7) will be repeated. The actuality of Yahwe's intervention is stressed: "Now it springs forth, do you not perceive it?" (vs. 19a) The realisation of this proclamation has commenced already. Here we find an allusion to the political condition. The Persian king Cyrus, who is about to overcome Babylon and to set free the exiles, has already started his advance. The theme is more explicit in Is. xli 2-3; xlv 1-7, 13; xlvi 11; xlviii 14.

[1] H. E. VON WALDOW, "... *denn Ich erlöse dich*", p. 50: "Unter dem 'Früheren' versteht Dtjes. die ganze Heilsgeschichte Gottes, die mit dem Auszug aus Ägypten begann, ... aber wegen der fortgesetzten Untreue des Volkes ihr Ende in der Zerstörung Jerusalems und der Deportation fand".

A way and water for the returning exiles are fixed themes in the expectations of our prophet: the way in xl 3-4; xlii 16; xlix 11; the water in xli 18; xlviii 21. The wild beasts are a bit strange in the context. They have a merely literary function. It would be wrong to regard them as symbols of a theological reality, as E. HESSLER does. As in the oracles analyzed above, the prophet uses strong, even exaggerated images. Here also, there is plenty of water (rivers) to such a degree that the wild beasts will glorify God for it. All this Yahwe does for his chosen people. Again his salvific act is a creative act that realizes wonders in nature.

Here also E. HESSLER searches for a hidden theological intention. The main idea would be not so much the way in the desert but rather the water. One should not accept too easily that this represents the exodus. Again the desert is the pagan country, where Israel receives the salvific gift which renovates its life. It is hard to make out what this gift exactly is: Cyrus? a Messiah? the Servant of Yahwe? The wild beasts would be Israel's pagan countrymen, who also have some part in its salvation.[1]

Now I return to the question about motif I: is it possible to regard vs. 18 as an allusion to the lament? It is, if one grasps the exact nuance of the verb *zkr*. The meaning of the verse is not simply: "Forget the first exodus for I am about to do something better". The verses 16b-17 may correspond to a motif of collective lamentation, viz. the reminiscence of Yahwe's former salvific acts. The psalmist recalls these acts to induce God to act again in the same way (Pss. xliv 2-4; lxxiv 2; lxxx 9-12; Is. lxiii 11-14; Mic. vii 15).[2] We may thus imagine that the oracle replies to a lamentation, in which the salvation out of the Reed Sea was recalled, after the manner of Is. lxiii 11-14. In vss. 16b-17, the prophet repeats a couple of verses of that lamentation. Then the verb *zkr* in vs. 18 does not mean simply "to remember" but it is a cultic term indicating the complaining commemoration of God's former salvific acts, as against the present condition of distress.[3] B. J. VAN DER MERWE has seen the possibility that vss. 16-17 allude to a motif in the psalms of lament, viz. the reference to the former salvific acts, *in casu* the exodus. But he did not take advantage of

---

[1] E. HESSLER, *EvTh.* XXV 1965, pp. 361-362.

[2] H. GUNKEL - J. BEGRICH, *Einleitung*, p. 130.

[3] So C. WESTERMANN, *Jesaja 40-66*, p. 105; A. BENTZEN, *Studia Theologica*, I 1947, pp. 183-189, also gives a cultic meaning to זכר in this context.

this view in interpreting vs. 18. On the contrary, he supposes *ri'šōnôt* to refer to the time of sin and punishment that ended in the exile.[1]

The final motif in vs. 21 is very simple. The nation which God made (*yṣr*, terminology of creation) will tell of God's praises. After the salvation, Yahwe's praises are declared in a song of thanksgiving. An important main constituent of the latter is the telling of God's act: "Come and hear, all you who fear God, and I will tell what he has done for me!" (Ps. lxvi 16).[2] The prophet puts a short song of that type into the mouth of the delivered people in Is. xlviii 20-21. There also, the event to be told is the wonderful water supply in the desert. Although here, the motif of final goal does not include a formula of recognition, it is not without relation to it. The praise-telling in Israel's mouth evidently has a kerygmatic function. It will lead to the acknowledgment of Yahwe. And at the same time it proceeds from such an acknowledgment by Israel. The oracle thus has the same theocentric conclusion as the former ones.

4. *Is. xlix 7-12(13)*

7 Thus says Yahwe,
the Redeemer of Israel and its Holy One,
to one deeply *despised*[a],
abhorred[b] by the nations, the servant of rulers:[c]
8 "In a time of favour I answer you,
on the day of salvation I help you;
(I have kept you, I have made you a covenant to the people),
putting you in possession of the land,
apportioning the desolate heritages,
9 saying to the prisoners: 'Come out',
to those in darkness: 'Appear'.
They shall feed along the ways,
on all bare heights shall be their pasture.
10 They shall not hunger or thirst;
neither scorching nor sun shall smite them,
for he who has pity on them will guide them,
and lead them to springs of water.

---

[1] B. J. van der Merwe, *Pentateuchtradisies*, pp. 62-65; his reference to P. Volz, *Jesaia II*, *ad loc.*, is without any foundation.

[2] Cf. H. Gunkel - J. Begrich, *o.c.*, pp. 318-319.

11 I will make all my mountains a way,
and my highways shall be raised up.
12 Lo, these shall come from afar,
and lo, these from the north and from the west
and these from the land of Syene.
7c Kings shall see it and arise,
princes, and they shall prostrate themselves;
because of Yahwe, who is faithful,
the Holy One of Israel, who has chosen you."

13 Sing for joy, O heavens, and exult, O earth,
break forth[d], O mountains, into singing!
For Yahwe has comforted his people,
he has had compassion on his afflicted.

[a] Lg לבזוי loco לבזה c IQIa.
[b] Lg למתֹעַב loco למתָעֵב c LXX: *βδελυσσόμενον*; Vg: ad abominatam gentem; Pesh: ܠܕܡܣܠ.
[c] Vs. 7cd transposed after vs. 12 and dl כה אמר יהוה.
[d] Lg ופצחו c Q; IQIa: פצחו.

The reader, who is acquainted with C. Westermann's works, will remark that here I skip a pericope (Is. xlv 14-17), which this scholar classifies with the proclamations of salvation in his form-critical articles.[1] Further on I shall show that such a designation is wrong and Westermann himself does not mention it again in his commentary.[2] We have to deal now with Is. xlix 7-12.

A number of interpreters reckon these verses partly (vss. 7-9) with the second Servant Song, according to others it belongs to the redactional extension of it. In vs. 7, however, a new unit commences, as the introductory formula and the shift of person suggest. The following analysis will also show a proper structure of the genre in the vss. 7-12.

The question is whether Is. xlix 7-12(13) contains one or two oracles. In commentaries as well as in form-critical studies Is. xlix (7)8-13 (with or without vs. 13) is generally regarded as one unit.[3] This was

[1] C. Westermann, *EvTh.* XXIV 1964, p. 366; *Forschung*, p. 120.

[2] C. Westermann, *Jesaja 40-66*, pp. 137-139.

[3] Cf. B. Duhm, *Jesaja*, p. 334; F. Feldmann, *Das Buch Isaias*, II, p. 124; C. C. Torrey, *The Second Isaiah*, p. 246; A. van Hoonacker, *Het boek Isaias*, pp. 241-242 (with a caesura after vs. 9a); P. Volz, *o.c.*, pp. 100-102 (same remark); H. Gressmann, *ZAW.* XXXIV 1914, p. 264; L. Köhler, *Deuterojesaja*, p. 38; S. Mowinckel, *ZAW.* XLIX 1931, p. 105; K. Elliger, *Deuterojesaja*, pp. 48-54; J. Begrich, *o.c.*, p. 13.

already the case in IQIa and probably in IQIb.[1] H. E. VON WALDOW was the first to question this unity and to conclude that these verses contain two salvation oracles: vss. 8-10 and 11-13.[2] The main idea of vss. 8-10 would be the deliverance from exile and the restoration of the homeland, dominated by the picture of the feeding flocks. On the contrary, vss. 11-12 would deal with the return from the diaspora, presented with the picture of the way through the desert. But my analysis shows that vss. 7-12 correspond to the structure of a proclamation of salvation in the sense proposed by WESTERMANN, thus rendering superfluous the separation between the vss. 10 and 11. As to their content, one may ask if vss. 9-10 do not deal with the journey through the desert, an idea which is continued in vs. 11 and enlarged in vs. 12 to include the return of the diaspora.

The pericope is a word of salvation, directed to Israel. This is self-evident, if one ignores the vss. 8-9. These verses indeed seem to be directed to an individual, who receives a mission with regard to the people. This has induced A. VAN HOONACKER and J. VAN DER PLOEG to relate them to Cyrus.[3] But xlix 8b must be eliminated.[4] This distich is a literal quotation from xlii 6, where it is at home in the Cyrus oracle. On the contrary, here it does not fit the context rhythmically (2 + 2, whereas the other verses are 3 + 3). It has been interpolated by the redactor who linked up this oracle with the second Servant Song. But then vss. 8-9 are no longer an oracle of mission. Yahwe himself is the subject of the infinitives *l^e^hāqîm*, *l^e^hanḥîl* and *lē'mōr*, which have a gerundival function.[5]

The first verse offers a problem (vs. 7). The expanded messenger's formula again has the typical epithets "Redeemer" and "Holy One of Israel". Also the recipient, Israel, is indicated in vs. 7b with expressions that clearly recall the lament to which the proclamation replies: "deeply despised, abhorred by the nations" (Pss. xxii 7; xliv 14-17; lxxix 4, 10, 22; lxxx 7; lxxxix 42, 51-52; cxv 2; cxxiii 3-4;

[1] Cf. M. BURROWS, *The Dead Sea Scrolls of St. Mark's Monastery*, I, plate XLI; E. SUKENIK, *The Dead Sea Scrolls of the Hebrew University*, plate 8.

[2] H. E. VON WALDOW, *o.c.*, pp. 19-20.

[3] A. VAN HOONACKER, *o.c.*, p. 241; J. VAN DER PLOEG, *Les chants du Serviteur de Jahvé*, Paris 1936, pp. 46-47.

[4] K. MARTI, *Jesaja*, p. 329; B. DUHM, *o.c.*, p. 335; P. VOLZ, *o.c.*, p. 99; K. ELLIGER, *o.c.*, p. 50; L. KÖHLER, *o.c.*, p. 38; S. MOWINCKEL, *a.c.*, p. 106; C. R. NORTH, *o.c.*, p. 130.

[5] Cf. JOÜON, § 124 o; the same opinion in E. N. P. SCHROTEN, "Het gerundium in Deutero-Jesaja", *NedTTs.* XVII 1962, p. 57.

Jer. xxxi 19; Lam. i 8, 11; iii 45; v 1),[1] a servant of rulers (Lam. i 1, 3; v 8). As an allusion to the lament motif of shame, verse 7b thus acts as motif I in the proclamation of salvation. But the remainder of the verse is not so easy to place. It announces a homage to Yahwe by foreign kings. The verse makes no sense on its own and should belong to a larger whole, because it refers to something the kings see and which is not expressly indicated.[2] In its content, it is a motif III, a sort of formula of recognition. I have already suggested in an earlier study that the verse should be placed after vs. 12, as the final motif of the oracle.[3] C. WESTERMANN defends the same opinion.[4] In the present text, the oracle has no final motif and vs. 7cd certainly is one. It is thus reasonable to think that originally it followed after vs. 12, particularly if we consider that the oracle underwent some more adaptations when it was attached to the second Servant Song. When attaching vs. 7cd to 7ab, the redactor of Is. xl-lv wanted to relate the homage by the kings directly to the Servant's activity. The deplacement also provoked the repetition of the messenger's formula in vs. 8.

One could imagine also that what the kings see in vs. 7c, is Israel, and then the verse would express the reversal of the situation described in vs. 7b. So the verse would be a motif II, 2, which is less probable, since 1) it is a good motif III; 2) the motif II, 2 would be placed before II, 1, followed again by II, 2; 3) the second messenger's formula remains unexplained.

According to the motif II, 1 (vs. 8a), God grants (answers) the prayer of his people and helps them. So Yahwe replies to the double supplication in the lament: "answer me" (Pss. iv 2; xiii 4; xvii 6; xxvii 7; xxxviii 16; lv 3; lxix 14), and "help me" (Pss. cix 26; xxx 11). The *perfecta executionis* have a similar function as in the A motif of the salvation oracle: the actuality of Yahwe's intervention is underlined. Yahwe acts on the day of salvation, which is also the time of favour (*rāṣôn*). The word *rāṣôn* means "things pleasing". In a religious

---

[1] Cf. H. GUNKEL - J. BEGRICH, *Einleitung*, p. 126. — H. L. GINSBERG, "Some Emendations in Isaiah", *JBL*. LXIX 1950, p. 59, reads גו, "back", instead of גוי, in parallel with נפש, which here would mean "neck". This correction is completely superfluous.

[2] A. CONDAMIN, *Le livre d'Isaïe*, p. 298, reads יראוך loco יראו; also A. VAN HOONACKER, *Het boek Isaias*, p. 239.

[3] A. SCHOORS, *De literaire en doctrinele eenheid van Dt.-Is.*, Diss. Leuven 1963, pp. 129 and 252.

[4] C. WESTERMANN, *Jesaja 40-66*, p. 173; cf. G. FOHRER, *Jesaja III*, p. 125.

context, quite different nuances can be given to this. Sometimes, it indicates God's favour, his goodwill which is concretely expressed in things pleasing (Deut. xxxiii 16, 23; Pss. v 13; xxx 8; li 20; lxxxix 18). In this meaning it appears in opposition to Yahwe's wrath (Pss. xxx 6; Is. lx 10). Its gratuitous character is hardly expressed. On the contrary, Yahwe's *rāṣôn* is implored (Ex. xxxviii 28; Ps. xix 15), and above all, the word became a technical term of cultic law. Here, *rāṣôn* is the quality which the one who offers invests as a fruit of his offering: i.e. the sacrifice renders him agreeable. In these texts the word sometimes is used with a suffix indicating the one who offers (Lev. i 3: *reṣōnô lipnê yhwh*; xix 5: *lireṣōnekem*; xxii 19-21; xxxiii 11). This meaning passed into prophetic literature (Is. lvi 7; lviii 5; lx 7; Jer. vi 20; Mal. ii 13). In Ps. xl 8-9, the psalmist says that he has been prescribed in the scroll to execute Yahwe's *rāṣōn*. Thus here *rāṣôn* is God's will as source of Israel's ethics.

The expression *'ēt rāṣôn* occurs only in one other place in the Old Testament: Ps. lxix 14, where it indicates the propitious moment for prayer. Here *rāṣôn* thus means the goodwill which the suppliant hopes to find with God. Remarkably enough the psalmist invokes the abundant *ḥesed* of Yahwe and the faithfulness of his salvation (*'ĕmet yēša'*). Yahwe's acceptance of the prayer is supported, according to this verse, by two qualities, which actually are only one: Yahwe's faithfulness to his covenant.[1] So we are able to interpret Is. xlix 8, since the verse is precisely Yahwe's reply to such a prayer (same word *'nh*). In this verse *yešû'â* // *rāṣôn* is thus Yahwe's salvific will. But the day of salvation or the time of favour is the moment when Yahwe intervenes and turns his salvific will into concrete salvation as described further on in the proclamation. J. VAN DER PLOEG is right in asserting that this time is concretely the moment of the return from exile.[2] But the broader literary and theological perspectives should not be neglected.

Yahwe's intervention (motif II, 2; vss. 8c-12) includes the fact that he will give the land again to Israel as a stable and patrimonial possession, exactly as he did at the time of the conquest. The verb *nḥl* is extremely frequent in the Hexateuch, indicating the occupation of the land by the Israelites.[3] The deliverance of captives undoubtedly

[1] See comments on Is. liv 7-10.

[2] J. VAN DER PLOEG, *Les chants du Serviteur de Jahvé*, p. 45.

[3] The root נחל always stresses the stable character of the possession rather than the transfer of possessed goods; cf. F. DREYFUS, "Le thème de l'héritage dans l'A.T.",

means the end of the exile.[1] Vss. 9b-11 can best be interpreted as referring to the protection on the march through the desert, in accordance with the most accepted view. In connection with xli 18-19 one could imagine also a *Naturwandlung* symbolizing the restoration of the land (remark *š**ᵉpāyim*).[2] But I have already pointed out that also in xli 18-19 the idea of the desert wonders is not absent. In Is. xlix 10a, typical desert dangers are mentioned: hunger, thirst, heat.[3] The allusion to the first exodus is apparent (cf. also xlviii 21). The image of the herdsman and his flock is applied to the exodus elsewhere in the O.T. (cf. Pss. lxxvii 21; lxxviii 52-53: *nhg*). In Is. xl 11 the prophet applies the same image to the return from exile. The exilic prophets had already used it in connection with the exile (Jer. xiii 7) and the deliverance from it (Jer. xxxi 10; l 19; Ez. xxxiv 11-16). The idea of a march through the desert is sustained in vs. 11, apparently akin to xl 3-4: Yahwe prepares the way for return.

In vs. 12, the prophet widens the horizon to the dispersed Jews all over the world. They come from afar, which apparently means the east, from the north, the seaside or west and from Sinim. During the 19th century, some scholars thought this was China,[4] but it is beyond any doubt that Elephantine, where the archives of an important Jewish colony have been discovered is meant. Firstly, it should be a southern region, as suggested also by Targum and Vulgate.[5] Moreover,

---

RScPhilThéol. XLII 1958, pp. 3-49, esp. p. 9. The parallel formula הקים ארץ means: "to put in possession of the land", owing to the meaning of קום, "to be established, confirmed (of purchase)", in Gen. xxiii 17, 20; Lev. xxv 30; xxvii 19 (oral suggestion of C. BREKELMANS). The root נחל occurs as a technical term of the conquest in Ex. xxiii 30; xxxii 13; Num. xxvi 55; xxxii 19; xxxv 8; Deut. xix 14; Jos. xiv 1 (Qal); Num. xxxiv 17-18, 29; Jos. xiii 32; xiv 1; xix 49 (Pi.); Num. xxxii 18; xxxiii 54; xxxiv 13 (Hitp.); and the hiphil as in our text: Deut. i 28; iii 28; xii 10; xix 3; xxxi 7; Jos. i 6; Jer. xii 14.

[1] F. DELITZSCH, *Commentar über Jesaja*, p. 487; K. MARTI, *o.c.*, p. 329: "Die Gefangenen und *die im Dunkel* sind die Deportierten".

[2] H. E. VON WALDOW, *Anlass und Hintergrund*, p. 187, note 37.

[3] The noun שרב appears in Is. xxxv 7, in parallelism with צמאון, "thirsty ground". In Aramaic, Syriac and Modern Hebrew the root שרב expresses the idea of scorching, cf. ZORELL, p. 881. — GB, p. 789 and KÖNIG, p. 527, think here of the scorching desert wind. Today in Israel the word indicates the *khamsin*, a characteristic heatwave of the country.

[4] T. K. CHEYNE, *The Prophecies of Isaiah*, II, pp. 20-23. J. KNABENBAUER, *o.c.*, p. 242, who refers to GESENIUS, SCHEGG, HITZIG, MAURER, SEINECKE, HAHN, NAEGELSBACH, MOVERS, LASSEN, LANGLÈS, FIELD, F. DELITZSCH, *o.c.*, pp. 448-489.

[5] Targ: ואלין מארע דרומא; Vg: et isti de terra australi.

1QIa reads *s*^{e}*wēniyyîm*, which indicates the inhabitants of *s*^{e}*wēnēh*, the place that, according to Ez. xxix 10; xxx 6, is the extreme south of Egypt, and that in the Elephantine papyri is called *swn*, the present Assuan, situated on the eastern bank of the Nile off Elephantine.[1] To our prophet, the coming salvation involves the return of the dispersed Israelites to their homeland. Just as in xliii 5-7, the prophet does not aim at geographical accuracy; he merely wishes to indicate all parts of the world.[2]

The motif III (vs. 7cd) holds very well with vs. 12, which is another argument in favour of the transposition I propose. Since the return from the diaspora is an event on the stage of the world, foreign kings will be witnesses of it and therefore they will prostrate themselves. There is no question of the kings joining Israel. That their homage is brought about by Yahwe's salvific act to Israel, is underlined in the verse: Yahwe remained faithful (*ne'ĕmān*) to the election (*wayyibḥārekā*).

Verse 13 does not belong to the proclamation of salvation but is a small song of thanksgiving. GUNKEL cites the verse with the hymns and GRESSMANN calls it the final hymn of xlix 8-13.[3] It is better to regard it as a *Volksdanklied*, with a hymnic introduction,[4] granting that the difference is not very great. Decisive in this respect is the so-called narrative motif, that tells about a concrete and recent act of Yahwe, which is proper to the song of thanksgiving. This interpretation is favoured also by the literary contact with other songs of thanksgiving (*nḥm, rḥm, 'ăniyyîm*; cf. Is. xii 1; Pss. ciii 13; cxvi 5). A song of this genre normally follows after the salvation word (Pss. vi 9-11; xxii 23-25; xxviii 6-8; xxxi 20-25; lvi 11-14). Taking into account the original sequence lament — oracle — song of thanksgiving,

---

1 Cf. letter 1, line 7 in E. SACHAU, *Aramäische Papyrus und Ostraka*, Leipzig 1911, p. 3; E. J. KISSANE, "The land of Sinim (Is. 49:12)", *The Irish Theological Quarterly*, XXI 1954, pp. 63-64. According to the latter, G. LAMBERT has definitively proven that the name "China" did not yet exist at the time of Dt.-Is. (cf. *NRT*. LXXV 1953, pp. 965-972).

2 On J. MORGENSTERN's objections against this text, cf. the comments on Is. xliii 5-7 and A. SCHOORS, *Orientialia Lovaniensia Periodica*, II 1971, pp. 132-135.

3 H. GUNKEL - J. BEGRICH, *Einleitung* § 2, 28, p. 52; H. GRESSMANN, *ZAW*. XXXIV 1914, p. 293.

4 H. GUNKEL - J. BEGRICH, *o.c.*, § 8, 32; J. BEGRICH, *Studien*, p. 54. J. ZIEGLER in a recension of BEGRICH's work, in *Th.* XXXIX 1940, p. 51, holds with GUNKEL's opinion.

it is quite probable that the prophet himself attached verse 13 to the preceding oracle.

5. *Is. xlix 14-26*

14 Zion says:
"Yahwe has abandoned me, my Lord has forgotten me".
15 "Can a woman forget her suckling child,
a mother[a] the son of her womb?
But even if these should forget,
I forget you not.
16 Behold, I have graven you on my hands;
your walls are continually before me.
17 *Your builders*[b] hurry;
your destroyers and those who laid you waste go forth from you.
18 Raise your eyes around you and look;
they all gather, they come to you.
As I live," — the oracle of Yahwe —,
"you shall put them all on as an ornament,
you shall bind them on as a bride does.
19 For your ruins and wasted places
and your devastated land, —
now you will be too narrow for your inhabitants,
and those who swallowed you up are far away.
20 The children of your bereavement
will yet say in your ears:
'The place is too narrow for me;
make room for me that I may settle.'"

21 You say to yourself:
"Who has borne me these?
I was childless and barren
(*exiled and put away*)[c],
but who has brought up these?
Behold, I was left alone;
whence then have these come?"
22 Thus says the Lord Yahwe:
"Behold, I lift up my hand to the nations,
and raise my signal to the peoples,
and they will bring your sons in their arms,
and your daughters will be carried on their shoulders.

23 Kings will be your foster fathers
and princesses your nursing mothers.
With their faces to the ground they will bow down to you,
and lick the dust of your feet.
You will know that I am Yahwe,
and those who hope in me will not be put to shame."

24 "Can the prey be taken from a strong man,
or the captive of a *mighty*[d] be rescued?"
25 Surely, thus says Yahwe:
"Even the captive of a strong man will be taken,
and the prey of a mighty be rescued.
It is I who will defend *your cause*[e],
it is I who will save your children.
26 I will make your oppressors eat their own flesh,
and they shall be drunk with their own blood as with wine.
Everybody shall know
that I am Yahwe your Saviour,
and your Redeemer, the Mighty One of Jacob."

[a] See comments, p. 106, note 2.
[b] IQIa: בוניך; LXX: *ταχὺ οἰκοδομηθήσῃ*; Theod, Aq: *οἰκοδομουντες*; Targ: יבנון: Vg: structores.
[c] See comments.
[d] IQIa: עריץ; Vg: robusto: Pesh: ܥܫܝܢܐ.
[e] See comments, p. 118, note 4.

In Is. xlix 14-21 we find a strong personification of Zion as Yahwe's spouse and the mother of the citizens. L. Köhler calls the pericope a disputation (*Streitgespräch*). He admits himself that the characteristics of the genre are very weak here, but, in his opinion, the content gives the decisive answer. In vs. 14 he recognizes the quoted accusation, in vs. 15 the judgment and in vs. 18 a declaration on oath.[1] Concerning this opinion I would first note that the author does not distinguish between disputation and trial speech, as I do in the following chapter. The elements which he recognizes in the pericope rather point to a trial speech. It is an ominous sign that neither the quoted accusation nor the declaration on oath has a parallel in the other *rîb*-pericopes of Dt.-Is. and that he cannot define the setting of vss. 19-21 in the genre he proposes. I hold with Begrich and

---

[1] L. Köhler, *o.c.*, pp. 111-114.

WESTERMANN in regarding the pericope as a proclamation of salvation.[1] I admit that vs. 14 quotes an assertion made by Zion, which in a certain way is contested in the following verses. But the refutation is made with a proclamation of salvation, so that the assertion of vs. 14 rather acts as the quoted lament. From the literature of lament, one can allege a series of similar complaints about being abandoned by God (Pss. xiii 2; xxii 2; xxiv 25; lxxiv 19; lxxvii 10; Lam. v. 20). Such a complaint of Jacob-Israel is quoted in Is. xl 27b.

The assurance of Yahwe's turning in favour (vss. 15-16) is expressed in a somewhat unusual form, viz. as a conclusion of a reasoning *a minori ad maius*,[2] that ends in the phrase: "I forget you not". A certain affinity to the disputation is undeniable. In Ps. xxvii 10, we find a cognate motif of confidence. In vs. 16, the assertion is repeated in a more poetic style: "I have graven you on my hands, your walls are continually before me".

Vs. 17 speaks of the reconstruction of the city, the other verses of its repeopling.[3] Against the theme of reconstruction one might object that the text has *bānayik*, "your sons". But the emendation to *bōnayik*, "your builders", is beyond any doubt according to the concordant testimony of IQIa, LXX, Theodotion, Aquila, Targum and Vulgate. H. M. ORLINSKY's objections to this reading do not render the MT more probable.[4] The antithetic parallelism with the next verse requires it also. Then it is clear that the walls, which are continually in front of Yahwe (vs. 16) are the ruined walls of the city.[5] Both ideas, of repeopling and of reconstruction, have distinct parallels in Is. xliv 26, 28 and xlv 13. In the present text, the prophet directly addresses Zion and he develops poetically the idea of repeopling: the returning exiles will be a bridal ornament to Zion.

Verse 21 offers a form-critical problem. Vss. 14-21 are unanimously taken for one unit. Only WESTERMANN reckons vs. 21 with the following pericope, having the function of a motif I: allusion to the lament.[6]

---

[1] J. BEGRICH, *Studien*, p 14; C. WESTERMANN, *EvTh.* XXIV 1964, p. 366.

[2] H. E. VON WALDOW, *o.c.*, pp. 16-17. Following *BHK*, instead of מֵרַחֵם, I read מְרַחֵם, a piel part. of רחם, denominative from רֶחֶם. The part. means "the one who has conceived, pregnant". It has no feminine ending, being naturally feminine.

[3] It is not necessary to transpose vs. 17 after 18, as proposed by WESTERMANN, *o.c.*, p. 178.

[4] H. M. ORLINSKY, *Tarbiz*, xxiv 1954, pp. 4-8.

[5] Cf. T. K. CHEYNE, *The Prophecies of Isaiah*, II, p. 17.

[6] C. WESTERMANN, *EvTh.* XXIV 1964, p. 367; *Jesaja 40-66*, pp. 177-179.

Both opinions can be defended. The verse expresses Zion's amazement at the great number of her children.[1] The demonstrative pron. *'ēlleh* gets its best sense, when it refers to *b^e^nê šikkulāyik* of vs. 20. Moreover, the messenger's formula in vs. 22 suggests that vs. 21 goes rather with the preceding verses. On the other hand, it cannot be questioned that vs. 21bc contains a motif of lament. In Lamentations, Jerusalem's childlessness belongs to the condition of distress (Lam. i 5, 20). The absence of complaints about childlessness in the psalms seems to be accidental. For childlessness was a misfortune (Gen. xxx 1), a shame (1 Sam. i 5) and a punishment from God (Is. xlvii 9; Jer. xviii 21; Hos. ix 12). It thus evidently can be an important theme of a lament. When we look at the next pericope (vss. 22-23), we remark also that it shows the structure of a proclamation of salvation (motifs II and III). Then motif I should be found in vs. 21.

I think one may combine both opinions. The prophet made a composition of two proclamations of salvation. Verse 21 is the link between them. It is a reflection of Zion on the first salvation word, but at the same time it acts as the beginning of another proclamation. Since the passage is fluent and nothing suggests a later reinterpretation, I assume that such a close connection of the oracles is due to the prophet himself.

Before analyzing the second oracle, let us consider for a moment the first one in its totality. From the themes of rebuilding and repeopling, it appears that the geographical Jerusalem is meant. It is not a theological reality in the first place. It certainly makes no sense to restrict the oracle to the ideal Jerusalem.[2] On the other hand, as mentioned already, the personification is very strong. In the first part, where reconstruction is the chief idea, personification does not appear so much. True, Zion is addressed in the second person (I forget you not...), but it is not certain that in vs. 14, Zion speaks as Yahwe's spouse, abandoned by her husband. However, in view of Is. l 1 and especially liv 6, where the verb *'zb* is also used, the idea is quite acceptable.[3] K. MARTI unduly invokes the further development of the oracle to reject it.[4] Precisely in vs. 18 the repeopled Zion is presented

---

[1] Cf. T. K. CHEYNE, *o.c.*, p. 19; A. BENTZEN, *Jesaja 40-66*, p. 85.

[2] Against T. K. CHEYNE, *o.c.*, p. 17.

[3] Cf. D. CORREA, *De significatione montis Sion in S. Scriptura*, Diss. Antonianum, Roma-Bogota 1962, p. 47; C. R. NORTH, *Isaiah 40-55*, p. 111.

[4] K. MARTI, *o.c.*, p. 330.

as a festively ornamented bride. In the second part, however, Zion is thought to be the mother of the citizens. She is a childless woman, who suddenly has plenty of children, so that they are short of room in the city. The prophet makes bold combinations. Not only are the images of lady Zion and city of Zion interwoven, but the returning inhabitants are called children of mother Zion as well as a garment of bride Zion.

Often the complaint in vs. 14 is connected with the condition of the exile [1] and the "children of your bereavement" are identified as the many who are born in the land of the *gôlâ*.[2] One cannot invoke the word *gôlâ* in vs. 21 in favour of this interpretation, since it is a later addition. The words "exiled and put away" are missing in the LXX and many critics delete them accordingly. I agree with these authors, for, beside the witness of LXX, we must remark that the words under consideration disturb rhythm and parallelism and that they are an apparent dittography of *glmwdh*, corrected afterwards to *glh wsrh*.[3] Thus the words become a gloss that offers an exact interpretation of the two preceding words. Owing to the prophet's interest in the return, the many sons certainly are the returning exiles, but the prophet may have in mind also a continuous fertility of Zion after the exile. F. Delitzsch justly thinks that the oracle views the community of the exile.[4] There are other instances of this community being addressed as Zion-Jerusalem or being assimilated to it (xl 1-2; xli 27; li 16; lii 9). The pericope under consideration does not expressly formulate this identity. But the oracle only makes sense, when it is intended for the community of the exiles or for the remnant in Judah. When the prophet addresses Zion, he metonymically means the whole community. One must keep the complex character of the Zion image in the oracle: Zion is the destroyed Jerusalem, that is to be rebuilt and repeopled, but it is also the community of God's people, and as such Yahwe's spouse and the mother of many sons.

We now come to vss. 22-23. To the slightly insinuated complaint

---

[1] E.g. F. Feldmann, *Das Buch Isaias*, II, p. 134: "In V.14 ist wieder ganz die Situation des babylonischen Exils gegeben".

[2] T. K. Cheyne, *o.c.*, p. 19: "The astonishment of Zion is caused by the vast multiplication of the comparatively few who had gone into exile". Cf. F. Feldmann, *o.c.*, p. 135; J. Fischer, *Das Buch Isaias*, II, pp. 111-112; A. Zillesen, "Israel in Darstellung und Beurteilung Deuterojesajas", *ZAW*. XXIV 1904, pp. 260-262.

[3] The Qumran documents offer clear examples of confusion between *samekh* and *mem* and between *daleth* and *resh*; cf. P. W. Skehan, *CBQ*. XXII 1960, p. 55.

[4] F. Delitzsch, *o.c.*, p. 489.

about bereavement, Yahwe replies with a new proclamation of salvation. It has no motif II, 1, but it immediately begins with Yahwe's intervention. The motif II, 1 of the former oracle seemingly also concerns vss. 22-23, which is one more argument in favour of the original connection of xlix 14-21 and 22-23.

Yahwe gives a sign to the nations and they bring back the children of Israel to mother Zion. According to WESTERMANN, "the intervention (vs. 22a) and its consequence (vss. 22b, 23a) are not in entire agreement. When God lifts up his hand against nations and raises his signal against them, this is a sign to join battle with them".[1] This is somewhat simplistic, because he does not sufficiently distinguish between *nṭh yād*, which is basically a punitive divine intervention,[2] and *nś' yād*, *hērîm* (ev. *nś'*) *nēs*, which have variated nuances. When Yahwe lifts up his hand, this may mean salvation (e.g. Ps. x 12; Ez. xx, passim) or a punitive intervention (Ez. xxxvi 7; xliv 12; Ps. cvi 26 with *l* of the *dativus incommodi*). Also the raising of the signal has several meanings. The image is a *topos* proper to Isaiah and Jeremiah.[3] In Is. v 26 it is directed against Israel (with *l*), in xiii 2 against Babylon (with *'al*). In Jeremiah, Yahwe is never the subject of the action. The signal is a sign to flee in Jer. iv 6 (cf. lx 6), a sign of triumph in Jer. l 2 and a sign to join battle with Babylon in Jer. li 2, 27 (with *'el*). Is. xi 11-12 offers both images in a context similar to the one of xlix 22: the gathering of the diaspora. Esvecially vs. 12a is eloquent: "God will raise an ensign for the nations (*laggôyim*), and will assemble the outcasts of Israel". If there is any literary contact between these texts, then xlix 22 seems to be anterior to xi 11-12. The latter is not very well constructed and gives the impression of being a reminiscence of Is. xlix 22-23. The fact that in xi 11, Yahwe lifts up his hand "again" may even refer to xlix 22, where he did it for the first time.[4] In any case, Is. xi 11-12 is post-exilic and probably originated in trito-Isaian circles (cf. Is. lx 4; lxii 10; lxvi 19-22). Also the regions named point to the same background.[5] Anyhow, Is. xi 11-12 cannot clarify xlix 22.

---

1 C. WESTERMANN, *Jesaja 40-66*, p. 179; engl. p. 221.

2 P. HUMBERT, "Etendre la main", *VT.* XII 1962, pp. 383-395. The author does not deal with *nś' yād*.

3 Cf. L. ALONSO-SCHÖKEL, *Estudios de poética hebrea*, Barcelona 1963, pp. 347-350.

4 The idea of "again" is to be found, not so much in שנית, which should be emended to שאת (cf. LXX), but in the verb יוסיף.

5 Cf. K. MARTI, *o.c.*, p. 114; B. DUHM, *o.c.*, p. 82; P. AUVRAY - J. STEINMANN, *Isaïe*, p. 66, note b.

Summarizing, we may hold that vs. 22a, according to the *topos* in other texts, may have a hostile meaning, but that in the present context it means only a sign to the nations, that they must bring Israel's children back home. The proclamation continues announcing a submission of these nations and their kings.

J. MORGENSTERN and, in some smaller degree, K. ELLIGER invoke the likeness between Is. xlix 8-26 and ch. lx, to prove the trito-Isaian character of the present pericope.[1] Let us first examine ch. lx. That it shows some contacts with ch. xlix is beyond any doubt. As a matter of fact, on this ground some critics have joined Is. lx-lxii to Is. xl-lv.[2] Chapter lx is a composition in which the poet sings the praises of the new Jerusalem in literary dependence on and even with literal quotations from Is. i-lv. From this book ch. xlix has been the main source of inspiration for the author of ch. lx. His verse 4a is a literal quotation from xlix 18, and 4b summarizes xlix 18-22 (cf. also xlix 12 and xliii 6). In vs. 9c, we find lv 5 literally. "The glory of Lebanon" in vs. 13 comes from Is. xxxv 2 and is joined to the series *b^{e}rôš tidhār ût^{e}'aššûr yaḥdāw*, borrowed from xli 19 (cf. lv 13). The submission of foreign kings (xlix 23) resounds in lx 14, 16a and, combined with xlix 17, it is related to the rebuilding of Jerusalem in lx 10 (cf. xlv 14). Again vs. lx 16b is literally taken from xlix 26, with this difference: "you shall know ..." (lx 16) as against "all flesh shall know ..." (xlix 26). The word *'ăzûbâ* (vs. 15) goes back to xlix 14 (*yhwh 'ăzābanî*) and liv 6 (*ka'ăšer 'ăzûbâ*) (cf. xlix 21). Also verse i 26 seems to have left traces in lx 14, 17. As to *šōd wāšeber* (vs. 18) one may refer to li 19 and lix 7.[3] There is no doubt that this chapter has been made, keeping in view all the cited texts. It is thus to be dated later and perhaps at a moment when Is. i-xxxix and xl-lv had already been united, owing to the fact that the author quotes both indistinctly, even if he has some preference for xl-lv.

As to the theme of the diaspora in ch. lx, MORGENSTERN attaches some importance to the fact that a section of the people must return

---

[1] J. MORGENSTERN, *The Message*, pp. 6-8; K. ELLIGER, *Deuterojesaja*, pp. 124-129.

[2] Cf. A. CONDAMIN, *Le livre d'Isaïe*, pp. 358-361; A. VAN HOONACKER, *o.c.*, p. 190 and *RB*. XVIII 1909, pp. 497-528; XIX 1910, pp. 537-572; XX 1911, pp. 107-114; 279-285; W. W. CANNON, "Isaiah c. 57, 14-21; cc. 60-62", *ZAW*. LII 1934, pp. 75-77.

[3] One could find some more connections, which, however, are more superficial. All commentaries refer to the most important related texts. A good systematic survey, verse by verse can be found in A. ZILLESEN, "Tritojesaja und Deuterojesaja", *ZAW*. XXVI 1906, pp. 240-242.

to Zion in ships (vs. 9). Hence it would appear that they come from across the Mediterranean. The clear implication would be, that they had been held as enslaved captives in the Greek regions. It is true that the ships of Tarshish come from across the Mediterranean, and MORGENSTERN's position is supported by the fact that no other region is mentioned, from which exiles return. But according to vss. 6-7, the wealth of the nations will come from Midian, Ephah, Sheba, Kedar and Nebaioth, to be used in the worship of Yahwe. The whole situation, presupposed here, viz. the destroyed city (vs. 10), the dispersion all over the world (vss. 4-9), the oppression in the country (vs. 14), fits in well with the framework of MORGENSTERN's hypothesis.[1] But this delineation is so general, that one cannot reach assured conclusions as to the date, perhaps because the poet gathers all these elements of restoration in an idealized eschatological picture.[2] The promise of rebuilding the wall and the temple sounds authentic in the whole period of the exile until Ezra.[3] For the return from the diaspora the same remark is pertinent.[4] Finally, the allusion to oppression can be a reminiscence of the situation shortly after 587, perhaps a hint at the relations with the Samaritans and other neighbours, or the injustice which is done in Israel itself. In any case, there is no trace whatsoever of the so-called slavery in Greek regions.

MORGENSTERN finds the national situation he deduced from lx 4, 8-22 also in Is. xlix 8-26. Above, we have seen that in vss. 7-12, the deliverance from Babylonia is broadened to the perspective of a return from the diaspora. Nowhere is the Greek world suggested, let alone put in evidence. In vss. 14-21, the repeopling of the city can refer to the return from the Babylonian *gôlâ* as well as from the diaspora. Nothing obliges us to think here of slavery on Greek soil. In vss. 22-23, there is a clear mention of a return from the diaspora, that goes together with the subjection of kings and nations to Israel. Here the contact with Is. lx really exists, but we just saw that the author of ch. lx

---

[1] Cf. p. 56, note 3.

[2] P. VOLZ, *o.c.*, p. 246.

[3] Cf. K. MARTI, *o.c.*, p. 383; B. DUHM, *o.c.*, p. 409; J. FISCHER, *Das Buch Isaias*, II, p. 171. — According to C. C. TORREY, *The Second Isaiah*, pp. 456-460, in Is. lx 10, the walls are in ruins since the exile, but he dates Dt.-Isaiah's activity about 400 and the rebuilding of the walls by Ezra in 384.

[4] A. VAN HOONACKER, *Het boek Isaias*, p. 269, finds here an allusion to the pilgrims who come every year from the diaspora to Jerusalem and the temple at the great festivals.

quoted and imitated these verses of ch. xlix. From an historical viewpoint, this allusion to a diaspora can be explained like that in xliii 5-7 and xlix 12. But the question must be asked whether the attitude of domination over foreign nations is in accordance with Dt.-Is. as a whole.

According to K. MARTI and B. DUHM, this idea is not dt.-Isaian: it does not fit in with the participation of the pagans in the coming salvation (xlv 23), but much more, it is in accordance with the pride of later Judaism (lx 10, 16; lxi 5).[1] Let us remark that the idea of subjection has a parallel in xlv 14. But the literary status of this verse is far from clear. Some scholars, such as MORGENSTERN and even WESTERMANN, contest its authenticity and transpose it to ch. lx.[2] A number of critics regard xlv 14-17 as one literary unit, but it is impossible to define its literary genre and probably the unit does not exist. Vss. 14, 15 and 16-17 seem to come from three distinct contexts. In that case an interpretation of vs. 14 becomes extremely difficult. As a matter of fact, the themes seem to be trito-Isaian (cf. lx 6-7; lxi 5-6; xxiii 18). But in vs. xlix 23b, the difficulty is not that great. The picture can be explained very well within the framework of the oracle. In 22b-23a, it has been said already that foreign nations and kings will bring back Zion's children and will be in their service. Verse 23b does not go beyond this. There is no mention, as in xlv 14, of their wealth, of chains, of a prayer in which Yahwe is worshiped. There is only a *proskynesis*. Such need not mean a special subjection of these nations. C. C. TORREY is right in his comment that vs. 23b does not describe the attitude of the lowest slaves.[3] The *proskynesis* is an expression of great veneration. Abraham performs it to the three men who came to visit him (Gen. xviii 2; cf. xix 1), or to the people with whom he negotiates about a bargain (Gen. xxiii 7, 12). We thus should not overdraw the text theologically. We may paraphrase the promise of salvation as follows: "The situation will be reversed. The nations, in whose service the Israelites are, now shall be in their service, in order to bring them home carefully". I fully agree with VOLZ who states: "The poet only deals with the act of bringing back, and, just as elsewhere he speaks of the transformation of the desert and foretells that to this purpose trees will grow and water will gush

---

[1] K. MARTI, *o.c.*, p. 332; B. DUHM, *o.c.*, p. 339; cf. K. ELLIGER, *o.c.*, p. 129.
[2] J. MORGENSTERN, *o.c.*, p. 113; C. WESTERMANN, *Jesaja 40-66*, p. 138.
[3] C. C. TORREY, *o.c.*, p. 387; C. R. NORTH, *Isaiah 40-55*, p. 113.

forth, so he presents here symbols of the protection and honorific fostering, which is the share of the returning people".[1]

The present proclamation of salvation ends in a motif of goal, which has the form of a formula of recognition. I have already treated the subject of such a formula (cf. xli 20). We here have a formula of recognition strictly speaking, according to W. ZIMMERLI's terminology. That means that the content of *yd'* is not: "Yahwe has done so and so", but "I am Yahwe (*'ănî yhwh*)". In this formula one recognizes Yahwe's self-presentation by means of his name. The phrase "I am Yahwe" probably originated in the cultic theophany.[2] But in the prophecy of Ezekiel and Dt.-Is., it has been separated from that original setting and now expresses that Yahwe in his name, i.e. in his personal mystery, is also recognizable in history.[3] If the formula really comes from cult and was known as such to the Israelites, then an oracle like Is. xlix 22-23 aims at the cultic self-presentation of Yahwe, being itself the proclamation of the historical proof that the divine claim, couched in the formula, is true.[4] That what is meant is not a speculative knowledge but a concrete knowledge of the salvific God, is expressed in an eloquent manner in the second part of the verse; "You will know that those who wait for me shall not be put to shame". So "I am Yahwe" means: "You can trust in me, I shall not put you to shame".

Again the prophet is thrown back upon formulas from the literature of lament. A frequent expression of confidence is: "We set our hope on thee!" (Is. xxxiii 2; Jer. xiv 22). Also in the individual lament, the hope in Yahwe is a current theme (Pss. xxv 5, 21; xxxix 8; lxxi 5; cxxx 5) and in the song of thanksgiving one refers to the fulfilled hope (Ps. xl 2). In a sound article WESTERMANN has made clear that "to hope in Yahwe" has precisely its original setting in the expression of confidence, a motif of the lament.[5] But the idea of hope is to be found

---

[1] P. VOLZ, *Jesaia II*, pp. 104-105: "Der Dichter redet nur vom Akt der Heimführung, und wie er sonst von der Verwandlung der Wüste spricht und weissagt, dass für diesen Zweck Bäume wachsen und Wasser sprudeln, so gibt er auch hier Gleichnisse der sorgsamen Hut und der ehrenden Pflege, die den Heimkehrern zuteil wird".

[2] Cf. W. ZIMMERLI, "Ich bin Jahwe", *Festschrift A. Alt*, Tübingen 1953, pp. 179-209 (= *Gottes Offenbarung*, pp. 11-40).

[3] W. ZIMMERLI, "Der Wahrheitserweis Jahwes nach der Botschaft der beiden Exilspropheten", *Festschrift A. Weiser*, Göttingen 1963, p. 139.

[4] W. ZIMMERLI, "Das Wort des göttlichen Selbsterweises", *Gottes Offenbarung*, p. 127.

[5] C. WESTERMANN, "Das Hoffen im Alten Testament", *Theologia Viatorum*, IV 1952, pp. 19-70 (= *Forschung*, pp. 219-265); esp. *Forschung*, p. 265.

in other settings, such as the promises to those who hope (Lam. iii 25; Ps. xxv 3), the incitement to hope (Ps. xxvii 14), and the vow (Ps. lii 11: "I will hope in your name"). All these expressions borrow their full meaning from the primary situation of hope in the lament's motif of confidence. The wording e.g. of Ps. xxv 3: "No one that hopes in thee will be put to shame", supposes that the hope in Yahwe is expressed in a prayer and that Yahwe replies to it with an oracle in the sense of Is. xlix 23c. Then Ps. xxv 3 expresses confidence with a formula taken from the salvation word. The sequence of form-critical dependence between the distinct formulas of hope is thus: Ps. xxv 5b>Is. xlix 23c>Ps. xxv 3.

Furthermore, WESTERMANN makes clear that to hope in Yahwe means to wait for him as for salvation. The original usage does not know persons as object of *qwh*: one hopes for something, for help. When in religious speech, one starts to speak of "hope in Yahwe", this is a kind of neologism. It expresses that, for the suppliant, God is the expected salvation: in his person he realizes that which the suppliant hopes for. The equation is nicely formulated in Ps. xxxix 8: "And now, Lord, for what do I wait? My hope is in thee". Such expressions of confidence are the background of Is. xlix 23c.

With vs. 24 we are confronted with another form-critical problem. What is the literary function of this question? According to BEGRICH and VON WALDOW, the vss. 24-26 are an oracle of salvation. These scholars regard vs. 24 as the quotation of a question in the lament, that expresses the suppliant's despair.[1] WESTERMANN calls the pericope a proclamation of salvation and he interprets vs. 24 in the same way. Because of the exile Israel became the prey of a strong enemy and it does not believe that it can be freed. In its lament it cites a motif of the *Feindklage*. To this the oracle replies: "Surely, the prey of a strong man will be rescued".[2]

Another possible approach deserves our attention. The authors just mentioned think that the captive of the strong man[3] is Israel in exile. DUHM, however, comments that the prey, which will not be rescued

---

[1] J. BEGRICH, *Studien*, p. 21; H. GUNKEL - J. BEGRICH, *Einleitung*, p. 127; H. E. VON WALDOW, *Anlass und Hintergrund*, pp. 17 and 182, note 12; cf. H. GRESSMANN, *ZAW*. XXXIV 1914, p. 276.

[2] C. WESTERMANN, *EvTh.* XXIV 1964, p. 367; *Jesaja 40-66*, p. 179.

[3] In vs. 24, I replace צדיק by עריץ, because of the testimony of Vg, Pesh and IQIa and the clear chiastic parallelism with vs. 25. So also *BHS*, and many commentators.

from Yahwe, is the oppressor of Israel, whom he will call to account.[1] The image of the tyrant then represents Yahwe. The whole problem consists in the relation between the question and the answer, in other words, in the meaning of the particle *gam*. Does it introduce a strong assertion ("surely, *adeo*")[2] or an improbable hypothesis or concessive clause ("even if, *etiamsi*")?[3] From a lexicographical standpoint, both meanings are possible.[4] The second parsing is supported by the parallel train of thought in xlix 14-15. There we have the question: "Can a woman forget her child?" Then follows the improbable eventuality: "Even if these forget ...", against which Yahwe stresses his fundamental fidelity. The opposition *gam-'ēlleh ... we'ānōkî* (vs. 15) has a good parallel in vs. 25. So it is possible to understand vss. 24-25 as follows: Yahwe asks: "Can the prey be taken from the mighty?", a question which suggests the answer: "Of course not".[5] But he goes on: "Even if it would be possible, my prey will not be taken from me, for I will contend with those who contend with you and I will save your children". Just as in vss. 14-15 this procedure would underline the strong certainty of Yahwe's promise. In this explanation, vs. 24 loses its character of cited complaint. Then Yahwe goes on speaking from vs. 22 to vs. 26.

In favour of this interpretation one may invoke the fact that Yahwe is regularly called *gibbôr*. He is compared to a *gibbôr* in Ps. lxxviii 65; Job xvi 14; Is. iii 2, and in a dt.-Isaian text, viz. xlii 13. Sometimes he is styled *hā'ēl haggibbôr* (Deut. x 17; Is. x 21; Jer. xxxii 18; Neh. ix 32) and elsewhere it is said that he is a *gibbôr* (Ps. xxiv 8; Zeph. iii 17). In Jer. xx 11, the prophet says in his confessions that Yahwe is with him as a *gibbôr 'ārîṣ*. Both epithets from Is. xlix 24-25 are here applied to Yahwe.

Moreover, the first approach, proposed by the form-critics, offers some problems. Verse 24 is not introduced as a saying of Zion, as against vss. 14 and 21. Nowhere in the literature of lament is there a similar question. On the other hand it must again be admitted that *'ārîṣ* is used in the psalms of lament to indicate the enemy (Pss. liv 5;

---

[1] B. Duhm, *Das Buch Jesaia*, p. 339.

[2] So Cheyne, Knabenbauer, Delitzsch, Feldmann, Torrey, Simon, de Boer, Auvray-Steinmann.

[3] So Rosenmüller, Marti, Duhm, Condamin, Köhler, Van Hoonacker, Fischer, Bruno, Elliger, Caspari.

[4] Cf. Siegfried-Stade, p. 125; GB, p. 128; Zorell, p. 154; GK § 160 b.

[5] The particle *hă-* corresponds to Latin *num.*

lxxxvi 14), and that the prayer for rescue from the hand of the enemy is a *topos* of these psalms (Ps. xxxi 16).

In favour of BEGRICH's opinion one can invoke the parallel structure of vss. 24-26 and 21-23. True, some authors regard vss. 22-26 as a continuous unit. K. ELLIGER points out that *kî-kōh 'āmar yhwh* (vs. 25) is not a formula of introduction but a *Weiterleitungsformel*. He also underlines the cohesion in form (*w^{e}yādāʿat ... w^{e}yād^{e}ʿû*) and content (the submission of the enemies).[1] Even if vss. (21)22-26 are an original composition, it still cannot be questioned that it consists of two parallel parts. This appears from the cola 23c and 26b, which ELLIGER himself calls *Schlusssätze*, and from the parallel content. The binary structure is illustrated by the repeated messenger's formula in vs. 25. This is not necessarily a *Weiterleitungsformel* and, in order to make it a formula of introduction, one need not delete *kî* (against MOWINCKEL). It suffices to parse the particle as an emphatic *kî*.[2]

We thus find in the vss. 21-26 two parallel pericopes, each of them containing a motif II, 2 (vss. 22-23b and 25-26a) and a motif III (vss. 23c and 26b) of a proclamation of salvation. Besides, vs. 21 is a motif I with regard to 22-23. Thus normally vs. 24 should be such a motif too. Such is finally confirmed by the place of the messenger's formula in vs. 25. Since the second oracle begins with vs. 24, several critics wanted the formula to be put before this verse.[3] There is no objective reason for doing so. On the contrary, the parallelism favours the conservation of the formula in vs. 25. In vs. 24 a new unit begins or at least a new part of a larger unit, but the verse is kept outside the divine utterance proper, which begins only in vs. 25. So vs. 24 corresponds to vs. 21 in its literary function and acts as a quotation of a complaint. I thus agree with BEGRICH and his followers, in spite of what I have written before.[4] The entire parallel structure is this:

Motif I	Messenger's formula	Motif II	Motif III
21	22aα	22aβ-23b	23c
24	25aα	25aβ-26a	26b

Now we have to go somewhat deeper into the oracle 24-26. The words "prey" and "captive" thus allude to the exile. J. MORGENSTERN

[1] K. ELLIGER, *o.c.*, pp. 123-124; cf. M. HALLER, *Das Judentum*, p. 52.

[2] Cf. J. FISCHER, *Das Buch Isaias*, II, p. 113.

[3] *BHK*, MOWINCKEL, KÖHLER, ELLIGER.

[4] Cf. A. SCHOORS, "שבי and גלות in Isa. 40-55; Historical Background", *Proceedings of the 5th World Congress of Jewish Studies*, Jerusalem 1969, pp. 90-101.

supposes that these verses date from the time, when in the general desolation after 485, a new hope arose. For his Greek campaign, Xerxes levied troops among the neighbouring nations (Ammon, Moab, Edom, Philistia), who were, with the help of that same Xerxes, the oppressors of Judah. These enemies were enfeebled by the levy so that they became victims of the Nabataeans. When, in these circumstances, Xerxes was succeeded by Artaxerxes, the time seemed to be auspicious to cast off the Persian yoke. Such would be the historical background of Is. lx 8-22; lxi 2-9; xlix 8-26; xlii 14 + lxii 1-12; liv 1-10, according to MORGENSTERN.[1]

The deep hatred against the enemies, expressed in vs. 26, could point in that direction. Dt.-Isaiah's attitude generally is one of derision of Babylon because of its vain confidence in idols. Sometimes the prophet says that the nations will submit to Israel (xlv 14, 24-25; lv 5; cf. lx 1-13; lxvi 18-19). Only in xlvii 1-5, Babylon is threatened with slavery and shame, childlessness and widowhood and other disasters, in a spirit of revenge and without a perspective of conversion. But here also the derision at the powerlessness of the Babylonian gods is in the background (cf. xlvii 9, 12-15). In Is. xlix 26 and also in xlix 23 and li 22-23, one may have the impression of a stronger hatred. But to conclude from this to the historical background of an oppression by their neighbours, after a supposed destruction of Jerusalem in 485, requires a strong imagination.

Others also have supposed that the sentiments of revenge, such as expressed in vs. 26a, are not in keeping with the message of Dt.-Is. (e.g. DUHM, ELLIGER). BEGRICH suggested that these severe text should be explained by the fact that the prophet takes up traditions, which he could not completely assimilate. The only possibility which remained for him was to put these stern features under the dominating light of the glorification of Yahwe in vs. 26b.[2]

WESTERMANN thinks he can demonstrate more precisely that Dt.-Is. has digested here an older oracle, directed against the enemies. It would be conserved in the vss. 22a, 23b, 25b and 26a.[3] Verse 22a then originally meant a sign *against* the enemies (see above). The *proskynesis* of vs. 23b should be understood in the strict sense of a submission. But I repeat that both verses can be sufficiently explained in the present context. Verse 25b replies to a prayer like Pss. xxxv 1;

[1] J. MORGENSTERN, "Jerusalem — 485 B.C.", *HUCA*. XXXI 1960, pp. 18-19.

[2] J. BEGRICH, *Studien*, p. 86.

[3] C. WESTERMANN, *Jesaja 40-66*, p. 179.

lxxiv 22. The noun *yārîb* designates the adversary at a lawsuit, at least in Ps. xxxv 1. If the word occurs in Is. li 22, which the consonantal text admits, then it means defender.[1] The reading of Jer. xviii 19 is critically uncertain, since LXX, Targum and Peshitta read *rîbî*, which fits the context better.[2] Even in Ps. xxxv 1, eight masoretic manuscripts and Peshitta read *rîbî*. The existence of the noun *yārîb* thus is not out of doubt and, anyhow, it is an unusual nominal formation.[3] In Is. xlix 25 one must undoubtedly read *rîbēk*, in accordance with LXX, Targum and Peshitta. Now IQIa has strengthened this testimony.[4] So vs. 25b*a* gets a positive meaning, so as to be more in accordance with 25bβ, and it is not necessarily borrowed from an older oracle against enemies. "I will defend your cause ..." is at home in a prophecy of Dt.-Is., who also in li 22 says about Yahwe, that he defends his people (*yārîb 'ammô*, ev. *y^erîb*), while 25bβ is perfectly dt.-Isaian.

Verse 26a seems to be most in contradiction to the general tenor of Is. xl-lv. In Is. ix 18-20 and in Jer. xix 9, similar images are used in an oracle of doom against Israel. The punishment there goes to the point of the Israelites devouring each other in a time of war and siege. One can imagine the same announcement in an oracle of doom against the nations. But such an oracle need not be the source of Is. xlix 26a. Dt.-Is. himself may have used this metaphor, adopting a common locution. From a similar phraseology in Is. ix 19; Jer. li 57; Zech. xi 9; Ps. xxvii 2; Eccl. iv 5, we learn that the picture of Is. xlix 26a is a metaphor for the idea: "to bring somebody to extreme distress". M. Dahood has shown that a similar metaphor is to be found in the Phoenician inscription of Kilamuwa (9th cent. B.C.).[5] In Akkadian we find it also in the treaty between Assurnirari V and Matiel of Arpad (754 B.C.) and in the treaties of Esarhaddon (672 B.C.).[6]

---

[1] Cf. p. 130, note 4.

[2] W. Caspari, *Lieder und Gottessprüche*, p. 42, justly remarks that the prayer: "Listen to my adversaries", is not quite convenient.

[3] M. Dahood, *Psalms I*, p. 210.

[4] LXX: *τὴν κρίσιν σου*; Targ: וית פורענותיך; Pesh; ܘܕܝܢ̈ܟܝ; IQIa: ריבך; not רובך, as *BHK* wrongly reproduces. The *yodh* has somewhat blotted, but is still clearly distinct from a *waw*. A superscript *yodh* suggests an emended reading ריביך (Plural). Cf. M. Burrows, *The Dead Sea Scrolls of St. Mark's Monastery*, I, plate XLI.

[5] M. Dahood, "Textual Problems in Isaia", *CBQ*. XXII 1960, pp. 404-406.

[6] *Ash N*, rev. IV, 10-11, in *ANET*, p. 533; *Esar*. 448-450; 547-550; 570-572, in *ANET*, pp. 538-540; cf. D. R. Hillers, *Treaty-Curses and the Old Testament Prophets*, Roma 1964, pp. 62-63.

We have already seen that Dt.-Is. likes strong metaphors. Now he announces distress for the enemy, Babylon, and this fits his message no less than xli 11-12, 15-16; li 22-23 and esp. xlvii. It does not appear proven to me that the prophet quoted a pre-existent oracle of doom against enemies. On the contrary, I think I have shown that the presence of vss. 22a, 23b, 25b and 26a needs no special explanation in the present context.

We can paraphrase the motif II, 2 in vss. 25-26a as follows: "Surely, even from the mighty Babylon will be taken its prey; for I myself (*'ānōkî*) will defend your cause and deliver your children (the oracle is directed to mother Zion). I will reduce your oppressors to extreme distress". The motif of goal in the form of a formula of recognition follows in vs. 26b. As against vs. 23c, the motif is formulated here in more universalist terms: "All flesh shall know ..." But to conclude that Dt.-Is. announces a universalist message, is somewhat rash. WESTERMANN comments that vs. 23c deals with what Yahwe's divinity means for Israel, vs. 26b with what it means for the world.[1] This is too systematic and does not correspond to the text. Vs. 26b clearly says that the whole world will know that Yahwe is the saviour and redeemer of Zion. The point still is what God means for Israel.

A participation of the pagans in salvation is out of the question here. The prophet explicitly deals with Yahwe's salvific activity on behalf of Israel, but the nations will witness it. Also the Egyptians learned to know Yahwe in their own ruin (Ex. xiv 4: *wᵉyādᵉʿû miṣrayim kî-'ănî yhwh*), but nobody regards this as a participation in salvation. Similarly, Ezekiel proclaims that one will recognize Yahwe in the destruction of Sidon (Ez. xxviii 22) without meaning a participation in salvation. These utterances are entirely theocentric and do not pronounce on the salvific statute of the pagan spectators.

The titles *môšîaʿ* and *gō'ēl* have been commented on above in connection with xliii 3 and xli 14. They often support the promise of salvation. Because Yahwe was the saviour and redeemer of Israel in history, he can warrant his word of salvation in the present distress. Now, the fulfilment of the word of salvation will make clear to the whole world that Yahwe indeed is that saviour and redeemer of Israel. In parallelism with "Yahwe" the prophet uses the ancient divine name "the Mighty One of Jacob" (cf. Gen. xlix 24; Is. i 24; lx 16; Ps. cxxxii 2). This name, an artificial deformation of "the Bull of

---

[1] C. WESTERMANN, *o.c.*, p. 180.

Jacob", has its roots in Canaanite mythology, where the bull was El's emblem.[1] It is impossible to make out whether in the present context the prophet intends anything more than a parallel of Yahwe. According to WESTERMANN, the phrase "Your redeemer is the mighty one of Jacob", co-relates the two aspects of divinity: the one who wields sovereign power is at the same time the saviour of Israel.[2] But let us remark that the epithet "Mighty One of Jacob" also contains a reference to salvation history.

We must deal with a last question, that of the original connection between the three proclamations in xlix 14-26. After the form critics had divided these verses into two or three oracles, WESTERMANN defended that the three proclamations together are one original composition. We have seen already that 14-21 and 22-23 originally belong together, verse 21 being the link. Vss. 21-23 and 24-26 show an entirely parallel structure. Another argument of WESTERMANN is that the three complaints are complementary: accusation of God (vs. 14), a complaint about their own distress (vs. 21) and a complaint about the enemy (*Feindklage*, vs. 24). Besides, I point to the climax from the formula of recognition in vs. 23 to the one in vs. 26. To me the main argument in favour of an original connection between 24-26 and the preceding verses is the absence of a motif II, 1 in the last proclamation as well as in the second one (vss. 21-23). This motif is essential to the genre. This way vss. 21-23 as well as 24-26 act as a further elaboration of the motif of turning in favour in xlix 15-16. The complete structure of the pericope is:

Motif I	Messenger's formula	Morif II,1	Motif II,2	Motif III
14		15-16	17-20(21)	
21	22aα		22aβ-23b	23c
24	25aα		22aβ-26a	26b

It is striking that none of the three proclamations of salvation is form-critically complete, but with three incomplete proclamations the prophet made a neat whole. In WESTERMANN's opinion, this whole has the character of a disputation, in which Yahwe refutes Israel's complaints. I shall return to the point in the next chapter. In any case, it seems to be a dialogue between Yahwe and Zion. The latter

[1] One has apparently changed the name אַבִּיר into אָבִיר for theological reasons; Ug. *ibr*; KB, p. 5.

[2] C. WESTERMANN, *l.c.*

complains of her abandonment (vs. 14), but Yahwe promises that her children will be so numerous as to make them short of room (vss. 17-20). Unbelief of Zion: "How is this possible?" (vs. 21) is followed by divine reply: "I will mobilize your oppressors and they themselves will bring back your children" (vss. 22-23). Zion's reaction: "Such is impossible, for my enemy is too mighty!" (vs. 24). But Yahwe has the last word: "I myself fight for you and against me your enemies are powerless" (vss. 25-26).

6. *Is. li 9-16*

9 Awake, awake, put on strength, O arm of Yahwe,
awake as in days of old,
the generations of long ago.
Was it not thou who didst cut Rahab in pieces,
who didst pierce the dragon?
10 Was it not thou who didst dry up the sea,
the waters of the great deep;
who didst make the depths of the sea a way
for the redeemed to pass over?
11 Let the ransomed of Yahwe return,
and come to Zion with a joyous shout;
may there be everlasting joy upon their heads,
may joy and gladness overtake them,
so that sorrow and sighing *flee away*[a].

12 I, I am he that comforts you;
who are you that you are afraid
of men who die,
of the sons of men who pass away *like*[b] grass,
13 and that you have forgotten Yahwe, your Maker,
who stretched out the heavens,
who lays the foundations of the earth,
and that you tremble continually all the day,
because of the fury of the oppressor,
when he sets himself to destroy?
Where is the fury of the oppressor?
14 He who is bowed down shall speedily be released;
he shall not die in the Pit,
neither shall his *strength*[c] fail.
15 (For I am Yahwe, your God,

who stirs up the sea so that its waves roar; —
Yahwe of hosts is his name.
16 I have put my words in your mouth,
and hid you in the shadow of my hand,
to plant the heavens and to lay the foundations of the earth,
and to say to Zion: "You are my people".)

[a] Lg ונס c IQIa; Targ: ויסוף; Vg: fugiet.
[b] Lg כחציר c LXX, Pesh and Vg.
[c] Cf. comments.

The original setting of the word of salvation is best approximated in Is. li 9-16, where the lament and the proclamation are transmitted together.[1] In application of his theory about the adaptation of Is. xl-lv by Trito-Isaiah, Elliger supposes that the latter had a large part in the formation of the pericope.[2] In this respect a couple of questions about authenticity will have to be solved in the next analysis. On the ground of the double imperatives of *'ûr* in li 9, 17 and lii 1, he prefers a larger composition, as do Volz and Westermann.[3] The argument is rather simplistic. In any case, the sections which open with the quoted verses, are relatively independent.

The lament (vss. 9-11) opens in vs. 9 with a general cry for Yahwe's intervention. It is an insistent prayer comparable with Pss. vii 7; xliv 24. Formally, the entreaty is directed to Yahwe's arm. In the O.T. the arm is a symbol of power. Yahwe's arm indicates divine power, such as it revealed itself in creation (Ps. lxxxix 11) and in Israel's deliverance from Egypt (e.g. Deut. iv 34).

Then the praying community puts forward the motives for Yahwe's intervention (vss. 9c-10). Already in vs. 9b we have the transition to these motives by the reference to the days of old (*kîmê qedem, dôrôt 'ôlāmîm*). They review Yahwe's former actions in order to induce him to a renewed intervention. Two facts from the primeval ages are viewed here: creation and deliverance from Egypt. Vs. 9c alludes to

---

[1] Parallels: Jer. iii 22b-iv 2; xiv 2-10; xiv 19-xv 2; Cf. H. Gunkel - J. Begrich *Einleitung*, pp. 136-138.

[2] K. Elliger, *Deuterojesaja*, pp. 204-213.

[3] K. Elliger, *o.c.*, pp. 264-265; P. Volz, *Jesaia II*, pp. 116-125: li 9-11, 17-23, lii 1-2, 7-12; C. Westermann, *EvTh.* XXIV 1964, pp. 368-369; *Jesaja 40-66*, pp. 192-194.

creation with the mythological picture of the fight and victory over Rahab, the sea monster. The affinity with Ps. lxxxix 11 is so close that one may suppose a direct literary dependence (*'ōz, zerôa', 'att, rahab, ḥll*). H. L. GINSBERG has remarked this similitude and pointed out Dt.-Isaiah's dependence on the psalmic literature. But he did not see that Is. li 9-11 is itself a psalm.[1]

The deliverance from Egypt is typified by the miracle of the Reed Sea, just like elsewhere in Dt.-Is. This is a frequent motif in the laments (cf. Pss. xliv 2-4; lxxiv 2; lxxx 9-12; Is. lxiii 11-14; Deut. ix 26). Verse 10a, the theme of which originally belongs to the creation myth, is a link between 9c and 10b. *Yām* and *tehôm rabbâ* are the names of the primeval ocean. The drying up of the sea is thus a reminiscence of creation (Gen. i 9-10) but at the same time it involves an allusion to the passage through the Reed Sea. We met the idea of the deliverance out of Egypt in the introductions of the words of salvation, either in the term *g'l* or in nearly the same metaphors as here (xliii 16). The theme of creation is often invoked in the first part of Dt.-Is., but never in this mythological form of the fight with the sea monster. But from the proclamation itself (vss. 13-14) it will appear that the prophet assimilates this image with that theme from xl-xlviii, since he speaks clearly of stretching out the heavens and laying the foundations of the earth. So, it is insufficient to explain Rahab only as an image of Egypt, as proposed by J. FISCHER and others. The prophet clearly has in mind both creation and exodus, and represents them in the image Rahab-Yam-Tehom.[2] According to BEGRICH, vss. 9c-10 are doubtful questions, which betray uncertainty.[3] This is a gratuitous affirmation. On the contrary, it seems to me that we have here rhetorical questions that underline the insistence uttered in vs. 9ab.

In vs. 11 follows the concrete entreaty for the return to Zion. Many critics deleted the verse as a gloss, borrowed from Is. xxxv 10. But the verse is needed in the literary context, for it is the appropriate entreaty of the lament. Moreover, there is no reason to suppose that

---

1 H. L. GINSBERG, "The Arm of Yhwh in Isaiah 51-63", *JBL.* LXXVII 1958, p. 153.

2 J. FISCHER, "Das Problem des Neuen Exodus", *Theologische Quartalschrift,* CX 1929, p. 116; more recently W. SCHMIDT, *Kõnigtum Gottes in Ugarit und Israel,* Berlin 1960, p. 40; the interpretation I defend has been proposed by B. J. VAN DER MERWE, *Pentateuchtradisies,* pp. 202-205; G. FOHRER, *Jesaja III,* pp. 146-147.

3 J. BEGRICH, *Studien,* p. 167.

xxxv 10 is more original. On the contrary, ch. xxxv seems to depend on Dt.-Is. in other points (cf. xl 3-5, 10, 29-31; xli 18-19; xliii 19-20; xlviii 21).[1] I thus feel obliged to keep the verse in this place. The meaning of the verse is quite clear: it is a simple prayer for a joyful return to Zion. VOLZ exaggerates in recognizing here the return of the *Urzeit* in the *Endzeit*.[2] The reference to creation and to the exodus in vss. 9-10 does not mean that a renewal of primeval times is asked for; it is a ground of confidence for the prayer: the God, who wrought such deeds in the past, will be able to redeem again.

According to VON WALDOW, Is. li 9-11 is a collective lament, as appears from the entreaty in vs. 11 and the motif of the exodus wonders, proper to these collective genres. BEGRICH thinks it is an individual lament as to the form, whereas the content is that of a collective lament (cf. Ps. lxxvii). The difference between these positions is negligible.[3] That BEGRICH is not completely wrong may appear from the salvation word, which is formulated in the second person singular (see below). But he wrongly considers it to be a lament by the prophet. It is surely meant in the name of the people.

It is a strange fact that in the proclamation, the prophet addresses a group (*m^e^naḥem^e^kem*) and then a feminine figure (fem. sing. *'att*). In vs. 13, we suddenly have a masc. sing. (*wattiškaḥ* ... *'ōśekā* ... *watt^e^paḥēd*). One may wonder if the text is not in disorder. But the textual tradition is entangled as well:

IQIa:	12	(fem.) מי אתי ותיראי ... (pl.) מנחמכמה
	13	(fem. + masc.) ותשכחי (!) את יהוה עשכה
LXX:	12	*παρακαλῶν σε* (sing.) ... *τίνα εὐλαβηθεῖσα ἐφοβήθης* (fem)
	13	*ἐπελάθου ... καὶ ἐφόβου*
Aq:	12	... *τις συ* (sing.)
Sym:	12	*παρηγορων σε ... τις ει* (sing)
Targ:	12	(all pl.) מנחמכון ... ממן אתון דחלין
	13	(masc. sing.) ואתנשיתא ...... ודחילתא
Pesh:	12	(fem. sing.) ܡܢ ܐܢܬܝ، ܕܕܚܠܬܝ، ... (pl.) ܡܒܝܐܢܘܟܘܢ
	13	(fem. sing.) ܘܛܥܝܬܝ، ܠܡܪܝܐ ܕܥܒܕܟܝ ... ܘܕܚܠܬܝ

[1] P. VOLZ, *o.c.*, p. 117, note f: "... Jes 35 ist in solchem Mass kompilatorisch, dass dort die Annahme der Entlehnung von vornherein das Gegebene ist".

[2] P. VOLZ, *o.c.*, p. 119.

[3] Good form-critical analyses of the pericope in J. BEGRICH, *o.c.*, pp. 166-168; H. E. VON WALDOW, *o.c.*, pp. 23-25; cf. H. GUNKEL - J. BEGRICH, *Einleitung*, § 4 and 6, nr. 17-21; H. GRESSMANN, *ZAW*. XXXIV 1914, p. 264.

Vg: 12 consolabor vos (pl.) ... timeres (sing.)
13 oblitus es (masc. sing.)

The reading *m^enaḥem^ekem*, with plural suffix (vs. 12), is very old, as appears from IQIa. Only LXX departs from it. However, the plural form is limited to this one word, except in Targum, where things are seemingly put in order. LXX offers the best reading and the difference in the other witnesses can be explained by dittography of the *mem*. A haplography in LXX is to be rejected, owing to the constant singular in the other morphemes. Do we have a masculine or a feminine singular, i.e. is the oracle directed to Israel or to Jerusalem? In Targum and Vulgate everything is masculine, in LXX [1] and Peshitta feminine. The Qumran-manuscript is in accordance with MT with this difference, that in vs. 13, it has *wtškḥy* instead of *wattiškaḥ*. This way the disorder in IQIa is still greater, for the masc. suffix in *'śkh* (MT *'ōśekā*) and the verb *wtpḥd* are in discord with the fem. *wtskḥy*. The *yodh* of *wtskḥy* can hardly be designated as a dittography, for the manuscript has *'t* between the verb and *yhwh*. If this *'t* is secundary, then the *yodh* may be due to an older dittography. It is impossible to make a choice between masculine and feminine, though the latter has the best witnesses in its favour. In any case the masoretic reading is as ancient as IQIa, and probably we can explain it satisfactorily. According to BEGRICH [2] a feminine personage is addressed. That much is certain, I think, that already the LXX knew of a feminine personage being addressed. But in principle, the suppliant in a lament is a man, so that the recipient of the oracle is regularly addressed in masculine singular (Is. xli 8; xliii 1; xliv 2; xlix 7; Jer. xxx 10). This style is so fixed, that this masc. sing. shows up, sometimes even in the case of a feminine personification. A parallel phenomenon is to be found in Is. xli 14-15. To me it seems much more acceptable that LXX only harmonized the context with the feminine forms already present, then that it changed into feminine a text which was originally completely masculine.

At the same time it becomes clear that the oracle is directed to Jerusalem, as a symbol of the community, and that the lament must be understood in the same perspective, as pointed out above.

---

1 The apparatus in *BHK* is wrong on this point.

2 J. BEGRICH, "Das priesterliche Heilsorakel", *ZAW*. LII 1934, p. 82; H. E. VON WALDOW, *o.c.*, p. 24.

The turning towards Israel in vs. 12 is stressed with the double *'ānōkî*. This repetition stylistically corresponds to the double *'ûrî* in vs. 9. So lament and oracle are strongly linked together. This is one more argument against ELLIGER and STEINMANN, who declare vss. 12-14 to be unauthentic.[1] Just as in li 3, Yahwe's turning is expressed with the word "to comfort" (*nḥm*). The series of questions that follows, acts as an elucidation: Yahwe protects against human enemies. The question *mî-'att wattîre'î* is a poetical allusion to the motif of assurance of salvation, that normally occurs in an oracle of salvation *sensu stricto*. Remark the neat stylistic opposition: "I am ... who are you?" to express the idea: I am such that you do not have to fear. The expansion of the name Yahwe in vs. 13 is a sort of substantiation, appealing to the creative power and thus referring to vs. 9.

From vs. 13c it appears that Zion is afraid of the oppressor (*ham-mēṣîq*). Most of the interpreters recognize in him the Babylonians. Strangely enough, A. VAN HOONACKER here detects a reminiscence of the oppression in Egypt.[2] But to this effect, he must delete vs. 11 and replace it by xlviii 21, an operation which is completely unacceptable. To L. WATERMAN it is a reminiscence of the sorrowful condition at the capture of Jerusalem by Nebuchadnezzar.[3] In the line of his easy method, J. MORGENSTERN places vss. 12-13 after 17-23 and changes some words. In the framework of his theory on the catastrophe of 485, the oppressor must be Xerxes and the allusion is to this catastrophe.[4] In my opinion, the oppressor, here as anywhere else in Dt.-Is., is the Babylonian. In the hypothesis of a persecution of Jews under Nabonidus, the text would be very well in place.

Verse 14 mentions the concrete outcome of Yahwe's intervention: the deliverance out of the oppressor's hand. The participle *ṣō'eh* indicates the prisoner, who is bowed down in chains. In the verse there is a climax, viz. from deliverance from prison to escape from death. That the latter is a topic of the literature of lament needs no proof. According to C. C. TORREY, the climax continues in the last words of the verse: "neither shall his bread fail". G. R. DRIVER justly remarks that we rather have an anticlimax: prison, death, indigence. He

---

[1] K. ELLIGER, *Deuterojesaja*, pp. 207-212; J. STEINMANN, *Le livre de la consolation*, p. 165.

[2] A. VAN HOONACKER, *Het boek Isaias*, p. 248.

[3] L. WATERMANN, *Forerunners of Jesus*, New York 1959, p. 62.

[4] J. MORGENSTERN, "The Oppressor of Isa. 51,13 — Who was he?» *JBL.* LXXXI 1962, pp. 25-34; cf. A. SCHOORS, *Orientalia Lovaniensia Periodica*, II 1971, pp. 107-108.

proposes to read *lēḥāmô*, i.e. *lēaḥ*, "strength", with the suffix *-mô* of the third person. The latter occurs also in Is. xliv 15; liii 8. Then the text may be translated: "His natural force will not fail". This way one obtains a parallel with the preceding stich and one conserves the climax.[1]

In the following verses, commentators generally delete something.[2] Though verse 15 is not absolutely necessary, it fits the context very well. It may act as a concluding substantiation of the oracle or even as a sort of motif of goal. Still, I regard it as a quotation from Jer. xxxi 35, added by a glossator, who did not even adapt the suffix in *šᵉmô* to the new context, where Yahwe is speaking and we thus should have *šᵉmî*. Verse 16 is still less acceptable. According to the rules of the genre we should not have an intervention by Yahwe after the motif of outcome. Moreover, an individual seems to be addressed and no longer the personified community. The verse also seems to quote lix 21 and xlix 2. Some scholars think it to be a fragment of a Servant prophecy.[3] This is possible. The verse sounds very dt.-Isaian: "to plant the heavens and to lay the foundations of the earth". To me this defies explanation in the present context, as well as "to say to Zion: You are my people". When parsing the infinitives as gerundives, as proposed by TORREY, the meaning does not become more clear.[4] The proclamation ends without a motif of goal.

7. *Is. li 17-23*

17 Rouse yourself, rouse yourself, stand up, O Jerusalem,
you who have drunk from Yahwe's hand the cup of his wrath,
who have drunk to the dregs the bowl of staggering.
18 There is none to guide you
among all the sons you have borne;

---

[1] C. C. TORREY, *The Second Isaiah*, p. 402; G. R. DRIVER, *JTS*. XXXVI 1935, pp. 402-403. The same explanation can be defended with regard to the difficult text Jer. xi 19. It is not necessary to dissolve the suffix מוֹ‎ into an enclitic *mem* and the common suffix וֹ‎, as proposed by M. DAHOOD, "Ugaritic Studies and the Bible», *Gregorianum* XLIII 1962, p. 66; cf. *Bib*. XLVII 1966, p. 409. But formerly the suffix מוֹ‎ may have originated from enclitic *mem* plus the common suffix.

[2] I.a. vs. 16: CHEYNE, HALLER, VON WALDOW; vss. 15-16: DUHM, MOWINCKEL, VOLZ, FISCHER; vss. 12-16: ELLIGER, STEINMANN. MARTI and FELDMANN hesitate.

[3] A. VAN HOONACKER, *o.c.*, pp. 248-249; J. FISCHER, *o.c.*, p. 124; H. E. VON WALDOW, *o.c.*, p. 190, note 54; M. HALLER, *Das Judentum*, p. 48.

[4] Cf. C. C. TORREY, *l.c.*

there is none to take you by the hand
among all the sons you have brought up.
19 These two things have befallen you:
— who will condole with you? —
devastation and destruction, famine and sword;
who will *comfort*[a] you?
20 Your sons lay fainting,
at the head of every street like an antelope in a net,
full of the wrath of Yahwe,
of the anger of your God.
21 So hear this, you who are afflicted,
who are drunk, but not with wine.
22 Thus says your Lord, Yahwe,
your God who defends the cause of his people:
"Behold, I take from your hand the cup of staggering,
the bowl of my wrath you shall drink no more.
23 I put it into the hand of your tormentors,
who have said to you:
'Bow down, that we may pass over',
so that you made your back like the ground,
like a street for people to pass over".

[a] Lg ינחמך c IQIa; LXX: *τίς παρακαλέσει*; Targ: דינחמניך; Vg: quis consolabitur; Pesh: ܡܢ ܢܒܝܐܟܝ.

According to all form critics, the pericope li 17-23 is an original unit. VON WALDOW calls it an oracle of salvation, BEGRICH, however, a word of comfort, an imitation of the words addressed to a suffering one by his friend (cf. Job's friends). But still he admits that in this pericope, the comfort rests upon the fact that the speaker has an oracle of salvation to communicate to the suffering person (vss. 22-23).[1] According to VON WALDOW, the oracle is preceded by an expanded introduction which resumes the description of distress from the lament.[2] From a literary point of view, his interpretation is preferable. The text certainly is a word of salvation which, according to WESTERMANN's classification, must be labeled a proclamation of salvation, as appears from its structure.

The prophet addresses Jerusalem, personified as a woman who is

---

[1] J. BEGRICH, *Studien*, p. 62; Cf. H. GRESSMANN, *ZAW*. XXXIV 1914, p. 276.
[2] H. E. VON WALDOW, *o.c.*, pp. 21-22.

drunk from the cup of Yahwe's wrath. The address is resumed in vs. 21 with an additional style *'ăniyyâ*. The vss. 17-20 constitute an elaborated reference to the lament. The latter is not directly quoted, as it is in li 9-11, but it is transposed into the second person and taken into the address. It is not hard to reconstruct the original lament:

(17) Thou hast given me to drink the cup of thy wrath,
hast given me to drink to the dregs the bowl of staggering.
(18) There is none to guide me
among all the sons I have borne;
there is none to take me by the hand
among all the sons I have brought up.
(19) These two things have befallen me
— who will condole with me? —
devastation and destruction, famine and sword;
who will comfort me?
(20) My sons lay fainting like an antelope in a net;
they are full of the wrath of Yahwe,
of the anger of my God.

One easily recognizes two motifs from the lament: the accusation of Yahwe (vs. 17bc) and the picture of distress (18-20). The nominal phrases are typical of the latter. The perfect tenses must be understood as a *perfectum praesens*.[1] WESTERMANN amply showed the affinity with the Book of Lamentations.[2]

K. MARTI, B. DUHM and K. ELLIGER eliminate vs. 18 because it treats of Jerusalem in the third person.[3] Such might seem an objection, but the shift from second to third person is quite usual in relative clauses.[4] True, the present verse is rarely understood as a relative clause, but it is one, though asyndetically built. I thus keep the verse, the dt.-Isaian physionomy of which is recognized by ELLIGER himself.

---

[1] Cf. H. GUNKEL - J. BEGRICH, *Einleitung*, p. 215; GK. § 106 g.

[2] C. WESTERMANN, *Jesaja 40-66*, p. 198: a complaint of Zion (Lam. i 6); Yahwe's wrath (ii 21-22; iv 11); Yahwe gives to drink bitterness and wormwood (iii 15, 19; cf. Ps. lx 5: the cup that dazes); complaint about the loss of children (i 18, 20); there is none to comfort her (i 2b, 16b, 17b, 21b); in vs. 20a, there are literal reminiscences of Lam. ii 19; iv 1. I do not see the connection between vs. 20a and Lam. i 15. Cf. T. K. CHEYNE, *o.c.*, p. 53; F. DELITZSCH, *o.c.*, pp. 525-526.

[3] K. MARTI, *o.c.*, p. 341; B. DUHM, *o.c.*, p. 350; K. ELLIGER, *Deuterojesaja*, p. 262, note 2.

[4] Cf. JOÜON § 158 n.

Distress, as it is pictured here, belongs to the topics of the prophet, as may appear from a comparison of vs. 17 with xl 2 and of vss. 19-22 with xlii 22-25; xliii 28 and xlix 19. The prophet uses the image of the cup of staggering (vss. 17, 21-23), which he borrows from his predecessors, esp. from Jeremiah (Hab. ii 16; Jer. xxv 15-27; xlviii 26; xlix 12; li 7; Ez. xxiii 31-34; Lam. iv 21; Ob. 16; cf. Ps. lxxv 9).[1] Verse 18 aims at the depopulation of the city, presented under the image of childlessness. The metaphor of the cup of staggering is continued in it. According to the Ugaritic legend of Danel, it is one of the children's duties to guide their parents when they are drunk.[2] An idea like this forms the background of vs. 18. Nothing indicates that *šōd* and *šeber* in vs. 19 suggest moral collapse, as Torrey supposes.[3] These words mean violence and destruction in a material sense. The delineated condition is probably a reminiscence of the tragedy of 587, described in vivid colours as in Lamentations.

The fresh address in vs. 21 evokes the miserable condition and connects it again with the cup of staggering. The messenger's formula typifies Yahwe as the one who defends the cause of his people.[4] Yahwe's turning to them consists in taking the cup of staggering from Zion's hand. In the motif II, 2, the oracle corresponds verbally with the lament: Zion will no longer have to drink the cup. In its content it is reminiscent of xl 2: Israel's punishment is ended. But the motif of outcome also contains the negative side, viz. the punishment of the enemies. Such is announced in the continued image of the cup of staggering, that passes to the hand of the oppressor. A certain spirit of revenge cannot be denied in vs. 23, since the oppression, of which the enemies rendered themselves guilty, is recalled. The picture

---

[1] In vss. 17b and 22c delete כוס, in accordance with LXX and several commentators. It has been added to explain the rare word קבעת, which is ancient and occurs in Ug. in parallelism with *ks*; cf. I Aqht: 216-218.

[2] 2 Aqht I: 31-32: *aḫd ydh bškrn mʿmsh kšbʿ yn*, "take his hand in drunkenness, support him when he is sated with wine», further 2 Aqht II: 5-6, 19-20; cf. U. Cassuto, "Daniel et son fils dans la tablette II D de Ras Shamra», *REJ*. V 1940, pp. 125-131. Also G. R. Driver, *Canaanite Myths and Legends*, Edinburgh 1956, p. 49, note 12, refers to Is. li 18.

[3] C. C. Torrey, *o.c.*, p. 404.

[4] In MT, there is an asyndetic relative clause: יריב עמו, "who defends the cause of his people». The transitive use of the verb ריב, however, is unusual (elsewhere, only in Is. i 17). One can also read יְרִיב עמו, "the defender of his people». But a nominal formation of the type *yārîb* is also rather unusual; cf. Joüon § 88 L, c, and my note 4, on p. 118.

is borrowed from the ancient eastern customs of war (cf. Jos. x 24; Ps. cx 1).

Just like the preceding pericope, this proclamation of salvation is not concluded with a motif of goal.

8. *Is. liv 7-10*

7 "With little emotion I abandoned you,
but with great compassion I gather you.
8 In overflowing wrath I hid
for a moment my face from you,
but with everlasting loyalty I have compassion on you",
says Yahwe, your Redeemer.
9 "For this is like the days of Noah to me:
as I swore that the waters of Noah
would no more go over the earth,
so I swear to be no more angry with you,
no more to rebuke you.
10 For even although the mountains depart
and the hills remove,
my loyalty shall not depart from you,
and my covenant of peace shall not remove",
says Yahwe, who has compassion on you.

After the oracle of salvation Is liv 4-6, which I have already analyzed, follows, in the present order of the book, a proclamation of salvation: liv 7-10. The critics differ in opinion about the delimitation of these verses. BEGRICH and VON WALDOW regard vss. 7-10 as an oracle of salvation.[1] I have already mentioned that WESTERMANN considers vss. 1-10 to be an original composition of three words of salvation: 1-3, 4-6, 7-10. At the same time I showed the proper structure of vss. 4-6. That in vs. 7 a new oracle commences, appears also from *'āmar 'ĕlōhāyik* in vs. 6, which is a formula of conclusion, just like *'āmar m^eraḥămēk yhwh* in vs. 10. The main argument, however, is the structure of a proclamation of salvation, which I shall show in the vss. 7-10, whereas vss. 4-6 clearly are a salvation oracle. M. HALLER speaks of Zion songs,[2] but such a name only indicates a theme and

---

[1] J. BEGRICH, *Studien*, p. 14; H. E. VON WALDOW, *o.c.*, p. 28.

[2] M. HALLER, *Das Judentum*, p. 58.

cannot pass for a definition of the genre. As a matter of fact, the oracle is directed to Zion, as appears from the suffixes in the feminine singular.

In vss. 7-8, the motifs I and II, 1 are antithetically interlaced. Verses 7a and 8a clearly suppose a motif of lament. J. ZIEGLER's doubts on this point are without foundation.[1] With vs. 7a one may suppose something like Lam. v 20: "Why dost thou so long forsake us?" and vs. 8a refers to a complaint like Pss. xliv 25; lxxxviii 15: "Why dost thou hide thy face?" (cf. Pss. xxx 8; civ 29; cxliii 7). In both cases we have a complaint against Yahwe. In the second part of both verses Yahwe enunciates his turning in favour, which is exactly the opposite of the accusation made by Zion. G. R. DRIVER has proposed a new interpretation of *rega'* in vs. 7. He supposes that the word does not only mean "moment" but also "movement" (cf. Lat. *momentum* / *movimentum*) and thus in a psychical sense "emotion". Thus the parallelism of the verse becomes perfect: "With little emotion I forsook you, but with great compassion I gather you." This interpretation can be supported somewhat by Targum and Peshitta, which certainly did not read "moment".[2] This rendering of *rega'* also fits Ps. xxx 6 very well, so that there is a biblical parallel.[3] DRIVER substantiates his interpretation linguistically only by a reference to Arab. *ra'aǧa*. The connection with the Hebrew root *rg'* only holds *per metathesim*, which is suspect. One could rather invoke the meaning "to stir" of the verb *rg'* in Jer. xxi 35 (= Is. li 15); Job xxvi 12. The verb is commonly used with that meaning in later and modern Hebrew and it is included as such in the dictionaries.[4] It is related to Arab. *raǧa'a*, "to turn back". But with respect to the text proper, DRIVER's proposal is fully acceptable. One may wonder whether the prophet would use the same word with two distinct meanings in one immediate context (vss. 7 and 8). It is not excluded that *rg'*, "moment" has other vowels than *rg'*, "movement". Moreover, why should he not make a pun? This play on two meanings of the same word is dear to

---

[1] J. ZIEGLER, *TR.* XXXIX 1940, p. 51 (recension of BEGRICH's *Studien*).

[2] Targ: ברגז זעיר; Pesh: ܒܪܘܓܙܐ ܙܥܘܪܐ; both translate רגע as "anger". Cf. G. R. DRIVER, "Studies in the Vocabulary of the O.T. VIII", *JTS.* XXXVI 1935, p. 299.

[3] M. DAHOOD, *Psalms I*, p. 182, translates רגע in Ps. xxx 6 as "perdition, death". But the justification seems farfetched to me.

[4] J. LEVY, *Wörterbuch*, IV, pp. 425-426; KB, p. 874; ZORELL, p. 757; cf. J. BACHMANN, *Präparation und Kommentar zum Deuterojesaja*, Berlin 1922, p. 96.

Dt.-Is., as appears from xl 12-13 (*tkn*), 19 (*ṣōrēp*); li 6-7 (*ḥtt*); lv 2-3 (*nepeš*), eventually liv 13 (*bnyk*); lv 1 (*kesep*) and some four instances in the Servant prophecies.[1]

According to Š. Porúbčan, the matrimonial theme which occurs in the prophet's other Zion oracles, is present also in these verses.[2] It may be, but there is no explicit reference to it. Some terms, such as *'zb*, *gō'ēl*, *ḥesed*, may belong to that theme, but nevertheless, it seems to me that the prophet expresses more directly the theology of election and covenant. The term *qbṣ*, "to gather", in vs. 7 points in the same sense. Because Yahwe had retired, the people fell apart. Here, there is certainly no image of a spouse. On the contrary, it appears that to the prophet Zion-Jerusalem coincides with the exiled inhabitants.[3]

Against his short absence Yahwe puts his eternal *ḥesed* (motif II, 1). This pronouncement must be understood in the light of the following comparison (motif II, 2). Negatively, he swears that he will be angry no more with Israel, just as he swore to Noah. Positively, his *ḥesed* and his covenant of peace will be stronger than hills and mountains. From the parallelism in vs. 10b it appears that to the prophet *ḥesed* and *b^erît* are connected to one another. That connection applies to old testament theology in general. *Ḥesed* expresses the attitude towards others because of a relation of kinship, friendship, hospitality or service. It could be translated best as "solidarity, joint liability", or as Latin *pietas*. The idea of *ḥesed* involves faithfulness (*'ĕmet*). The formula *ḥesed we'ĕmet* thus is a hendiadys, in which *'ĕmet* sets forth the firmness of the *ḥesed*. In any case, since the thorough study by N. Glueck, one can no longer translate *ḥesed* simply as "grace".[4]

A *b^erît* is based on a solemn act, whereas *ḥesed* as an obligation arises of itself, as soon as there is a close relationship between both parties. But both contain substantially the same duties.[5] Moreover, the covenant is one of the relationships that occasion *ḥesed*. On the other hand, partners that are connected by *ḥesed*, may confirm this

---

[1] G. R. Driver, "Linguistic and Textual Problems: Isaiah XL-LXVI", *JTS.* XXXVI 1935, p. 406; C. C. Torrey, *The Second Isaiah*, pp. 199-202.

[2] Š. Porúbčan, *Il Patto nuovo in Is. 40-66*, p. 177-178.

[3] Cf. A. Zillesen, "Israel in Darstellung und Beurteilung Deuterojesajas", *ZAW.* XXIV 1904, pp. 266-267; F. Delitzsch, *Commentar*, p. 562; K. Marti, *o.c.*, p. 354.

[4] N. Glueck, *Das Wort* hesed *im alttestamentlichen Sprachgebrauch*, Giessen 1927. The translation of LXX (ἐλεός) and Vg (misericordia) is misleading here.

[5] KB³, p. 323.

bond with a covenant. "So *ḥesed* constitutes the object of a *b^{e}rît* and it can also be called its content. The possibility of a covenant being concluded and maintained is based upon the existence of *ḥesed*."[1]

In Israel, a covenant thus is not a merely external reality. It rests upon and creates a close bond between the contracting parties. The *ṣ^{e}dāqâ* or *mišpāṭ*, the observance of the clausulas, is only the expression of this solidarity or fidelity. All this applies also to the covenant between Yahwe and his people. Therefore, *b^{e}rît* and *ḥesed* are a fixed word pair in the Hebrew Bible, underlining the connection between the two realities (Deut. vii 9, 12; 1 Kings viii 23; Pss. xxv 10; lxxxix 29, 34-35; ciii 17-18; cvi 45; Is. lv 3). There is even a hendiadys *b^{e}rît w^{e}ḥesed* to express the loyalty to the covenant (Deut. vii 9, 12; 1 Kings viii 23; 2 Chron. vi 14; Neh. i 5; ix 32; Dan. ix 4). In liv 10, the prophet thus adheres to a well-known tradition. God's *ḥesed* is his attitude to his people based on his connection with them. This attitude includes fidelity and justice. It also underlines God's help (*yš'*) and redemption (*g'l*, cf. vs. 8b), and as such is related to his power and mighty deeds (Pss. lix 10-11, 17-18; lxii 12-13; cxxxvii 2-3). It is the result of a promise, an oath or a covenant.

In the present oracle, Yahwe's *ḥesed* is associated with his mercy. In the parallelism between vss. 7 and 8, *ḥesed* (vs. 8) is balanced by *raḥămîm* (vs. 7). Furthermore, the concrete act of *ḥesed* is expressed with the verb *riḥamtîk*. In the conclusion *'āmar yhwh*, Yahwe once more is called *m^{e}raḥămēk*. This proves that something more than loyalty is operating in Yahwe. Actually, with its sins Israel had infringed upon the covenant. Yahwe was no longer obliged to loyalty. But still he keeps it. Here loyalty passes into mercy and grace. It becomes a manifestation of spontaneous love, which is not required by any obligation. Loyalty and mercy are thus closely connected, not identical. As appears from vs. 10b, *ḥesed* remains a relationship of covenant, *raḥămîm* is forgiving love.[2] We may put it this way: out of mercy, Yahwe turns again to his people and he restores the covenant and the *ḥesed* which it implies.

---

[1] N. GLUECK, *o.c.*, p. 13: "Ḥesed macht den eigentlichen Gegenstand einer berith aus und kann fast als ihr Inhalt bezeichnet werden. Die Möglichkeit des Entstehens und Bestehens eines Bundes beruhte auf dem Vorhandensein von *ḥsd*". Cf. W. EICHRODT, *Theologie des A.T.*, I, p. 150; A. R. JOHNSON, "Hesed and Hasîd", *Festschrift S. Mowinckel*, Oslo 1955, pp. 100-112.

[2] N. GLUEK, *o.c.*, p. 48: "Ḥesed ist die gemeinschaftsgemässe Treue, raḥamim die vergebende Liebe".

One more word about the background of the covenant idea, which is central in old testament theology.[1] In Israel the divine *ḥesed* is sealed with a covenant that Yahwe has concluded with his people on his own sovereign initiative. According to J. BEGRICH, this sovereign character belongs to the essence of a covenant. A *b^erît* originally was not bilateral. It meant a relationship between two unequal parties: a stronger partner granted the covenant to a weaker one (Jos. ix; 1 Sam. xi; 1 Kings xx 34). Only the stronger committed himself with the *b^erît*, while the recipient was passive.[2] BEGRICH unduly simplifies the evidence. As. R. KRAETSCHMAR had pointed out already, one should accept some variation of different types of treaty, and it is impossible to arrange them in a line of evolution.[3] This has been confirmed by the more recent studies on the subject.[4] The Ancient Near East had parity treaties and vassal treaties, the latter corresponding somewhat to BEGRICH's unilateral covenant. The form of the vassal treaty fits best the condition of a covenant between Yahwe and Israel or its king. But the Bible also knows other forms of covenant, such as the more ritual form practiced by the nomads and semi-nomads (cf. the account of the Sinai-covenant).[5]

Anyhow, BEGRICH's distinction between bilateral and unilateral covenant became irrelevant to the subject which occupies us. The vassal treaty stresses the vassal's duties, while reducing the great king's obligation mostly to the guarantee of the vassal's possession of the throne. And even though many a vassal treaty will have been forced upon a weaker king, the latter was juridically supposed to agree in some way. So the vassal treaty was not unilateral, in spite of the distinct roles of both sides. Deuteronomy also knows Yahwe's gracious initiative together with his fidelity to the covenant (*šōmēr habb^erît w^ehaḥesed*; Deut. vii 9, 12).[6] At the same time it stresses the

---

[1] Cf. P. VAN IMSCHOOT, art. "Verbond", BW³, col. 1453-1457; W. EICHRODT, *Theologie*, I, pp. 9-32: "Das Bundesverhältnis"; Š. PORÚBČAN, *Il Patto nuovo*, pp. 5-81; "Il Concetto del Patto (berît)"; V. HAMP, art. "Bund, I, Altes Testament", *LTK*. II, Freiburg i.B. 1958, col. 770-774.

[2] J. BEGRICH, "Berit", *ZAW*. LX 1944, pp. 2-3.

[3] R. KRAETSCHMAR, *Die Bundesvorstellung im A.T.*, Marburg 1894, pp. 29-30; 40.

[4] Cf. G. E. MENDENHALL, *Law and Covenant in Israel and the Ancient Near East*, Pittsburg 1955; K. BALTZER, *Das Bundesformular*, Neukirchen 1960; R. SMEND, *Die Bundesformel*, Zürich 1963; D. J. MCCARTHY, *Treaty and Covenant. A Study in Form in the Ancient Oriental Documents and in the Old Testament*, Rome 1963.

[5] D. J. MCCARTHY, *Treaty and Covenant*, p. 175.

[6] Cf. J. SCHARBERT, *Bib.* XXXVIII 1957, p. 135. The same formula occurs in Neh.

obligations and the privilege of Israel as the people of the covenant. It points out Israel's agreement as a partner (Deut. xxvi 16-19; Ex. xix 7). In the popular mind this went as far as the pretention of invoking the covenant against Yahwe's judgment. Jeremiah's and Ezekiel's reaction was directed against this attitude. They lay a stronger stress on the covenant as a decision of God's mere grace alone (Jer. xxxi 31-34; xxxii 38-42; Ez. xvi 59-63; xxxiv 25; xxxvii 26).[1] In Is. liv 10, Dt.-Is. is close to this view. God is the only initiator; there is no word of *quid pro quo*. Yahwe himself swears (*nišba'tî*) and what is involved is *his* covenant and *his* fidelity (suffixes of the first person). We may apply to this text the summary by T. C. Vriezen: "The covenant between God and the people has put both 'partners' not into a relation of treaty, but into a community of life, proceeding from Yahwe, in which Israel was completely commited to and dependent on him."[2]

The covenant is described as a *b^erît šālôm*. The genitive *šālôm* does not add a new meaning to *b^erît*; it is a *genitivus appositionis* or *epexegeticus*, defining the true content of the covenant. The expression occurs already in the treaty between Mursilis II and Niqmadu of Ugarit: *ri-kil-ta ša-la-ma*. When somebody concludes a covenant with a weaker partner, then he offers him *šālôm*.[3] In the Old Testament "peace" means welfare, material and spiritual prosperity of the individual as well as of the community (Ex. xviii 23; 1 Kings v 4-5). With this broad sense, peace is a gift from Yahwe, on account of his covenant.

And finally, what is involved here, is an eternal covenant. Already in vs. 8 the covenant is ascribed to a *ḥesed 'ôlām*. Also in vs. 9, its definitive nature is stressed by means of a comparison with the Noahite covenant. The simile in vs. 10 again confirms this firmness, for the mountains are a symbol of stability (Ps. xxxvi 7; Hab. iii 6). One may assert that the prophet has in view a *b^erît 'ôlām*, as expressly in lv 3. Does this mean a new, eschatological covenant? I

---

i 5; Dan. ix 4; 1 Kings viii 23; 2 Chron. vi 14. All of these instances seem to be dependent on Deut.

[1] Cf. P. Van Imschoot, *a.c.*, col. 1457; W. Eichrodt, *o.c.*, pp. 25-28.

[2] T. C. Vriezen, *Hoofdlijnen der Theologie van het Oude Testament*, Wageningen 1966, pp. 184-185.

[3] J. Begrich, *ZAW*. LX 1944, p. 2. Cf. P. Van Imschoot, *a.c.*, col. 1454; Š. Porúbčan, *o.c.*, p. 53; W. Zimmerli, *Ezechiel*, p. 845. Cf. *PRU*. IV, 17.340, line 14'.

refer to a paper in which I have already dealt with the question.[1] Eschatology probably includes the expectation of a new order but certainly involves a definitive one, otherwise the word "eschatology" becomes meaningless. The prophet does not explicitly state that the covenant is a new one, as against Jeremiah's clear affirmation in his pericope on the new covenant (Jer. xxxi 31-34). The interpreters too rashly speak of a new covenant in their comments on Is. liv 7-10.[2] One might point to the definitive nature of the *b^{e}rît ʿôlām*. But in this respect one should not overdo the impact of that formula. It occurs so frequently and in such varied contexts, that it must be considered a current expression.[3] *B^{e}rît ʿôlām* means a guaranteed covenant, in which God becomes seriously engaged. Whether it is eschatological must be inferred from each distinct context. As far as the covenant of lv 3 is concerned, I shall come back to the point below. We shall be able to see that the continuity with the past is stressed, rather than an eschatological reality. Is. liv 10 undoubtedly refers to Yahwe's lasting fidelity: his covenant is unshakable, because it is the expression of his divine, i.e. eternal *ḥesed*. Yahwe's salvific will is everlasting (cf. comments on li 6, 8). One should relate these texts to xl 27-28, a disputation in which Yahwe is called *'ĕlōhê ʿôlām*. The prophet does not intend to ascribe to Yahwe an abstract metaphysical quality. His attention is focused on the history of Israel and the nations. He wants to reply to the objection: "Yahwe can no longer save us" (vs. 27). In the word of salvation liv 7-10, he replies to the complaint: "Yahwe has forsaken us". As will appear from the disputations, the exile seemed to be a proof to the Israelites that Yahwe was without power or unfaithful. Now, behind the title *'ĕlōhê ʿôlām* is the idea of Yahwe's mastery of all temporality, his activeness in all conditions, in spite of the seeming defeat, his faithfulness to himself and his commitments.[4] Thus Yahwe is able to give a *b^{e}rît ʿôlām*, being himself an *'ĕlôhê ʿôlām*. And on the other hand, every covenant which he concludes, is a *b^{e}rît ʿôlām*.

---

[1] A. Schoors, "L'eschatologie dans les prophéties du Deutéro-Isaïe", *Recherches bibliques*, VIII, Bruges 1967, pp. 124-127.

[2] E.g. M. Haller, *Das Judentum*, p. 59; B. Duhm, *Das Buch Jesaia*, p. 371; K. Marti, *Jesaja*, p. 355.

[3] Cf. Gen. ix 16; xvii 7-8, 13; Ex. xxxi 16; Lev. xxiv 8; Num. xviii 19; xxv 13; 2 Sam. xxiii 5; Is. xxiv 5; lv 3; lxi 8; Jer. xxxii 40; l 5; Ez. xvi 60; xxxvii 26; Ps. cv 10 (= 1 Chron. xvi 17).

[4] E. Jenni, *Das Wort ʿôlām im Alten Testament*, Berlin 1953, pp. 68-69.

At the first sight, the point of Is. liv 7-10 consists in underlining that Yahwe is faithful to his *still existing* covenant. True, the verbs *mûš* and *mûṭ* are used to indicate the eschatological cataclysms (Is. xxiv 19-20), but they also occur in various other contexts. Their occurence here is no argument in favour of the eschatological interpretation. But the problem remains if the comparison with the Noahite covenant does not involve an eschatological perspective.

When consulting the account in Genesis, we should remember that two traditions are present in it. We find the J version of the end of the flood in Gen. viii 20-22 and P in Gen. ix 1-17. When comparing the present oracle to Gen. viii 20-22, we do not see any conformity, unless the general idea of no punishment any more. There is nothing about an oath or a covenant. On the contrary, Yahwe speaks to himself (vs. 21: *'el-libbô*). But there is an unquestionable connection with P. God concludes a covenant (Gen. ix 9), which is a valuable parallel to the oath in Is. liv 9, for the conclusion of a covenant involves an oath (Gen. xxxi 44-53; Deut. iv 31; viii 18; xxix 11-12; Jos. ix 15; 2 Sam. xxi 7).[1] Further, the prophet uses the word *'ereṣ* just as P does (vs. 11) in opposition with *'ădāmâ* in J (Gen. viii 21). Finally P considers the Noahite covenant as a *b^{e}rît 'ôlām*, just like Dt.-Is. in lv 3 and *quoad sensum* in liv 10. The reference to J by DUHM and MARTI is completely out of place.[2] It rests upon a wrong application of the widely accepted theory that J is the oldest tradition, whereas P would be post-exilic. One should avoid using such dates too mechanically. Although P may have been finished only in the 5th century, it went, however, through a long history of formation, including the exile [3] and probably already began before the exile.[4] It is quite possible that Dt.-Is. quotes the tradition about Noah in a protosacerdotal version.

In the article already mentioned, I wrote that the comparison with the Noahite covenant involves the announcement of a stable salvific order without punitive justice. Such would give a certain eschatological impact to the covenant the prophet has in view, the

---

[1] Cf. J. PEDERSEN, *Der Eid bei den Semiten*, Strassburg 1914, pp. 21-51; D. J. Mc CARTHY, *o.c.*, pp. 47 and 125.

[2] B. DUHM, *l.c.*, "Wieder eine Frucht aus der Lecture des Jahvisten (Gen. 8. 20-22)". — K. MARTI, *l.c.*

[3] Cf. J. DE FRAINE, *Genesis*, Roermond 1963, p. 13: between 570 and 445; O. EISSFELDT, *Einleitung*, pp. 275-276; *La Sainte Bible* (*BJ*), p. 5.

[4] T. C. VRIEZEN, *De Literatuur van Oud-Israël*, Den Haag 1961, p. 99.

more so as the comparison includes a reference to the *Urzeit* and a universalist perspective.[1] This interpretation, while being possible, is not at all certain. *In recto*, the comparison only bears upon vs. 9c: *'ăšer* (ev. *ka'ăšer*) ... *kēn*. DUHM paraphrases the comparison very well: "Just like Yahwe swore after the flood, that there would be no more flood, so he now swears that he will not punish Israel again with exile". Such is the obvious sense of the comparison. When Dt.-Is. uses *qṣp* and *g'r*, he always means Yahwe's anger, which found concrete expression in the exile (cf. xlvii 6; liv 8; li 20). The comparison does not view a complete similarity. The situation is similar but not the same: the flood was a universal cataclysm, whereas the exile was not. That is why we should not overstress the comparison.

In vs. 10 a comparison appears between Yahwe's *berît* / *ḥesed* and the mountains. This does not belong to the comparison with the Noahite covenant. One will look in vain for a parallel to vs. 10 in the account of the flood.

Summarizing, we may paraphrase vss. 9-10 as follows: "The condition resembles the one in Noah's time. Just as I swore then, that I would not again send the flood, so I swear now, not to punish you again with exile. As a guarantee I recall to you my covenantal faithfulness, which is more unshakable than mountains and hills". The eschatological intention of such an assertion is not evident.[2]

9. *Is. liv 11-17*

11 "O afflicted one, storm-tossed, and not comforted,
behold, I set your stones in antimony,
and your foundations in sapphires.
12 I make your pinnacles of rubies,
your gates of carbuncles
and all your walls of precious stones.
13 All your sons shall be instructed by Yahwe,
and great shall be the prosperity of your sons,
14 in salvation you shall be established.
You shall be far from oppression,
for you need have nothing to fear,

---

[1] A. SCHOORS, *a.c.*, p. 127. A mistake escaped the vigilance of the corrector; read "sanction punitive" instead of "sanction primitive".

[2] Cf. the cautious statement by J. L. McKENZIE, *Second Isaiah*, p. 140: "But the vision of the prophet here approaches the eschatological".

and from terror, for it should not come near you.
15 If any one attacks, it is not *from me*,[a]
whoever attacks you, shall fall because of you.
16 Behold, I have created the smith
who blows the fire of coals,
and produces a weapon for its purpose;
and I have created the destroyer for ruin.
17 No weapon fashioned against you, shall prosper,
and you shall prove guilty
every tongue that rises against you in judgment.
This is the portion of the servants of Yahwe,
and their salvation from me", —
oracle of Yahwe.

[a] Lg מֵאִתִּי c IQIa and LXX: δι' ἐμοῦ..

The last two words of salvation in Dt.-Is. (liv 11-17; lv 1-5) offer some difficulties, as to the structure of the genre. The delimitation of the former pericope is generally accepted. BEGRICH and VON WALDOW classify the pericope with the oracles of salvation. But the structural elements are hard to distinguish, since the oracle opens immediately with a very concrete description.[1] In its content, the pericope certainly is a proclamation of salvation. Moreover, we shall recognize the structure of that genre, though somewhat obscured.

The address reminds one of a lament (vs. 11a). Zion is addressed as afflicted (*'ăniyyâ*) as in li 21. It is well known that the suppliant is often styled as *'ānî* (Pss. x 2; xxii 22; xxxv 10; xl 18; lxix 35; lxxvi 1; lxxxviii 16). Furthermore *sō'ărâ lō' nuḥāmâ* points to a condition of distress.

In vs. 11b, the prophet passes to the turning of Yahwe (motif II, 1). The particle *hinnēh* and the participle *marbîṣ* underline the actuality of Yahwe's intervention. The following perfect tenses thus are *perfecta executionis*. But the wording of the motif is so concrete, that these verses could be reckoned with the motif of outcome. That is what I meant by an obscured structure. For the first time in the Bible the image of the splendid city appears, which will be adopted later in Tob. xiii 16-17 and Apoc. xxi 18-21.[2] In the text there is no ground

---

[1] J. BEGRICH, *Studien*, p. 13; H. E. VON WALDOW, *Anlass und Hintergrund*, pp. 22-23.

[2] There is some discussion about the meaning of פוך in vs. 11. It is often understood as a black powder, with which women coloured their eyelids in order to bring out their

to suppose that the prophet would have imagined Jerusalem as a great royal castle and not as a city.[1] It is evident that Yahwe announces a glorious restoration of Zion. It is not certain that the description of the splendour involves a further design. According to F. STUMMER, these verses are reminiscent of the Babylonian building inscriptions, where it is written that the king has had constructed a palace or a temple with precious stones. We have here, as STUMMER points out, not only *lapides pretiosi* but *gemmae*. With this the prophet would mean that Jerusalem will surpass Babylon in glory.[2] A perspective of this kind is possible and fits in with the whole of the dt.-Isaian message, especially of his trial speeches, where Yahwe's superiority to the Babylonian gods is continually at stake.

WESTERMANN supposes that the description presents Jerusalem as the city of God, radiating God's majesty in its splendour.[3] The intent certainly reaches further than a purely material restoration, but it is questionable whether it reaches as far as WESTERMANN supposes. In favour of his thesis, one may invoke vs. 13a, at least when reading *bōnayik* instead of *bānayik*: "Your builders are taught by Yahwe". This reading is proposed by MARTI, DUHM and WESTERMANN. It fits logically in the context and so one avoids a repetition of *bānayik*. The phrase would mean that the builders learn directly from Yahwe the plan of the city which is to be rebuilt, as Moses in the desert received the plans of the tabernacle directly from God (Ex. xxv 9, 40; xxvi 30; xvii 8; Num. viii 4), or as Bezalel was filled by Yahwe with his spirit to make the tabernacle and the cult objects (Ex. xxxi 3). The reading *bōnayik*, however, has no support whatever in the textual tradition.[4] Moreover, the masoretic reading also matches the context very well. It brings out more clearly the spiritual nature of

---

eyes (2 Kings ix 30); cf. already S. JEROME, *ad loc.*: "in stibio, in similitudinem comptae mulieris, quae oculos pingit stibio, ut pulchritudinem significet civitatis". The splendour of the stones, set in פוך, antimony, is brought out more nicely (so also DELITZSCH, KNABENBAUER, VAN HOONACKER). According to B. DUHM, *o.c.*, p. 371 and F. FELDMANN, *Das Buch Isaias*, II, p. 178, the word should be explained with 1 Chron. xxix 2, where the expression אבני־פוך, LXX: λίθους πολυτελεῖς, occurs, which would mean splendidly shining stones.

[1] Against K. MARTI, *o.c.*, p. 355 and B. DUHM, *o.c.*, p. 372.

[2] F. STUMMER, "Einige keilschriftliche Parallelen zu Jes 40-66", *JBL.* XLV 1926, pp. 188-189.

[3] C. WESTERMANN, *o.c.*, p. 224.

[4] LXX: υἱούς; Targ: בנך; Vg: filios; Pesh: ܒܢ̈ܝܟܝ. Strangely enough, IQIa suggests for בניך² the reading בוניכי with a superscript *waw*.

the restoration. The city is rebuilt in splendour and its inhabitants are disciples of Yahwe.

The expression "disciples of Yahwe" is *hapax*, but in its meaning it joins Jer. xxxi 34: "They will no longer teach (*y^elamm^edû*) each other, saying: 'Know Yahwe', for they shall all know me". In the context it is said that Yahwe himself will write his *tôrâ*, his instruction in their heart. We find a similar line of thought in Jer. xxiv 7 and Ez. xxxvi 26-27. If Dt.-Is. has in mind these texts, one may ask whether he makes his the whole theology of the new covenant. This is not proven. The first mentioned text from Jer. suggests that this prophet announces a recognition of Yahwe by fulfilling his law. When Yahwe puts his law in the heart, this not only leads to knowing it but also to living it.[1] The Hebrew *yd'* always means an active and vital knowledge.

According to BEGRICH, a new oracle of salvation begins in vs. 14. However, it is impossible to see in vss. 14a + 13a + 14b-17 the structure of a salvation oracle, nor the structure of the proclamation of salvation in WESTERMANN's system. Yet the latter too supposes that a new unit opens with vs. 14, which he further defines as a *Segenszusage* (14a, 13b, 14b-17). Originally this is a cultic type, which can be found in Pss. xci; cxxi and Job v 17-26. The difference between the promise of blessing and the word of salvation is this: "The latter is God's answer to a lament, and it promises the removal of the suffering there lamented. The former, on the other hand, promises God's constant presence, help, protection and blessing".[2] As a matter of fact, the pericope can be a distinct promise of blessing. The inclusion with *ṣ^edāqâ* points in that direction: a general promise of *ṣ^edāqâ* at the beginning (vs. 14a), a concrete elaboration in the following verses, and a conclusion which refers to the introduction: "This is the *ṣ^edāqâ*, which my servants receive from me" (vs. 17b). The similarity of the texts, alleged by WESTERMANN, is unquestionable. We may complete his argumentation with the following considerations.

The themes of safety from oppression and protection against the enemy belong among the topics of a promise of blessing (Pss. xli 3-4; xci 5-11; cxxi 7-8; cxxvii 5; Ps. Sal. vi 2).[3] It is quite normal also

---

[1] B. N. WAMBACQ, *Jeremias*, Roermond 1957, p. 208; W. RUDOLPH, *Jeremia*, Tübingen 1958, pp. 184-195; J. COPPENS, "La nouvelle alliance en Jer 31, 31-34", *CBQ*. XXV 1963, pp. 17-19.

[2] C. WESTERMANN, *l.c.*, quoted from the English edition, pp. 278-279.

[3] H. GUNKEL - J. BEGRICH, *Einleitung*, p. 301; S. MOWINCKEL, *Psalmenstudien. V. Segen und Fluch in Israels Kult und Psalmdichtung*, Kristiania 1924, p. 131.

that the content of a promise of blessing is summarized in the word *šālôm* (vs. 13b). In Ps. xxix 11, the formula of blessing is: "May Yahwe bless his people with peace" (cf. Ps. cxxii 6-9). To me the imperative *raḥăqî* (vs. 14b) is decisive. In the context of liv 11-17, whether or not considered as a word of salvation, this form seems strange. Therefore, it is sometimes suggested that it be emended to an imperfect tense.[1] But the imperative is a usual form in the promise of blessing, and only in the framework of the genre, can it be understood (cf. Gen. i 28; xii 2; xxiv 60; Ps. cxxviii 5-6).[2] Thus WESTERMANN has seen correctly, and it surprises me that GUNKEL and MOWINCKEL did not cite Is. liv 13b-17 in their fine expositions of the promise of blessing.

The question is whether or not the prophet has absorbed the promise of blessing into a larger whole, that would be a word of salvation (vss. 11-17). One cannot be certain. As a matter of fact the transition from 13a to 13b is fluent, and would point in that direction. The promise of blessing on its own, without introduction, would start rather abruptly. Moreover, the form of the promise of blessing is not absolutely pure, since vs. 16 is a kind of substantiation, which is out of place in that genre but current in the dt.-Isaian oracles and proclamations of salvation. There is thus a good presumption in favour of the original unity of liv 11-17, where the prophet would have combined a promise of blessing with a proclamation of salvation.

The shift of vss. 13b and 14a, as proposed by WESTERMANN, is superfluous. It is certain that both stichs belong together, so that the masoretic punctuation should be emended, as proposed in *BHS*. In vs. 14a, the image of the city still seems to be present in *tikkônānî*, but from *ṣ^edāqâ* it appears that not only the material city is meant. Put in parallelism with *šālôm*, the word *ṣ^edāqâ* will have a meaning, that comes close to that parallel term. In the comments on xli 10, we have seen that *ṣedeq* / *ṣ^edāqâ* there meant something like the divine salvific will. In the present verse the same meaning is acceptable: "The peace of your sons shall be great, (for) you shall be established

---

[1] E.g. in *BHS*.

[2] H. GUNKEL - J. BEGRICH, *o.c.*, p. 295; S. MOWINCKEL, *o.c.*, pp. 30; 56; cf. GK § 110 c. D. N. FREEDMAN in J. L. MCKENZIE, *Second Isaiah*, p. 138, suggests the reading רחקי, an absolute infinitive in *i*. This form, known from the Amarna letters, has no parallel in Dt.-Is. and an absolute infinitive in the present context would have exactly the same meaning as an imperative has. It must be admitted that an absolute infinitive, continuing a finite verb, would render the phrase somewhat smoother.

in my salvific will". However, the concrete import of the word seems to be more objective. In some instances in Dt.-Is., *ṣᵉdāqâ* means the realized salvation, parallel with *yᵉšû'â* in xlvi 13; li 5, and still more clearly in xlviii 18, where also *šālôm* is the parallel word.[1] The same meaning is present in vs. 17. The interpretation of *ṣᵉdāqâ* as moral loyalty to the covenant [2] is unacceptable, for it has no support in the context and it is rather contradicted by *mē'ittî*, "from me", in vs. 17. Here the *ṣᵉdāqâ* is a gift from Yahwe. Within the framework of a promise of blessing the word surely means the same as *šālôm*,[3] and the prophet has kept that meaning in his proclamation of salvation.

Salvation involves protection against the enemies (vss. 15-17a). Yahwe can assure this too, since he is the creator of the enemy. The objection that vs. 15 disturbs the context is without any foundation.[4] The verse is not easy to translate. J. KNABENBAUER reads it as a programme of proselytism: "En habitando habitabit (qui) non est mecum; advena quondam tuus adiungetur tibi". He invokes the Vulgate, Septuagint, Peshitta and Targum.[5] Others translate *gûr* as "to fight, to attack"[6] or "to assemble against",[7] or they substitute *gôy* for *gôr* and translate: "When a nation attacks ...".[8] C. C. TORREY

---

[1] Cf. P. VOLZ, *o.c.*, p. 16; F. FELDMANN, *o.c.*, p. 181; ad vs. 17: "... der ihnen von Gott zustehende Anteil am Heil, dass den Zustand äusseren und innern Glückes bezeichnet". — Cf. K. MARTI, *o.c.*, p. 356; B. DUHM, *l.c.*; T. K. CHEYNE, *The Prophecies of Isaiah*, II, p. 58.

[2] So T. K. CHEYNE, *o.c.*, p. 57 and perhaps Š. PORÚBČAN, *o.c.*, p. 169.

[3] Cf. S. MOWINCKEL, *Psalmenstudien*, V, p. 118.

[4] Against K. MARTI, *l.c.*; B. DUHM, *o.c.*, p. 373; A. CONDAMIN, *Le livre d'Isaïe*, p. 347; with F. FELDMANN, *o.c.*, p. 180.

[5] Cf. K. KNABENBAUER, *o.c.*, p. 349; Vg: Ecce accola veniet qui non erat mecum, advena quondam tuus adiungetur tibi; LXX: *ἰδοὺ προσήλυτοι προσελεύσονταί σοι δι' ἐμοῦ καὶ ἐπὶ σὲ καταφεύξονται*; Pesh: ܘܟܠ ܕܡܬܦܢܝܢ ܡܢ ܠܘܬܝ̈ ܢܣܩܘܢ ܠܟܝ. ܘܬܗܘܝܢ ܒܝܬ ܓܘܣܐ ܠܥܡܘܪܝܟܝ, "and all who are away from me will go up to you. And you will be a refuge for your inhabitants"; the Targ. supports this interpretation only partly, and partly mine: הא אתכנשא יתכנשון ליך גלות עמיך לסופא מלכי עממיא דמתכנשין לאעקא ליך ירושלם בגויך יתרמון, "Behold, the exiles of thy people shall be gathered together unto thee at the last; the kings of the peoples that gather together to oppress thee, O Jerusalem, shall be cast down in thy midst" (transl. J. F. STENNING, *The Targum of Isaiah*, p. 184).

[6] B. DUHM, *l.c.*; A. CONDAMIN, *l.c.*; F. FELDMANN, *l.c.*; A. VAN HOONACKER, *o.c.*, pp. 262-263; L. KÖHLER, *Deuterojesaja*, p. 54; P. VOLZ, *o.c.*, p. 135.

[7] F. DELITZSCH, *l.c.*; SIEGFRIED-STADE, p. 119.

[8] J. FISCHER, *Das Buch Isaias*, II, p. 144.

and U. E. SIMON translate *gûr* in the first colon as "to combat" and in the second one as "to dwell".[1] J. BACHMANN thinks the pronoun *mî* is interrogative and moreover, he reads *'apsām 'ittî*, which he translates as: "so ist ihr Ende in meiner Hand".[2] J. STEINMANN explains *'ālayik* as "because of you".[3] The translation of the *RSV* is well defended philologically and it also fits best in the present context:

If any one stirs up strife, it is not from me;
whoever stirs up strife with you shall fall because of you.

Here one regards *hēn* as a conditional particle, *mî* as an indefinite relative pronoun (cf. Is. l 10), one reads *mē'ittî* instead of *mē'ôtî*, and one translates *gûr* as "to attack".[4]

The oracle concludes, not with a motif III, but with a proverb of wisdom, that has its parallels in the proverbs in which the pious or the wicked are typified (Job xviii 21; xx 29; xxvii 13). Because of this, MARTI and DUHM want to drop verse 17b.[5] However, its presence here is fully justified. The verse, its *Ausleitungformel* included, rhythmically matches the whole oracle. I have already mentioned the inclusion with *ṣ^e^dāqâ*. Furthermore, sapiential instruction and promise of blessing go together, in the sense that the poet of wisdom uses promises of blessing when typifying the happiness of the pious.[6] We have something of this kind in our text. The promise of blessing liv 13b-17 ends with a sapiential proverb. This way, vss. 13b-17 as a whole receive a sapiential character. This fact, together with the retention of the imperative *raḥăqî* (vs. 14) make certain that Dt.-Is. has adopted an existing sapiential promise of blessing in his proclamation of salvation. In the original promise of blessing the pious were meant by "servants of Yahwe". In the salvation word the expression indicates more precisely the Israelites, children of Zion (vs. 13).

In summary, Is. liv 11-17, with its varying imagery and its unusual structure, makes a balanced oracle with regard to the content. We

---

[1] U. E. SIMON, *A Theology of Salvation*, p. 230; C. C. TORREY, *The Second Isaiah*, p. 425.

[2] J. BACHMANN, *Präparation und Kommentar zum Deutero-Jesaja*, p. 123, note 1.

[3] J. STEINMANN, *Le livre de la consolation*, p. 179.

[4] Cf. JOÜON, § 167 k; GK § 137 c; as to גור, cf. גרה and Arab. *ǧâra 'al*; same meaning in Ps. lix 4; KB, p. 176; ZORELL, p. 147; G. R. DRIVER, "Studies to the Vocabulary of the O.T. IV", *JTS*. XXXIII 1931, pp. 38-47. Remark that all translations that do not hold with גור = to dwell, differ from *RSV* only in minor details.

[5] K. MARTI, *o.c.*, p. 357; B. DUHM, *o.c.*, p. 374.

[6] Pss. i 1-3, xxxii 1-2; xxxiv 9; xci; xciv 12; cxii; Prov. iii 13-18; viii 32-36; etc. Cf. H. GUNKEL - J. BEGRICH, *Einleitung*, p. 392.

can distinguish these components of salvation: splendid restoration of Zion (vss. 11-12), great prosperity, in which the sons of Zion are instructed directly by Yahwe (vss. 13-14), unshakableness in face of the enemy (vss. 15-17). In this last element, vs. 16 acts as a motivation: Yahwe, by his creative power, also dominates the enemy and his weapons.

10. *Is. lv 1-5*

1 Ho, every one who thirsts, come to the waters;
and you who have no money, come,
buy and eat *without money*,[a]
and without paying, wine and milk!
2 Why do you spend money for that which is not bread,
and the wages of your labor for that which does not satisfy?
Listen carefully to me, and eat what is good,
and let your desire regale itself with fatness.
3 Incline your ear and come to me,
listen and you will live.
I will make with you an everlasting covenant,
my steadfast loyalty to David.
4 Behold, I made him a witness for the peoples,
a leader and commander of nations.
5 Behold, you shall call a nation that you know not,
a nation that knew you not shall run to you,
because of Yahwe, your God,
and the Holy One of Israel, for he glorifies you.

[a] Del ולכו ושברו c IQIa, LXX and Pesh.

In Is. lv 1-5, the structural problem is in the introduction. According to WESTERMANN's structural scheme, we may call the pericope a proclamation of salvation, of which motif I has been enlarged into a long introduction. If there is an allusion to the lament, it would be in the one word *ṣāmē'*, with which elsewhere in Dt.-Is., the condition of distress is indicated (Is. xli 17; xliv 3). Some need is certainly expressed in vs. 1a. How can we further typify this introduction?

According to BEGRICH, vss. 1-3a are formally an invitation on the part of Wisdom to be guests at her table.[1] Just as in Sir. xxiv

[1] G. R. DRIVER, *JTS.* XXXVI 1935, p. 404, made the interesting proposal to translate כסף in vs. 1a as "food", because of the parallelism and on the ground of Akk. *kispu* (ev. *kusāpu*), "food, meal".

19-22, there is a transition from the image of the table to the reality meant: "Listen to me..." As in Prov. ix 11, this invitation culminates in a promise of life. In its content, the text has no connection with the doctrine of wisdom. From vss. 3b-5 it appears that Yahwe himself is actually speaking. BEGRICH does not clarify why the prophet would have used a sapiential genre.[1] H. E. VON WALDOW prefers to consider the verses as an imitation of the cries of watersellers and other street-vendors, since the invitation is not to a table but to a bargain. That the prophet opens his oracle with such a cry would be due to the situation, viz. the crisis of belief in Yahwe, which is also the background of the disputations. WESTERMANN offers the same form-critical approach, without referring to VON WALDOW.[2] Both interpretations can be defended. However, it is more important to know what the prophet means with his cry.

The summonses are certainly to be taken metaphorically, since image and reality are put together: "Eat ... listen". J. FISCHER supposes the invitation is directed to those who hunger and thirst for spiritual or divine things (Prov. ix 5-6).[3] According to a theme of the psalms of lament (*ṣāmē' lē'lōhîm*), one would rather think of those who thirst for God himself (cf. Pss. xlii 3; lxii 2). It is clear that vs. 2 puts the word and gift of Yahwe over against something that, in the eyes of the prophet, is unreal and worthless. In FELDMANN'S opinion, the prophet has in mind the efforts to acquire terrestrial prosperity in Babylon.[4] This comment is correct in as much as the desire to stay quietly in Babylon, rather than to undertake the journey to the homeland, revealed a lack of confidence in Yahwe. But, since the prophet so often in the *rîb*-pericopes stresses the vanity of the pagan gods (xl 18-20, 25-26; xli 6-7; xliii 9-10; xlvi 5-9; xlviii 5; cf. next chapter), the chief idea here will be: Yahwe is the only one who can offer everlasting salvation, which the promise of salvation proper (vss. 3-5) will announce. What the idols have to offer is as worthless and nonexistent as themselves. Rather than an opposition between worldly and eternal goods, as VOLZ supposes, there is an opposition between Babylonian gods and Yahwe.[5] The gods are

---

[1] J. BEGRICH, *o.c.*, pp. 59-60.

[2] H. E. VON WALDOW, *o.c.*, pp. 22 and 153; C. WESTERMANN, *Jesaja 40-66*, p. 227.

[3] J. FISCHER, *o.c.*, p. 145.

[4] F. FELDMANN, *Das Buch Isaias*, II, p. 183; J. FISCHER, *o.c.*, p. 146.

[5] P. VOLZ, *Jesaia II*, p. 138.

capable of nothing, but when one goes to Yahwe and listens to him, then one has true life. "Therefore, listen to what I have to say you ..."

In the motif II, 1 (vs. 3b), Yahwe promises he will conclude an eternal covenant with the Israelites. This covenant is immediately explained as the "steadfast graces to David". The plural *ḥasdê* involves a reference to the different manifestations of Yahwe's covenantal loyalty. According to B. DUHM and C. C. TORREY, this text must be interpreted in a messianic sense, as a promise of restoration of the Davidic dynasty.[1] But this is justly contested by P. VOLZ and J. MUILENBURG.[2] The stress is upon a lasting covenant with the Israelites (plural), as promised in liv 10. According to the song of victory Is. lii 7-10, Yahwe himself reigns in Zion. Furthermore, the restoration of the dynasty is not foretold in any salvation word of Dt.-Is. On the contrary, the prophet applies the title "Yahwe's anointed" to Cyrus (xlv 1) and he uses the word "king" only to indicate foreign kings (xli 2; xlv 1; xlix 9, 23; lii 15) or Yahwe himself (xli 21; xliii 15; lii 7). Verse 3bβ thus means that the promise, made to David, now applies to the people: the lasting covenant with Israel is the continuation of it.[3] This had already been suggested by K. BUDDE.[4] Perhaps one may here suppose an objection by the auditors who allege the fall of David's house. Or better, one may imagine as *Sitz im Leben* a preceding complaint in the sense of Ps. lxxxix 39-52 or Lam. iv 20.

One cannot invoke the terminological contact with 2 Sam. vii 8-16 (*nāgîd*, *'ad-'ôlām*, *ḥasdê*, *ne'ěmān*) to support the messianic interpretation. It is to be expected that, in order to apply the davidic promises to the people, the prophet cites the tradition about these promises (2 Sam. vii 8-16; Ps. lxxxix 25-30; 2 Chron. vi 42). The approach of Ps. lxxxix, for example, and Is. lv 1-5, to the davidic covenant is completely different, as O. EISSFELDT has shown conclusively: the psalmist prays for restoration of the dynasty, whereas

---

[1] B. DUHM, *o.c.*, pp. 375-376; C. C. TORREY, *o.c.*, pp. 142 and 427.

[2] P. VOLZ, *o.c.*, p. 139; J. MUILENBURG, *The Book of Isaiah. Chapters 40-66*, New York 1956, pp. 644-646.

[3] J. BEGRICH, *Studien*, p. 92; P. VOLZ, *l.c.*; G. VON RAD, *Theologie des A.T.*, II, München 1965, p. 254; C. WESTERMANN, *o.c.*, p. 228; A. SCHOORS, *Recherches bibliques*, VIII, Bruges 1967, p. 125.

[4] K. BUDDE, "Das Buch Jesaja. Kp. 40-66", in E. KAUTZSCH, *Die heilige Schrift des A.T.*, I, Tübingen 1922, p. 645: "Was David zugesagt war, bleibt fest bestehen und soll an Israel seine Erfüllung finden".

the prophet announces the continuation of the covenant under a new form.[1]

In verse 4, it is further explicated in what consist the *ḥasdê dāwid*: "witness to the nations, leader for the nations". In *n^e^tattîw*, the suffix refers to David. It should not be emended to *n^e^tattîkā*, since the masoretic reading is too well attested (against AUVRAY-STEINMANN). As a matter of fact, the verse does not belong to the motif II, 2, which comprises only vs. 5a, but it is a transition to it. In the motif of turning in favour, Yahwe says: "I transfer the davidic covenant to you, Israel". This covenant implied a mission (vs. 4). Now Israel will accomplish that mission (vs. 5a; motif II,2). With the repeated particle *hēn*, the two verses are put together as past and present. Here, the shift of tense (*n^e^tattîw* ... *tiqrā'*) should be given its full weight.

Which mission is meant? David was a leader and commander of the peoples. This is a reminiscence of his conquests in the style of Ps. xvii 44: "Thou didst make me the head of the nations; people which I had not known served me". The literary contact with Is. lv 4-5a is obvious. But the prophet also calls David a "witness". He surely does not restrict his mission to a political domination. With WESTERMANN we must understand the connection in the text as follows: with his victories, David bore witness to the might of his God. According to F. DELITZSCH, David's witness consisted in composing the psalms and in his religious activity in general.[2] WESTERMANN's proposal is much better.

Now the whole people is entrusted with David's mission (vs. 5a). In his disputations also the prophet sometimes appeals to the mission of witness (xliii 10; xliv 8) and there too it has something to do with demonstrating Yahwe's might and superiority. Israel will call an unknown nation. This *qr'* expresses Israel's authority as a master of foreign nations. "The renewed people will be, instead of a slave of foreign rulers, a strong, commanding people, respected by everyone, like Israel in David's time".[3]

The oracle is concluded with a theocentric motif of goal *in forma* (*l^e^ma'an*; vs. 5b), however without using a formula of recognition:

---

[1] O. EISSFELDT, "The Promises of Grace to David in Is. 55, 1-5", *Festschrift J. Muilenburg*, New York 1962, pp. 196-207.

[2] C. WESTERMANN, *o.c.*, p. 229; F. DELITZSCH, *Commentar*, p. 570.

[3] P. A. H. DE BOER, *Second-Isaiah's Message*, p. 56; cf. B. DUHM, *o.c.*, p. 376.

all this happens because of Yahwe. After verse 5a, which induces many interpreters to universalist comments, the exclusive relationship between Yahwe and Israel is stressed with the titles "your God" and "the Holy One of Israel", and with the last word *pē'ărāk*: God glorifies you! It is striking that the relationship between Yahwe and Israel has a different nuance in xlix 7 and lv 5. In the first-mentioned verse, the prophet refers to the election (*bḥr*), to which Yahwe is faithful (*ne'ĕmān*). Also lv 5 is reminiscent of it with God's titles, yet the verb is not *bḥr* but *p'r*, "to glorify". The first motif is more properly theological; in the other, the prophet gives more attention to Israel's glorious position in the coming salvation.

Is the oracle eschatological? As in liv 10, the eternal character of the covenant implies an opening to eschatological explicitation. Yet, in my opinion, the point of the oracle is Yahwe's steadfast fidelity, as in liv 7-10. Yahwe's covenant is unshakable, as it is the expression of his divine (i.e. eternal) *ḥesed*. Likewise, verse lv 3 makes clear that the everlasting covenant, which Yahwe offers his people, is the continuation of the promises to David. Yahwe's covenant with David did not exclude defection and punishment, it even foresaw them (2 Sam. vii 15; Ps. lxxxix 31-34). In lv 1-5, the same is neither said nor denied about the covenant. Nowhere in the oracle is it asserted or suggested that the eschaton is near.[1]

11. *Is. xlvi 12-13*

12 Hearken to me, you, stubborn of heart,
you who are far from deliverance.
13 I bring near my deliverance, it is not far off,
and my salvation will not tarry;
I will manifest salvation in Zion
and my glory in Israel.

The pericope Is. xlvi 12-13 is a very short proclamation of salvation, which I deal with only at the end of the list, because of its uncommonly compact form. In vs. 13, Yahwe announces that he will give salvation (*t^ešû'â*) in Zion and his glory (*tip'eret*) to Israel.

---

[1] Cf. A. Schoors, *a.c.*, p. 126. In accordance with his predilection for uncommon and fanciful hypotheses, J. Morgenstern supposes the whole oracle refers to Zorobabel and should be dated in 520; cf. J. Morgenstern, "Two Prophecies from 520-516 B.C.", *HUCA*. XXII 1949, pp. 368-383.

The content points to a word of salvation. The delimitation of the literary unit is not easy, as appears from the variety of propositions on this point. But vss. 12-13 can be treated as one unit. Not only is vs. 11b formally a good conclusion and vs. 12 a good beginning of an oracle (cf. xlii 18; xlvi 3; xlviii 1; xlix 1; li 1), but moreover, two genres must be distinguished here. Whereas vss. 5-11 consitute a *Disputationswort* (cf. next chapter), we have a proclamation of salvation in 12-13. This has been accepted by BEGRICH, VON WALDOW and FOHRER, and finally also by WESTERMANN, who, however, puts these verses in the framework of chapter xlvi.[1] I shall return to this question after the analysis of vss. 5-11. Let us remark also that ELLIGER did not prove convincingly that both verses are inauthentic.[2]

In the address, the prophet says something about the condition of his hearers. The MT reads "stubborn of heart", as do Targum, Vulgate and Peshitta; the LXX however has "dejected in heart" (*'ōbᵉdê lēb*).[3] As the second colon expresses the absence of Yahwe's *ṣᵉdāqâ*, one could be inclined to prefer the LXX reading (MARTI, DUHM). But the question is what *ṣᵉdāqâ* exactly means here. The word occurs also in vs. 13 in parallelism with *tᵉšû'â*, where at the same time it is said that Yahwe brings his "righteousness" near, clearly in opposition to its being far in vs. 12. Thus righteousness is certainly not a moral quality which the hearers lack (subjective righteousness). According to the parallelism, it rather has something to do with salvation. The same parallelism, with *yᵉšû'â* however, we find in Is. li 6 (cf. liv 14; Pss. xxiv 5; lxix 28; xcviii 2; Prov. viii 18; Job xxxiii 26). The word *ṣedeq* also occurs in Dt.-Is. and elsewhere in parallelism with *yᵉšû'â*, resp. *yēša'* (Is. xlv 8; li 5; Ps. xl 10-11; cf. Is. xli 2, 10; xlii 6; xlv 13; lviii 2; Pss. lxv 6; lxxxv 11).[4] In xlvi 13, salvation and righteousness are regarded as emanating from Yahwe: this appears from the suffix of the first person and from the verb forms *qērabtî*

[1] J. BEGRICH, *Studien*, p. 14; H. E. VON WALDOW, *Anlass und Hintergrund*, p. 28; G. FOHRER, *Jesaja III*, p. 103; C. WESTERMANN, *Jesaja 40-66*, p. 149.

[2] K. ELLIGER, *Deuterojesaja*, pp. 183-185.

[3] Targ: תקיפי לבא; Vg: duro corde; Pesh: ܥܫܝܢܝ ܠܒܐ; LXX: *οἱ ἀπολωλεκότες τήν καρδίαν.*

[4] Cf. GB, pp. 674-675; KB, pp. 794-795; C. C. TORREY, *The Second Isaiah*, p. 367, translates צדקה[1] as "righteousness", and צדקה[2] as "triumph". Also J. STEINMANN, *Le livre de la consolation*, p. 143, translates "victoire" and paraphrases: "Le prophète annonce que la conquête militaire n'est que le prodrome d'une autre victoire religieuse, le salut de Sion".

and *nātattî*. Seen in this light, *ṣ^edāqâ* must coincide with salvation, in as much as it is an expression of Yahwe's justice, his loyalty or salvific will.[1] The frequent parallelism with the root *yš'* and in xlviii 18 even with *šālôm* warrants such a conclusion. MOWINCKEL has expounded very well how in Israelite thought salvation and justice are connected and even coincide. Dt.-Is., as the Norwegian scholar points out, has emphatically and repeatedly set forth this connection, but it was known before him. He does not prove the last point, but we find the idea in Deut. xxxii 4, 35-36; Hos. ii 21; Mic. vii 9, and more clearly in some psalms: lxv 6; lxxi 15-16; xcviii 2-3.[2]

Because of the opposition to vs. 12, we must say that the salvation, which God brings near, is a salvation for the Israelites.[3] In vs. 13b, salvation is defined as *tip'eret*. Is. xliv 23 offers an interesting parallel. This small hymn summons Nature to joy. The reason for this is the redemption of Jacob (*g'l*) and the manifestation of Yahwe's glory. Although *g'l* (xliv 23) and *yš'* have not necessarily the same meaning, they may indicate the same reality. The term *g'l* I have explained already above.[4] According to Jer. xxx 10 and Zech. viii 7, *yš'* may also refer to the liberation from exile. Although it is not expressly said, the proclamation in Is. xlvi 12-13 must be a promise of return from the exile and of restoration. Even if the prophet also has in mind a more distant future, nevertheless to him salvation starts with the liberation by Cyrus, as J. KNABENBAUER correctly remarks.[5] If the prophet himself has composed the vss. 12-13 in direct connection with 5-11, this idea is even expressly formulated. In xliv 23, Jacob's redemption by Yahwe is put on a level with Yahwe's glorification in Israel: by redeeming Jacob, Yahwe will glorify himself in Israel. The hitpael *yitpā'ār* here is synonymous with *nikbad*: Yahwe shows his glory. The preposition *b* must be taken in its fulness, indicating the place but with an apparent nuance of instrument: Yahwe shows his glory *in* but also *through* Israel whom he redeems.[6] According to xlvi 13, Yahwe will give his salvation *b^eṣiyyôn*. Here the same nuance of *b* is obvious: Zion becomes again the salvific centre of Israel, the centre of God's favour. The parallel phrase says that Yahwe "gives

---

1 Cf. pp. 53-55.

2 S. MOWINCKEL, *Psalmenstudien*, II, pp. 275-276.

3 Against P. VOLZ, *Jesaia II*, p. 80: "Das Heil ist wohl als Weltheil gedacht ...".

4 Cf. pp. 62-63.

5 J. KNABENBAUER, *Comment. in Is.*, II, p. 198.

6 Cf. JOÜON, § 133 c.

his glory to Israel". The substantive *tip'eret* means "beauty, ornament", and like the hithpael of *p'r* it is sometimes used to indicate Yahwe's glory and majesty, being synonymous with *k^ebôd yhwh* (2 Chron. xxix 11; Pss. lxxi 8; xcvi 6; Jer. xiii 11; xxxiii 9). Although it does not occur elsewhere in Dt.-Is. with that meaning, in xlvi 13 the suffix of the first person removes any doubt. Is this colon a nominal phrase: "my glory (is) for Israel", or is *tip'artî* object of *nātattî*? In both suppositions, the meaning might be the same, but if one adopts the second one, the analogy with xliv is more clear: *nātattî tip'artî* then has the same sense as the hithpael *hitpā'artî*. The verb *ntn* in this case means *edere, manifestare*.[1] In xlvi 13, however, Israel is more the recipient of this manifestation of glory. Nevertheless, the preposition *l* has a broad range of nuances, and because of its vague meaning it sometimes continues another preposition, the meaning of which it adopts.[2] So in xlvi 13b, *l* comes very close to *b* of the first colon. The verse is thus strictly parallel with xliv 23 and its full meaning is: "I give salvation in Zion and so I show my glory in Israel".

The whole oracle is theocentric. Yahwe brings near his salvation and this involves his glorification. His salvation and his glory belong together, somewhat as in classical dogmatic expositions concerning the aims of creation. J. MORGENSTERN aptly stresses this theocentrism, when paraphrasing *tip'artî* as "my glorious presence, i.e. Myself".[3] Since the prophet reassumes the theology of Yahwe's salvific presence in Zion, as appears from other pericopes (e.g. lii 7-10), this paraphrase is fully justified. The deliverance out of exile is the concrete content of the promise in xlvi 12-13. But the point of his promise is deeper: it asserts that Yahwe, through that deliverance and the following restoration, will again be present in Zion with his glory, as the God of salvation. From this we must conclude that Zion is not a mere symbol of Israel, in the sense that the name could have been replaced by "Jacob" or "Israel". Here Zion is the holy place, where Yahwe comes to his people and thus shows his glory to and in Israel.

The analysis of the complete pericope thus strengthens the LXX reading, as the parallel phrase speaks about the absence of God's salvation. Still the masoretic reading is more acceptable. It is better attested and is *lectio difficilior*. It also has a good sense in Dt.-Isaiah's

---

[1] Cf. GB, pp. 529-530; KÖNIG, p. 292; ZORELL, p. 539.

[2] JOÜON, § 133 d.

[3] J. MORGENSTERN, *The Message of Deutero-Isaiah*, p. 98.

mouth. When dealing with the disputation, we shall see that the prophet must defend his message against unwillingness to accept it. Especially the role of Cyrus in the coming salvation will appear to be challenged. Therefore the prophet can call his hearers stubborn. Moreover, vs. 12b then gets an ironical nuance: "You who think you are far from salvation", and so remains a perfect parallel to vs. 12a.

I may point out that in this very limited text all elements of a proclamation of salvation are present. We find the reference to the lament in vs. 12b. Certainly, the existing literature of lament does not offer a complaint about salvation being far away but the farness of God himself is a well attested theme (Pss. xxii 2, 12; xxxv 22; lxxi 12). In vs. 13, Yahwe's intervention and his turning in favour are intertwined. Verse 13bβ, as I interpreted it above is a very convenient motif of goal, since this motif always presents the final goal of Yahwe's intervention as a manifestation of his divine might and glory.

12. *Is. li 1-8*

1 Listen to me, you who pursue salvific justice,
you who seek Yahwe,
look to the rock from which you were hewn,
to the quarry from which you were dug.
2 Look to Abraham your father,
and to Sarah who bore you,
for when he was but one I called him,
and I blessed him and made him many.
3 For Yahwe comforts Zion,
he comforts all her ruins;
he makes her wilderness like Eden,
her desert like the garden of Yahwe.
4 (Listen to me, my people,
give ear to me, *nations*,[a]
for teaching will proceed from me,
and my judgment as light to the peoples.
5 In an instant I will bring near my justice,
my salvation shall come forth,
my arms shall judge peoples;
the islands wait for me,
and for my arm they hope).
6 Lift up your eyes to the heavens

and look at the earth beneath;
for the heavens will vanish like smoke,
the earth will fall in pieces like a garment
and they who dwell on it will die like *gnats*;[b]
but my salvation will be for ever
and my salvific justice will not be shaken.
7 Listen to me, you who know salvific justice,
you people in whose heart is my teaching.
Fear not the reproach of men,
and be not dismayed at their revilings.
8 For the moth will eat them up like a garment,
and the cockroach will eat them like wool.
But my salvific justice will be for ever,
and my salvation from generation to generation.

[a] Plural c 9 mss, ± LXX.
[b] Conj כִּנִּים, haplography of כמו־כנים ימותון.

Is. li 1-8 could be regarded as a disputation, although it does not show the components of that genre very neatly.[1] Furthermore, in the course of the investigation, I shall have to make clear where the limits of the literary unit are. Some scholars consider li 1-3 as a distinct oracle.[2] It is clear that a unit begins in vs. 4, according to form (*Heroldsruf* as introduction in vs. 4a) as to content as well. S. Mowinckel and K. Elliger suppose the first oracle to be continued in vs. 6, and this is quite acceptable.[3]

What is the sense of vss. 4-5? Some scholars delete them as inauthentic, a position to which also J. Begrich inclines.[4] According to A. Van Hoonacker, Is. li 4-8 would be a Servant poem and W. B. Stevenson says the same about li 4-6.[5] As a matter of fact,

---

[1] H. E. von Waldow, *Anlass und Hintergrund*, p. 36.

[2] H. Gressmann, *ZAW*. XXXIV 1914, p. 264; J. Begrich, *o.c.*, p. 13.

[3] S. Mowinckel, *ZAW*. XLIX 1931, p. 108; K. Elliger, *Deuterojesaja*, pp. 199-204.

[4] S. Mowinckel, *l.c.*; K. Elliger, *l.c.*; J. van der Ploeg, *Les chants du Serviteur de Jahvé*, Paris 1936, p. 207; C. R. North, *The Suffering Servant in Deutero-Isaiah*, Oxford 1956, p. 137; W. Rudolph, "Der exilische Messias", *ZAW*. XLIII 1925, p. 114, note 2; W. Staerk, *Die Ebed-Jahwe-Lieder in Jes. 40ff.*, p. 43; J. Begrich, *l.c.*: "... sehr wahrscheinlich für unecht zu gelten ...".

[5] A. Van Hoonacker, *Het boek Isaias*, pp. 235-236; W. B. Stevenson, "Successive Phases in the career of the Babylonian Isaiah", *Werden und Wesen des AT*, Berlin 1936, p. 89, note 2.

vss. 4-5 remind us of the Servant songs. The word pair *mišpāṭ* — *tôrâ* we find in xlii 4, as well as the phrase *yāṣā' mišpāṭ* in xlii 1 and the expression "light of the nations" in xlix 6 (here however *gôyim* instead of *'ammîm*). The first colon is akin to xlix 1a. For the "arm of Yahwe" one can refer to liii 1. "The islands hope for me" (li 5) reminds one of "the coastlands hope for his teaching" (xlii 4). Some contact between li 4-5 and xlii 1-4 cannot be denied. J. van der Ploeg and C. R. North justly pointed out that the Servant can hardly be speaking here; expressions like "my justice, my righteousness (*ṣidqî*), my salvation, my arm" can only be ascribed to Yahwe.[1] As to the content, the text seems more akin to Is. ii 2-4 and in a high degree also to xlv 20-25. From a literary standpoint, the most plausible solution is, that we have a composite interpolation, combining proto- and dt.-Isaian elements with the proper flavour of the Servant prophecies.[2] Whether the redactor has conserved some parts of an original oracle is hard to decide. J. Fischer supposes that vs. 5a, somewhat emended, would be authentic and would involve a promise of salvation to Israel or Zion. He reads:

> In an instant I bring near my justice,
> my salvation shall come forth like a light,
> and my arms shall judge peoples.[3]

In that case, *špṭ* would not necessarily indicate a salvific judgment. Yahwe's arm is a symbol of his dominion for doom as well as for salvation (cf. xl 10-11; li 9-10; lii 10; liii 1; lix 16; lxii 8; lxiii 12).[4] Whatever value the reconstruction has, the present text of both verses certainly announces salvation for the nations. In favour of the plural *'ammîm* and *le'ûmmîm* one may invoke: 1. the witness of twelve manuscripts and Peshitta; 2. the parallelism with xlix 1; 3. the plural form of the verbs which is unusual immediately after a singular vocative; still, a *constructio ad sensum* remains possible; 4. above all, *le'ōm* is used nowhere else with a suffix of the first person

---

[1] J. van der Ploeg, *o.c.*, p. 206; C. R. North, *o.c.*, p. 136.

[2] Cf. W. Staerk, *l.c.*; W. Rudolph, *l.c.*; J. Fischer, *Isaias 40-55 und die Perikopen vom Gottesknecht*, Münster 1916, pp. 54-58; J. van der Ploeg, *o.c.*, p. 207. The authenticity is defended by J. Muilenburg, *Isaiah chs. XL-LV*, pp. 592-593. He also points to an echo of the Ebed-Yahwe pericopes.

[3] Lg ארגיע אקריב c *BHK*: יֵצֵא pro יָצָא; add כאור c LXX: ὡς φῶς. Same reading in J. L. McKenzie, *Second Isaiah*, p. 118.

[4] Cf. J. Fischer, *Das Buch Isaias*, II, p. 121.

and it never indicates Israel. From S. SMITH's translation: "Attend to Me, O My people; O nations give ear to Me", it appears that he has an interesting position: he reads *'ammî* and *le'ûmmîm*, following nine manuscripts and perhaps the LXX.[1] So he meets the objections against *le'ûmmî* which do not apply to *'ammî*. In that case the verse would be directed to Israel and the nations at the same time, and it becomes understandable, why further on, it speaks about the nations in the third person. Moreover, this is in keeping with the normal use of *'am* and *le'ōm*. In my opinion, SMITH is right. Anyhow, the text testifies to a high degree of universalism. Yahwe's *mišpāṭ* will be a light to the nations. The islands hope for his arm. In vs. 5b Yahwe's arm thus has a positive salvific value. Then it is impossible that the judgment of his arm in 5a would have a sense of doom. So, one must agree with P. VOLZ, who considers *špṭ* as a salvific act and translates it as *zurechtbringen, zum Recht bringen.* The term *yēša'* here has a universal connotation: the salvation which comes forth from Yahwe is intended for all nations. Then, Yahwe's righteousness also should be salvific (cf. xlv 8; lix 17).[2] T. K. CHEYNE understands it as Yahwe's "consistent adherence to his revealed line of action, which involves deliverance".[3] It seems to me, he confuses it with *'ĕmet.* I cannot agree with K. CRAMER either, who understands *ṣedeq* and *yēša'* to be correlative: punitive justice and as reverse, salvation for Israel.[4] For, in the present context, there is no party to be condemned.

In the proclamation proper, the Israelites are addressed in plural. The address resembles the one in vs. 7. In vs. 1, the addressees are styled as those who pursue justice, in vs. 7 as those who know justice. It is not evident that the same justice is meant in both cases. K. CRAMER distinguishes the two: in vs. 7, *ṣedeq* would mean the relation between Yahwe and Israel, whereas in vs. 1, it views Yahwe's judgment over the nations, for which Israel is waiting. F. FELDMANN also discovers a difference: those who pursue justice are those who willingly accept the promises and look forward to Israel's salvation. Verse 7 would be addressed to the same, but characterized now as those who know justice and care about it. K. FAHLGREN makes the same dis-

---

1 LXX: *λαός μου καὶ οἱ βασιλεῖς*; cf. S. SMITH, *Isaiah. Chapters XL-LV*, London 1944, p. 60.

2 P. VOLZ, *o.c.*, p. 115; F. DELITZSCH, *Commentar*, p. 520.

3 T. K. CHEYNE, *The Prophecies of Isaiah*, II, p. 29.

4 K. CRAMER, "Der Begriff צדקה bei Tritojesaja", *ZAW.* XXVII 1907, pp. 89-90.

tinction.[1] According to P. Volz, in both verses those who pursue salvation are meant, in other words, who live the eschatological expectation, although ethical traits are not completely absent.[2] To be satisfactory, the interpretation must account also for the ideas expressed in the parallel verses. In vs. 7, knowing justice is tantamount to having God's *tôrâ* in one's heart. This explains why Feldmann ascribes an ethical meaning to the expression here. In vs. 1, "to pursue justice" is parallel with "to seek Yahwe".

The last mentioned formula is not univocally used in the O.T. To seek Yahwe (*drš*) means to go to him in his sanctuary (Deut. xii 5; 2 Chron. i 5), often with the intention of consulting him, either with the help of a man of God (Gen. xxv 22; Ex. xviii 15; 1 Sam. ix 9; 1 Kings xxii 8) or of a book (Is. xxxiv 16). The expression with the verb *biqqēš* particularly means the seeking of Yahwe's protection, especially when the object is "Yahwe's face" (Jer. xxix 13; Hos. v 15; 2 Sam. xxi 1; 1 Chron. xvi 2 (= Ps. cv 4); Pss. xxiv 6; xxvii 8). All these meanings are related. One seeks Yahwe's face to obtain his protection, and this is manifest in his oracles. Both verbs are also used in parallelism (1 Chron. xvi 11; Zeph. i 6). The prophets Amos and Hosea, although knowing this cultic sense, gave an ethical meaning to the formula *biqqēš* (*drš*) *yhwh*. Amos has this eloquent paraphrase: "Seek good and not evil" (Am. v 14; cf. vss. 4 and 6; Hos. iii 5; x 12; Zeph. i 6).[3] At the beginning of the proclamation in Is. li 1-8, the expression "to seek Yahwe" no doubt is connected with the literature of lament. It suffices to refer to Pss. xxvii 8; xl 17; lxix 7; lxx 5, where *biqqēš* is used, and to Pss. ix 11; xxii 27; xxxiv 5; lxix 33; lxxvii 3, where *drš* occurs. The address thus contains the allusion to the lament, as is usual in the proclamation of salvation.

The God who is invoked in the suggested lament is the *'ĕlōhê ṣedeq* (cf. Ps. iv 2). The psalmists often appeal to God's *ṣedeq* / *ṣ^{e}dāqâ* (Pss. ix 5; xxxi 2; xxxv 24; lxxi 2; cxix 40; cxliii 1, 11) or their

---

[1] F. Feldmann, *Das Buch Isaias*, II, pp. 146-148; K. Fahlgren, Ṣ^{e}dāḳā, *nahestehende und entgegengesetzte Begriffe im A.T.*, pp. 94 and 101.

[2] P. Volz, *o.c.*, p. 110: "... Leute, die *dem Heil nachjagen*, es sehnsüchtig erstreben, die das kommende Heil fassen und sich darum kümmern".

[3] Cf. A. Greiff, *Das Gebet im Alten Testament*, Münster 1915, p. 22; J. Herrmann, art. "εὔχομαι; C. Das Gebet im A.T.", *TWNT*. II, p. 787, note 186; H. Greeven, art. "ζητέω κτλ.". *TWNT*. II, p. 895, note 5; *BJ*, p. 1232, note c; for Amos and Hosea, cf. also D. Deden, *De kleine profeten, ad loca*; H. W. Wolff, *Dodekapropheton* 2, Neukirchen 1969, p. 294.

prayer intends to obtain it (Ps. v 9). Even if vs. 7, together with Amos and Hosea, invites us to an ethical interpretation of vs. 1, I prefer a different understanding. The prophecy is directed to those who call upon Yahwe in their distress, reckoning on his righteous benevolence. The divine *ṣedeq* here is God's will to keep his salvific order, to which the Israelite appeals, when he prays to Yahwe.[1] This meaning fits also vs. 7 as we shall see further on. It may be surprising that WESTERMANN did not remark this form-critical import of vs. 1a. But it is understandable when one knows that this scholar elsewhere asserts that nowhere in the O.T. is the prayer to Yahwe called "seeking".[2] Man, so WESTERMANN maintains, is not able to do anything in this respect, only God can bridge the gap between himself and man. Obviously, the author is victim of a christian *a priori*. It is unquestionable that *biqqēš* (*p^enê*) *yhwh* sometimes indicates a cultic act, and more precisely a humble prayer to Yahwe. It is unmistakably a cultic act in Hos. ii 9; v 6. In Hos. v 15, the meaning is not necessarily cultic but the expression can be understood only as an invocation of Yahwe in distress, owing to the context: "In their distress they seek me (*šḥr*)". The cultic meaning again is very clear in Zeph. i 6. Furthermore, in Jer. xxix 13, the parallelism with *qr'* and *hitpallēl*, and in Zech. viii 21, the parallelism with *ḥillâ 'et-p^enê yhwh* points in a sense "to pray, to invoke". But the chief witness is 2 Sam. xii 16, where David prays and fasts for the salvation of his sick child: *way^e-baqqēš dāwid 'et-hā'ĕlōhîm b^e'ad hanna'ar*. Actually, the verb is used here with the preposition *b^e'ad*, as is usual with *hitpallēl*, *nāśā' t^epillâ* (cf. Gen. xx 7; 2 Kings xix 4; Is. xxxvii 4; Jer. vii 16; xi 14; etc.). The expression thus has the meaning which I propose and in the context of a lament it certainly is preferable to that of a general religious attitude (*pietas*).[3]

The second colon of vs. 1 is a *crux interpretum*. The repetition of *habbîṭû* suggests parallelism with vs. 2a. The sense of the latter is

---

[1] Cf. p. 54; in a similar sense J. MUILENBURG, *Isaiah chs. 40-66*, p. 590; differently A. SCHOORS, *De literaire en doctrinele eenheid*, p. 254.

[2] C. WESTERMANN, "Die Begriffe für Fragen und Suchen im Alten Testament", *Kerygma und Dogma*, VI 1960, pp. 2-30; esp. p. 6: "An der Stelle wirklichen Suchens Gottes steht im AT das Flehen, die Klage, des Gebet ... Das aber wird im AT *niemals* Suchen Gottes genannt".

[3] Cf. GB, KB and ZORELL *sub verbo* בקש; H. W. WOLFF, *Hosea*, Neukirchen 1965, p. 148; A. PETITJEAN, *Les oracles du Proto-Zacharie*, Paris 1969, p. 431; H. J. KRAUS, *Psalmen*, p. 197: "בקש und דרש sind termini technici für die Wallfahrt zum Heiligtum".

quite clear: the prophet points to the ancestors Abraham and Sarah, in order to offer a motive of confidence. Though Abraham was alone when God called him, God's blessing made him a great nation. Is this apt to throw light on vs. 1b? It is commonly accepted that the images of the rock and the pit refer to Abraham and Sarah. According to VAN DER MERWE, the image would have been chosen in connection with Sarah's sterility. In this way the miraculous origin of the numerous offspring would be more strongly suggested and thus the motive of confidence be strengthened.[1] This interpretation is traditional in Jewish as well as in Christian circles.[2] Perhaps Mt. iii 9 (par. Lk. iii 8) supposes the same interpretation. It can be expressed in this translation: "Look to the rock, from which you were hewn, and to the hole of the pit, from which you were dug". Grammatically this translation can be defended, when one regards the verbs *ḥuṣṣabtem* and *nuqqartem* as asyndetic relative clauses. The ancient versions understood it this way, expressing the relative pronoun with the preposition.[3] But the image is strange, especially concerning Sarah. P. A. H. DE BOER has made a study of the subject, in which he proposes a new and stimulating interpretation. The LXX has the verbs in the active aorist, which the consonantal text allows, and which gives a better sense, particularly with regard to the pit: "look to the hole, the cistern, you dug".[4] To this I would add that IQIa has the same consonantal text as MT. This means that according to the manuscript an active parsing remains possible. A number of pual forms are written *plene* in that manuscript (cf. i 6; ix 5; xiii 16; xv 1; xxiii 1, 14; xxv 6; l i; li 20; lii 5, 15; liii 4, 5, 8; lxv 20). Beginning from col. xxviii, i.e. ch. xxxiv, the *scriptio plena* is more frequent. But the copyist is not consistent on this point and the number of defective pual forms is much larger, even in the second part of the manuscript.[5] DE BOER

---

[1] So in A. LOISY, *La consolation d'Israël*, p. 113; B. J. VAN DER MERWE, *Pentateuchtradisies*, p. 113.

[2] Cf. b. Yebamot 64ab; ExR. li 7; EsthR. vii 10; THEODORET OF CYRRHUS, *Exploratio in Is.*, *PG.* 80, col. 436; HAYMO OF HALBERSTADT, *PL.* 116, col. 975.

[3] JOÜON, § 158 c; GK. § 155 k. Sym: ὅθεν; Th: ἐξ ἧς, ὅθεν; Targ: מן; Pesh: ܡܢܗ; Vg: unde, de qua.

[4] LXX: ἣν ἐλατομήσατε, ὅν ὠρύξατε..

[5] *Scriptio plena*: 16 times; *defectiva*: 37 times. Also IQIb has נקרתם, but this ms. is much closer to MT, as far as spelling is concerned. Cf. E. L. SUKENIK, *The Dead Sea Scrolls of the Hebrew University*, pp. 30-31. Further J. T. MILIK, "Note sui manoscritti di 'Ain Fesḫa". *Bib.* XXXI 1950, p. 88; J. HEMPEL, "Beobachtungen an den "syrischen" Jesajarolle vom Toten Meer (DSIa)", *ZDMG.* CI 1951, pp. 138-173; esp. pp. 141-143.

further points out that the verb *ḥṣb* occurs almost exclusively in qal forms. The root *nqr* has an important derivative, *neqārâ*, "hole, cleft, cavern". In Ex. xxxiii 22 and Is. ii 21, it indicates caverns wherein one can find a hiding-place in times of danger. The noun *bôr*, perhaps a gloss for elucidation of the unusual *maqqebet*, means a cistern, hewn in the rock to keep the collected water. According to some biblical texts, the rock is water-bearing: Ex. xvii 6; Deut. viii 15; Pss. lxxvii 20; cv 41; cxiv 8; Is. xlviii 21.

It is from this, according to DE BOER, that we must try to interpret the metaphorical use of the term rock. The rock in metaphorical language is never a place of wilderness. Rock is a name of Israel's God as the protector and provider of life and security, as in Pss. xviii 3; xix 15; lxxviii 35 and in Is. xliv 8. The main idea seems to be the rock as a hidingplace and source of life, as water-bearing, being a rock with caves and cisterns. Those who hew out the rock are those who seek refuge in Yahwe. "They dig the well", is said also of the covenanters of Damascus.[1] Later Judaism would have changed the active into passive, maybe because of some hesitation to use the metaphor: hewing out in the rock, digging the pit, for "seeking Yahwe". Thus the masoretic vocalisation would have much of a *tiqqûn sopherim*.[2]

DE BOER's argumentation shows some weak points. Firstly, the reference to CDC is not acceptable, since it is expressly said there that the well is the torah. Furthermore, it is an overstatement to say that in the O.T. the rock is water-bearing. All cited texts are about the same episode of the miraculous water in the desert. Precisely the wonder is stressed that God made water gush forth even out of a rock. Contrarily to my previously expressed opinion, I now think the traditional interpretation is the best.[3] I call attention to the following considerations. The passive forms of the verbs are conserved also in the Lucianic recension of the LXX, which borrowed them from Theodotion.[4] In the Bible the verb *nqr* occurs exclusively in connection with the eyes, whereas *qûr* is used for digging (2 Kings xix 24; Is. xxxvii 25). If in the present context the root *qûr* is used, which is more probable, the consonants *nqrtm* are a nifal and thus passive. Moreover, it seems

[1] CDC. iii 16; vi 3-4.

[2] P. A. H. DE BOER, *Second-Isaiah's Message*, pp. 58-67: "The Rock".

[3] A. SCHOORS, *Recherches bibliques*, VIII, p. 117, note 5.

[4] *L* = Th: ἐξ ἧς ἐλατομήθητε ; ἐξ οὗ ὠρύχθητε..

that the unusual word *maqqebet*, "hole, opening" has been chosen here because of the association with *n*^{e}*qēbâ*, "woman", a noun of the same root. The word *bôr*, "pit", is nowhere used as a metaphor for a woman, but one uses the related *b*^{e}*'ēr*, "well" with that sense in Prov. v 15; xxiii 27; Cant. iv 15, as well as *ma'*^{e}*yān*, "spring" in Prov. v 16; Cant. iv 12, 15.[1] The word *bôr*, however, most probably is a gloss, as is also suggested by DE BOER: when we suppress it, the verse gets the same rhythm as 2a (3 + 2). Then we may completely avoid the strange image, if we understand *maqqebet* as a quarry, which is fully acceptable.[2] The glossator wanted to elucidate the unusual *maqqebet* and he may have been under the impression that it referred to the metaphoric use of *b*^{e}*'ēr*, which I have just mentioned.

I admit that the use of "rock" as a metaphor for Abraham is wholly unknown in the Bible, whereas the noun is applied to God 33 times. In the later Jewish tradition, there are some hints to such a metaphorical use. So in *Midrash B*^{e}*midbar*, the *ṣûrîm* from Num. xxiii 9 are considered as an indication of the patriarchs. In a saying from *Y*^{e}*lamm*^{e}*denu* in *Yalqut Shim'oni*, Abraham is expressly called a rock when the same text is connected with Is. li 1.[3] The idea that Israel came forth from a rock is not absent from the Bible: we find it in Deut. xxxii 18, with regard to God, "the Rock that begot you". Finally, there is a strong argument from the fact that this interpretation beyond any doubt best fits the context.[4]

The promise of salvation consists in a comfort of Zion. The prophet certainly has in view the real city, which is in ruins, but this promise makes sense only if this city is seen as the religious centre of the nation. The verse contains the theme of the renewal of paradise. According to GRESSMANN, FOHRER and many others, we are dealing

---

[1] To be sure, in Prov. v 15, בור is used also, but as a synonym of באר; we are dealing here with living water, as appears from vs. 16: מעינתך. — Cf. B. J. VAN DER MERWE, *o.c.*, p. 106, note 7.

[2] Cf. ZORELL, p. 467: lapidicina; further *RSV*; J. L. MCKENZIE, *Second Isaiah*, p. 118; cf. נָקַב, "mine", according to KB, p. 632. מַקֶּבֶת is a *maqtal(t)* form, very often indicating the place where an operation is done.

[3] Cf. STRACK-BILLERBECK, I, p. 733: "Als aber Gott auf Abraham schaute, der erstehen sollte, sprach er: Siehe, ich habe einen Felsen gefunden, auf dem ich die Welt bauen und gründen kann. Deshalb nannte er Abraham einen Felsen: Blicket auf den Felsen, aus dem ihr gehauen seid".

[4] A good exposition in B. J. VAN DER MERWE, *o.c.*, pp. 104-115, who, however, keeps the strange idea of "being dug from a pit".

here with an eschatological theme.[1] What does the prophet mean exactly? Yahwe makes Jerusalem's wilderness a paradise, or, giving its full weight to the *kaph comparationis*, he will make Jerusalem something *like* a paradise. With the image of the wilderness, the ruined city is indicated (cf. Jer. l 12; li 43; Zeph. ii 13). To the prophet the prediction of Jer. ix 10 has been fulfilled: "I will make Jerusalem a heap of ruins, a lair of jackals; and I will make the cities of Judah a desolation, without inhabitants".

What is the exact meaning and backgroud of the idea of paradise in the present context? The South African scholar VAN DER MERWE has devoted a careful study to the question. In his opinion, the O.T. knows more than one idea of paradise. It knows the garden where the first man lived (Gen. ii), — we may call it the primeval paradise —, but also the very beautiful and fertile garden of God (*gan-'ĕlōhîm*: Ez. xxviii 13; xxxi 8-9). The two are not completely different, but we may put it this way: the primeval paradise may be a garden of God (Gen. ii 8-9; iii 8, 24; its particular fertility: ii 9; iii 2), but the garden of God is not always the primeval paradise. On the contrary, nowhere do we meet the idea of a return of the primeval paradise. But the "garden of God" is used as a term of comparison in contexts where it is opposed to *midbār* or a catastrophe (Gen. xiii 10; Ez. xxxvi 35; Joel ii 3). We have to do with a locution that has a metaphorical meaning. The Genesis account is not the source of the other references to a Garden of God, but the various references or allusions all invoke the same general tradition about a paradise. The conclusion then is obvious: Is. li 3 does not speak about a return of the primeval paradise, but the verse refers to a familiar popular tradition, just as Gen. xiii 10 and the other cited texts.[2] The prophet only says with an impressive image: Zion, that now is in ruins, will be restored in all its splendour. The parallel instance, Ez. xxxvi 35, confirms this interpretation, and here also a *kaph* points out the comparative character of the assertion. Formerly, GRESSMANN had already suggested the same idea.[3] Thus one avoids inferring here a falling back on the *Urzeit* for the description

---

[1] Cf. H. GRESSMANN, *Der Ursprung der Israelitisch-jüdischen Eschatologie*, Göttingen 1905, p. 248; G. FOHRER, "Die Struktur der alttestamentlichen Eschatologie", *TLZ.* LXXXV 1960, pp. 406, 415-416.

[2] B. J. VAN DER MERWE, *o.c.*, pp. 41-51.

[3] H. GRESSMANN, *o.c.*, p. 217. Here one comes close to the use of divine names to indicate the superlative: e.g. Gen. xxx 8: נפתולי אלהים: mighty wrestlings.

of the *Endzeit*.[1] When J. STEINMANN understands from this text that Zion's restoration will abolish the punishment for Adam's sin, this is a gross extrapolation.[2]

If there is any reference to a kind of beginning era, it should be in the introduction. In the vss. 1-2, the lot of Abraham acts as a motive of confidence. Just as God brought Abraham from childlessness to a great offspring, so he will transform Zion from a wilderness to a garden of Yahwe. The reference to Abraham's great fertility suggests the idea of repeopling, when speaking of Zion's restoration (cf. Is. xlix 21; xlv 1-6). The joy and the songs of thanksgiving that are found in the city perhaps suggest the new presence of inhabitants also (cf. Jer. xxx 19).

I already mentioned the possibility of vs. 6 being the continuation of vs. 3. Vss. 7-8 are a short proclamation of salvation, which will appear to be composed in connection with 1-3, 6. In other words, vss. 1-8, with the exclusion of 4-5, are one literary unit, in which vs. 6 cannot be omitted.

Through a comparison with the created cosmos, the everlasting character of salvation is stressed, just as in liv 10, the covenant of peace is called everlasting. Like the mountains and hills in the verse just mentioned, so in li 6, heaven and earth are a symbol of firmness, but they will perish. Yahwe's salvation, however, will be for ever. Yahwe's everlasting salvation is put in opposition also with the transitoriness of men, who die *kemô-kēn*. This word can be translated as "in like manner".[3] Since in the preceding verses the perishable things are compared to smoke and a garment, this is a rather pale translation. One might find a concrete simile, when reading *kemô-kinnîm*, "like gnats", which supposes a haplography.[4] Another explanation has been proposed by J. REIDER. He reads *kemôkēn* and translates *môkēn* as "locusts", invoking the Arabic root *mkn*, "to lay eggs" (said of lizards and locusts), whence *makûn-* and *mumukin-*, "lizard, locust, etc.". Since, then, that reading has found a fresh support in IQIb and it has been adopted by D. W. THOMAS in *BHS*.

---

[1] P. VOLZ, *Jesaja II*, pp. 112: "... ein Motiv aus der uralten Zeit: die Endzeit kehrt in die Urzeit zurück". According to C. C. TORREY, *The Second Isaiah*, p. 397, the author of this verse has read Genesis.

[2] J. STEINMANN, *Le livre de la consolation*, p. 136.

[3] LXX: *ὥσπερ ταῦτα*; Vg: sicut haec; Targ: הכין; Pesh: ܐܟܘܬܗ̇. Cf. P. A. H. DE BOER, *o.c.*, p. 54; C. C. TORREY, *o.c.*, p. 398.

[4] So *BHK*; *RSV*; cf. KÖNIG, p. 182.

Moreover, Dt.-Is. is not unfamiliar with the idea, as he wrote in xl 22: *w^e^yōš^e^beyhā kāḥăgābîm.*[1] Whether gnats or locusts, it does not make much difference. One of both certainly is exact.

Again the question arises whether an eschatological promise of salvation is meant in vs. 6. DUHM dismisses the idea with the remark that Dt.-Is. only uses poetical language. His judgment may be somewhat rash, but he is essentially right.[2] We should not follow J. BEGRICH, inferring from the perfect tense *nimlāḥû*, "the heavens have vanished like smoke", that the eschatological distress has set in.[3] This perfect form, followed by two imperfect tenses, is certainly in the sphere of future, and expresses a firm certainty.[4] I call attention to the fact that *y^e^šû'â* and *ṣ^e^dāqâ* are again parallel and have Yahwe as subject (suffixes of the first person). Both come forth from Yahwe. In agreement with J. FISCHER and K. CRAMER, we better understand both nouns as indicating qualities of Yahwe, who brings about his salvific order. Both have a subjective sense, as they indicate Yahwe's salvific will and righteousness, which are everlasting.[5] An eschatological meaning then is less obvious. One may paraphrase the connection between vss. 3 and 6 as follows: "Zion will be restored; be sure of that, because my salvific will and righteousness are everlasting, i.e. they keep operating even in the present precarious condition". The verse is thus rather a motive of confidence than an eschatological promise. As far as I can see, nobody has put forward this so clear as B. J. VAN DER MERWE: "As to Is. li 6 and liv 10, it is apparent that not the suppression of the present world order is announced, but that the transitoriness of the world is stressed in order to underline better the durability of Yahwe's loyalty and salvation".[6]

---

[1] J. REIDER, "Contributions to the Hebrew Lexicon", *ZAW*. LIII 1935, pp. 270-271. According to the Talmud, there are 800 different species of locusts (p. Hul. 63b). All of the nine species, mentioned in the Bible, except חגב, are indicated with a collective singular.

[2] B. DUHM, *Das Buch Jesaja*, p. 346: "Dtjes aber hat gewiss keine eigentliche eschatologische Idee vor Augen, er spricht wie ein Dichter". Cf. A. SCHOORS, *Recherches bibliques*, VIII, p. 118.

[3] J. BEGRICH, *Studien*, p. 21.

[4] Cf. JOÜON, § 112 g-h.

[5] J. FISCHER, *Das Buch Isaias*, II, pp. 121-122; K. CRAMER, "Der Begriff צדקה bei Tritojesaja", *ZAW*. XXVII 1907, p. 91.

[6] B. J. VAN DER MERWE, *o.c.*, p. 155: "Wat Jes. 51:6 en 54:10 betref is dit duidelik dat hierin nie die opheffing van die huidige wêreldorde verkondig word nie, maar dat die verganklikheid van die wêreld hierin benadruk word om die bestendigheid van die trou en heil van Jahwe des te beter te beklemtoon".

Vss. 7-8 resemble the preceding text. We find in these verses the constitutive elements of a proclamation of salvation, just as in 1-3, 6. Moreover, it appears that they go together with 1-3, 6 in one composition. As to the content, they offer a further specification of the preceding verses, as I will show immediately. As far as form is concerned, vss. 1-3, 6-8 are a fine work of parallelisms, associations and chiasms, made with artful variation, as is apparent in this scheme:[1]

1 שמעו אלי רדפי צדק (1)
הביטו (2)
2 הביטו (2)
6 והביטו (2')
כבגד (3)
וישועתי לעולם תהיה (4) וצדקתי לא תחתת (5)
7 שמעו אלי ידעי צדק (1)
אל תחתו (5)
8 כבגד (3)
וצדקתי לעולם תהיה (4) וישועתי

It is almost unacceptable that this can be the work of a glossator. It becomes completely unacceptable when one knows that the typical dt.-Isaian play upon words is present in these verses. As I have already remarked, the prophet likes to use the same word twice with a different nuance of meaning.[2] So we find here the root *ḥtt* in vss. 6 and 7. In the first instance it means "to be shattered, to be destroyed", the opposite of "to be for ever", whereas in vs. 7 it means "to be filled with terror", parallel with *yr'*. Also *habbîṭû* has in vss. 1-2 the more spiritual meaning of "to pay attention to, to keep in mind", — the object is something in the past — whereas in vs. 6 the same word has the material sense of "to look", having the visible heaven and earth as object.[3]

What do these verses mean? The *Heroldsruf* (vs. 7a) is a stylistic articulation that refers to the first verse. But there are some important shifts. True, *ṣedeq* has the same meaning as in vs. 1, and I thus reject FELDMANN's ethical interpretation. But the verb *rdp* has been replaced

---

[1] The numbers (1), (2), etc. indicate the expressions which are mutually parallel or associated.

[2] Cf. p. pp. 132-133.

[3] Also P. VOLZ, *o.c.*, p. 109, has pointed out the literary unity of vss. 1-3, 6-8, however without showing sufficently the stylistic connection of the whole.

by *yd'*. The hearers not only pursue Yahwe's salvific will, they also have experienced it. Fundamentally, the same idea is expressed in vs. 7a: they have God's *tôrâ* in their heart. I refer to my comments on xlii 21, where *tôrâ* and *ṣedeq* are also put together. The *tôrâ* is the revelation of God's salvific will in history. The hearers thus bear in their hearts that revelation, they know God's salvific will. They know it will not cease and they have thus nothing to fear. In this case, *ṣedeq* has the same sense as in vs. 1. We thus see that the parallelism *ṣedeq* / *tôrâ* in vs. 7 has not merely a moral significance.

In vs. 7b, we find the allusion to the lament, which ran in the sense of Pss. xii 7; xxxix 9; lxix 22: "Make me not the scorn of my ennemies".[1] To this the prophet answers with the assurance of salvation "Fear not", which recalls the cultic oracle of salvation, but which here expresses, in a negative form, God's turning in favour. The motif of outcome is found in vs. 8a. One can imagine that in these verses the prophet makes clear by means of a simile that Yahwe's salvation will last longer than human transitory existence. However, here the opposition has a deeper meaning than in vs. 6. There, heaven and earth, as symbols of only seeming stability, are cited in order to underline the real stability of Yahwe's salvation. On the contrary, in vs. 8 the passing away of men is adopted as a negative component (threat) in the promise of salvation itself. We have to do with the enemies of Israel, who are only men and who will be exterminated. The precarious condition which I mentioned in my paraphrase of vs. 6, is alluded to here. In that sense vss. 7b-8 offer a further specification of vs. 6. The positive formulation points out Yahwe's everlasting salvific will, just as vs. 6 does. The meaning of the verse is identical with that of vs. 6, and so is not eschatological. It is a motive of confidence that must remove the dismay of the hearers, who are put to shame by their enemies.

I think I have sufficiently shown that Is. li 1-3, 6-8 is an artfully built, twofold proclamation of salvation.

§4. Conclusion

Let us now summarize the results of the analysis of the salvation words.

1. The distinction, made by WESTERMANN between the oracle of salvation and the proclamation of salvation, has proved fruitful.

---

[1] Cf. further for חרפה: Pss. xxxi 12; xliv 14; lxxix 4; lxxxix 42; cix 25.

We succeeded in placing all words of salvation from Is. xl-lv in one of these classes, without important modifications of the text. We are also allowed to confirm WESTERMANN's idea that the oracle of salvation shows a very fixed structure, while the proclamation of salvation has a looser one.[1] The question now is this: is the distinction merely formal or does a distinct theological content correspond to each class?

According to WESTERMANN, the oracle addresses the individual and the proclamation the community. In Is. xl-lv the former is a fiction, of course. Actually, all words of salvation are intended for the Judaean community. When an oracle is formulated in the singular, it is only possible through a personification of the community. Thus, all of Dt.-Isaiah's oracles of salvation, except one, are directed to the personified Jacob-Israel. But, contrary to what WESTERMANN asserts, most of the proclamations are also directed in a fiction to an individual. Only in Is. xliii 18; xlvi 12-14; li 1-8 and lv 1-5, does the prophet, literarily speaking, address a group. In xli 17-20 and xlii 14-17 he speaks in plural about third persons. But he speaks to Zion in the singular in xlix 14-26; li 12-14, 17-23; liv 7-10, 11-17. This singular involves a true personification, for Zion-Jerusalem is presented under the image of the mother and the spouse.

It is remarkable that the oracles of salvation are intended for Jacob-Israel, while the proclamations of salvation are for Zion-Jerusalem. What does this mean? Firstly, it be remarked that the distinction is not absolute, since in xlix 7-12 and lv 1-5 the prophet directs a proclamation to Israel and in liv 4-6 an oracle to Zion. Nevertheless, the distinction is not without importance from a form-critical point of view. It corresponds to an intention of the prophet, as will appear from a complete comparison of both genres.

The individual style of the salvation oracle is maintained better than the one of the proclamation of salvation. The epithet "servant" in the address of the oracle of salvation is individual (xli 8-9; xliv 1, 2). The same applies to the image "worm" in xli 14. The messenger's formula occurs only twice in this genre, and both times it is expanded with the definition of God as the one who created, formed, made the recipient (xliii 1a; xliv 2a). In xliv 2, it is said that Yahwe has formed him from the womb. The individual character of such expressions is obvious as I have pointed out sufficiently in the analysis. We hear the same individual sound in the nominal substantiations:

---

[1] C. WESTERMANN, *Forschung*, p. 123.

"I am your *gō'ēl*, I am with you, I hold your right hand, you are mine, I am your husband" (xli 10a, 13, 14b; xliii 1b; liv 5), as well as in the verbal ones: "I help you (*'zr*), I redeem you (*g'l*), I call you by name" (xli 10, 13, 14; xliii 1b; liv 6). In this connection, it should be remarked again that the *gō'ēl*-relation involves a family tie. I also point to the fact that the root *'zr* belongs to the individual lament, whereas it is almost completely absent from the collective lament.[1] This individual style is often continued in the motif of outcome (cf. xli 11-12, 15-16a; xliii 2-4; liv 4b). I wish to recall that in xli 11-12, Israel's enemies are typified as personal enemies. But as this motif announces concrete salvific facts, it is inevitable that sometimes the prophet passes to the plural, as in xliii 5-6 in connection with the return from the diaspora, or in xliv 3-4 in connection with the promise of fertility.

When we turn our attention to the proclamations of salvation, we remark that more than once the personification is abandoned in the course of the pericope. Such is the case in xlix 7-12, 14-26 (passage from the image of the woman to the image of the city); liv 7-10 (I will gather you) and 11-17 (image of the city). WESTERMANN is thus quite right. But on this point the distinction between both genres is not complete. In liv 17-23, the individual style is maintained very well, and in other proclamations too, the departure from personification is rather slight.

Characteristic of the proclamation is the motif I: the allusion to the lament. When investigating this motif in the various proclamations, we see that it mostly refers to a collective lament. But here also there are exceptions. I cite xlix 7, 14, 21, where the prophet certainly alludes to an individual lament.[2] Also the motif of seeking Yahwe, which we found in li 1, occurs only in individual psalms. On this point WESTERMANN's position should be qualified.

The oracle of salvation also differs from the proclamation through the assurance of salvation "Fear not" and the nominal substantiation. Both give an actual character to the oracle. The prophet assures the recipient, appealing to an existing relationship between him and his God. The point of the oracle is precisely in this assurance. With the

---

[1] Cf. Pss. xx 3; xxii 20; xxvii 9; xxxvii 40; xxxviii 23; xl 14; lxx 6; lxxi 12; lxxxv 17; xciv 16; cix 26; cxviii 13; cxix 86, 173, 175. Collective context in Ps. lxxix 9.

[2] Cf. Pss. xxii 7; xxxi 12; xiii 2; xlii 10; xxii 2; lxxi 9, 11, 18. Cf. H. GUNKEL-J. BEGRICH, *Einleitung*, § 6, nr. 6-7.

proclamation the point is more in the announcement of coming salvation. Here we see a clear distinction between the genres, but it should not be overstressed. For every oracle of salvation includes a proclamation of salvation. I mean the motif of outcome or, in BEGRICH's system, the B motif. On the other hand, the motif II, 1 sometimes gives an actual character to the proclamation of salvation. So in xliii 19, where the participle *'ōśeh* and the particle *'attâ* underline this actuality. Also in xlix 8a; li 12-13, 22bc; liv 8b, the actuality of Yahwe's intervention is pointed out by a participle or a *perfectum executionis*. But it remains a striking fact that the motif II, 1, which in the proclamation of salvation expresses Yahwe's turning in favour, is mostly formulated in the imperfect.

It is respectively in their motif of outcome and their motif II,2 that oracle and proclamation of salvation most resemble one another. When comparing the classes on this point, we remark that the oracles have more general promises, which remain mostly in an individual context, while in the proclamations we find a great variety of collective goods, as may be seen from the following table:

TABLE IV

	Oracle	Proclamation
destruction of enemies	xli 11-12,15-16	xlii 15-16; xlix 25-26; li 8, 22-23
deliverance	xliii 3	xlix 25-26; li 14
protection: — general	xliii 2	
— on the march		xli 18-19; xlii 15-16; xliii 19-20; xlix 8-11
return from diaspora	xliii 5-7	xlix 12, 22-23
promise of fertility	xliv 3-5	xlix 17-20
restoration of land/city		xlix 8-11, 17-20; li 3; liv 11-17
lasting covenant		liv 9-10; lv 4-5

Even the parallel themes, such as deliverance and destruction of the enemies, are treated in a more individual or collective sphere, according to the genre.

Summarizing, we may say that the oracle addresses the hearers more personally, as it were more individually. We feel this from the very beginning, the address, in the assurance of salvation and its substantiations and in the promises of the B-motif. The proclamation is more tuned in to the community, be it personified or not as lady

Zion. The personification of Zion is a figure of speech, behind which one clearly recognizes the city or the community. True, the name Jacob-Israel certainly means the nation taken all together; nevertheless, owing to the individual style, the message of the oracle of salvation is meant to affect more each individual member of that nation. Now we grasp the connection between the genre and the chosen personification. In the name "Zion" the prophet could not bring into evidence the individual aspect of salvation. To this the name "Jacob-Israel" was more apt, as, in their mind, it was originally a personal name. Zion-Jerusalem, the centre of the nation, was a good symbol of the whole community. In xli 1-2 the prophet puts "Jerusalem" in parallelism with "my people".[1] And with regard to the image "Zion" the prophet is more free: he can treat it as a personification, as an indication of the city (e.g. xlix 16: *ḥômōtayik*), or as a symbol of the community. In this way, in his proclamations, he is able to deal more specifically with salvation in all its phases : deliverance, return under divine protection, rebuilding and repeopling, spiritual restoration.

But all this requires many nuances. Naturally, both types remain very much akin so we should expect some overlapping. At certain points the boundaries between them have faded. And in both the same prophet is speaking of the same salvific reality.

One more word about the motifs of final goal. In principle, they are the same in both genres. They give a theocentric perspective to the words of salvation: Yahwe acts for the sake of his own honor. This motif is formulated in various ways, but in a few instances the prophet uses a traditional formula of recognition at the end of a proclamation of salvation (xli 20; xlix 23c, 26b). This probably is the original formulation, but the prophet freely expresses the same idea in other phrases. I have already pointed out that the word of salvation thus becomes an *Erweiswort*. Only one oracle of salvation has a motif of goal (xli 16) and this is built so loosely, that originally the motif will have belonged only to the proclamation of salvation.

2. Let us now summarize Dt.-Isaiah's message as he presents it in

---

[1] In the inauthentic text li 16, we read: "... to say to Zion: You are my people" Cf. G. Fohrer, "Zion — Jerusalem im A.T.", *TWNT*. VII, p. 307; *Jesaja III* p. 16.

his salvation words.[1] The theological fundament of the coming salvation is historical. The election of Israel by Yahwe created a particular relation between God and his nation. Although the election (*bḥr*; xli 8; xliv 1) is an historical deed from the past, it is still effective. As focuses of the history of election the prophet considers above all the deliverance out of Egypt (*g'l*; theme of the exodus in general) and the vocation of Abraham (xli 8). By the election, Yahwe became the God of Israel. Israel became a nation through him, so that he is its maker, creator and former (*'ōśeh, bōrē', yōṣēr*). Yahwe rightly regards Israel as his own people, which is sanctified by his belonging to the holy Yahwe (*qᵉdôš yiśrā'ēl*). The relationship which originates in this way makes Israel an *'ebed yhwh,* who rightly expects that Yahwe will help and save him in his distress. For Yahwe is Israel's *gō'ēl*: he has undertaken the obligation to redeem Israel when strangers have it in their power. In other words, between Yahwe and Israel there is a bond of *ḥesed.* These themes are mostly suggested with a few basic words in the introductions and substantiations of the oracles of salvation.

In the light of all this, the prophet cannot accept that the condition of distress will continue. He surely knows that Yahwe intervenes. To this effect God will not hesitate to destroy the enemies of his people or to deal with them severely. He makes an end to the condition of bondage and oppression. This means that he will bring back the exiled Israelites from Babylon to Zion. Faithful to his original salvific deeds, he will again take care of his people on the way home which is a second exodus. Once back in the homeland, Yahwe will go on protecting Israel. The land and especially Zion will be rebuilt. The children of Israel will come back from all countries. The weakened people will become numerous and strong. In the restored nation there will be welfare, the condition of *šālôm* involving all goods. The dynasty indeed went to ruin, but not the covenantal graces which Yahwe intended with his promises to David (*bᵉrît, ḥasdê dāwid*). This restoration has a religious dimension: it involves a growth of the yahwistic community (xliv 5) and a witness of Israel to Yahwe before foreign nations (lv 4-5).

The whole message of Dt.-Is. is theocentric. The most striking

---

[1] Cf. A. Schoors, *Recherches bibliques*, VIII, pp. 108-110, where most of the textual evidence has been collected.

expression of it is to be found in the final motif of the proclamation of salvation. Yahwe's deeds reveal his glory. From his deeds Israel will recognize who Yahwe is. The stage whereon this revelation happens is history, the object of it is Yahwe's greatness and might. Therefore honor and praise are his due. The goals of the divine activity can be paraphrased: "The people whom I formed for myself will tell my praises" (Is. xliii 21). But, as Yahwe acts on the stage of the world-events, foreign nations will also see Yahwe's glory and the revelation will be universal. How precisely this universalism must be described, will be clear only after the analysis of the other texts. As yet, we only know that foreigners will be serving Israel (xlix 22-23), that everybody will know Yahwe's intervention (xlix 26b), that a foreign nation will come to Israel because of Yahwe's deeds (lv 5).

S. Herrmann has claimed that the exodus tradition, as well as the other great traditions of salvation, have only a restricted importance to Dt.-Is., viz. as a reminiscence but not as actually binding.[1] After my analysis, it is needless to say that I contest this position, at least concerning the tradition about the exodus and the davidic covenant. If the references to the exodus seem to be at times quite external (xliii 16-17; xlix 10; li 9), this does not mean that the exodus is of no importance to Dt.-Is. His wording indeed shows a certain literary freedom with respect to the formulas of tradition. It is known that Dt.-Is. is not tied down by the letter of any tradition. He adapts them to his own style and message.[2] But the deliverance out of Egypt is to him the basic event of history. It must be read in the depth of such phrases as "who formed Israel in the womb" (xliv 2a). Moreover, in li 10, the prophet uses the reference to the miracle of the Reed Sea as a motive of confidence in a lament. Indeed to him this event motivates the certainty of Yahwe's present salvific activity. This is much more than a reminiscence. I shall be able to defend more thoroughly the importance of the exodus to our prophet when I have analysed the allusions to it in the other genres.

As to the three categories or, in the terminology of Gressmann, the three motifs, which the prophets use in their salvation words, we

---

[1] S. Herrmann, *Die prophetischen Heilserwartungen im A.T.*, Stuttgart 1965, pp. 297-298: "So scheinen die älteren grossen Heilstraditionen Israels für Deuterojesaja nur noch eine relative Bedeutung zu haben, die Bedeutung heilsgeschichtlicher Reminiszensen, jedoch nicht mehr die einer direkten aktuellen Verbindlichkeit".

[2] B. J. van der Merwe, *Pentateuchtradisies*, pp. 174; 244.

may conclude that in Dt.-Is. we find political, natural and ethico-religious motifs.[1] But he uses them on different levels. The natural motifs (water in the desert, vegetation, etc.) have a symbolic meaning: they refer precisely to the other motifs. The political expectations are concretely directed to destruction of the oppressor, deliverance, return, restoration of the homeland, protection against enemies and to a certain supremacy over the other nations. But restoration and relation to the other peoples belong at the same time to the religious sphere (e.g. xliv 3-5; liv 13; lv 4-5). The latter predominates through the theocentric character of the message, as I have already pointed out.

3. Now it is possible to take a stand on the actual *Sitz im Leben* of the dt.-Isaian words of salvation. I recall briefly the opposite theories of BEGRICH and VON WALDOW. According to the former, the words of salvation are literary imitations of cultic oracles. On the contrary, VON WALDOW thinks they are real salvation oracles, pronounced in collective liturgies of lament. In my opinion, the latter has convincingly demonstrated, on the ground of data from Pss. xliv; lxxiv; lxxix; Lam. v; Zech. vii 1-5; viii 18-19, that after 587 a liturgy of lament, in which the fall of Jerusalem was commemorated, came to be celebrated in the ruins of the temple. The deuteronomic redaction of Solomon's prayer at the inauguration of the temple (1 Kings viii 46-50) also proves that the exiles held such a liturgy, the temple as the only legal cult place being replaced by their facing Jerusalem.[2] His opinion is justly agreed upon by H. J. KRAUS.[3]

In the dt.-Isaian salvation words, VON WALDOW finds several features that indicate their original setting in such liturgies. Their content proves that they are directed to the community. Moreover, some words of salvation (called proclamations by WESTERMANN) commence with an allusion to the preceding lament. Also the verb *'nh* in xli 17 and xlix 8 only makes sense when referring to a lament. Finally, in li 9-15, the preceding lament is preserved *in extenso*.[4] There is no objection against these arguments.

But the distinction between oracle and proclamation of salvation complicates the problem. In principle, the former genre is a reply to

---

[1] Cf. p. 33.

[2] H. E. VON WALDOW, *Anlass und Hintergrund*, pp. 112-123.

[3] H. J. KRAUS, *Psalmen*, pp. 514-515; 550-551; *Klagelieder*, Neukirchen 1960, pp. 8-13.

[4] H. E. VON WALDOW, *o.c.*, pp. 100-108.

an individual lament and thus finds its place in an individual liturgy of lament. We have seen the degree to which Dt.-Is. has respected this form, although the message it carries concerns the community. The tension between form and content points to a distance from the original *Sitz im Leben.* In other words: Dt.-Is. imitates the form of the individual oracle of salvation in oracles that are destined for the community. The proclamation of salvation on the other hand is a reply to a collective lament and thus belongs to a collective liturgy. Here we do not feel the same tension between form and content. But as the prophet imitates in the former genre, there is the supposition that he does so too in the other. Against this presumption the cited arguments of VON WALDOW are not decisive. The features which he invokes, can be explained sufficiently as conscious and accurate imitations of existing genres. This he admits himself,[1] but in the further development of his study he abandons this more nuanced view. Some contaminations with the individual oracle, e.g. in the allusion to the lament, also jar with a setting in an actual collective liturgy. And finally, an elaborate proclamation such as Is. xlix 14-26 can hardly be anything but an imitation. Thus VON WALDOW's position on the *Sitz im Leben* is partly wrong, partly unproven as well as being improbable. But it must be admitted that the type of the dt.-Isaian words of salvation is pure, i.e. it is not a mixed type, and that the prophet uses many topics and formulas from the liturgy of lament. Although he imitates, he has nevertheless a close contact with the cultic setting, in which the adopted genres originated. It is hardly possible to arrive at a more positive result concerning the actual *Sitz im Leben.*

---

[1] H. E. VON WALDOW, *o.c.*, p. 108: "... alle die herangezogenen Stellen lassen sich auch als bewusste und naturgetreue Imitationen erklären".

CHAPTER THREE

THE POLEMIC GENRES

§1. Definition of the Genre

From the beginning of form criticism, some sections of a contentious nature have been recognized in Is. xl-lv. But scholars neither call them by the same names, nor do they subdivide them along the same lines. The confusion can be clearly seen from table V, on page 177. The borderlines do not always seem to be very neat and one gets the impression that these genres, hardly distinct as they are at times, are connected with each other. Before analyzing the pericopes, I would like to clarify somewhat the distinction between these genres and their proper rules.

1. *Connection and Characteristics of the Polemic Genres*

From the summary of Gressmann's article in my first chapter it appeared, that we do not learn much from him about the typology of these genres.[1] He does not tell us how we can distinguish a threat (*Drohung*), or a rebuke (*Scheltwort*). He only points to the close connection between them in classical prophetism[2], where the rebuke acts as a foundation of the threat, a connection which would be disrupted in Dt.-Is. Concerning the *Gerichtsworte*, he mentions the typical formulas of introduction and a couple of *topoi* such as "to witness" or "to prove".

With H. Gunkel the harvest is not much better. He regards the rebuke as secondary, in the sense that the prophets used it only in the later stage of development to justify their pronouncement of the threat with a reference to Israel's sins. The rebuke is added to the threat with a "because" or, when it precedes, the threat is introduced with "therefore" (Am. iv 12; v 11; vi 7; Is. v 13; x 16; xxix 14; Jer. ii 9). In the second case, the rebuke regularly opens with *hôy* (Is. i 4; v 8, 11, 18, 20-22; xxix 15; xxx 1; Am. v 18; vi 1; Jer. xxii 13) or with

---

1 Cf. chapter I, § 2.

2 Also H. Gressmann, *Die älteste Geschichtschreibung und Prophetie Israels*, Göttingen 1910, p. 326; *Der Messias*, p. 69.

The polemic genres in Is. xl-lv

TABLE V.

	Gressmann	Köhler	Mowinckel	Caspari	Begrich	von Waldow	Westermann
xl 12-17		Streitgespr.			Disputation	Disputation	
18-20		Streitgespr.	Streitgespr.		Disputation	Disputation	
21-24		Streitgespr.	(+xli 6-7)		Disputation	Disputation	Disputation
25-26					Disputation	Disputation	
27-31					Disputation	Disputation	
xli 1-5	Gerichtsw.	Streitgespr.	Streitgespr.		Gerichtsrede	Gerichtsrede	Gerichtsrede
6-13			(-6-7)				
21-24	Gerichtsw.	Streitgespr.	Streitgespr.		Gerichtsrede	Gerichtsrede	Gerichtsrede
25-29							
xlii 18-25	Scheltw.	Streitgespr.					Gerichtsrede
xliii 8-13	Gerichtsw.	Streitgespr.	Streitgespr.	Streitgespr.	Gerichtsrede	Gerichtsrede	Gerichtsrede
14-15	Drohung				Gerichtsrede	Gerichtsrede	
22-28	Scheltw.				Gerichtsrede	Gerichtsrede	Gerichtsrede
xliv 6-8	Gerichtsw.			Streitgespr.	Gerichtsrede	Gerichtsrede	Gerichtsrede
9-20							
21-22						Disputation	
24-28					Disputation	Disputation	
xlv 9-10	Scheltw.				Disputation		
11-13						Disputation	Gericht/disp.
18-19					Disputation	Disputation	+ Disp.
20-21	Gerichtsw.						Gerichtsrede
22-25							
xlvi 5-11					Disputation	Disputation	
xlviii 1-11	Scheltw.		Scheltrede		Disp+Gericht	Disputation	
12-13	Gerichtsw.		Streitgespr.		Disputation	Disputation	
14-15		Streitg.(+16)					
xlix 14-21		Streitgespr.		Streitgespr.			Disputation
22-26							
l 1-3	Scheltw.				Disp+Gericht	Gerichtsrede	Gerichtsrede
li 1-3						Disputation	
lv 8-13						Disputation	

the summons "Listen you who ..." (Am. iv 1; viii 4).[1] Later on, the rebuke had a separate existence, because of the ethical interest of the prophets. Often such a rebuke is clothed in the form of a trial speech (e.g. Is. iii 13-15; i 18-20; Mic. vi 1 ff.; Jer. ii 4-9; Hos. ii 4ff.). Therein we sometimes have traces of an interrogatory.[2] On the other hand, the prophets often are in opposition to their listeners or to their prophetical adversaries. Hence the type of disputation originates. The sayings of the people or the adversaries are often quoted, to refute them (e.g. Am. v 14; Is. xxii 12; xxviii 9 ff.; xxx 16; Zeph. i 12; etc.). This type sometimes leads to the use of parables.[3]

The connection between rebuke and threat has repeatedly been stressed since GRESSMANN and GUNKEL, either as an original unity in one genre [4] or as a secondary combination of two genres, which were originally distinct.[5] At the same time H. GRESSMANN, A. BALLA, J. HEMPEL and R. B. SCOTT pointed out that the threat is the divine word proper, whereas the rebuke is rather to be considered a prophetic word. All this has been formulated less technically by B. DUHM, where he stated that already Amos's and Hosea's prophetic message consisted in the announcement of the destiny which Yahwe had decided for Israel and in the justification of this decision by referring to Israel's sin.[6]

In his dissertation on the *Redeformen des israelitischen Rechtslebens*, H. J. BOECKER has touched on the same question. In his opinion, there is a separate *Scheltrede*, which originated as an imitation of the accusation in the profane judicial practice. He shows that the profane accusation is directed to the court, speaking about the accused in the third person. But in the prophetic accusations the second person prevails, because they are pronounced in the name of God, who is

---

[1] H. GUNKEL, *Die Propheten als Schriftsteller*, p. LXV. I had to correct several of GUNKEL's references.

[2] H. GUNKEL, *o.c.*, pp. LXV-LXVI: "Es lag den Propheten nahe solche Scheltreden in die Form einer '*Gerichtsrede*' Jahwes an Israel zu kleiden".

[3] H. GUNKEL, *o.c.*, pp. LXIX-LXX. The textual references are illchosen; few of them belong to the genre of disputation.

[4] H. W. WOLFF, "Die Begründung der prophetischen Heils- und Unheilssprüche", *ZAW*. LII 1934, pp. 1-21.

[5] E.g. O. EISSFELDT, *Einleitung in das A.T.*, pp. 106-107; E. BALLA, *Die Droh- und Scheltworte Amos*, Leipzig 1926; R. SCOTT, "The Literary Structure of Isaiah's Oracles", *Studies in O.T. Prophecy*, Edinburgh 1950, pp. 175-186. Somewhat between them is J. HEMPEL, *Die althebräische Literatur*, Potsdam 1934, p. 61.

[6] B. DUHM, *Israels Propheten*, Tübingen 1922, p. 94; cf. also pp. 104ff. and 114ff.

both accuser and judge.[1] This bringing together of distinct functions in one person has been underlined also by B. GEMSER and J. BEGRICH.[2] Besides, BOECKER knows an original combination of rebuke and threat, which has its origin in the structure of the judicial sentence (*Gerichtsspruch*), which in its complete form contains a judgment (*Urteil*) and a penalization (*Urteilsfolgebestimmung*).[3] In this respect, he judges the distinction between divine and prophetic word to be secondary. It would come forth from the pastoral feeling of the prophets, who think they may convince the people better when not confronting them directly with a word of Yahwe. This is in agreement with R. RENDTORFF's position that the distinction between *Begründung* and *Drohwort* does not coincide with that between prophetic and divine word (Cf. 1 Sam. ii 27-36; 2 Sam. xii 7b-10; 1 Kings xiv 7-11; xx 42; xxi 19).[4]

In his *Grundformen prophetischer Rede*, C. WESTERMANN gave a satisfactory solution to these problems by combining *Botenspruch* and *Gerichtswort*. In an incisive analysis of the profane genre of the message (*Botenspruch*), he shows that this has not only a typical introduction but also a binary structure: it contains a description of the situation (perfect tense) and an instruction, a desire or something like that (imperfect tense). There are several types, one of which is important for our purpose: in the message of a king to a colleague the description of the situation is sometimes an accusation and the imperfect part is replaced by an appeal to a divine judgment, in practice to weapons (cf. Jud. xi 16-27), i.e. by a declaration of war. In the prophetical texts from Mari, the prophetic message was directed to the king and it is striking that in the historical books of the Bible, also, the prophecies are directed to an individual, mostly to the king. Therefore WESTERMANN first analyzes the *Gerichtswort* to the individual. With three examples, viz. Am. vii 16-17; 1 Kings xxi 17-19; 2 Kings i 3-4, he shows its basic structure: summons to listen, accusation, messenger's formula, announcement of penalty. Accusation and penalization of course are the main components, the former being the

[1] H. J. BOECKER, *Redeformen des israelitischen Rechtslebens*, Diss. Bonn 1959, pp. 95-96.

[2] B. GEMSER, "The RÎB- or Controversy-Pattern", *SVT*. III 1955, p. 124; J. BEGRICH, *Studien*, pp. 43-44.

[3] H. J. BOECKER, *o.c.*, pp. 159-162.

[4] R. RENDTORFF, "Botenformel und Botenspruch", *ZAW*. LXXIV 1962, p. 175, note 30.

foundation (*Begründung*) of the latter. Moreover, the penalization is the divine message proper. Therefore, in the most pure examples, it is immediately preceded by the messenger's formula. This, according to WESTERMANN, is the basic type of a prophetic saying.[1] The connection with the form of the profane message is obvious.

The *Gerichtswort* against Israel is only a further development of this type. Its basic structure is this:

- Foundation (*Begründung*)
  - Accusation (*Anklage*)
  - Unfolding of the accusation
- Messenger's formula (*Botenformel*)
- Pronouncement of the sentence (*Gerichtsankündigung*)
  - God's intervention (*Eingreifen Gottes*)
  - Consequence of the intervention (*Folge des Eingreifens*)

In this structure, C. WESTERMANN justly recognizes the basic type of the *Gerichtswort* but he is flexible enough to accept variations and further developments. The *Gerichtswort* is the fundamental genre of the prophetic utterances, combining in itself foundation and pronouncement of the sentence, which his predecessors called rebuke and threat. He does not give many details about the shaping of the two main components. The foundation, which he calls accusation, is sometimes worded as an accusing question (e.g. 1 Sam. ii 29; 2 Sam. xii 9; Is. vii 13; xxii 15; xxxvii 23; Jer. xxii 15). The most original form is a simple assertion, which secondarily developed into a *kî*-clause.[2] I am not convinced of this secondary nature of the *kî*-clauses. Anyhow, they are quite frequent. The accusation in its assertive form coincides with what BOECKER calls the judgment (*Urteil*).

About the shaping of the accusation/rebuke we find more details in the *Einleitung* of GUNKEL-BEGRICH, who find the genre also in a couple of psalms (Pss. l 16-20; liii 1-4, 5-6; lxxxi 9-12). Beside the summons "Hear" and the indignant question, there is the quotation of sayings of the accused (e.g. Is. v 19-20; x 8-11, 13-14; xxviii 15;

---

[1] C. WESTERMANN, *Grundformen prophetischer Rede*, München 1960, p. 41: "In diesen beiden Erkenntnissen: a) der Prophetenspruch hat seine 'Normalform' in der Einheit von Begründung und Ankündigung; b) das eigentliche Botenwort (= Gotteswort) ist die Ankündigung, ist die wesentliche Bestimmung der Grundformen prophetischen Redens gegeben".

[2] C. WESTERMANN, *o.c.*, pp. 102-104.

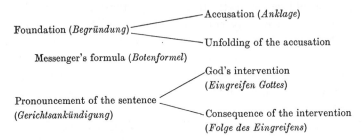

xxix 15; Am. vi 13; viii 5-6; Hos. ii 7). More than once the accusation involves an historical summary, to oppose Israel's guilt to Yahwe's benevolence (Am. ii 9-12; Hos. xi 1-4; Jer. ii 1-13; Mic. vi 3-5). The accused is addressed in the second person or he is the object of the accusation in the third person.[1]

In the footsteps of GUNKEL and GRESSMANN, WESTERMANN also asserts that the prophets, instead of pronouncing their *Gerichtswort* in the shape of a message, sometimes put it in the literary framework of a lawsuit or a disputation. In the former case the prophet describes a lawsuit, at least in part (cf. Is. i 18-20; iii 13-15; v 1-7; Mic. vi 1-5; Hos. ii 4-7; iv 1-10; xii 3-15; Jer. ii 5-37).[2] WESTERMANN shows briefly that, in the quoted instances, the lawsuit is only a scenic representation (*szenische Einkleidung*) of what happens in every other *Gerichtswort*. At times, as in Hos. iv 1-3 or xii 3-15, it is only the introductory sentence which refers to a lawsuit scene, whilst the rest of the utterance is a clear *Gerichtswort*. We are dealing with the genre, that since GUNKEL, is called trial speech (*Gerichtsrede*). The disputation is fairly close to the type of trial speech, and in practice it is not always easy to distinghuish between them. As typical samples WESTERMANN cites Mic. ii 6-11; Is. xxviii 23-29; Jer. iii 1-5; ii 23-25, 29-30, 34-45.[3] According to this German critic, both types become fully elaborated only with Dt.-Is. I shall try now to delineate more precisely their proper characteristics.

2. *The Trial Speech*

a. Structure and Proper Style

In his *Deuterojesaja*, L. KÖHLER devotes a few paragraphs to the disputation (*Streitgespräch*). But from his exposition it appears that by this name he means the same as GUNKEL and others when they use *Gerichtsrede*. By *Streitgespräch* he understands a *rîb*, i.e. a lawsuit or an imitation of it. From him we learn the following *topoi* of the genre: the convocation of the witnesses, the summons, declarations under oath, the quotations of the accusation, questions to the adversary, the final judgment. Further different technical terms: *rîb*, the trial; *dîn*, the judgment; *špṭ*, to help a man to his right; *mišpāṭ*,

---

[1] H. GUNKEL - J. BEGRICH, *Einleitung in die Psalmen*, pp. 362-363.

[2] C. WESTERMANN, *o.c.*, pp. 143-144: "Die Rechtsverhandlung".

[3] C. WESTERMANN, *o.c.*, pp. 144-145: "Das Streitgespräch oder Disputationswort".

the court (e.g. Is. iii 14);[1] *'ăṣāmôt*, proofs; *ṣaddîq*, the man whose behaviour is examined and found correct, guiltless; *ba'al hammišpāṭ*, opponent in the trial; *hiršîa'*, to declare guilty; *y^ešû'â, ṣ^edāqâ*, the help given by an arbiter.[2] Although he creates some confusion with his appellation *Streitgespräch*, Köhler has delineated the characteristics of the trial speech better than any of his predecessors.

Gunkel-Begrich also paid some attention to the trial speech. The speech is preceded by a description of the trial (Is. iii 13). In the speech of the accuser heaven and earth are designated as judges (Is. i 2; Ps. l 6). It opens with a summons to the accused (Jer. ii 4; Ps. l 7), it addresses the opponent in the second person (Is. iii 14-15; Jer. ii 5ff., 22ff.; Mic. vi 3ff.; Ps. l 8, 9, 12). Or it opens with a question to the opponent (Is. iii 14; Ps. lxxxii 2). It refutes his arguments and then passes to the attack (Is. xliii 22ff.; Ps. l 8ff.). The speech of the judge commences addressing the accused, it casts the disputed point in his face, it states that the opponent has nothing to reply (in the third person). The guilt is declared and finally the judgment passed, in the second person (cf. Ps. lxxxii 2ff.; xli 21-29). The distinction between judgment and penalization is not clearly made here, as appears from the text references. In the same exposition some themes of the genre are listed: Yahwe as accusing his people, Yahwe as judge, the people as accused, accusations of exaggerating the value of cult with neglect of other obligations, violation of right.[3]

J. Begrich was the first to offer a systematic treatment of the trial speech.[4] *Gerichtsrede* is, in his opinion, a collective name for several types with relation to lawsuit: appeal of the accused or the plaintiff for a judicial sentence, pleadings, the sentence itself and, finally, the description of the lawsuit. An *Appellationsrede* of the accused was somewhat as follows: a question to the accuser about the charge (Gen. xxxi 36b; 1 Sam. xxiv 10), then the refutation of the charge (1 Sam. xxiv 11-12) sometimes in the form of a question (Gen. xxxi 37), the counter-charge (1 Sam. xxiv 12; Gen. xxxi 41-42), an appeal to the court (Gen. xxxi 37; 1 Sam. xxiv 13). The sequence

---

[1] The expression בוא במשפט עם rather means "to enter into judgment with" (cf. Ps. cxliii 2; Job ix 32; xxii 4). The meaning "court" for משפט is not proven and improbable. But משפט as a judicial term certainly has several concrete meanings. Cf. the dictionaries.

[2] L. Köhler, *Deuterojesaja*, pp. 110-116.

[3] H. Gunkel - J. Begrich, *o.c.*, pp. 364-365.

[4] J. Begrich, *Studien*, pp. 26-48.

of the motifs is relatively free, also in the *Appellationsrede* of the accuser. In the latter we may distinguish the following motifs: an appeal to the court (Gen. xvi 5; Is. i 18; xli 1) and the charge in perfect tense (Gen. xvi 5). When a claim is disputed reciprocally, the method of question and reply is often used (e.g. Is. xli 2-4).

In the pleadings of both parties at the court the same motifs obviously occur. The pleading of the accused asks for the reason of the charge (Jer. ii 5, 29; Mic. vi 3) and the legitimacy of the conclusion drawn from it (Jer. ii 5b-6; Joel iv 4b), it asserts the good he has done (Jer. ii 7a; Mic. vi 4-5), it alleges a counter-charge (Jer. ii 7b-9, 29-30; Joel iv 5-6; Is. l 1c), it asks for his witnesses, it tries to impress the judges (Jer. ii 12-13). Here also the sequence is free. Some formulas are typical of the genre. Such is the question: "Why do you plead (*rîb*) with me?" (Jer. ii 29). Further, after a question, the summons: "Answer me (*'nh*)" (Mic. vi 3). So the verb *'nh* becomes a technical term for the reply of one party to the other in a lawsuit (Job ix 3, 14, 15; xxxiii 13). Other technical terms are *bô'*, "to enter into judgment", a shortened form of the expression *bô' b^e^mišpāṭ*, and *qr'*, "to summon to court" (Is. lix 4).

The accuser directs his speech to the judges, speaking of his opponent in the third person (Is. i 2b-3; v 3-5), or he directly addresses the opponent (Ps. l 7 + 21c). He uses motifs similar to those the accused uses in his pleadings (cf. Ps. l 16 ff.; Is. iii 14-15) and alleges aggravating circumstances (Is. i 2-3). As to the pronouncement of the judge, BEGRICH only suggests the possibility of the judge being at the same time a party. Throughout his exposition we pick up some more technical terms: *'md*, "to present oneself to the judge", *'rk*, "to bring proofs" (Ps. l 21; Job xiii 18; xxiii 4); *yô'ēṣ*. The author does not make clear what meaning he ascribes to the last mentioned word.

H. E. VON WALDOW also devotes a paragraph of his dissertation, which I summarized in the firs chapter, to the trial speeches.[1] I pointed out the distinction between a cultic and a secularized type of trial speech. He finds both types in Dt.-Is. As a characteristic common to both he only mentions the use of juridical terms, which suggests the situation of a lawsuit. The secularized type is recognizable by the rejection of an accusation, which Israel would have moved against Yahwe and by Yahwe's invitation to the opponent to defend himself.

---

[1] H. E. VON WALDOW, *Anlass und Hintergrund*, pp. 37-47.

In the cultic type, as represented in Dt.-Is., he finds two main components: the *Beweisaufnahme* and the judgment. This clearly is the basic structure of the *Gerichtswort*, which, as we have seen, was detected by WESTERMANN. It thus is not a secundary formation, as VON WALDOW wrongly supposes.

In his doctoral dissertation, H. J. BOECKER made an exhaustive analysis of the judicial types.[1] Schematically he comes to these subdivisions:

A. Utterances before the lawsuit

- I. Types of the private discussion before the lawsuit
  1. Formula of accusation
  2. Formula of defence
- II. Transition to the lawsuit: *Appellationsreden*
  1. in the mouth of the accused
  2. in the mouth of the accuser
  3. appeal to a *Feststellungsverfahren* (not about a delict but about a claim)

B. Utterances during the lawsuit

- I. Accusations
  - — joined to a request for condemnation (Jer. xxvi)
  - — by witness (1 Kings xxi)
  - — by the account of the injured (1 Kings iii)
- II. Defence
  - — self-defence
    - — with couter-attack
    - — proof of innocence only
  - — defence of others
- III. Formulations of avowal
- IV. Proposals for a settlement

C. Decisive pronouncements

- I. Judgment
  1. pronouncement of guilt
  2. pronouncement of innocence
  3. settlement (in case of legal contest)
- II. Penalization (*Tatfolgebestimmung*)

---

[1] H. J. BOECKER, *Redeformen des israelitischen Rechtslebens*, Diss. Bonn 1959; republished: *Redeformen des Rechtslebens im A.T.*, Neukirchen 1964. Further I refer to this later edition.

In general BEGRICH's considerations have been confirmed here. It is impossible to go into details of BOECKER's study, but I use it fully when analyzing the texts. Just let us remark that an *Appellationsrede* addresses the opponent in the second person, while an accusation in court more than once speaks of the opponent in the third person. BOECKER has summarized the motifs of these genres but his list is hardly different from what we found in BEGRICH.

C. WESTERMANN confines himself to the trial speeches in Dt.-Is. He distinguishes between two groups, viz. the trial speeches "Yahwe — the nations" and "Yahwe — Israel". He proposes this general scheme of structure:

I. Summons (*Vorladung*)
II. The trial (*Verhandlung*)
  a) words of the parties
  b) interrogation of the witnesses
III. Judgment.

He opposes a more concrete subdivision, because we are dealing here with a very abstract stylization, not an imitation of real lawsuits. He does not study the proper style of the genre.[1]

From a quick reading of the form-critical literature about the trial speech, we may conclude that it is a real genre, with its proper style, *topoi* and terminology and with well defined subgenres.

b. Sitz im Leben

According to most of the form critics, this genre is an imitation of the corresponding genres in the administration of justice. "The internal connection,—thus BEGRICH,—of the different types of the trial speech is due to the fact that they are situated at distinct moments of the same trial. To show this is to delineate their *Sitz im Leben*".[2]

E. WÜRTHWEIN has contested this. Examining form and content of the trial speeches, he points in particular to the phrase "Yahwe has a *rîb* against ..." and to the fact that the background of the

---

[1] C. WESTERMANN, *Forschung*, pp. 134-144; *Jesaja 40-66*, pp. 16-18.

[2] J. BEGRICH, *Studien*, p. 27: "Der innere Zusammenhang der verschiedenen Gattungen der Gerichtsrede ist damit gegeben, dass sie ihren Standort an verschiedenen Stellen ein und desselben rechtshandels haben. Dies nachzuweisen, heisst zugleich ihren 'Sitz im Leben' schildern". — L. KÖHLER, *Deuterojesaja*, p. 110; H. W. WOLFF, *Das Zitat im Prophetenspruch*, München 1937, pp. 62-69.

accusation is mostly the covenant. The royal psalms also speak of a trial by Yahwe (Pss. xcvi 11-13; xcix 7-9; xcvii 5-6; lxxvi 8-10; l 1-7). WÜRTHWEIN considers that the cultic origin of these psalms is proven. The cultic drama thus knows a judgment by Jahwe through cultic persons (esp. Pss. l; lxxxvi; lxxxii). What is more likely, asks WÜRTHWEIN, than the bringing together of prophetic and cultic trials? So the prophetic trial speech is not an imitation of a profane one, but it has its origin in a cultic trial.[1] However, he excepts the dt.-Isaian trial speeches, because they have a different content from classical prophetism. I shall return to the question in the comments.

An important nuance has been introduced by F. HESSE. He thinks that only the trial speeches against the foreign nations can be reduced to this cultic setting as appears from the psalms alleged by WÜRTHWEIN and from the fact that the cultic nabis were prophets of salvation.[2] In his dissertation, VON WALDOW agrees with WÜRTHWEIN. The decisive argument, in his opinion, is the identity of accuser and judge in the person of Yahwe, which would be completely impossible in the profane administration of justice (contrast BEGRICH).[3] The priests have to watch over the covenantal faith of the people and thus also to "judge" in the framework of the covenantal cult. Such a cultic act can be considered the *Sitz im Leben* of the trial speech. The prophets imitate such a cultic situation. That this is imitation appears from the fact that the prophets developed the trial speech after the manner of the profane administration of justice. Hence VON WALDOW's distinction between a more cultic and a more profane type in the prophetical trial speeches.[4]

In any case, BOECKER's dissertation conclusively demonstrates by a thorough analysis of form and structure, that the prophets adopted the genres which were current in the profane trial. In his *Promotionsvortrag*, he demonstrated it once again.[5] WESTERMANN agrees with

---

[1] E. WÜRTHWEIN, "Der Ursprung der prophetischen Gerichtsrede", *ZTK.* XLIX 1952, pp. 1-16.

[2] F. HESSE, "Wurzelt die prophetische Gerichtsrede im israelitischen Kult?" *ZAW.* LXV 1953, pp. 45-53.

[3] Cf. p. 21.

[4] H. E. VON WALDOW, *Anlass und Hintergund*, pp. 37-39.

[5] H. J. BOECKER, "Anklagereden und Verteidigungsreden im Alten Testament", *EvTh.* XX 1960, p. 400.

him, and VON WALDOW, in his turn, under the influence of BOECKER's exposition, has abandoned his original view.[1]

An interesting approach to the problem has been made by J. HARVEY.[2] In the prophetical *rîb* he recognizes the following motifs:

I. Introduction
II. Interrogation with implicit accusation
III. Requisitory: accusation, reminder of Yahwe's benefits, ingratitude of Israel
IV. Reference to the uselessness of ritual compensation or foreign cults
V. Pronouncement of guilt and threat of total destruction or demands to change attitude (according to whether it is a *rîb* of condemnation or a *rîb* of warning).

Of the biblical material, he cites in particular Deut. xxxii 1-25; Is. i 2-3, 10-20; Mic. vi 1-8; Jer. ii 2-37; Ps. 1. The origin of this genre is to be found in international law, whence also the covenant pattern has been borrowed. In that international juridical context the *rîb* of condemnation is a declaration of war by the suzerain on the unfaithful vasal, the *rîb* of warning amounts to an ultimatum. This explanation is substantiated by some very ancient Akkadian and Hittite documents; the *epos* of Tukulti-Ninurta I, the *rîb* of Yarîm-Lim of Aleppo to Yašûb-Yaḫad of Dîr (Mari), the so-called letter about Milavata, the pleading against Madduwataš, the letter of Anum-ḫirbi to Waršama of Kaniš. In these documents the whole contest is a question of sacral law. The dispute with the opponent is regarded as a lawsuit. When nobody gives in, the decision is left to a divine judgment, i.e. to war.[3] The biblical *rîb*-prophecies are akin to these diplomatic transactions. The prophets pronounce, in the name of Yahwe, the condemnation or the ultimatum against the rupture of the covenant. They are the bearers of sacral law. Since this kind of *rîb* in international affairs is conducted through ambassadors, HARVEY is able to explain at the same time why the prophetic *rîb* often has the form of a message

[1] C. WESTERMANN, *Grundformen prophetischer Rede*, p. 97; H. E. VON WALDOW, *Der traditionsgeschichtliche Hintergrund*, p. 9.

[2] J. HARVEY, "Le 'Rîb-Pattern', réquisitoire prophétique sur la rupture de l'Alliance", *Bib.* XLIII 1962, pp. 172-196, further developed in his book *Le plaidoyer prophétique contre Israel après la rupture de l'alliance*, Bruges 1967, where the same structure is divided in a somewhat different way: I. Convocation; II. Interrogatory; III. Requisitory; IV. Pronouncement of guilt; Va. Condemnation and threats; Vb. Demands to change attitude (cf. p. 54).

[3] A. GOETZE, *Kleinasien*, München 1957, p. 127: "Die Auseinandersetzung mit dem Gegner wird als ein Prozess angesehen; gibt sich keiner schuldig, so muss ein Gottesgericht — eben der Krieg — herbeigeführt werden".

(*Botenspruch*). It should be noticed also that this position is in full accord with the structure of the genre as proposed by WESTERMANN.

Independently of HARVEY and by a different way, VON WALDOW came to similar conclusions in his monograph about trial speeches. After having admitted that BOECKER has proven the profane origin of the prophetic trial speech, he asks the question: which traditions and ideas induced the prophets to adopt this profane type? Moreover, the problem of the identity of party and judge in Yahwe remains. The solution is in the idea of covenant. In political treaties the gods were guarantors of loyalty to the treaty. When it was broken, the injured appealed to the intervention of these gods, who had to punish the offender. But in the biblical theology of covenant, Yahwe is at the same time a party and protecting God. In the case of rupture of the covenant, he accuses the people and condemns them at the same time. So VON WALDOW reaches a satisfying synthesis. In their form the prophetic trial speeches are rooted in the administration of justice, but in their contents they are in the tradition of Yahwe's covenant with his people. The identity of judge and party, necessarily resulting from the theology of covenant, gives their peculiar structure to the prophetic trial speeches, so that, besides all their connection with profane trial speeches, they keep a proper character.[1] We must take into account this complex *Sitz* when analyzing a trial speech.

3. *Disputation*

The prophets, thus BEGRICH, used the genre of disputation in order to defend their message and to convince their hearers (Cf. Am. iii 3-6, 7-8; ix 7; Is. x 8-11; xxviii 23-29; Jer. viii 8). Frequent forms in the genre are question and answer, statement and counterstatement. The aim is to convince and to refute objections. This is distinctive of the genre. The disputation often commences with a question about the point at issue or about a parallel truth which the opponent does agree to. On the ground of this truth one tries to convince the opponent of the point at issue. Often one does not formulate the conclusion but leaves it to the opponent to draw it for himself. Some *topoi* are questions like: "Do you not know ... ?" or an invitation like: "Remember ...". Finally BEGRICH points to the fact that Dt.-Is. more than once uses hymnic themes and forms in his disputations.[2]

---

[1] H. E. VON WALDOW, *Der traditionsgeschichtliche Hintergrund*, pp. 12-25.

[2] J. BEGRICH, *Studien*, pp. 48-53.

According to VON WALDOW, all of Dt.-Isaiah's disputations show this structure: A. the *Disputationsbasis*, the starting point, which the adversary is supposed to have already agreed to; B. the conclusion (*Schlussfolgerung*) which is drawn from A. The first member aims at finding a common base. Such is done with a question, a quotation of a known hymn, a reference to known facts. Sometimes the thesis which is to be refuted precedes (xl 27) or the thesis which is to be proven (xlv 18d). The member B may have various forms (comparison, questions, word of salvation, etc.). In view of their very simple structure, according to VON WALDOW, the disputations of Dt.-Is. are not literary imitations; they must be real disputations.[1]

WESTERMANN points out that in the pericopes in question, we never have an exact copy of a dispute. Only one side is speaking and one could better call it a *Bestreitung*. The forms which it adopts are so various that we would not have to do with a genre properly. Further, WESTERMANN only analyzes the disputes in Dt.-Is. We too shall turn now to the texts.

§2. THE TRIAL SPEECHES IN IS. XL-LV

1. *Is. xliii 22-28*

22 You did not call me, Jacob,
you did *not* [a] weary yourself for me, Israel.
23 You have not brought me your sheep for burnt offerings,
or honored me with your sacrifices.
I have not made you serve me with grain offerings,
nor wearied you with frankincense.
24 You have not brought me sweet cane with money,
or sated me with the fat of your sacrifices.
You made me serve with your sins,
you have wearied me with your iniquities.
25 I, I am he who blots out your transgressions,
for my own sake I remember your sins no more.
26 Bring a charge against me! Let us go into court!
Set forth your case, that you may be proved right!
27 Your first father sinned,
and your spokesmen rebelled against me.

[1] H. E. VON WALDOW, *Anlass und Hintergrund*, pp. 28-36.

28 Therefore I slew the princes of the sanctuary,
I delivered Jacob to utter destruction
and Israel to reviling.

[a] לא c LXX, Vg. Cf. parallelism.

The utterance Is. xliii 22-28 is the one that comes closest to the basic structure described by Westermann in his *Grundformen prophetischer Rede*.[1] Its delimitation is easy and it can be found already in IQIa.[2] The inclusion "Jacob-Israel" (vss. 22 and 28) marks the delimitation stylistically.

Yahwe is speaking and the speech is directed against Israel. In the vss. 22-24 we have the accusation, which mainly consists in a rejection of a complaint against Yahwe. So, along with Begrich and Boecker, we can characterize the pericope as an *Appellationsrede* of the accused, a genre we meet also in Gen. xxxi 32, 37, 41-42; Jud. xi 27; 1 Sam. xxiv 10-16 and in a prophetic context in Jer. ii 5ff.[3] They think, however, that here the accused does not defend himself against an accusation but against a claim. Israel would think Yahwe obliged to help it thanks to some favors it did for him. According to Westermann, on the contrary, Yahwe defends himself against a straight accusation, which is quoted in the last verse: "You delivered Jacob to destruction ..." Then the vss. 22-24 do not allude to a claim for the future but rather to a demand from the past: "How could you act this way, Yahwe, whereas we served you faithfully?" In the same sense, von Waldow supposes that an accusation of rupture of the covenant, proferred by Israel against Yahwe, is at the base of this pericope.[4] The interpretation proposed by Westermann and von Waldow, is the best, as it gives better account of the whole pericope. We find a similar accusation in Ps. xliv. The refutation by Yahwe follows this line: "You did not serve me, but you only burdened me with your sins; so I had to deliver Jacob to destruction".

Let us now consider the details in order to throw more light on the prophet's message. The accusation, after an impressive series of *lō'*,

---

[1] C. Westermann, *Grundformen*, p. 122; cf. p. 180.

[2] Cf. M. Burrows, *The Dead Sea Scrolls of St. Mark's Monastery*, I, pl. XXXVII.

[3] J. Begrich, *Studien*, p. 27; H. J. Boecker, *Redeformen*, pp. 54-55; cf. H. E. von Waldow, *Traditionsgeschichtliche Hintergrund*, p. 44.

[4] C. Westermann, *Forschung*, p. 142; *Jesaja 40-66*, p. 107; H. E. von Waldow, *Anlass und Hintergrund*, p. 40.

comes to the decisive attack (vs. 24b); clearly marked by the particle *'ak*. Israel thinks that it has merited Yahwe's protection by its accomplishments, but this pretension is energetically rejected by Yahwe through the striking opposition between 23b and 24b: *lō' he'ĕbadtîkā - he'ĕbadtanî*; *lō' hôga'tîkā - hôga'tanî*. This throwing back of the accusation is a classical motif in the *Appellationsrede* of the accused (cf. 1 Sam. xxiv 12bβ; Jud. xi 27aβ; Jer. ii 6-7).

The first verses are related to the sacrificial cult, which is presented in all its variety. The prophet mentions holocausts (*'ōlôt*), sacrifices (*zebāḥîm*), grain offerings (*minḥâ*), frankincense (*lebônâ*). The cane (*qāneh*), mentioned in vs. 24a, must have something to do with cult also. Jer. vi 20 has *qāneh ṭôb*, parallel with *lebônâ*, coming from a far country. It is a sweet smelling cane, used for the incense offering. The same is meant in Is. xliii 24 with the shortened expression *qāneh* (cf. Ez. xxvii 19; Cant. iv 14).[1] The LXX renders it as θυμίαμα. With his negative attitude toward cult the prophet is in the line of his predecessors: Am. v 21-25; Hos. v 6; vi 6; Is. i 10-15; Mic. vi 6-8; Jer. vii 22. Indeed, I do not accept that the reproach is directed against the neglect of cult, as asserted in *Bible de Jerusalem*.[2] The *Appellationsrede* precisely supposes that Israel asserts his care of cult. And I cannot see how such a reproach could be historically justified. The reproach only concerns the formalistic cult without righteousness (see vs. 24b). True, Israel has performed its cult, but the prayers and sacrifices did not reach God. This idea, as is usual in Dt.-Is., is expressed in very radical terms: "You did not worship me". But the nuance is: "It is not me you worshipped", as appears from the order of words in vs. 22a: *lō'-'ōtî qārā'tā*. Since these are the very first words of the pericope, they bear upon the interpretation of the following verses.

There has been a lot of discussion about the anti-cultic attitude of the prophets. R. HENTSCHKE cites an impressive list of scholars who deal with the problem as to whether the prophets radically

---

[1] Cf. KB, p. 844. It is unnecessary to postulate a root *ṭwb* II. KB invoke Arab. *ṭîbon*, "perfume", but this also is derived from *ṭwb*, "good", as well as the adj. in Akk. *qanû ṭābu*. The adj. *ṭôb* in Semitic languages often has a concrete meaning according to the object it defines: sweet, agreable, solid, attractive; cf. e.g. J. AISTLEITNER, *Wörterbuch der ugaritischen Sprache*, p. 119; C. F. JEAN - J. HOFTIJZER, *DISO*, p. 99.

[2] *La Sainte Bible*, p. 1032, note b: "Cet oracle, où Yahvé reproche à Israël d'avoir négligé son culte ...".

rejected cult or only opposed pagan deviations or cultic formalism.[1] He himself stands in an intermediate position. The prophets attacked cult in so far as it was a cult of nature, proceeding from a false religiosity, but, as they did not know a better cult, their opposition concretely was an absolute rejection of cult.[2] However, H. WILDBERGER has made it clear that, in Is. i 10-15, the disposition and the behaviour of the people who participate in the cult, is rejected. The same is true of Hos. vi 6: "One cannot replace covenantal loyalty (*ḥesed*) by sacrifices", and of Am. v 21-25 (social justice), the most ancient witnesses of prophetical polemics against cult. The same interpretation seems to be the best also with regard to Mic. vi 6-8 and Jer. vii 22, *pace* W. RUDOLPH.[3] The prophets oppose cult because it is an alibi for the people in their ethical iniquity. That Dt.-Is. is in the same tradition is evidenced from vs. 24b: the counter-accusation. Israel did not bring a true cult to Yahwe, it only committed sins. GUNKEL-BEGRICH sharply summarize the accusation: "overestimation of cult and neglect of other duties" (cf. Ps. l 8ff.).[4]

The rejection of Israel's pretension based on its cult includes something more. Not only did their cult not reach Yahwe, but Yahwe had not asked that much. It was not his fault that the sacrifices became a kind of slavery and a tiring occupation (vs. 23b). Here we hear the same blame of over-estimation of cult. One would rather expect: "You did not burden yourselves with grain offerings nor weary yourselves with frankincense". This idea is not well expressed in the actual verse. One has the impression that the prophet chose the causative formulation because of the opposition between vss. 23b and 24b, which I pointed out above. But in this way a new idea emerges: the overestimation of cult is not wanted by God. Yahwe did not compel his people to slavery.

---

[1] R. HENTSCHKE, *Die Stellung der vorexilischen Schriftpropheten zum Kultus*, Berlin 1957, p. 1, note 4.

[2] R. HENTSCHKE, *o.c.*, pp. 122-125.

[3] H. WILDBERGER, *Jesaja*, Neukirchen 1965, pp. 38-39; H. W. WOLFF, *Dodekapropheton* 1, Neukirchen 1965, p. 154; D. DEDEN, *De kleine profeten*, Roermond 1953, pp. 147 and 225; W. RUDOLPH, *Jeremia*, Tübingen 1958, pp. 51-54. — Cf. W. EICHRODT, *Theologie des A.T.*, I, pp. 244-247; 103, note 348: "Es handelt sich also in der Polemik der Propheten darum, ob der Bundesbruch durch Opfer geheilt werden kann oder ob sie nur unter der Voraussetzung des intakten Bundesverhältnisses einen Sinn haben, nicht aber um die Ersetzung des Kultus durch Moral". — Cf. also K. ROUBOS, *Profetie en cultus in Israël*, Wageningen 1956.

[4] H. GUNKEL - J. BEGRICH, *Einleitung*, p. 365.

On the contrary, Israel enslaved Yahwe with its sins. WESTERMANN correctly points out the profound condemnation of Israel, which is pronounced here. "God is Lord: in all Semitic religions what consitutes the nature of divinity is lordship. If God is made into a *'ebed*, if he is made to serve, he has his divinity taken from him".[1] The whole depth of Israel's sins is illustrated by the three terms the prophet uses to indicate them. Israel's sin consists in transgressions against Yahwe's law, against the clauses of covenant (*ḥaṭṭa'â*); it comes from a wrong attitude towards him (*'āwōn*); it is a rebellion against the lord, the suzerain of the covenant (*peša'*).[2]

All the evil is on Israel's side, whereas Yahwe, and He alone, wipes out the sins of his people. The double *'ānōkî* underlines this divine initiative which has nothing to do with the people's perfomance. The adjunct *l^ema'ănî* expresses the same idea. In his *Appellationsrede*, Yahwe thus opposes his own forgiveness to the continuous sins of his people. The opposition is expressed also in the rhythm, vs. 25 being 4 + 3 surrounded by 3 + 3 verses. It is wrong to emend the verse because of rhythm.[3] The verse thus expresses what Yahwe has always done, in contrast with Israel's iniquity; it is not an announcement of forgiveness.[4]

The appeal to a trial properly speaking follows in vs. 26. Such is not expressed directly. Yahwe feels his position to be so strong that he does not need to appeal to a trial. But he suggests that his adversary do so, if he wants to. Both *hizkîr* and *sippēr* are technical terms for a judicial accusation. The first word means "to denounce a crime" in a juridical sense (cf. *hizkîr 'āwōn*; Num. v 15; 1 Kings xvii 18; Ez. xxi 28).[5] The other means "to tell, to expound" and in connection with an accusation it indicates the exposition of the case by the injured side.[6] The verse thus means: "Bring a charge against me,

---

[1] C. WESTERMANN, *Jesaja 40-66*, p. 107; Eng. ed. p. 131.

[2] Cf. H. E. VON WALDOW, "... *denn Ich erlöse dich*", p. 80. In my opinion, the author wrongly connects the idea of rebellion with עון and that of guilt with פשע. Cf. KB, pp. 689 and 785.

[3] Against L. KÖHLER, *Deuterojesaja*, p. 22. If at the end of the verse we add the particle עוד as in IQIa, we even have a 4 + 4 verse.

[4] Differently in A. SCHOORS, "The Rîb-Pattern in Isaiah xl-lv", *Bijdragen*, XXX 1969, pp. 27-28.

[5] Cf. ZORELL, p. 209; J. BEGRICH, *Studien*, p. 33, note 94. A more extensive treatment in H. J. BOECKER, *Redeformen*, pp. 106-110.

[6] An example of such an exposition in 1 Kings iii 17-21. Cf. H. J. BOECKER, *o.c.*, p. 74, note 3.

let us go into court! Set forth your case, that you may be proved right". The transition from vs. 25 to 26 is a typical dt.-Isaian wordplay. The root *zkr*, used twice in the same context, has two concretely distinct meanings.

The prophet repeats the accusation in a more historical perspective. Israel's whole history is full of sin. Israel's father is Jacob and with him began the history of sin in God's own people. One generally accepts that the allusion is to the way in which Jacob stole the birthright from Esau. Some scholars supposed that Adam or Abraham were meant. But B. J. VAN DER MERWE has convincingly shown that a reference to Jacob is more probable.[1] Adam plays no part in Dt.-Is. The idea that in this context Abraham is the father of Israel dates back to old Jewish traditions and occurs in JEROME, RASHI, DELITZSCH and others.[2] An argument in favour of this opinion is Is. li 2: "Abraham, your father", and xli 8: "offspring of Abraham". But the theme of Abraham's sin plays no part in the whole Bible and, if Abraham were meant, Is. xliii 27 would be completely isolated. The arguments in favour of an identification with Jacob are better. In the first place, there is a chiastic parallelism with vs. 28:

your father	*m^eliṣeykā*
śārê qōdeš	Jacob-Israel

Further, it appears from xlviii 1 and xliv 5a, that the people in Dt.-Isaiah's time attached importance to the name Jacob-Israel. But above all, in xliii 27, Dt.-Is. resumes a prophetic tradition, which we find in Hos. xii 4-5 and to which also Jer. ix 3 alludes. This tradition seems to continue after the exile, as e.g. in Mal. iii 6.

After Jacob the *m^elîṣîm* of Israel also rebelled against Yahwe. The Hebrew *lîṣ* or *lûṣ* seems to derive from a double Semitic root. *Lûṣ* I, protosem. *lṣ*, as e.g. in Arab. *lâṣa,* means "to deviate from the right way". In this sense, the participle is often used in sapiential literature to indicate the wicked, the haughty, the arrogant (e.g. Prov. i 22; ix 7-8; xiii 1; etc.). In the Phoenician inscription from Karatepe, the part. yiph. *mlṣm* means "rebels" and is used in parallelism with *r'*.[3] In the O.T., the participle *mēlîṣ* designates an inter-

[1] B. J. VAN DER MERWE, *Pentateuchtradisies*, pp. 130-139.

[2] S. JEROME, *Comment. in Isaiam, Liber XII, ad loc.*: "... quando Domino terram repromissionis semini illius pollicente, respondit: In quo sciam quia possidebo eam?" Cf. STRACK-BILLERBECK, vol. I, pp. 118; 284; 855; vol. II, p. 174.

[3] Cf. H. DONNER - W. RÖLLIG, *KAI*, nr 26, A, 8; C. F. JEAN - J. HOFTIJZER, *DISO*, p. 138.

preter (Gen. xlii 23), legates (2 Chron. xxxii 31), magistrates (Sir. x 2), an advocate (Job xxxiii 23). In a Phoenician inscription from Abydos also *mlṣ* seems to designate a similar function.[1] I agree with ZORELL that *lûṣ* II is used here, though he incorrectly relates it to Arab. *lâza* or *lâḏa*.[2] All known texts thus allow a definition of the function of a *mēlîṣ* in general terms as that of a "spokesman, a mediator". In Is. xliii 27 the leaders of the people are meant, but it is hard to decipher whether this refers to the political leaders, or the priests or the prophets. The first meaning is adopted in the Peshitta,[3] but this does not prove anything. The present trial speech comes very close to the classical genre in its form. Thematically also we met older prophetical traditions in the criticism of cult and the reference to Jacob's sin. It thus is acceptable that, also in vs. 27b, Dt.-Is. adopts the prophetical motif of criticism of the priests and official prophets.

The final verse offers a small textcritical problem. When one accepts the MT, the verse does not make much sense in the mouth of our prophet: he would be announcing to Israel a coming punishment, which does not match any of his other utterances. Verse 28b can easily be rendered as: "I delivered Jacob to *ḥērem* and Israel to reviling". Then one reads *wā'ettēn* with conversive *waw*, at the condition that a past tense precedes. Such is the reading of LXX and Vulgate,[4] and it is only a minor problem of vocalisation. One might have the impression that the term "officials" (vs. 28a) is in continuity with "father" and "spokesmen" of vs. 27. Then one should read something like: "Your leaders profaned my sanctuary", which is the reading of LXX and Peshitta.[5] C. F. WHITLEY proposed: *wayyeḥallelû śāreykā šemî*, "your leaders profaned my name".[6] This emendation is too arbitrary. It is better to connect the colon with the following: "I profaned the officials of the sanctuary". So one keeps the consonantal text intact. The first verb then needs a conversive *waw*, which has

---

[1] Cf. H. DONNER - W. RÖLLIG, *KAI*, nr 49, 17; vol. III, p. 66.

[2] Cf. ZORELL, pp. 394-395. Protosem. *lz* and *lḏ* would both result in a Heb. or Phoen. לוז.

[3] Pesh: ܡܫܠܛܢ̈ܝܟ.

[4] LXX: ἔδωκα; Vg: dedi.

[5] So HOUBIGANT, KLOSTERMANN, CHEYNE, CONDAMIN, AUVRAY-STEINMANN. LXX: ἐμίαναν οἱ ἄρχοντες τὰ ἅγιά μου;; Pesh: ܘܛܢܦܘ ܪ̈ܘܪܒܢܝܟ ܡܩܕܫܐ.

[6] C. F. WHITLEY, "Textual Notes on Deutero-Isaiah", *VT*. XI 1961, pp. 457-461.

the value of a *waw conclusivum.*[1] But what does it mean? WESTERMANN deletes *śārê qōdeš we'ettenâ* without any justification.[2] In some Phoenician inscriptions of the V-IVth century the title *śr qdš* is an epithet of the god Eshmun.[3] If one supposes a divine epithet in Is. xliii 28 also, then the prophet says that Yahwe profaned gods. This makes a good sense, if it means that he deprived them of their divinity, that he showed their "undivine" nature. Such would fit very well the dt.-Isaian polemic against the pagan gods. But it is not clear what it has to do in the present context. One may think of the anointed king but most probably the expression indicates the priests. This is suggested by the plural and by the chiasm in which *śārê qōdeš* balances *melîṣeykā*, but above all by 1 Chron. xxiv 5, where the same title is applied to the priests. A last remark about *ḥll*: it is better to abandon the traditional rendering "to profane", and to take *ḥll* II, "to pierce", which provides a better parallel with *'ettenâ laḥērem.*[4]

Yahwe delivered Israel to *ḥērem.* It is known that *ḥērem* is a term which originally belonged to the holy war and had a religious meaning. The defeated enemy and his possessions were made *ḥērem*, which meant a consecration to the victor's deity (cf. Stela of Mesha, line 17; Num. xxi 2-3; Jos. vi 21; 1 Sam. xv). But the religious meaning gradually got lost, and so it became possible that, besides Israel, also other nations and even Yahwe were subject of the verb *heḥĕrîm* or *ntn leḥērem.* The word then simply means "to destroy" (e.g. 2 Kings xix 11; 2 Chron. xx 23; Is. xxxiv 2).[5] Precisely Jeremiah's threatening Judah with *ḥērem* is a good antecedent of Dt.-Is. (cf. Jer. xxv 9). The *ḥērem* can hit somebody as a punishment, especially for idolatry (Ex. xxii 19; Lev. xxvii 29; Deut. xiii 13-19). So the sense of Is. xliii 28 is this: because of its sins Israel is punished by Yahwe with utter destruction. I think that an allusion to the holy war, in the sense that Nabuchadnezzar would have made Yahwe's holy war against his own people, cannot be proven.[6]

---

1 JOÜON, § 118 i; so Vg: et contaminavi principes sanctos. P. VOLZ, *Jesaja II*, p. 44, translates vs. 28b as follows: "So musste ich Jakob dem Bann hingeben, Israel der Verhönung". On the cohortative form for phonetic reasons, cf. GK, § 108 g.

2 C. WESTERMANN, *Jesaja 40-66*, p. 106.

3 Cf. *RES*, I, nr 287, 5-6; 289, 4; 294, 5.

4 Cf. J. L. McKENZIE, *Second Isaiah*, p. 58.

5 C. BREKELMANS, *De* ḥerem *in het Oude Testament*, Nijmegen 1959, pp. 51-52; 114-123; cf. *BW*3, col. 118-119.

6 Against H. E. VON WALDOW. "... *denn Ich erlöse dich*", pp. 84-86.

After the accusation, the classical *rîb* would have a condemnation. Indeed, vs. 28 still bears the remembrance of a judgment. The verse is not a pronouncement of sentence, but rather the statement of a *fait accompli*, referring to the defeat of 587 and the Babylonian exile. Is. xliii 22-28 is an *Appellationsrede*, which still clearly reflects the classical *rîb*-structure. But the prophet changes the pronouncement of the sentence into a simple statement about the judgment that is accomplished already. The prophet, or better, Yahwe through his prophet, shows why he had to punish. He justifies the destruction of Israel with a reference to its sins throughout its history, especially the sins of its leaders. Here too is a traditional feature of the *Gerichtsworte*. Dt.-Is. keeps the moral gravity of his predecessors. Although Yahwe is the one who forgives and forgets the sins, the events of the exile prove that he does not fail to punish, when he has to.

2. *Is. l 1-3*

1 Thus says Yahwe:
"Where is your mother's bill of divorce,
with which I dismissed her?
Or which of my creditors is it
to whom I have sold you?
Behold, for your iniquities you were sold,
and for your transgressions your mother was dismissed.
2 Why, when I came, was there no man,
when I called, was there no answer?
Is my hand too short for it to rescue,
or have I no power to deliver?
Behold, by my rebuke I dry up the sea,
I turn rivers into a desert;
their fish stink for lack of water,
and die of thirst.
3 I clothe the heavens with blackness,
and make sackcloth their covering.

This pericope is clearly delimited by the preceding salvation words (xlix 14-26) and the following Servant poem. At the commencement, the messenger's formula strengthens this delimitation. But the inner structure of the pericope is not very obvious and the form critics are divided as to the genre. Let us analyze the text.

According to vs. 1, we have to do with the saying of an accused, comparable to Jer. ii 4-13, 29-30; Mic. vi 3-5. As BEGRICH rightly remarks, it is a speech of a man, who has been accused by his sons of having repudiated their mother and sold themselves.[1] On this point the situation is the same as in xliii 22-28. Again Yahwe stands in court as the accused. In figurative speech the catastrophe of 587 is evoked. Yahwe's spouse, the mother of the Israelites, is Zion, as far as it is a symbol of the whole nation. Yahwe would have broken his covenant with Israel like one who has divorced. Such would have happened concretely in the exile, as vs. 1b clearly suggests with the image of the sale of the children to the creditors. Similar complaints are expressly formulated in Jer. xiv 19 (a lament of Jeremiah) and Ps. xliv 13. This accusation is not expressly contradicted, though the rhetorical question involves a certain retort. Yahwe rather justifies his deed. He was obliged so to act because of Israel's sins.[2] Although here the mode of expression is more succinct, the train of thought is the same as in Is. xliii 22-28.

Judging from the terminology, verse 2a continues the trial speech, as BEGRICH rightly pointed out. The verb *bô'* is an abbreviation of *bô' b^e mišpāṭ* (cf. Ps. cxliii 2; Job ix 32; xxii 4). Further, *qr'* means the question from one party to the other, perhaps more the challenge to court (cf. Job ix 16; xiii 22; Is. lix 4), while *'nh* indicates the rejoinder of the adversary (Mic. vi 3; Job ix 3, 14, 15; xiii 22; xxiii 5; xxxiii 12).[3] What is the meaning of the verse? According to BEGRICH, the accusers withdrew, so that the accused can say: "What am I pleading here, there is no longer anybody who attacks me". It may be better to suppose that nobody accepts his challenge to go to court. At any rate, the plaintifs have no answer. A similar phrase is found in another trial speech of the prophet (Is. xli 28). This interpretation certainly surpasses the one proposed by some scholars, who explain the verse with reference to the rejection of the prophetic message, be it past or present.[4]

---

[1] J. BEGRICH, *Studien*, p. 38.

[2] Cf. P. VOLZ, *Jesaia II*, p. 107.

[3] Cf. *Bible de Jérusalem*, p. 609, note f: "Litt. 'lui répondre'. Le verbe a souvent un sens judiciaire".

[4] L. G. RIGNELL, "Jesaja Kap. 50", *SvTKv.* XXIX 1953, p. 110; C. R. NORTH, *The Second Isaiah*, p. 149; F. DELITZSCH, *Commentar*, pp. 513-514; B. J. VAN DER MERWE, *Pentateuchtradisies*, p. 149; J. KNABENBAUER, *Commentarius in Isaiam prophetam*, II, p. 253.

In BEGRICH's opinion, the pericope now passes into a disputation, in which the prophet opposes the idea that Yahwe was not able to help. A similar position is defended by VON WALDOW. From his trial speech Yahwe would draw the conclusion: if he is able to punish his people, he is able to restore it also. Such would be illustrated with a reference to his unlimited power, which became manifest at the exodus (vs. 2cd).[1] As we shall see below, such a topic is not alien to the disputations of our prophet. A dispute about Yahwe's power to save Israel is accepted by WESTERMANN too. The latter, however, considers this to be the second motif of the complaint against Yahwe, so that in vs. 2b the trial speech is continued. In this respect, he incorrectly asserts that vss. 2b-3 have a parallel in xliii 22-24.[2] The theme of Yahwe's lack of power is completely absent from that trial speech. The choice between the opinions is difficult but WESTERMANN's interpretation has the advantage of saving the unity of type.

In order to prove that his hand is not "too short to rescue", Yahwe invokes his dominion over nature. It is clear that the concrete picture involves an allusion to the exodus and the connected episode of the plagues of Egypt. The prophet again uses cultic traditions: in Ps. cvi 9 we read: *wayyigʿar beyam-sûp wayyeḥěrāb*; in Ps. cvii 33: *yāśēm nehārôt lemidbār* (cf. Is. xlii 15). The verse member 2cβ may contain an allusion to the passage of the Jordan. In Ps. lxvi 6 too, the passage of the Reed Sea and that of the Jordan are mentioned in the same breath. B. J. VAN DER MERWE prefers to see here mythical reminiscences of creation rather than historical reminiscences of the exodus.[3] We can reject his appeal to Ps. civ 7, since the above-cited texts offer parallels that are much more striking. A valuable argument for his opinion he may find in Nah. i 4: "He rebukes the sea and makes it dry, he dries up all the rivers (*gʿr, yām, nehārôt, heḥěrîb*). Yet the parallels I adduced are closer to Is. l 2. Furthermore, vs. 2d refers to the traditions about the plagues of Egypt (Ex. vii 18-19; viii 10; *dāgâ, mût, bāʾaš, nehārôt*).[4] Against this, too, VAN DER MERWE raises

---

[1] J. BEGRICH, *o.c.*, p. 52; H. E. VON WALDOW, *Anlass und Hintergrund*, p. 41; *Der traditionsgeschichtliche Hintergrund*, p. 143.

[2] C. WESTERMANN, *Forschung*, p. 143.

[3] B. J. VAN DER MERWE, *o.c.*, p. 152.

[4] J. MORGENSTERN thinks that at the end of the verse the word בהמה got lost. Cf. J. MORGENSTERN, "The Loss of Words at the Ends of Lines in Manuscripts of Biblical Poetry", *HUCA*. XXV 1954, p. 62. Cf. also DUHM, KÖHLER, WESTERMANN, *BHS*.

objections, which do not convince me. He artificially disjoins the members c and d. When one reads them together, I do not see how one can elude my interpretation. I do not understand VAN DER MERWE's reserves on this point, the more so as in many oracles the prophet deduces Yahwe's creative power from history. He even uses terminology of creation to indicate Yahwe's historical interventions (e.g. Is. xlii 9; xliii 19; xlviii 3, 7).[1] In the present context also we have to do with Yahwe's creative power, as manifest in the facts of the exodus. This blending of creation- and exodus-motif is rightly recognized by C. STUHLMUELLER. However, his conclusion, that "Dt.-Is. is announcing a new exodus in which Yahwe vigorously renews or re-creates the whole realm of Israel's existence", goes beyond the actual range of the context.[2]

One may wonder if vs. 3 does not allude to the plague of darkness in Egypt. There is no verbal contact with Ex. x 21 or Ps. cv 28. Nevertheless, this interpretation fits the context very well. Of itself, the verse could suggest a thunder-storm, in which Yahwe manifests his power.[3] BEGRICH sees in the verse the description of an eschatological phenomenon in nature. Also WESTERMANN thinks that it suggests apocalyptic. He gives the impression that the verse does not belong to the pericope, which, in his opinion, is broken off.[4] Such cannot be proved, although the trial speech gives an impression of being unfinished. VAN DER MERWE correctly rejects an eschatological interpretation of vs. 3, but he is wrong again in not accepting an historical interpretation, viz. referring to the plagues of Egypt. If we want to keep the verse in the present context, the allusion to that episode offers the best interpretation. The South African scholar gives no own positive explanation.

In the framework of the trial speech we may paraphrase vss. 2b-3 as follows: to the accusation of having abandoned his people, Yahwe retorts: "Do you think I am not able to deliver you? I proved in Egypt that I am able to. If I have not yet done it, then it must have been for another reason". From vs. 1 we know that this reason was Israel's sin.

---

[1] Cf. A. SCHOORS, "L'eschatologie dans les prophéties du Deutéro-Isaïe", *Recherches bibliques*, VIII 1967, p. 114.

[2] C. STUHLMUELLER, *Creative Redemption in Deutero-Isaiah*, Rome 1970, pp. 91-92.

[3] J. KOENIG, *Bible de la Pléiade*, II, p. 177.

[4] J. BEGRICH, *o.c.*, p. 83; C. WESTERMANN, *Jesaja 40-66*, p. 182.

3. *Is. xlii 18-25*

18 Hear, you deaf!
and look, you blind, that you may see.
19 Who is blind but my servant
and deaf like my messenger, whom I send?
(Who is blind like *m^e^šullām*,[a]
and blind (deaf) like the servant of Yahwe?)
20 *You have seen*[b] much, but did not heed it,
your ears were open, *but you have*[c] not heard.
21 Yahwe wished, because of his salvific will,
to make his teaching great and *glorious*.[d]
22 But this is a people plundered and spoiled,
they are all of them *trapped in holes*,[e]
they are hidden in prisons.
They became a prey, there was none to rescue,
a *spoil*[f] and none said: "Restore!"
23 Who among you hearkens to this,
attends and listens for the time to come?
24 Who gave up Jacob to the *spoiler*,[g]
and Israel to the plunderers?
(Is it not Yahwe, against whom we sinned,
in whose ways they would not walk,
and to whose teaching they would not listen?)
25 (Who) poured upon him the *heat of*[h] his anger
and the fury of war?
It scorched him round about, but he did not understand,
it burned him, but he paid no attention.

[a] See comments.
[b] Lg רָאִיתָ c K; IQIa: ראיתה.
[c] Lg תשמע c 60 mss; LXX: ἠκούσατε; Pesh: ܫܡܥܬܘܢ ܐܢܬܘܢ; unless we accept a shift from the second to the third person, עבד יהוה of vs. 19 being subject of ישמע.
[d] LXX: *κύριος ὁ θεὸς ἐβούλετο ἵνα δικαιωθῇ καὶ μεγαλύνῃ αἴνεσιν*; Vg: Et Dominus voluit ut sanctificaret eum et magnificaret legem, et extolleret.
[e] Lg הֻפָּחוּ בְּחוֹרִים loco הָפֵחַ בַּחוּרִים; cf. LXX and parallel colon.
[f] IQIa: למשוסה loco משסה. Cf. Targ. Pesh. Vg. But the rule of the double duty prefix suffices to explain MT.
[g] Lg משוסה c K, IQIa.
[h] Lg חמת c IQIa; LXX; Tg; Vg.

I hesitate somewhat to analyze Is. xlii 18-25, after reading BEGRICH's confession that he does not understand this pericope, and seeing WESTERMANN's question-mark, when he lists it with the trial speeches.[1] The pericope certainly has a polemic character. But it is hard to decide whether it is a trial speech or a disputation. It is to this problem that I turn now.

The summons in vs. 18 can be the introduction to a trial speech. L. KÖHLER points in the same direction, as he defines vs. 18 as a *Zweizeugenruf*.[2] Why the hearers are called blind and deaf will appear from the following verses. The rhetorical question in vs. 19 also makes a good sense in the framework of a trial speech. One may suppose that Yahwe defends himself against the charge that he is blind and deaf. To this he retorts with the question: "Who is blind but my servant?" The charge against Yahwe would be the same as the one quoted in xl 27: Yahwe is blind and deaf to Israel's burden of suffering. The pericope thus would be an *Appellationsrede* of an accused. This interpretation, proposed by WESTERMANN, is the best I know, and it allows the present pericope to rank with xliii 22-28 and l 1-3.[3] Further analysis will confirm this.

The explanation of details reveals a lot of problems. Therefore, it is not surprising that many exegetes delete some parts as inauthentic; for example K. MARTI (vss. 19, 21-22a), B. DUHM (vss. 19b-22a), A. CONDAMIN (vs. 22a), S. MOWINCKEL (vss. 19-23), K. ELLIGER (id.), J. STEINMANN (vss. 19b, 21), G. FOHRER (vss. 19-21, 24-25). I am convinced that the whole pericope must be preserved, except perhaps vss. 19b and 24b, which are very dubious.

With the servant in vs. 19a the whole nation is meant. The LXX even has the plural.[4] But what about the messenger in the member β? The Vulgate reads: nisi ad quem nuntios misi. If this reading is correct, the verse makes good sense. The MT permits this reading, at least according to the consonants. The messengers who were sent to Israel then are the former prophets.[5] But parallelism favours the strict masoretic reading. The question is, to whom Israel is sent as a messenger. According to P. VOLZ, the prophet refers, with the epithet "my messenger" to Israel's task to be Yahwe's witness in the world.[6] This task is not strange to our prophet's message, as is

---

1 J. BEGRICH, *Studien*, p. 13; C. WESTERMANN, *Forschung*, p. 141.
2 L. KÖHLER, *Deuterojesaja*, p. 113.
3 C. WESTERMANN, *Jesaja 40-66*, p. 90.
4 LXX: *οἱ παῖδές μου*. Cf. S. D. LUZZATTO, *Il profeta Isaia*, Padova 1867, p. 472.
5 Cf. J. KNABENBAUER, *Commentarius*, II, p. 120.
6 P. VOLZ, *Jesaia II*, p. 33; B. DUHM, *Jesaia*, p. 285.

evident from Is. lv 4-5, which we dealt with above, and from xliii 10 and xliv 8.

Verse 19b seems to be tautological after 19a. Therefore most of the exegetes consider it as inauthentic.[1] As a matter of fact, in Dt.-Is. parallelism is always variable. But the colon is attested in the most ancient witnesses and in the further textual tradition it is missing nowhere. Perhaps one should replace *wᵉʿiwwēr* in 19b by *ḥērēš*, as we find in two masoretic manuscripts and Symmachus. We have a *crux interpretum* in *mᵉšullām*. This word is well attested in the O.T. and the Elephantine documents as a personal name. According to M. NOTH, the name is derived from the piel of *šlm*, with the sense of "to replace", and it would express gratitude to the deity for having replaced a dead child by another one.[2] If vs. 19b is a gloss, which is quite probable, then a personal name may be meant here, too. The glossator would have applied vs. 19a to a certain Meshullam, whom he calls a servant of Yahwe also. But it is impossible to identify this Meshullam. According to J. L. PALACHE, Meshullam here is the name of the enigmatic Servant of Yahwe in the so-called Servant Songs. He should be identified as Meshullam, the son of Zerubbabel. However, this solution is untenable since it requires a construction of too many hypotheses one upon the other.[3]

If the colon is from Dt.-Is., then the word is an epithet for Israel. What does it mean? LXX, οἱ κυριεύοντες αὐτῶν, Heb. *mōšᵉlêhem*, offers no solution. To T. K. CHEYNE the word means "the surrendered one", like Arab. *muslim*.[4] The *Bible de Jérusalem* following K. MARTI, emends the word to *mᵉšullāḥî*, "the one I have sent".[5] This emendation is favoured by the chiastic parallelism with the preceding colon. The remark is valuable even if vs. 19b is a gloss. The piel of *šlm* means i.a. "to recompense, to repay". So one could render the pual part. as

---

[1] K. ELLIGER, *Deuterojesaja*, p. 168: "Das die Hälfte des Textes als Variante ausgeschieden werden muss, ist eine fast allgemein geteilte Erkenntnis".

[2] M. NOTH, *Die israelitischen Personennamen im Rahmen der gemeinsemitischen Namengebung*, Stuttgart 1928, pp. 174; 250, nr 912.

[3] J. L. PALACHE, *The 'Ebed-Jahweh Enigma in Pseudo-Isaiah*, Amsterdam 1934.

[4] T. K. CHEYNE, *The Prophecies of Isaiah*, I, p. 271; cf. H. VINCENT, "Nouvelle intaille israélite", *RB.* XI 1902, p. 435, where the same interpretation is given to the name משלם, found on a seal. According to S. D. LUZZATTO, *o.c.*, p. 472, the same interpretation has been proposed by DÖDERLEIN and GESENIUS.

[5] K. MARTI, *Jesaja*, p. 292; P. AUVRAY - J. STEINMANN, *Isaïe*, p. 177; J. L. MC KENZIE, *Second Isaiah*, p. 45.

"repaid", i.e. "servant".[1] But this meaning is hardly applicable to Israel who is not in Yahwe's service as a wage-worker. A more suggestive interpretation is that of C. R. North. He connects the word with the expression *b^e^rît š^e^lômî*, "my covenant of peace". The hiphil of the root *šlm* indeed means "to make peace with somebody". Thus, one could read here a hophal part. meaning "the one who has been granted a covenant of peace" (cf. Job v 23).[2] Some transcriptions in the LXX render a hophal quite probable, as e.g. in 1 Chron. v 13: *Μοσολάμ* (cf. 1 Chron. iii 19; ix 11). D. Diringer suggests a similar meaning concerning this name, found on certain seals.[3] Since the text is critically dubious and these different explanations have about the same value, I agree with C. Westermann that the exact explanation has not yet been found.[4]

In vs. 20 follows the accusation, which explains the address (vs. 18) and the rhetorical question (vs. 19). Israel has seen and learnt a lot during its history, but did not realize it. Therein consists its blindness and deafness. Israel remained unheeding to the message, which was sent to it throughout its history.

The authenticity of vs. 21 is largely contested. K. Marti, B. Duhm, S. Mowinckel and K. Elliger delete it, adducing quite divergent arguments. That the prophet does not use the word *tôrâ* is a gratuitous supposition. A more serious argument is that proposed by Mowinckel who remarks that the verse is not poetical nor symmetric. The word statistics of K. Elliger are not conclusive: he finds that the verb *ḥpṣ* in Is. xl-lxvi is only used by Trito-Is. (lviii 2; lxii 4; lxv 12; lxvi 3-4; liii 10), that *ṣedeq* as a divine quality rather indicates Dt.-Is. (xli 10; xlii 6; xlv 13), that the hiphil forms of *gdl* and *'dr* are *hapax legomena* in Is. xl-lxvi, and that *tôrâ* occurs only in Dt.-Is. (xlii 4; li 4, 7).[5] C. Westermann calls the verse a gloss without any proof.[6] The verse might be a gloss but one cannot prove it. If one keeps it, it expresses what Israel has seen and heard in its history, without heeding it. The verse links up nicely with what precedes: "Yahwe wished, because of his righteousness, to make his teaching great and glorious". The verbs *yagdîl* and *ya'dîr* act as asyndetic object clauses

[1] Cf. KB, p. 980.

[2] C. R. North, *The Second Isaiah*, p. 118; cf. Zorell, pp. 852-853.

[3] D. Diringer, *Le iscrizioni Antico-Ebraiche Palestinesi*, Firenze 1934, p. 213.

[4] C. Westermann, *o.c.*, p. 91.

[5] K. Marti, *l.c.*; B. Duhm, *l.c.*; S. Mowinckel, *ZAW*. XLIX 1931, p. 96, note 3; K. Elliger, *o.c.*, p. 171.

[6] C. Westermann, *o.c.*, p. 92.

to *ḥāpēṣ*.[1] When Yahwe made his *tôrâ* great, he did so because of his righteous salvific will (*ṣedeq*). Here *tôrâ* means more than "law". With this word, the former prophets meant also God's word, which was active through themselves (Is. viii 16, 20; xxx 9-10). *Tôrâ* means a divine teaching, either formulated as a law, or given by a priest (Lam. ii 9; Ez. vii 26; Mal. ii 4-9), or pronounced by a prophet regarding a concrete situation. Thus the divine authority is formally distinctive of the *tôrâ*.[2] The *tôrâ* is the totality of God's revelations of his will. Also for Deuteronomy the word has this comprehensive sense of the complete divine revelation, although in this respect deuteronomic milieus paid less attention to the actual prophetic word. They thought of the totality of God's revelations as comprised and completed in the deuteronomic synthesis (cf. Deut. xiii 1; iv 2).[3] All this fits very well the context of the present oracle. God's word was great and strong in Israel's history, but the chosen nation did not heed it.

So the punishment was bound to come. It is described in vs. 22. The text offers some minor difficulties (cf. translation), but the literal sense is clear. Concerning this verse one might raise the historical problem: does the condition described here correspond to the reality of the exile, or should we ascribe the text to a different period because of its historical background? The vast majority of interpreters think that the condition of the exile is meant. They invoke the figurative and hyperbolic language of the prophet and are convinced that one cannot undo this with the remark that the condition of the *gôlâ* was not that bad.[4] Only B. DUHM induces from the description in this verse that the prophet did not know the real condition in Babylonia, which is an argument in favour of his thesis that Dt.-Is. did not live there.[5] Even J. MORGENSTERN conserves these verses in his purged Dt.-Is. and understands them as referring to the exile.[6] But in this

---

1 GK § 120 c; JOÜON, § 157 b.

2 Cf. W. GUTBROD, νόμος κτλ., *TWNT*. IV, p. 1038; J. SCHARBERT, "Gesetz. I. Im Alten Testament", *LTK*. IV, col. 816.

3 Cf. G. VON RAD, *Theologie des A.T.*, I, München 1966, pp. 234-236.

4 T. K. CHEYNE, *The Prophecies of Isaiah*, I, pp. 271-272; J. KNABENBAUER, *o.c.*, p. 123; F. DELITZSCH, *Commentar*, p. 440; K. MARTI, o.c., p. 293; F. FELDMANN, *Das Buch Isaias*, II, pp. 65-66; P. VOLZ, *o.c.*, p. 34; J. FISCHER, *Das Buch Isaias*, II, pp. 59-60; J. STEINMANN, *Le livre de la Consolation*, p. 119; H. E. VON WALDOW, *Anlass und Hintergrund*, p. 186, note 2.

5 B. DUHM, *Das Buch Jesaia*, p. 286.

6 J. MORGENSTERN, *The Message of Deutero-Isaiah*, p. 130; Cf. A. SCHOORS, *Orientalia Periodica Lovaniensia*, II, 1971, pp. 119-120.

he is inconsistent, claiming for other texts a post-exilic setting on the ground of "an oppressive captivity". Recently C. WESTERMANN has strengthened the above-mentioned appeal to figurative speech with his form-critical remarks. He points out that all the clauses in vs. 22 are taken from a lament, with a change of person. They need only to be converted into the first person to be seen to be taken from a collective lament, more specifically from a *Wir-klage.*[1] Yet, the literature of lament continues using certain terms and metaphors to delineate the condition of distress. The statements in vs. 22 "are long-established technical terms and metaphors used by Israel to describe its plight as it made lamentation in the presence of God".[2] Since Dt.-Is. has numerous links with the lamentations, this explanation of our verse is fully acceptable. Besides the well attested *'ên maṣṣîl* (Pss. vii 3; l 11; lxxi 11; Job v 4; x 7) one can refer to the use of *šsh* in Ps. xliv 11 or *šss* in Ps. lxxxix 42 and the metaphor of the bird-trap (*paḥ*), which is current, though the verb *pḥḥ* is a *hapax* in the O.T.

Verse 23 remains in the sphere of the accusation. The people do not pay attention, they do not understand or draw the conclusions for the future.[3] Therefore, in the following verses, the prophet resumes his argumentation, now with all desirable clarity: Yahwe himself gave up his people because of their sins. In vs. 24a we must prefer Ketib *m^e^šôseh* to Qere *m^e^šissâ*. Although Qere is supported by LXX, Vulgate, Peshitta and Targum, the consonantal text is made sure by IQIa.[4] Indeed, we need a word that means "spoiler" because of the parallelism with *bōz^e^zîm*. The form *m^e^šôseh* parses as a pōel part. of the verb *šsh*, which is used in a pōel perf. in Is. x 13 also.[5] This interpretation is better than G. R. DRIVER's, who conserves *m^e^šissâ* or *m^e^šussâ* and renders *bōz^e^zîm* as "spoliation", an abstract substantive of the type *qôt^e^lîm*.[6]

According to C. WESTERMANN, vs. 24bβγ is not authentic because

---

[1] Cf. C. WESTERMANN, "Struktur und Geschichte der Klage im A.T.", *ZAW*. LXVI 1954, pp. 44-80 = *Forschung*, pp. 266-305; cf. esp. pp. 277-279.

[2] C. WESTERMANN, *Jesaja 40-66*, p. 92.

[3] S. D. LUZZATTO, *o.c.*, p. 474, thus paraphrases the verse: ומי היה בכם שיקשיב ומתוך כך ישמע לאחור, יבין מה אחרית דבר.

[4] LXX: *εἰς διαρπαγὴν*; Vg: in direptionem; Pesh: ܠܒܙܐ; Targ: לעדי; IQIa: למשוסה.

[5] On the pōel form cf. JOÜON, § 59 a.

[6] G. R. DRIVER, "Notes on Isaiah", *Von Ugarit nach Qumran* (*Fs. O. Eissfeldt*), Berlin 1958, p. 47.

of its prose style. Along with K. Marti and B. Duhm one may add that the word order *bidrākāyw hālôk* is an aramaism. Also the passage from first to third person is in favour of Westermann's opinion. But then the colon 24b*a* has no parallel. Further, the use of *zû* as a relative pronoun is unusual in Dt.-Is. The reading *zh* in IQIa is a correction, as appears from the parallel case in xliii 21. This suggests that the whole of 24b is a gloss. In this connection Marti and Duhm point out that Dt.-Is. usually does not answer his own rhetorical questions.[1] Above all, in vs. 25 *'ālāyw* refers to Israel in vs. 24a, as if there were no vs. 24b.

The final verse makes a sort of inclusion with the first sentence, at least according to the sense. Israel's blindness and deafness (vs. 18) are explained here: Israel does not grasp what Yahwe intends with the calamities he has sent upon his people. To conclude, I therefore agree with Westermann: Is. xlii 18-25 is a trial speech in the line of xliii 22-28 and l 1-3. Yahwe justifies his punishing judgment of Israel, by turning back against Israel the complaint which was directed against him. Yahwe does not fail them, but he was obliged to punish his people because of its sins. Actually, von Waldow should have classified this pericope with what he calls the *profanisierte Typ* of the trial speech.[2]

4. *Is. xli 1-5*

1 Be silent before me, islands,
nations, *draw near and come.*[a]
Let them approach, then let them speak;
let us come together for judgment.
2 Who stirred him up from the east,
whom victory meets at every step?
Who gives up nations before him
and *dethrones*[b] kings?
His sword makes them like dust,
his bow like driven stubble.
3 He pursues them and passes on safely,
not touching the path with his feet.
4 Who performs and does this?
He who calls the generations from the beginning.

---

[1] K. Marti, *l.c.*; B. Duhm, *l.c.*; C. Westermann, *o.c.*, p. 93.
[2] H. E. von Waldow, *Anlass und Hintergrund*, p. 40.

I, Yahwe, am the first,
and with the last I am he.
5 The islands see it and are afraid,
the ends of the earth tremble.

[a] From vs. 5; see comments.
[b] Lg יוריד c IQIa.

The pericope, which I want to analyze now, is called a trial speech by all form-critics, but H. GRESSMANN and S. MOWINCKEL unduly expand it as far as vs. 13. K. MARTI, too, has recognized this literary character of the pericope.[1] BEGRICH specifies that the pericope is an *Appellationsrede* of the accuser (cf. Gen. xvi 5; Is. i 18-20). Materially, L. KÖHLER comes to the same specification where he calls it a *Zweizeugenruf* and a summons to court at the same time.[2] More correctly H. J. BOECKER typifies the genre as an *Appellationsrede* which introduces a trial revolving around a claim (*Feststellungsverfahren*). He has been followed by VON WALDOW and FOHRER and also WESTERMANN underlines that the background is not a criminal case dealing with an offence and its punishment, but a civil one which turns on a claim and its admission or dismissal.[3] BEGRICH, too, was aware that the point at issue was a claim, but, inconsistently, he continued using the term "accuser". The same inconsistency is to be found in VON WALDOW's former works.[4]

In vs. 1 we read the summons to court. Here the technical term is *mišpāṭ*, meaning "trial", synonymous with *rîb*.[5] The speaker passes from second to third person. In vs. 1a, *yaḥălîpû kōaḥ* seems not to belong to the original text but an expression from the preceding verse (xl 31) which invaded this context. But the wording is attested by all textual witnesses. Also S. THOMAS AQUINAS succeeded somewhat in giving a sense to the phrase in the context of a trial speech: "mutent fortitudinem, idest confortent se quasi renovati in fortitudine ad

---

[1] K. MARTI, *o.c.*, p. 278.

[2] J. BEGRICH, *o.c.*, p. 27; L. KÖHLER, *o.c.*, p. 113.

[3] H. J. BOECKER, *Redeformen des Rechtslebens im Alten Testament*, p. 69: "... bei zwei gegeneinander stehenden Behauptungen die eine für richtig, die andere für falsch zu erklären". — H. E. VON WALDOW, *Der traditionsgeschichtliche Hintergrund*, p. 45, note 5; G. FOHRER, *Jesaja III*, p. 34; C. WESTERMANN, *o.c.*, p. 136.

[4] J. BEGRICH, *o.c.*, p. 35; H. E. VON WALDOW, "... *denn Ich erlöse dich*", p. 64.

[5] ZORELL, p. 485: "actio judicialis". Cf. J. MORGENSTERN, *The Message of Deutero-Isaiah*, p. 152.

disceptandum mecum".[1] It is hard to decipher what was written originally, but the expression must have been in some way parallel with *haḥărîšû 'ēlay*. The suggestion of *BHK* is not satisfactory: *yaḥălû nikᵉḥî*. The preposition is not appropriate with the verb and the latter itself is not a satisfactory parallel for the first member. C. WESTERMANN and H. E. VON WALDOW suggest the possibility that the last two words of vs. 5, certainly superfluous there, formerly stood here.[2] The suggestion is valuable, the more so as in vs. 5 IQIa has *w'tywn* instead of *wayye'ĕtāyûn*, which, together with *qrbw*, may be the trace of an imperative. With reserve we thus may read: "nations, draw near and come".

In vs. 1b, *qrb lammišpāṭ* and *ngš* are synonymous and both technical terms of judicial language (cf. Deut. xxv 1). There is no reason to emend the third person (against MARTI). The passage from second to third person is not unusual at all. Or perhaps there are two distinct groups. This is possible when we accept that Yahwe addresses the forum of the nations (vs. 1a) and begs their attention for his contest with the pagan gods (vs. 1b). The pagan gods are also the opponent party in the trial speeches, which we have to study shortly. To be sure, the nations sometimes are associated with the gods they worship (xlv 20-21; xliii 8-13). But in the present pericope I rather have the impression that the nations are the witnesses of the contest between Yahwe and the gods. This explanation, proposed by J. MORGENSTERN, is acceptable, even if he unduly changes the text.[3] It is supported by the fact that there is a contradiction between 1a and 1b, if in the former the islands are commanded to be silent and in the latter to speak. It is not so sure that the foreign nations are formally challenged here, and they are certainly not accused, as suggested by VON WALDOW. In his doctoral dissertation he has himself remarked the difference between vss. 1a and 1b: the first is directed to the nations, the other speaks about their gods.[4]

In vss. 2-4aα the point at issue is expounded and the judgment follows in vs. 4aβb. The problem of the pericope is: Who stirred "him" up from the east? Almost unanimously, the interpreters relate this

---

[1] S. THOMAS AQUINAS, *In Isaiam prophetam, ad loc.*

[2] C. WESTERMANN, *Jesaia 40-66*, p. 53, note 1; H. E. VON WALDOW, *Anlass und Hintergrund*, p. 203, note 19; cf. K. MARTI, *l.c.* Now also *BHS*.

[3] J. MORGENSTERN, *o.c.*, pp. 146-147.

[4] H. E. VON WALDOW, *Der traditionsgeschichtliche Hintergrund*, p. 45; *Anlass und Hintergrund*, pp. 43-44.

to the Persian king Cyrus (cf. xliv 28; xlv 1). Already THEODORE OF HERACLEA (4th century) expressly mentions this interpretation.[1] True, the Targum of Jonathan applies vs. 2 to Abraham: "Who openly brought Abraham from the east?" But among modern scholars, only C. C. TORREY made this his opinion.[2] According to U. E. SIMON, these verses are about the Messiah. Along with the Vulgate he reads *ṣaddîq* (justum) instead of *ṣedeq*, and he adds this word to vs. 2a*a* as object of *hēʿîr*.[3] Both interpretations are due to a wrong grammatical approach of the sentence. From my analysis it seems that Cyrus fits the pericope very well and the reading of the other trial speeches will make clear that he is the only possible candidate. Therefore it is not yet necessary to call Is. xli 1-15 a Cyrus song, as M. HALLER does.[4] We have no song here and "Cyrus song" does not designate a genre but it may indicate the topic of the pericope. In this respect, it will appear that the point of the prophecy is not Cyrus.

Meanwhile, the translation of vs. 2a is not free from problems. The ancient translations, as well as IQIa, understood *ṣdq* as object of *hēʿîr*. The Isaiah scroll shows it with a *waw* before *yiqrāʾēhû*. The Septuagint and Peshitta read *ṣedeq*, the Vulgate *ṣaddîq*, which must also underlie the Targum paraphrase "Abraham".[5] But one can give value very well to the MT when regarding 2aβ as an asyndetic relative clause, the antecedent of which is not expressed. In this sense it is explained by DUHM, VOLZ, BEGRICH, SMITH, FOHRER and WESTERMANN.[6] Such a construction is far from rare in the Hebrew Bible.[7] Thus Cyrus is presented as the one, "whom *ṣedeq* meets at every step". In the expression *l^eraglô* I accept the preposition *l^e* as "according to, *secundum*, κατὰ", thus "according to his foot, his steps".[8] This can

---

[1] THEODORE OF HERACLEA, *Ex interpretatione in Isaiam*, *PG*, XVIII, col. 1333: "*Περὶ Κύρου λέγει, ὃν δικαίως ἐπήγειρε Βαβυλῶνι.*"

[2] Targ: מן איתי בגלי ממדנחא אברהם. C. C. TORREY, *The Second Isaiah*, pp. 33; 312; ID., "Isaiah 41", *HarvTR*. XLIV 1951, pp. 121-136.

[3] U. E. SIMON, *A Theology of Salvation*, pp. 70-72; 247, note d.

[4] M. HALLER, "Die Kyros-Lieder Deuterojesajas", *ΕΥΧΑΡΙΣΤΗΡΙΟΝ* (*Fs. Gunkel*), I, Göttingen 1923, pp. 261-277.

[5] LXX: *δικαιοσύνην*; Pesh: ܙܕܝܩܘܬܐ; Vg: justum.

[6] B. DUHM, *o.c.*, p. 269; P. VOLZ, *Jesaja II*, p. 14; J. BEGRICH, *l.c.*; S. SMITH, *Isaiah chs. XL-LV*, p. 49; G. FOHRER, *o.c.*, p. 33; C. WESTERMANN, *Jesaja 40-66*, p. 53.

[7] Cf. Is. xli 24; Ex. iv 13; Mal. ii 16; Pss. lxv 5; cxli 9; Job xxix 12, 16; Prov. viii 32; etc.; cf. GK, § 155,2.

[8] Cf. KB, p. 465, sub 21; ZORELL, pp. 381-382, sub 4, d.e.; so B. DUHM, *l.c.*: "dem Sieg begegnet auf Schritt und Tritt". Cf. *RSV*.

also mean concretely that *ṣedeq* meets him, as fast as he goes (cf. Gen. xxxiii 14), the more so as in vs. 3, it is precisely the speed of his march which is alluded to. Thus the *ṣedeq* keeps up with the pace of his advance. What is the meaning of *ṣedeq*? We have seen already that one of the spheres to which the word belongs is that of war (cf. comments on xli 10), and then it means victory.[1] From the following verses it appears that Cyrus's military successes are meant. According to C. R. NORTH, G. FOHRER and C. WESTERMANN, the prophet more precisely views the war with Croesus and the fall of Sardis (546).[2] As the prophet's historical allusions are always vague, it is impossible to make this sure. More important is the fact that the victories are not conceived as won by Cyrus, they are given to him by Yahwe, as K. CRAMER correctly remarked, they are a salvific reality.[3]

This is illustrated in vs. 2b with a question which we may paraphrase thus: "Who gave these successes to Cyrus?" In this sense the question at issue is specified. Scholars generally suggest the emendation of *yard* to *yār ōd*, while IQIa reads *yôrîd*. The first reading is more picturesque but both mean almost the same. I prefer the latter, because of its attestation in IQIa, supported by the LXX. The picturesque reading corresponds more to the Targum paraphrase.[4] The question does not continue in vs. 2c, but the circumstances of the subjection are described. The colon 2c rather goes along with vs. 3: here the man from the east is the subject, directly in vs. 3 and indirectly in vs. 2c through the suffix of *ḥarbô* and *qaštô*. Sometimes it is suggested, on the authority of the LXX, to read this suffix as a plural and to give the translation: "Who makes their sword like dust?" I object that the LXX is isolated in the textual tradition.[5] It is not God who makes the sword of the enemies like dust, but Cyrus's sword

---

[1] Cf. KB, p. 794, sub 4; GB, p. 674; ZORELL, p. 683; K.H. FAHLGREN, Ṣedâḳâ, *nahestehende und entgegengesetzte Begriffe im A.T.*, pp. 102-103; H. H. SCHMID, *Gerechtigkeit als Weltordnung*, pp. 18-22; esp. p. 21.

[2] C. R. NORTH, "The 'Former Things' and the 'New Things' in Deutero-Isaiah", *Studies in Old Testament Prophecy*, Edinburgh, 1950, p. 120; G. FOHRER, *o.c.*, p. 35; C. WESTERMANN, *o.c.*, p. 8.

[3] K. CRAMER, "Der Begriff צדקה bei Tritojesaja", *ZAW*. XXVII 1907, p. 89; cf. also P. VOLZ, *o.c.*, p. 19; "*Ṣedeḳ* heisst nicht Sieg, den Cyrus schafft, sondern Heil, das von Jahwe zukommt".

[4] LXX: ἐκστήσει; Targ: תבר; the correction יוריד has been proposed before by L. KÖHLER, *Deuterojesaja*, p. 10.

[5] LXX: τὰς μαχαίρας αὐτῶν... τὰ τόξα αὐτῶν; Vg: gladio eius ... arcu eius; Targ: קדם חרביה... קדם קשתיה; Pesh: ܣܝܦܗ .. ܩܫܬܐ.

that makes the enemies like dust. Therefore some suggest the reading *yitt^enēm* instead of *yittēn.*[1] This emendation is in accordance with the meaning of the text, but is superfluous, since the object is sufficiently expressed in the immediate context (vss. 2b and 3 - *yird^epēm*).

Verse 3 completes the picture with a description of the speedy progress of the Persian king. S. SMITH finds here an allusion to the speedy march of Cyrus from the Halys to Sardis and to the fact that the Lydian army did not offer any resistance.[2]

The question which is at issue in the trial speech, is repeated in vs. 4 and answered immediately. Only one can have stirred up Cyrus: he who calls the generations from the beginning, i.e. he who dominates history. In vs. 4b this enigmatic answer is made explicit and is deepened theologically. Yahwe is the first and "with the last he is still he". Here Yahwe's eternity is expressed: he precedes the movements of history and also terminates them. WESTERMANN rightly points out that this eternity is not an abstract quality, but a permanent active presence. The expression "with the last I am still he" expresses Yahwe's eternal *gegenüber*, his lasting creative presence in history.[3] N. WALKER sees in *'ănî-hû'* an echo of the divine name *'ehyeh* or *yahweh.* True, in both expressions the same theological reality may be intended, but the author's suggestive philological remarks are open to criticism on more than one point.[4] It is not sure at all that here the prophet wittingly alludes to the account of Ex. iii. At any rate, it is clear now that only Yahwe was able to stir up Cyrus, for he is the only one who dominates history.

H. J. BOECKER doubts whether vs. 5 still belongs to the pericope. Actually, it makes the impression of being outside the trial speech proper. J. BEGRICH tries to remedy this by changing the verbal forms into imperatives, invoking the witness of 32 manuscripts collated by KENNICOTT.[5] But the verse, as it stands, can easily be joined to the preceding ones. The inclusion *'iyyîm* is an indication in that direction.

---

[1] Thus *BHS*; B. DUHM, *l.c.*; M. HALLER, *o.c.*, p. 21; C. WESTERMANN, *o.c.*, p. 53, note 3.

[2] S. SMITH, *o.c.*, p. 50.

[3] C. WESTERMANN, *o.c.*, p. 56. — Cf. M. HALLER, *l.c.*

[4] N. WALKER, "Concerning hû' and 'anî hû'", *ZAW*. LXXIV 1962, pp. 205-206. Esp. his appealing to Aramaic and Syriac *hw'* to prove that also in the oldest Hebrew there was a form *hawa'*. In Aramaic itself the form *hw'* is younger than *hwy*.

[5] H. J. BOECKER, *Redeformen des Rechtslebens*, p. 70, note 1; J. BEGRICH, *o.c.*, p. 36.

The verse is a final statement in Yahwe's mouth. The islands and the ends of the earth are afraid when seeing Cyrus's *Blitzkrieg*. Even better, the nations tremble, because they are aware that Yahwe is at work in these world-shaking events, which is precisely the issue in this trial speech. Fear is a fixed component in a theophany. In vs. 5 too, the shuddering and dismay are an element of theophany: they are the effect of Yahwe's theophany in history.

5. *Is. xli 21-29*

21 "Set forth your case", says Yahwe,
bring forth your proofs", says the King of Jacob.
22 Let them *approach*[a] and tell us
what is to happen.
The former things, what did they foretell about them,
that we might consider them?
Or declare to us the things to come,
that we may know their *outcome.*[b]
23 Tell us what is to come hereafter,
that we may know that you are gods.
Do something, either good or evil,
that we may be dismayed and *afraid.*[c]
24 Behold, you are nothing and your work is naught,
an abomination is he who chooses you.
25 I stirred up one from the north, and he came;
from the rising of the sun *he was called*[d] by name.
He *treads*[e] governors as clay,
as a potter tramples mud.
26 Who declared this beforehand, that we might know,
and beforetime, that we might say: "He is right"?
There is none who declares it, none who proclaimed,
none who heard your words.
27 I first *declared it*[f] to Zion,
and I gave to Jerusalem a herald of good tidings.
28 I look — but none is there;
among these there is no counsellor,
who, when I ask, gives an answer.
29 Behold, they are all *nothing,*[g]
their works are nothing,
wind and emptiness are their images.

[a] Lg יִגְּשׁוּ c LXX: ἐγγισάτωσαν; Targ: יתקרבון; Vg: accedant; Pesh: ܢܩܪܒܘܢ.
[b] Transposition of both hemistichs.
[c] K: ונרא; Q: וְנִרְאֶה.
[d] Lg יִקָּרֵא בשמו c IQIa. See comments.
[e] Lg ויבס loco ויבא c Köhler.
f See comments.
[g] Lg אין loco און c IQIa, Targ.

The pericope Is. xli 21-29 is generally termed a trial speech. The prophet himself begins with the term *rîb*. According to J. Begrich and G. Fohrer we here have a word of the judge. I shall return to this point further on. L. Köhler exaggerates, when dividing the pericope in two distinct units, viz. 21-24 and 25-29. Not only can we easily recognize the internal continuity between the two sections, but their literary unity is clearly marked by a striking word parallelism. To be sure, there is a certain caesura after vs. 24, but we see in the first part a sequence *yaggîdû* (vs. 22a) — *wenēdeʿâ* (vs. 22c) — *hēn... mēʾayin* (vs. 24) — *ʾepes* (vs. 24 emended), which is to be found exactly in the second one: *mî-higgîd* (vs. 26) — *wenēdāʿâ* (vs. 26) — *hēn ʾayin* (vs. 29) [1] — *ʾepes* (vs. 29). We have, beyond any doubt, two parts forming one unit.

Also the content proves it. As there is no address, we must wait until vs. 23, before we know to whom the oracle is directed, viz. to the pagan gods. Yahwe challenges his adversaries to lay their arguments before him in a concrete manner in a *Weissagungsbeweis* (vss. 21-23a) When it appears that they are not able to do so, he makes a concession by accepting as a proof any act, either good or harmful (vs. 23b). But the gods cannot perform even that and the obvious conclusion is: "You are nothing". That is the first part. In the second Yahwe comes to his own defence: his claims are based on the fact that he rules the whole of history—he stirred up Cyrus (vs. 25)—, and that he foretold all these events (vss. 26-27). The same self-evident conclusion is stated.

After this short reading of the pericope, some details need further elucidation. The formula "says Yahwe" is not exactly a messenger's formula. It occurs almost exclusively in the book of Isaiah and it is typical of *rîb* pericopes (cf. Is. i 11, 18; xl 25; lxvi 9). It is thus better not to think of it as a messenger's formula that introduces no message, thus becoming a rather stylistic expedient, while losing its original vigour. There is no odd combination of a prophetic form of discourse

---

[1] MT: און; according to IQIa and Targ: אין.

with one of an entirely different kind.[1] Yahwe is called "king of Jacob". In this quality he is also judge.[2] *Rîb* is a juridical term, and also *ʿăṣumôt* seems to be one. Since KÖHLER's work, this fem. plur. of *ʿāṣûm*, "strong", is rendered as "strong words, arguments". One may suppose the same meaning in Prov. xviii 18, as there *ʿăṣûmîm* is used in parallelism with *midyānîm*. The proverb can be translated: "The lot puts an end to lawsuits and decides between the arguments".[3] So it may be superfluous to emend the word to *môʿăṣôtêkem* in xli 21, as proposed by BEGRICH on the ground of the Peshitta, or to *ʿaṣebôtêkem*, as suggested by HALLER.[4]

The emendation of *yaggîšû* to *yiggešû* (vs. 22), as suggested in my translation, can be substantiated by referring to the same *topos* in the other trial speeches (xli 1; cf. 1 8). Yahwe makes clear what he means with "proofs": "Tell us what is to happen". He is convinced that the gods will not be able to tell, since they were not able to do so before. This is the sense of the rhetorical question in vs. 22b. We meet here the expression *riʾšōnôt*, which occured also in the salvation word xliii 16-21. There the word concretely designated the exodus from Egypt. The question is whether, in the present trial speech, the expression has exactly the same content. I refer again to my article, which I resume briefly.[5] Here the expression *riʾšōnôt* seems to designate the former events in general: What did the gods reveal about the foregoing things? Verse 22b is mostly not rendered as "What did they foretell about them (the former things)?" but: "The former things, tell us what they were". Such is the meaning of MT, which appears in the ancient versions too. But I think I have sufficiently defended my own translation. To be sure, *higgîd* mostly has a different meaning

---

[1] Against L. KÖHLER, *o.c.*, pp. 106-107: "Die Benutzung der Formeln als blosses Kunstmittel tritt dadurch noch klarer zu Tage, dass auch der Inhalt der Botschaft: 'Bringt euern Streit herbei!' ... in den Bereich des Streitgesprächs weist". The formula occurs also in Ps. xii 6 and in Is. xl 1, where the context is not that of a *rîb*.

[2] J. MUILENBURG, *Isaiah chs. 40-66*, p. 460; cf. also G. VON RAD, *Theologie des A.T.*, I, pp. 334-335; G. FOHRER, *Jesaja III*, p. 45.

[3] L. KÖHLER, *o.c.*, p. 14; cf. KB, p. 728; ZORELL, p. 620; J. MUILENBURG, *l.c.*; F. FELDMANN, *Das Buch Isaias*, II, p. 51.

[4] J. BEGRICH, *o.c.*, p. 44, note 148. It is not apparent why BEGRICH does not invoke the LXX (*αἱ βουλαὶ ὑμῶν*). — M. HALLER, *o.c.*, p. 22.

[5] A. SCHOORS, *ETL.* XL 1964, pp. 25-31; cf. also "Het thema van het vroegere en het nieuwe in Deutero-Isaias", *Handelingen van het XXVe Vlaams Filologencongres*, Antwerpen 1963, pp. 129-133.

than "to foretell". The main senses are "to report" and "to explain".[1] But in Eccl. vi 12 and x 14, the meaning is clearly "to foretell".

The word is very frequent in Dt.-Is. In Is. xlv 19 it means "to tell" without further specification. In a series of other dt.-Isaian texts the meaning "to foretell" is obvious. So e.g. in xlii 9 and xlviii 5, where "before they spring forth" in the parallel verse removes any doubt. "Things to come" or "what is to come hereafter" as object of *higgîd* point to the same meaning in xli 23; xliv 7; xlvi 10. As in these texts the adverbs *mē'āz* (xlviii 5), *mē'ōlām* (xliv 7) and *miqqedem* (xlvi 10) underline this meaning, it is clear that elsewhere also the same words in similar contexts require the meaning "to foretell" for *higgîd* (xliv 8; xlv 21; xlviii 3). Recently this has again been demonstrated convincingly by E. VOGT.[2]

Verses xlviii 14 and xli 26 can only be understood in the same sense. Only about xliii 12 there is some doubt, but the sense "to explain" is certainly not better than "to foretell". I conclude that the same word in an identical context has the same meaning. Indeed, also in xlii 9 and xlviii 3, the *ri'šōnôt* are the object of fulfilled predictions. The *Weissagungsbeweis* commences at the word *higgîdû* in vs. 22b.

Apart from that, my interpretation leaves the consonantal text unchanged. I only change *haggîdû* into *higgîdû*. The clause *mâ hēnnâ* is usually explained as an indirect question, in nominal form, depending on *haggîdû*: "Tell us what they (the former things) were". In this case, the verse would be a challenge to interpret the past events. I admit that this idea is not senseless in the present context.[3] But we can render this couple of words as *quid earum*, on the understanding that in Hebrew an accusative of limitation corresponds to the Latin genitive. The same construction occurs in 1 Sam. xx 10; xxvi 18; 2 Sam. xix 29; xxiv 13; 1 Kings xii 16; Jer. ii 5; Eccl. xi 2; Esther vi 3.[4] Then *hāri'šōnôt* is a *casus pendens*. In a more prosaic form the sentence

[1] SIEGFRIED-STADE, p. 399; GB, p. 482; KÖNIG, p. 262; KB, p. 591.

[2] E. VOGT, "Einige hebräische Wortbedeutungen. I. 'Voraussagen' in Is. 40-48", *Bib.* XLVIII 1967, pp. 57-63. Cf. T. K. CHEYNE, *The Prophecies of Isaiah*, I, p. 261.

[3] See e.g. the good comments of C. WESTERMANN, *o.c.*, pp. 71-72.

[4] Cf. JOÜON § 144 d. A. VAN HOONACKER renders: "De vroegere dingen hoe hebben zij die verkondigd?" This interpretation is close to mine. Grammatically, he makes הנה object of הגידו and מה an adverbial accusative, "how?". This is hardly acceptable, because in classical Hebrew the absolute pers. pronoun is not used as a direct object; one should have אותן.

would run thus: *mâ hāri'šōnôt higgîdû*, "what did they predict about the former things?"

The transposition of 22cα and 22cβ, as suggested by *BHS*, is obvious and is generally accepted. To *ri'šōnôt* the prophet does not now oppose *ḥădāšôt* (cf. xlii 9; xliii 18-19; xlviii 3-6) but twice "things to come" (*habbā'ôt* and *hā'ōtiyyôt*). Both expressions occur only in Dt.-Is., viz. *bā'ôt* here, and *'ōtiyyôt* in xli 23 and xlv 11 also.[1] We have here a proper terminology of the prophet, with which he designates the coming events in general.[2] He does not view concrete events but the total future of Israel and the whole world. "That we may know their outcome", means "that we may know that the facts tally with your predictions" (cf. vs. 26). The sentence is not about the insight in the meaning of history, as supposed by J. MUILENBURG.[3]

If the adversaries are able to predict the future, it will be proved that they are gods. Here it appears clearly what is at issue in this trial speech. The contest is no longer about the question, who stirred up Cyrus, but who is actually god: the pagan gods or Yahwe. In vs. 23b Ketib *wenirā'* must be preferred to Qere *wenir'eh.* I refer to my comments on xli 10, where the same parallelism *šť* // *yr'* occurs. This interpretation is certainly better than the one proposed by M. DAHOOD. He parses *yaḥdāw* as a form of the substantive *yaḥad*, a formation of the verb *ḥdh*, "to see". The word thus would mean "face". The author himself presents his suggestion with all reserve. His arguments are valuable and they offer a possible explanation of Is. xl 5. But in this verse parallelism is completely different from the one in xli 23. DAHOOD is obliged to link up the beginning of next verse with the word, reading *yaḥdêhen.* "Their face" means the face, i.e. the shape of things to come. This renders the suggestion only more improbable.[4] One may see in 23bβ a parallel to 23aβ: fear is caused by the recognition that they are gods.[5]

---

[1] Dubious in xlv 11; the only באות outside Is. xl-lv, namely in Ez. xvi 16 is inauthentic.

[2] So also W. STAERK, *Die Ebed-Jahwe-Lieder in Jes., 40ff.*, Leipzig 1913, p. 275; cf. KB, p. 101. In my opinion, the distinction between באות and אתיות, proposed by M. HARAN, בין ראשונות לחדשות, p. 42, is artificial. To him באות designates the future from now on, and אתיות the future with regard to a certain moment (even in the past).

[3] J. MUILENBURG, *o.c.*, p. 461: "Where history is viewed as filled with meaning, men will inquire about the outcome or issue of events".

[4] M. DAHOOD, "Some Ambiguous Texts in Isaias", *CBQ.* XX 1958, pp. 46-49.

[5] The translation by GESENIUS-BUHL, p. 853, "sich gegenseitig ansehen = sich im Kampf messen", is not easy to defend, even if one parses נשתעה a hitp. of שעה.

In verse 24 the decisive declaration is pronounced: those gods are nothing, their works are nothing. I emend *'āpa'* to *'āpes*, according to Targum and the requirements of parallelism (cf. xl 17), whereas twice there is a dittography of *mem.*[1] The apologetics of our prophet are historical. If the gods are unable to foretell the events, such means that they do not dominate history, that they are unable to do anything (vss. 23b-24). They are gods who cannot be experienced in history (*yd'*: vss. 22, 23, 26). Hence the prophet concludes that these gods do not exist. It is not sure at all that the prophet only means the nothingness of their works, and not the non-existence of the gods. I think that WESTERMANN asserts this too easily.[2] I rather have the impression that both aspects should not be separated: working and existence are a unity. Non-existence appears from the nothingness of the works. At any rate, it is clear that the so-called gods are no gods. The last member of the verse is a condemnation of the worshippers of such gods. It recalls the classical *rîb* of the pre-exilic prophets, which ended in a condemnation. The reading of this member *tōhû wᵉrûaḥ 'aṣᵉbêkem*, as proposed by H. L. GINSBERG, is critically unjustifiable.[3] The worshippers of the pagan gods are called *tô'ēbâ.* This word originally designated a tabu and, esp. in Deuteronomy, became a technical term for anything not in keeping with pure Yahwism. It designates a segregation, something to avoid, an abomination.[4]

It is generally accepted that vs. 25 concerns Cyrus. Only C. C. TORREY and U. E. SIMON are exceptions to this point, the former holding with Abraham, the latter with the Messiah.[5] The last words of vs. 25a create a problem. Sometimes *yiqrā' bišᵉmî* is changed into *'eqrā' bišᵉmô.*[6] Now one invokes also IQIa which reads *wyqr' bšmw.* This reading, however, is completely isolated in the textual tradition and it supports only partly the proposed emendation. Its meaning is not quite clear either. Perhaps the *waw* before *yqr'* is secondary and the

---

1 Targ: לא מדעם ; מאפע is missing in IQIa.

2 C. WESTERMANN, *o.c.*, p. 72: "Die Nichtigkeitserklärung bezieht sich auf das Tun ... In einer Gerichtsverhandlung wäre eine Bezeichnung als nicht existent im Sinn des Nichtvorhandenseins sinnlos ...".

3 H. L. GINSBERG, "Some Emendations in Isaiah", *JBL.* LXIX 1950, p. 58.

4 Cf. P. HUMBERT, "Le substantif *to'ēbā* et le verbe *t'b* dans l'Ancien Testament", *ZAW.* LXXII 1960, pp. 217-237.

5 C. C. TORREY, *HarvTR.* XLIV 1951, pp. 121-136; U. E. SIMON, *A Theology of Salvation*, p. 80.

6 So *BHK*; C. WESTERMANN, *o.c.*, p. 69; K. MARTI, *Das Buch Jesaia*, p. 284; G. FOHRER, *Jesaja III*, p. 44.

verb form is niphal. Then vs. 25a would mean: "From the east he is called by his name". Such seems to me the only meaning one can give to IQIa. Then the proposed emendation is in keeping with the reading of the scroll in its content. Also xlv 3 favours the emendation, where it is said that Yahwe calls Cyrus by his name (*haqqôrē' bešimekā*). One cannot invoke parallelism, as this is assured in the masoretic reading as well.[1] The real reason of the emendation is that one does not know what to do with a Cyrus who invokes Yahwe. I prefer the reading of IQIa, as explained above, especially because of the parallel in xlv 3. The passive form of *qr'* is attested by LXX too.[2] One may ask if the masoretic reading has not been influenced by an application of the verse to the Servant of Yahwe or any messianic figure.

Verse xli 25a is related to xli 2 and xlv 13, where the hiphil *hē'îr* is used in connection with Cyrus. In his commentary, WESTERMANN has justly pointed out that here Dt.-Is. joins a tradition, which finds expression in Is. xiii 17; Jer. l 9; li 1, 11. In all these texts Yahwe announces that he will stir up a nation or a king against Babylon, in order to deliver Israel. Formerly, the same word was used in the prophecy of doom, denoting God's stirring up of Israel's enemies in order to punish his people (Ez. xxiii 22; cf. 1 Chron. v 26; 2 Chron. xxi 16). The verb *hē'îr* thus is sort of a technical term for Yahwe's action with reference to Israel through foreign nations or kings. Although Cyrus's appearance is presented in other texts as somewhat new (*ḥădāšôt*) it is in the line of what has been announced formerly and of Yahwe's former actions with reference to his people.[3] Cyrus tramples down rulers, as the potter tramples clay, thus vs. 25. There is no reason to change *segānîm* into *gôyim*, as suggested by GINSBERG. The Akkadian loanword *sāgān* (Akk. *šaknu*) fits in well with Dt.-Is., where Akkadian influence is noticeable in more than one place.[4]

As we have seen already in the first part of his trial speech, the argumentation is about predictions. Such appears again in vs. 26: none of Yahwe's adversaries has foretold Cyrus's activity. The expression *wenō'mar ṣaddîq* is a juridical formula. As KÖHLER has noticed, it expresses that the court agrees with a statement: *ṣaddîq*

---

[1] Against C. WESTERMANN, *o.c.*, p. 73.

[2] LXX: κληθήσονται; cf. now also *BHS*.

[3] C. WESTERMANN, *o.c.*, pp. 73-75.

[4] H. L. GINSBERG, *JBL*. LXIX 1950, p. 59. Cf. M. ELLENBOGEN, *Foreign Words in the Old Testament*, London 1962, p. 120.

means "*Es stimmt*".[1] Such a verdict about former predictions makes sense only if they are fulfilled. The same idea is behind the first hemistich: *w^e^nēdā'â* is an indirect cohortative,[2] which means: "... that we may recognize (that the fulfillment tallies with the prediction)". The contest thus is not simply about the mere fact of foretelling but about the inner connection between foretelling and fulfillment. Yahwe did not only stir up Cyrus, he has announced him beforehand.

The last idea is expressed in vs. 27, which is a *crux interpretum*, especially because of its first half. The second half reads: "I gave to Jerusalem a herald of good tidings". Elsewhere I have accepted the correction *higgadtîhā* for *hinnēh hinnām* (*BHK* and MARTI), *-hā* having a neuter value and referring to what was to be foretold, i.e. the content of vs. 25. The translation then is: "I first declared it to Zion".[3] In my article I have discussed the other explanations.[4] To these I have to add the one proposed by N. J. McELENEY. He thinks that vs. 27 continues vs. 26 in the sense that it reflects the content of *'imrêkem*. His translation is:

26 ... No one to hear your words:
27 "The first news for Zion: Behold, here are they!"
Or "to Jerusalem I am sending a messenger".[5]

This interpretation has the advantage that vs. 27 does not interrupt the line of thought from vs. 26 to 28. Both verses state that the gods have nothing to tell, which idea is interrupted by vs. 27 in my interpretation. But this is no real difficulty. It is not strange at all that Yahwe underlines his positive intervention in the midst of the failure of his adversaries. The more so when we notice the same line of thought in the other trial speeches of Dt.-Is. In xliii 8-13 e.g., the same question (*mî-yaggîd*, vs. 9) is followed by the answer (*'ānōkî higgadtî*, vs. 12). Moreover, in McELENEY's interpretation *ri'šôn* receives no satisfactory explanation. Why translate it as "the first news"? Finally, though vss. 26 and 28 say materially the same, they have a somewhat different function (cf. below).

---

1 L. KÖHLER, *o.c.*, p. 114; cf. J. BEGRICH, *Studien*, p. 46, note 151.

2 Cf. JOÜON, § 116 c; GK, § 108 d.

3 A. SCHOORS, *ETL*. XL 1964, pp. 28-29. Cf. *RSV*.

4 Namely the one of Vg, followed by KNABENBAUER, DELITZSCH, CONDAMIN, AUVRAY-STEINMANN; further the explanations of DUHM, GRESSMANN, MOWINCKEL, LOWTH, VOLZ, G. R. DRIVER.

5 N. J. McELENEY, "The Translation of Isaias 41,27", *CBQ*. XIX 1957, pp. 441-443.

The interpretation which I defend has been accepted and strengthened by C. F. WHITLEY. He supposes that *ri'šôn* is a deformation of *mērō'š*. The *mem* would have dropped out by haplography and the desinence *-ôn* would have been added by assonance with *leṣiyyôn*. So the answer in vs. 27 would completely fit the question in vs. 26. This correction, though not indispensable, is nevertheless very suggestive.[1] Moreover, the LXX with its reading ἀρχὴν represents the stage between the dropping of the *mem* and the addition of *-ôn*, which has not been noticed by WHITLEY. In the LXX, Hebrew *ri'šôn* is translated ἀπ'/ἐξ ἀρχῆς, whereas *rō'š* is mostly rendered as ἀρχή.[2] We may conclude, as it seems, that in Is. xli 27, Yahwe asserts that he has announced the rise of Cyrus to Zion-Jerusalem.[3] As in xl 2, Zion-Jerusalem here stands for the whole nation. In the other trial speeches of Dt.-Is., it is never said that this prediction was for Jerusalem but for Israel. Some exegetes search for the concrete oracles where these predictions are contained. They refer to pre-exilic predictions of the fall of Babylon or the deliverance of the exiles. F. FELDMANN, in the footsteps of C. VON ORELLI, cites Is. xiii 17; xxi 2; Jer. li 11, 28, where Medes and Persians are expressly mentioned.[4] But these texts are exilic.

A question, which I dealt with in the cited article, is this: is it possible to give a more concrete content to the *ri'šōnôt* and *bā'ôt* of vs. 22, on the ground of vss. 25-29? This is impossible. In the first part of the trial speech Yahwe challenges the gods either to make clear what they foretold about the former events, or to foretell now the things to come. With the case of Cyrus he proves that they are unable to. Nobody but Yahwe has foretold the victories of this king. Hence it follows that Cyrus's appearance (vs. 25) belongs to the things already fulfilled, but not foretold by the gods, i.e. the *ri'šōnôt* in vs. 22. But nothing indicates that in this way the full content of the word is designated. The deliverance and the return through the desert,

---

1 C. F. WHITLEY, "A Note on Isa. XLI, 27", *JSS.* II 1957, pp. 337-338.

2 Cf. E. HATCH - H. REDPATH, *A Concordance to the Septuagint*, I, Graz 1954, p. 164.

3 Cf. A. VAN HOONACKER, "Questions de critique littéraire et d'exégèse touchant les ch. XL ss. d'Isaïe", *RB.* XX 1911, p. 111; F. FELDMANN, "Das Frühere und das Neue", *Festschrift E. Sachau*, Berlin 1915, p. 160; ID., *Das Buch Isaias*, II, p. 53; J. STEINMANN, *Le livre de la consolation*, p. 107; W. STAERK, *Die Ebed-Jahwe-Lieder*, p. 81; J. FISCHER, *Isaias 40-55 und die Perikopen vom Gottesknecht*, Münster 1916, pp. 21-22.

4 F. FELDMANN, *Das Buch Isaias*, II, p. 55.

repeatedly announced in Is. xl-xlviii, certainly belong to the *bā'ôt*. But in vs. 22 the content of the word is larger: it views the future in general. For here we have to do with the principle of prediction (cf. xliii 12; xliv 7), which is concretely applied to Cyrus only further on.[1]

While vs. 26 states that nobody ever foretold something, it is said in vs. 28 that now everybody remains silent. This verse is the beginning of the final conclusion. According to J. BEGRICH, the prophet even suggests that the adversary silently left the court.[2] I have the impression that BEGRICH has too concrete an idea of the *Sitz im Leben*. At any rate, Yahwe concludes his trial speech with the statement that the adversary gives no answer. Verse 29 resumes vs. 24.

After this analysis I may conclude that Is. xli 21-29, just like xli 1-5, is a trial speech in the framework of a "civil" lawsuit, turning on a claim. It is not as much a speech of a judge as of one of the parties. Yahwe defends his claim and contests that of his adversaries. He does not say *totis verbis* that he alone is God, but he shows that the pagan gods are not. Therefore, the comparison made by GUNKEL-BEGRICH between this pericope and Ps. lxxxii 2-7 is not very apt. The two pericopes are called a speech of the judge, containing these elements: address of the accused (vs. 21; Ps. lxxxii 2), disclosure of the point at issue (vs. 24; Ps. lxxxii 2-4), the adversary has nothing to object (vss. 24, 26, 28; Ps. lxxxii 5), the judgment (vs. 29; Ps. lxxxii 6-7).[3] This comparison overlooks the fundamental distinction between a criminal lawsuit and an *Anspruchsstreit*. While Ps. lxxxii 2-7 is a speech of the judge, Is. xli 21-29 cannot be assimilated to one of the subtypes elaborated by BEGRICH and later by BOECKER. We find something of the *Appellationsrede* (21-23), the defence (25-27) and the judgment, more precisely the *Feststellungsurteil* (vss. 24 and 29). In this sense, Yahwe could be party and judge at the same time. But it seems more likely that this so-called judgment is only the conclusion of the defender's speech.

6. *Is. xliii 8-13*

8 *Bring*[a] forth the people which is blind but has eyes,
and the deaf, who have ears.
9 All the nations are gathered together,

---

[1] A similar position in P. VOLZ, *Jesaia II*, p. 25.

[2] J. BEGRICH, *o.c.*, p. 46.

[3] H. GUNKEL - J. BEGRICH, *Einleitung in die Psalmen*, pp. 364-365.

and the peoples have assembled.
Who among them announces this?
Let them tell us the former things.
Let them bring their witnesses, that they may be justified,
that we may hear and say: It is true.
10 You are my witnesses, — oracle of Yahwe —
and my servant whom I have chosen,
that you may know and believe me
and understand that I am he.
Before me no god was formed,
nor shall there be any after me.
11 I, I am Yahwe,
and besides me there is no saviour.
12 I announce, I save, I proclaim;
there is no strange (god) among you.
You are my witnesses, — oracle of Yahwe —:
I am God,
13 and also *henceforth*[b] I am he.
There is none who delivers from my hand.
I act and who thwarts it?

[a] Lg הוציאו c IQIa. LXX: *ἐξήγαγον*.
[b] LXX: *ἄπ' ἀρχῆς*; Vg: ab initio; Targ: מן עלמא. Perhaps add מעולם after אני־אל.

Is. xliii 8-13 is a trial speech which is akin to the previous one. When trying to offer some further specification, BEGRICH calls the pericope a lawsuit (*Gerichtsverhandlung*); to him it is a quasi-scenic description of a lawsuit. This way he can give a place to different phases of a lawsuit, that had been recognized already by KÖHLER: summons (vss. 8-9), appeal to witnesses (vss. 10 and 13), judgment (vss. 11 and 13).[1]

The speaker orders that the people that is blind and deaf be brought forth. This can only mean Israel. The paradoxical qualification of Israel as "blind, and yet it has eyes" and "deaf, and yet it has ears" must be seen in the light of xlii 18-21 (cf. supra). It has experienced Yahwe's action in history, but it did not learn anything from it. The people is summoned not as a party but as a witness, as appears from vss. 10 and 12. Therefore the paradoxical saying of vs. 8 is important. Although Israel did not draw lessons from history — it

[1] J. BEGRICH, *o.c.*, pp. 27 and 47; L. KÖHLER, *o.c.*, pp. 113-114.

is blind and deaf—, nevertheless, it did experience sufficiently Yahwe's intervention in history—it has eyes and ears—. It thus is able to witness in favour of Yahwe's claims. BEGRICH gives free course to his imagination when stating: "The text shows that the witnesses firstly are in a separate place and do not see the court, perhaps in order not to be influenced".[1]

From vs. 9 it appears that the other nations also are convoked. With their gods they are the opponent party. Again the lawsuit turns on the proof of prediction. Verse 9 reads: "Who among them foretells this (*zō't*)? And let them tell us the former things!" The second member is often rendered as a question, in accordance with the LXX: "Who tells us the former things?"[2] This requires only a slight change of vocalisation: *yašmî'ēnû* instead of *yašmî'unû*. Since MT expresses the same idea as the interrogative clause, this emendation is superfluous. IQIa reads *yšmy'w*.

What is referred to by the pronoun *zō't*? It could be identical with *ri'šōnôt* or the opposite, indicating a present prediction, e.g. concerning Cyrus and his role in the deliverance. The former pericope points to the second alternative. There the word pair *ri'šōnôt* / *bā'ôt* refer respectively to things foretold and fulfilled already, and to not yet fulfilled predictions. If the pronoun *zō't* is not identical with *ri'šōnôt*, then it seems to designate an important fact among the *bā'ôt*. It coincides then with what in other texts is called *ḥădāšôt* or *ḥădāšâ* (xlii 9; xliii 19; xlviii 6). In the preceding chapter I explained that in xliii 19, this means the return from exile, presented as a new exodus. Elsewhere I have demonstrated that also in xlii 9 and xlviiii 6, the prophet intends the fall of Babylon and deliverance from exile.[3] To accept the same concrete content for *zō't* in Is. xliii 9 seems to be the most obvious explanation. More precisely, the prophet views the role of Cyrus.[4] A hint of that sense is the argumentation of the trial speech xli 1-5, which is based on the fact that Cyrus's activity is wholly in Yahwe's hand and realized by him only. It is expressed more explicitly in xli 25-27: Yahwe asserts that he stirred up Cyrus

---

[1] J. BEGRICH, *o.c.*, p. 47.

[2] E.g. Vg, *RSV.*, CONDAMIN, FELDMANN, VAN HOONACKER, SMITH, SIMON, AUVRAY-STEINMANN, WESTERMANN.

[3] A. SCHOORS, *ETL.* XL 1964, pp. 39-42.

[4] So also S. D. LUZZATTO, *Il profeta Isaia*, p. 477: מי בהם יגיד זאת: מי שמגיד עניני כֹּרֶשׁ.

and that he leads him to victory, and then he asks: "Who foretold this?" It would be quite easy to replace vs. 26a with xliii 9bα.

How should we understand *ri'šōnôt* in xliii 9? All the texts analyzed so far point in the same direction. Here also the expression designates facts of Israel's past. If the gods had foretold these facts, they would have shown their divinity. But such did not happen. Only Yahwe foretold them (cf. vs. 12). The text is too close to xli 21-29 and xliv 6-8 (cf. below) to allow another interpretation.[1] We can understand the passage as follows: "Who among the gods foretells Israels deliverance (*zō't*)? And who can tell former things, i.e. facts which he has predicted and which are now fulfilled? Only Yahwe". WESTERMANN as well as VON WALDOW thinks that vs. 9bβ does not view fulfilled predictions but, rather, the interpretation of past history.[2] As in xli 22, this is possible, but in the setting of the dt.-Isaian trial speeches, which are based on the *Weissagungsbeweis*, and in the framework of all texts about the theme *ri'šōnôt*, such a standpoint is untenable.[3] FELDMANN rightly remarks that, in the second part of vs. 9b, Yahwe asks for evidence of predicted and already fulfilled facts.[4]

The adversaries may adduce witnesses in order to be put in the right. Here the verb *ṣdq* means "to carry one's point at a contest". In criminal cases it designates acquittal, in a trial on claims the fact of being justified.[5] One may ask who is the subject of the verbs in vs. 9cβ. According to FELDMANN they are the witnesses, who listen and then say: "It is true".[6] But the role of the witness is rather to speak. This is the way it is conceived in IQIa, since there we read a hiphil *wyšmy'w*. But IQIb has the qal, as MT, Vulgate and some LXX manuscripts.[7] The qal thus is well attested and allows the same interpretation of the hiphil, if one supposes a change of subject: "they (= one) will hear (the witnesses) and say: it is true". This translation fits the context best. The expression *w^{e}yō'm^{e}rû 'èmet* is parallel to

[1] Against CONDAMIN and STAERK, who, in this text, relate ראשונות to Cyrus.

[2] H. E. VON WALDOW, *o.c.*, p. 65; C. WESTERMANN, *o.c.*, p. 100.

[3] Cf. A. SCHOORS, *a.c.*, pp. 25-42.

[4] F. FELDMANN, *l.c.*: "... in der zweiten Halbzeile Angabe geweissagter bereits eingetroffener Ereignisse". Cf. already S. D. LUZZATTO, *l.c.*

[5] K. FAHLGREN, Ṣ^{e}dāḳā, *nahestehende und entgegengesetzte Begriffe*, p. 166, did not notice this distinction.

[6] F. FELDMANN, *l.c.*

[7] Namely in B *L C*. In others the verb is missing, while ORIGEN has it under asterisk.

w^eyiṣdāqû. Yet, the adversaries will make win their case if the court, after having heard the witnesses, will declare: it is true.

Yahwe, however, has "his" witnesses. Israel has to witness for Yahwe because of its peculiar relation to him, which is expressed with the terms *bḥr* and *'ebed*. The emendation of *'abdî* to plural *'ăbāday*, as suggested by *BHS*, Marti and Duhm is grammatically more in keeping with the first part of the phrase.[1] But this reading has no support in the textual tradition. The singular must be conserved, especially since it appeals to the theology of Israel as Yahwe's servant (xli 8-9; xlii 19; xliv 1-2, 21; xlv 4).[2] By its election Israel is made capable of witnessing, for it has been chosen precisely in order to know and believe that "he is he". I refer the reader to my discussion of the *Erkenntnisformel* in the comments on Is. xli 20. In my opinion, however, W. Zimmerli gave an incorrect explanation of the formula of recognition in the present context. According to MT God chose Israel to recognize him. Zimmerli however comments that Israel should witness that the nations may recognize him. To do so he must, along with Begrich, change the verbal forms from second to third person.[3] In the textual tradition there is no argument for this. The only reason for this emendation is that the text thus fits better the interpretation advanced by both these scholars, which is a weak argument in textual criticism. In a salvation word the promised salvation is the token that leads to recognition; that is why the formula of recognition is placed in the motif of goal. In the present trial speech the whole past history, as a realisation of election (*bāḥartî*), is a token meant to make Israel recognize that only Yahwe is God.

According to E. Nielsen, behind the phrase "You are my witnesses, I am God", lies a tendency to make the pre-deuteronomic and deuteronomic covenant formula "You are my people, I am your God" theocentric.[4] It is hard to see any direct indication of this tendency in the context of the present trial speech.

The enigmatic phrase "I am he" is explained further in the text. It means that Yahwe is the only God. Such is underlined in the conclusion of the oracle by the double *'ănî hû'* (vss. 10 and 12), cor-

---

1 K. Marti, *Jesaja*, p. 296; B. Duhm, *Das Buch Jesaia*, p. 290.

2 A. Condamin, *Le livre d'Isaïe*, p. 261.

3 W. Zimmerli, "Erkenntnis Gottes nach dem Buche Ezechiel", *Theologische Bücherei*, 19, p. 70.

4 E. Nielsen, "Deuterojesaja, Erwägungen zur Formkritik, Traditions- und Redaktionsgeschichte", *VT*. XX 1970, pp. 190-205; esp. p. 204.

roborated by the repeated *'ānōkî* and *'ănî-'ēl* in vss. 11 and 12. Really, one cannot get rid of this exclusivity of Yahwe! Before him no god was formed nor shall there be any after him. Here the prophet alludes to the Akkadian myths, like *Enuma eliš*, where the formation of gods is related.[1] Besides Yahwe there is no saviour (*môšîa'*, vs. 11). Again the salutary aspect of monotheistic faith is underlined. That Yahwe is the only God is not the object of a theoretical or abstract statement. The point is that he is the only one who can save. Nobody can undo his salvific act. He manifests his salvific functions in his acts (*hôšîa'*) and his words (*higgîd*; *hišmîa'*). The word *hôša'tî* in vs. 12 might be a gloss.[2] But this does not appear in the textual tradition and the word fits the context very well. Firstly, *'ānōkî hôša'tî* is clearly in contrast with "besides me there is no saviour", and furthermore, together with the phrases about God's word, it forms a global expression of Yahwe's salvific action: to act and to speak. C. STUHLMUELLER is right in pointing out that "the contrast of identical verbs, *ngd* and *šm'*, used in the perf. for Yahwe and in the imperf. for false gods, is impressive. The perf. tenses in xliii 12 call attention not so much to "time"—in past, present or future—..." But how can he prove that they call attention to the effectiveness of Yahwe's word? Why not say that they simply refer to the fact that Yahwe *actually* predicted the coming events? STUHLMUELLER searches unnecessarily here for indications of Yahwe's "creative word".[3] This oracle, it can be said, inculcates the monotheistic dogma with an impressive vigour.

In comparison with the trial speeches which I have analyzed so far, Is. xliii 8-13 shows two important features. In the conclusion the strictly monotheistic belief of the prophet is emphatically professed. Secondly, Israel receives the role of a witness. Before the forum of the world it must witness to Yahwe's unicity, a witness based on the historical experience of Yahwe's salvific action. So this trial speech uses a theme which shows up also in the final motif of some salvation words: through his activity in favour of Israel, Yahwe reveals himself to the nations (cf. xli 20; esp. xlix 26b; lv 5b). In this connection one can speak of an historical world theophany of Yahwe. In the conclusion of the proclamation of salvation in xliii 21, this revelation is realized also by the witness of God's people.

---

[1] F. STUMMER, "Einige keilschriftliche Parallelen zu Jes 40-66", *JBL.* XLV 1926, p. 180.

[2] Cf. e.g. *BHK*; C. WESTERMANN, *o.c.*, p. 98; J. BEGRICH, *o.c.*, p. 48, note 158.

[3] C. STUHLMUELLER, *Creative Redemption in Deutero-Isaiah*, p. 46.

7. *Is. xliv 6-8*

6 Thus says Yahwe, the King of Israel
and its Redeemer, Yahwe of hosts:
"I am the first and I am the last;
besides me there is no god!
7 Who is like me? Let him proclaim it,
let him declare and set it forth before me.
Who has announced from old the things to come?[a]
And let them tell us what is yet to be.
8 Fear not, be not *afraid.*[b]
Have I not told it from old? *Surely*[c] I declared it.
You are my witnesses: is there a god besides me?
There is no rock; I know not any".

[a] See comments.
[b] Lg תירואו c IQIa.
[c] See comments.

Is. xliv 6-8 is a short trial speech along the same line of thought as the preceding one. BEGRICH defines the genre as a speech of the plaintiff (*Kläger*) in court.[1] My analysis also will show that here Yahwe's situation is the same as in xli 21-29 and xliii 8-13. Indeed, Yahwe defends his claims, but this he does also in xli 21-29, which BEGRICH calls an utterance of the judge, and in xliii 8-13, which he regards as a description of the trial. It appears that BEGRICH, starting from the *Sitz im Leben* in the profane administration of justice, comes to an artificial subdivision of the trial speeches. H. J. BOECKER too calls the pericope a trial speech, which is a plea for judicial confirmation of certain claims.[2] So he renders the point of the speech correctly.

The introduction invokes Yahwe's titles *gō'ēl*, *yhwh ṣ^ebā'ôt* and *melek-yiśrā'ēl*. I dealt amply with the first and the second in the chapter on the salvation words.[3] The third has a parallel in another trial speech (*melek ya'ăqōb*: xli 21) and in the difficult pericope xliii 14-15 (*malk^ekem*). At any rate, the term expresses a peculiar relation between Yahwe and Israel. According to Is. lii 7-10, it seems that

[1] J. BEGRICH, *o.c.*, p. 27.
[2] H. J. BOECKER, *Redeformen des Rechtslebens*, pp. 162-163.
[3] Cf. pp. 62-63 and 84.

Yahwe becomes king by delivering Israel from exile.[1] But here and in xli 21; xliii 15, the title refers to a condition that exists, just like the other epithets such as Saviour, Redeemer, Holy One of Israel, etc. It is wrong to ascribe a universalist impact to the title by referring to lii 7-10, for there it is in a different literary and theological context and, at any rate, in lii 7-10, Yahwe's kingship is not universalist either.[2] Especially in xliii 15, the title is used in parallelism with "Holy One" and "Creator of Israel" as a motive of assurance. As xliv 6 offers *gō'ēl* as parallel, a term belonging to the same theological complex, there can be no doubt. *Melek-yiśrā'ēl* is a title which, in Dt.-Isaiah's message, is connected with his theology of election.

The topics of vs. 6a, and also the use of a messenger's formula, are unusual at the beginning of a trial speech. All this seems rather to belong to a word of salvation. This creates a problem to which I have to return further on.

The speech proper opens with the claim (vs. 6b), which is the same as in the *Appellationsrede* Is. xli 1-5: Yahwe is the only eternally present and active God. Such is expressed in the word pair first/last (cf. xli 4). Yahwe's strict exclusiveness, which we found in xliii 13, is again sharply formulated: besides Yahwe there is no god. Even the existence of other gods is denied as in xli 24.

In vs. 7 Yahwe addresses the adversaries challenging them to bring objections against him. The first colon has two forensic terms. The verb *qr'* designates the question of one party to the other (cf. Is. lix 4; Job ix 16; xiii 22). Especially *'rk* is used in the sense of "produce arguments in a trial" (cf. Ps. l 21; Job xiii 18; xxiii 4; xxxiii 5).[3] Several scholars add *ya'ămōd* after *mî-kāmônî*, invoking the LXX.[4] This reconstruction is not convincing. Admittedly, L. KÖHLER obtains a uniform rhythm 3 + 3 in the whole pericope, but his distribution of accents is arbitrary.[5] Furthermore, the LXX is isolated in the

---

[1] Cf. A. SCHOORS, *Recherches bibliques*, VIII, pp. 122-123.

[2] Against *BW*³, col. 1230; W. EICHRODT, *Theologie des A.T.*, I, pp. 124-125: "Aber diese Stellen sind nun nicht zu trennen von der weltweiten prophetischen Hoffnung: Jahwe erweist sich als der König Israels, indem er mit der Befreiung seines Volkes auch der Völkerwelt das Heil verschafft, vgl. besonders 52, 7 und 10". H. J. KRAUS, *Die Königsherrschaft Gottes im A.T.*, Tübingen 1951, p. 101. — Cf. A. SCHOORS, *l.c.*

[3] J. BEGRICH, *o.c.*, pp. 39 and 42; M. DAHOOD, *Psalms I*, p. 30.

[4] LXX: *στήτω*; cf. *BHS*; L. KÖHLER, *Deuterojesaja*, p. 23; A. LOISY, *La consolation d'Israël*, Paris 1927, p. 77; J. BEGRICH, *o.c.*, p. 42; C. WESTERMANN, *o.c.*, p. 113.

[5] It is not clear why he gives two accents to אני ראשון (vs. 6b) and only one to ואני אחרון. On the other hand, in vs. 7a he takes the very short לי for a separate foot.

textual tradition and it must be noticed that the Greek text has only three verbs, at least in A Q S. The fourth verb ἀναγγειλατω in B *L C* was missing in ORIGEN's Septuagint also (⁜). A. VAN HOONACKER, too, seems to be inspired by the LXX when he suggests that *yiqrā'* be emended to read *yiqreh*, "let him come forth".[1]

The next verse is a famous *crux interpretum*. MT *miśśûmî 'am-'ôlām we' ōtiyyôt* literally means "from my placing an eternal people and things to come". Generally the following emendation is proposed: *mî hišmîa' mē'ôlām 'ōtiyyôt* (*BHS*), but one looks in vain for justification. I myself formerly accepted the proposed reading.[2] The textual witnesses are strikingly concordant:

IQIa: (> יואמר in MT) משומי עם עולם ואותיות יואמר

LXX: *ἀφ' οὗ ἐποίησα ἄνθρωπον εἰς τὸν αἰῶνα καὶ τὰ ἐπερχόμενα πρὸ τοῦ ἐλθεῖν ἀναγγειλάτωσαν ὑμῖν.*

Vg: ex quo constitui populum antiquum, ventura et quae futura sunt annuntient eis.

Targ: משויותי עמא דמן עלמא ודאתין ודעתידן למיתי יחוון לנא

(since I appointed the people that is from everlasting; and the things that are coming, and that are about to come let them declare to us).[3]

Pesh: ܡܢ ܕܣܡܬ ܥܡܐ ܠܥܠܡ : ܘܐܬ̈ܝܬܐ ܕܐܬ̈ܝܢ ܢܚܘܘܢ

Thus the proposed correction has no support in textual tradition. But it is not so different from the consonantal text, expecially when one reads *yašmîa'* instead of *hišmîa'*. Between מי ישמיע מעולם אתיות (emended text) and משומי עם עולם ואתיות, the difference is only one of a couple of *waws* and *yods* which are very unstable consonants. From a literary standpoint the suggested reading is supported by *hišma'tîkā* in the following verse. So one has the same verb in both verses. The corrected version means: "Who has announced beforehand the things to come? Let them tell us what is yet to be".

Finally this interpretation fits the dt.-Isaian trial speeches, as I have shown in the cited article. For these reasons I think DAHOOD's

---

When we take it together with the preceding word, we have a 2 + 2 rhythm without adding יעמד.

1 A. VAN HOONACKER, *Het boek Isaias*, p. 210.

2 A. SCHOORS, "Les choses antérieures et les choses nouvelles" *ETL*. XL 1964, p. 31, note 49.

3 Translation of J. F. STENNING, *The Targum of Isaiah*, p. 148.

proposal is unacceptable: "Since I have fixed till (*'im*) eternity the thing that are to come".[1] It is a good suggestion but it does not put the verse in the context of the present trial speech and of Dt.-Is. in general. Again the prophet invokes the argument of prediction, which turns on the foretelling of former events (7bα) and the present prediction of what is still to come (7bβ). Comparing the verse with Is. xli 22, *'ōtiyyôt* corresponds to *ri'šōnôt* and *'ăšer tābō'nâ* to *habbā'ôt*.

Should not *'ōtiyyôt* refer to future things, in contrast with the *ri'šōnôt* of xli 22, which are situated in the past? The fem. participle of *'th* occurs only in the polemical texts of Dt.-Is., i.e. here and in xli 23 and xlv 11. From this viewpoint it is certainly related to *ri'šōnôt*. There is no reason why we should not be allowed to understand the term as designating a relative future. So in vs. 7 the *'ōtiyyôt* can denote events that were "to come" for the one who, formerly, had to foretell them. When the prophet is speaking, they may be past already. Thus I think that *'ōtiyyôt* here and *ri'šōnôt* in xli 22 designate the same event.[2] The line of reasoning of the prophet is the same in both pericopes.

A last critical remark about *lāmô*. This form generally designates a third person plural.[3] In vs. 7 some scholars emend it to *lānû*, with reference to the Targum.[4] But very probably *lam-* is a variant form of *l-* (compare *kāmō-* and *bᵉmô-*, Ug. *lm, km, bm*). So one can understand that *lāmô* sometimes designates a third person sing. (e.g. Is. xliv 15). In the present text one should read *lammû*<*lamnû* (so also in Pss. xxviii 8; xliv 11; lxiv 6; lxxx 7; Is. xxvi 16; Job xxii 17). The large number of instances renders this explanation, proposed by DAHOOD, very probable.[5]

After having noticed that the introduction of this trial speech is akin to the words of salvation, we now meet the assurance of salvation in vs. 8: "Fear not ..." The word *tirhû* is *hapax legomenon*. Its meaning

1 M. DAHOOD, *Ugaritic-Hebrew Philology*, Rome 1965, p. 32. Cf. *'m 'lm*, "to eternity" in 'nt V : 39.

2 Cf. C. R. NORTH, "The 'Former Things' and the 'New Things' in Deutero-Isaiah", *Studies in Old Testament Prophecy*, p. 123; the same interpretation of אתיות in M. HARAN, בין ראשונות לחדשות, p. 42.

3 JOÜON, § 103 f; GK, § 103f.

4 So e.g. *BHK*, LOISY, BRUNO, MCKENZIE; Targ: לנא; LXX: *ὑμῖν* is regarded then as a corruption of *ἡμῖν*.

5 M. DAHOOD, "Hebrew-Ugaritic Lexicography", *Bib.* XLVII 1966, p. 409. Cf. GK, § 103 k.

is sometimes connected with Arab. *r'h*, which means the rippling movement of water. This etymology is very doubtful. Along with IQIa a better reading is *tîr'û*.[1] The prophet comes to the same conclusion as in the trial speech just analyzed: Yahwe is the only rock. This means that one can expect salvation only from him. In Is. xvii 10 we find a parallelism between "the God of your salvation" and "the rock of your refuge". The salvific meaning of the term "rock" is most clearly expressed in the formulas "the rock of our salvation" (Pss. lxxxix 27; xlv 1) and "my rock and my redeemer" (Pss. xix 15; lxxviii 35).[2] This contest is not about the mere existence of Yahwe, but about his presence as the God of salvation. It is significant that Yahwe formulates this idea in a direct address to his witnesses and in connection with the typical formula of the assurance of salvation. There is a sort of salvation oracle in this trial speech.

Yahwe made predictions in the past. They are a reassurance for the chosen people. Yahwe dominates history. He is the only rock of refuge. Since Israel is summoned to witness, it must be able to found its witness on predictions that are already fulfilled. The Israelites should not fear, for Yahwe has shown with fulfilled predictions that he dominates history. It is this reliability of Yahwe's words and deeds which is the connection between salvation oracle and trial speech.

There is a problem about the extent of the pericope. The verses 9-20 certainly are an independent unit, which we may call a satire on the manufacture of idols. But DUHM, followed by WESTERMANN, proposes that vss. 6-8 and 21-22 be joined together to form one unit.[3] The latter thinks that vss. 21a and 22b (imperatives) are later additions made by disciples, when the pericope 9-20 had already been inserted. The remainder contains the nominal and perfective substantiation of the assurance in vs. 8a. Thus in the vss. 6-8, 21-22 a trial speech and an oracle of salvation would have been united in one unit.

This standpoint certainly offers an explanation of the presence of an assurance of salvation in the trial speech. The imperatives, however, make vss. 21-22 an admonition. And it is quite arbitrary to regard them as later additions. Moreover vss. 21-22 are in the singular,

---

[1] So already MARTI, BACHMANN, CONDAMIN, *BHK*. Vg: conturbemini.

[2] K. MARTI, *Das Buch Jesaja*, p. 144; P. A. H. DE BOER, *Second Isaiah's Message*, p. 64: "The rock is God as the protector and provider of life and security".

[3] B. DUHM, *o.c.*, p. 302; C. WESTERMANN, *Jesaja 40-66*, pp. 113-114.

whereas in vs. 8 the Israelites are addressed in the plural. The only exception is *hišmaʿtîkā*, but the suffix *-k* is a forgotten emphatic *kî* which goes with the following verb. It should be remembered also that the assurance "Fear not" is always in the singular in the salvation oracles of our prophet. Thus WESTERMANN's position about the original connection between xliv 6-8 and 21-22 seems to be unacceptable.

8. *Is. xlv 18-25*

18 Thus says Yahwe, who created the heavens,
— he is God —
who formed the earth and made it,
— he established it
he did not create it a chaos,
he formed it to be inhabited—:
"I am Yahwe, there is no other.
19 I did not speak in secret,
in a land of darkness;
I did not say to the offspring of Jacob:
'Seek me in vain'.
I, Yahwe, speak salvation, I declare what is right.
20 Assemble yourselves and come,
draw near together, you survivors of the nations.
They have no knowledge, who carry about their wooden idols
and pray to a god who cannot save.
21 Declare and present your proofs,
yes, take counsel together;
Who told this long ago, declared it beforehand?
Was it not I, Yahwe?
There is no other god besides me,
there is no righteous and saving god besides me.
22 Turn to me and be saved,
all the ends of the earth.
For I am God, and there is no other.
23 By myself I have sworn,
from my mouth salvation goes forth,
a word that does not return:
To me every knee shall bow,
every tongue shall swear.

24 Only in Yahwe, *it will be said*,[a]
there is salvation and strength.
To him *shall come*[b] and be ashamed,
all who were incensed against him.
25 In Yahwe all the offspring of Israel
shall triumph and glory".

[a] See comment.
[b] Lg יבואו c mss, Seb, IQIa, LXX, Vg, Targ.

Is. xlv 18-25 is a debated pericope, with regard to its limits as well as to its genre. According to GRESSMANN it is a trial speech, which passes into a missionary motif (vss. 22-24a); the introduction would be a hymn (vss. 18-19) and the conclusion would be a motif of certainty.[1] BEGRICH and VON WALDOW list the pericope with the disputations. But the latter notices several departures from the pure form of that genre and BEGRICH points to relations with the trial speech.[2] In my opinion, the pericope is undoubtedly a trial speech, comparable to xli 21-29; xliii 8-13; xliv 6-8, as accepted by WESTERMANN also.[3] One may doubt whether vss. 18-19 belong to the pericope or not. Vs. 20 certainly is a good beginning of a trial speech and vss. 20-25 suffice to make the genre. But vss. 18-19 cannot be a separate unit. I shall deal with them after 20-25.

In vss. 20-21a we have the challenge to appear in court (cf. *qbṣ* in xliii 9; *ngš* in xli 1; l 8) which, in contrast with the other trial speeches, is directed to the "survivors of the nations". The exact meaning of *pālîṭ* is nicely formulated by ZORELL: "qui salvus seu superstes est, aliis pereuntibus, post proelium".[4] Here we have to do with people who have escaped from a lost battle. Spontaneously, one thinks of the fall of Babylon. This does not mean that the oracle has been pronounced after this defeat. The prophet speaks about this imminent fall with prophetic certainty (cf. xlvi 1-2; xlvii). It has not been proved that the survivors here are an eschatological entity.[5] Recently D. E. HOLLENBERG has suggested that the survivors of the nations

[1] H. GRESSMANN, *ZAW*. XXXIV 1914, pp. 278-279.

[2] J. BEGRICH, *Studien*, pp. 49-51; H. E. VON WALDOW, *Anlass und Hintergrund*, pp. 29-32.

[3] A. SCHOORS, *De literaire en doctrine'e eenheid van Dt.-Is.*, p. 259, note 3; C. WESTERMANN, *a.c.*, p. 135; *Jesaja 40-66*, p. 142.

[4] ZORELL, p. 651.

[5] G. FOHRER, "σῴζω und σωτηρία im A.T.", *TWNT*, VII, pp. 979-980.

are rather survivors among the nations or crypto-Israelites, who have fled away into the nations and escaped the crisis which befell Israel.[1] This interpretation is suggestive, but very hypothetical. If it were correct, it would be necessary to apply it to all the instances of Dt.-Is. where nations or islands are mentioned. This is superfluous as there is really no positive reason to do so.

Verse 20bc is a condemnation of idolatry. It is stupid to carry around idols in procession and to pray to them. According to WESTERMANN the verse is a gloss, which was meant originally for xlvi 1-2.[2] Indeed, the verse somewhat interrupts the movement of the challenge, but it does not clash with the context. The idea is even close to vs. 21: the figure of a god, who does not save (*lōʾ yôšîaʿ*) is connected to the idea of Yahwe as the only saving God (*ʾēl môšîaʿ*).

Verse 21 reminds us of the trial speeches, which I have analyzed above. The object of *haggîšû* are the arguments and not the idols (cf. xli 21).[3] The second colon appeals to the argument of prediction. The question is to what the demonstrative *zōʾt* alludes. I cannot agree with M. HALLER in relating it to the mighty deeds of creation (xlv 18-19), for these deeds never were the object of predictions.[4] I refer to my interpretation of xliii 9, viz. that the demonstrative designates the fall of Babylon and the deliverance from exile, especially the role of Cyrus in these events.[5] It is not necessary that Babylon has already been captured, but the events show that defeat is approaching. Such is clearly expressed in the texts, which deal with Cyrus explicitly (e.g. xlv 11-13; xlvi 9-11). The analysis of xlviii 14, where the demonstrative *ʾēlleh* is explained, will remove any doubt: "Who among them has declared these things? Yahwe's friend shall perform his purpose on Babylon".

The conclusion again is: "Besides me there is no saving god". Then follows an admonition to draw the suitable conclusion from this statement. When the hearers do so, they will be saved (vs. 22). The

---

[1] D. E. HOLLENBERG, "Nationalism and 'the Nations' in Isaiah xl-lv", *VT*. XIX 1969, p. 31.

[2] C. WESTERMANN, *Jesaja 40-66, l.c.*

[3] Against C. C. TORREY, *The Second Isaiah*, p. 362.

[4] M. HALLER, "Die Kyros-Lieder Deuterojesajas", *ΕΥΧΑΡΙΣΤΗΡΙΟΝ. Festschrift Gunkel*, I, pp. 265-266.

[5] So already A. VAN HOONACKER, *RB*. VIII 1911, p. 284: "... le salut d'Israël à procurer par Cyrus". Also J. STEINMANN, *Le livre de la consolation*, p. 152. Against J. FISCHER, *Isaias 40-45 und die Perikopen vom Gottesknecht*, Münster 1916, pp. 23-24.

trial speech thus passes into an admonition (*Mahnwort*), which is an important new feature in comparison with the foregoing trial speeches. The invitation is directed to "the ends of the earth". In the framework of an absolute and universal monotheism, salvation might have a universal character.[1] According to the present text, Israel's salvation would not only be seen by the world, as is said in other pericopes, but the whole world itself would be invited to be saved. This is the most obvious meaning of this text. Nevertheless, it would be the only text of Dt.-Is. where such a universal conversion is viewed. From vs. 25 it appears that Israel's salvation is the point of the pericope: the prophet announces the salvation of all Israel (*kol-zeraʿ yiśrāʾēl*). This might give us a clue for the explanation of vs. 22: the idea of totality in "all the ends of the earth" seems to refer to the totality of Israel with an allusion to the diaspora (cf. xliii 5-7; xlix 12).[2] Moreover, the other nations, all Israel's enemies, will be ashamed (vs. 24). In the same sense the totality expressed in "every knee" and "every tongue" may refer to the totality of Israel. And even if these words be taken literally, they still do not involve universal salvation, but only universal recognition of Yahwe's power (cf. xl 5; xlii 6; xlv 14-17; lv 3-5).[3] Finally it must be noticed that, even if the salvation in vs. 22 concerns the other nations, it is put in a context of admonition and it is not announced like Israel's salvation in vs. 25.

I have noted already more than once that in Dt.-Is. *ṣᵉdāqâ* / *ṣedeq* often means "victory" or "salvation". So in vs. 21 Yahwe is called *ṣaddîq* and *môšîaʿ*: a saving God. In vs. 24 we have the plural *ṣᵉdāqôt* in parallelism with *ʿōz*. This plural designates, —as in Jud. v 11 and Mic. vi 5—the mighty deeds of Yahwe, with which he protects Israel. Those who recognize and worship Yahwe do so because they see that he alone is able to perform such salvific deeds, i.e. that he proves his divine exclusivity in historical salvific acts.

The little textcritical problem *lî ʾāmar* is easily solved with an emphatic *lamed* and the imperfect *yōʾmar* or *yēʾāmēr*. IQIa, too, has an imperfect. Already A. VAN HOONACKER pointed in that di-

[1] With some exaggeration J. STEINMANN, *Le livre de la consolation*, p. 152: "On ne saurait exagérer l'importance de cette première profession d'universalisme absolu dans la Bible".

[2] Thus also with some hesitation P. A. H. DE BOER, *Second Isaiah*, p. 90. A similar though not identical view in D. E. HOLLENBERG, *VT.* XIX 1969, p. 32.

[3] Cf. A. SCHOORS, *Recherches bibliques*, VIII, p. 124; D. E. HOLLENBERG, *l.c.*

rection, relating *lî* to the assertive particle *lû*, current in Assyrian, and which he thought to be used in other Hebrew texts (e.g. Ex. viii 22).[1]

Wrongly, in my opinion, W. CASPARI gives a merely forensic meaning to *ṣdq* in the present context. It apparently means Yahwe's salvific acts and in vs. 25, the verb must be understood in the same sense: Israel will obtain salvation through Yahwe. But using this root, the prophet gives to God's salvific acts a forensic overtone. What takes place now is like a great legal contest in which nations and gods are involved. Such appears in the trial speeches: in a lawsuit with the nations and their gods, Yahwe defends his divine claims. To man, more precisely, to Israel, it is important to choose the good side, viz. Yahwe. There is salvation only with him. That means, in the excellent comment of DUHM: only with him one is able to surmount all crises, whereas without or against him, one's lot can only be shame, as a partisan of the ἥττων λόγος, the *causa inferior.*[2]

Thus, Is. xlv 20-25 is a trial speech ending in an admonition, the latter being based on Yahwe's unique salvific power. The genre is thus not pure. The combination shows that the point of a dt.-Isaian trial speech, viz. the unicity of Yahwe, has something to do with the salvific message of the prophet. He wants to reinforce his hearers' trust in the only God who can save them.

When, after an analysis of vss. 20-25, we return to 18-19, we clearly see that both verses go together with the following ones. The point of 20-25, viz. Yahwe's unicity as the God of salvation is put forward already in vs. 18d: "I am Yahwe and there is no other". WESTERMANN also regards vs. 18 as the introduction to vss. 20-25. But I cannot agree with him, when he relates vs. 19 to xlvi 1-13.[3] The verse in question clearly refers to 23-25 and makes with them a sort of inclusion. To *zeraʿ yaʿăqōb* corresponds *zeraʿ yiśrāʾēl* (vs. 25), whereas *dōbēr ṣedeq* undoubtedly announces *yāṣeʾā* (MT *yāṣāʾ*) *mippî ṣedāqâ* (vs. 23). On the other hand there is no specific contact with ch. xlvi.

The whole of vs. 18a-c is a hymnic development of the messenger's

---

[1] A. VAN HOONACKER, *Het boek Isaias*, p. 218. On emphatic lamed cf. now M. DAHOOD, "Hebrew-Ugaritic Lexicography", *Bib.* XLVII 1966, p. 407, with bibliography.

[2] B. DUHM, *Das Buch Jesaja*, p. 314. Cf. K. MARTI, *Jesaja*, p. 314; J. STEINMANN, *l.c.*; K. CRAMER, *ZAW.* XXVII 1907, p. 89; W. CASPARI, *Lieder und Gottessprüche*, p. 160.

[3] C. WESTERMANN, *o.c.*, pp. 140-141.

formula. Strikingly, the theme is not historical but it refers to the theology of creation. So we find new thematic contact with 20-25 in the form of a theological substantiation. Since Yahwe created heaven and earth, he is the only God (*hû' hā'ĕlōhîm*, vs. 18a). Vs. 18c carries an idea which is unique in Dt.-Is.: God did not create the earth a chaos, he formed it to be inhabited. This means that he did a good job. His creation proves that one can trust him. At the same time this may involve an allusion to restoration. The substantive *tōhû* describes the ruined land of Edom in Is. xxxiv 11 and the desolation of Judah in Jer. iv 23. So, when it is said that Yahwe did not create the earth a *tōhû*, this means that the ruins of Judah will not exist indefinitely.

Yahwe says that he does not speak in secret, and that what he says is true and right. This clearly views the reliability, the salvific value of the word that he is about to announce. The phrase thus is complementary to vs. 18: in his creation and his words, Yahwe shows that one can trust him. That *māqôm* here means "grave", as suggested by DAHOOD, or *sēter*, "sheol", as proposed by N. J. TROMP, is possible but not proven and it does not render the text more clear.[1] Yahwe's word has been clearly audible. This may involve an anticipatory allusion to the former predictions which are expressly mentioned in vs. 21. It is not sure that it also means a contrast with the pagan gods, whom one can hear only through complicated mantic techniques.[2] However, the second colon points to this sense, where the verb *biqqēš* designates the oracular questioning of Yahwe (cf. 2 Sam. xxi 1; 1 Kings x 24; Hos. v 15; Pss. xxiv 6; xxvii 8; Ex. xxxii 7). Yahwe is not questioned in vain; he gives a clear answer. He speaks *ṣedeq* and *mêšārîm*. In connection with what I here said above, *ṣedeq* refers to God's salvific justice. Therefore WESTERMANN and VOLZ render it as "salvation". Both translate *mêšārîm* as "truth".[3] Being parallel to *ṣedeq* it also means "justice" in the sense just explained. Nowhere does the word mean "truth", but several times it is synonymous with *ṣedeq* or *mišpāṭ*, making a word pair which comes close to Akkadian *kittum u mēšarum*, which indicates total law[4].

---

[1] M. DAHOOD, *Bib.* XLVIII 1967, p. 430; N. J. TROMP, *Primitive Conceptions of Death and the Nether World in the O.T.*, Rome 1969, p. 97.

[2] P. VOLZ, *o.c.*, p. 71; C. R. NORTH, *Isaiah 40-55*, p. 93.

[3] P. VOLZ, *l.c.*; C. WESTERMANN, *o.c.*, p. 139.

[4] Cf. KB, p. 520; ZORELL, p. 433. A. E. SPEISER, "Authority and Law in Mesopotamia", *JAOS*. Suppl. 17, Baltimore 1954, pp. 12-14.

Conclusion

Let us now summarize the message of the eight pericopes and answer a couple of questions formulated in the first paragraph of this chapter.

1. First of all, the distinction made by WESTERMANN between trial speeches against Israel and against the nations must be confirmed. The first group consists of xliii 22-28; l 1-3 and xlii 18-25, which therefore I analyzed together. The three pericopes belong together, not only because they are directed to Israel, but also because they follow the same line of thought. They are a reply to an accusation against Yahwe that he has abandoned his people. The retort is that he had to do so because of their sins. The exile thus is willed by God and it is not a token of his powerlessness (esp. l 1-3). Israel's sin is present in its whole history beginning from the first ancestor (xliii 27), and although Yahwe continually tried to educate his people, they did not learn anything (xlii 18-21). On the other hand, Yahwe is the one who always forgives (xliii 25). With this *rîb* against Israel, the prophet continues prophetical tradition: he confirms the accusations uttered by his pre-exilic predecessors. But he departs from them in not announcing punishment any more but simply justifying the punishment undergone.

The trial speeches against the nations develop a completely different thought. The fact that they are directed to the gods constitutes a remarkable difference with the classical *rîb*. One could list these pericopes with the *rîbôt* against the nations, since the nations are closely connected with their gods and share their destiny. The nations are summoned together with their gods (e.g. xliii 9; xlv 20). But it must be noticed that, by having Yahwe address the gods directly, Dt.-Is. has at least shifted the point of the genre. The trial speech is no longer an accusation followed by a condemnation, but it becomes an *Anspruchsstreit*, a defence of Yahwe's claims. To be sure, there is a note of accusation: the pagans are wrong when they claim divine prerogatives for their gods. There is even a condemnation of the worshippers of such gods (xli 24). But this is not where the stress lies. Instead of accusations we have challenges and arguments, instead of condemnation there is the conclusion that the claims of the adversary are false. All this makes the dt.-Isaian *rîb* a reality *sui generis*. We cannot put it on a level with the prophetic requisitory against the breach of covenant, which constitutes the definition of a *rîb* according to J. HARVEY,[1] a valuable definition of the traditional *rîb*, but too narrow to embrace our prophet's trial speeches.

The trial speeches of the second group have a very characteristic theological intent. The central theological idea is not that of the covenant and the people's behaviour with regard to it. The only concern is to establish Yahwe's sovereign greatness against the nothingness of the pagan gods. So the trial speeches express one of the main themes of Dt.-Is., viz. his very strict monotheism. The prophet elaborates in the form of a trial speech an apologia for this monotheism. He bases the apologia on history. The absence of any direct appeal to Yahwe's creative acts is striking.[2] Yahwe challenges the gods to prove their existence by means of a *Weissagungsbeweis*, a prediction proof. But the gods are not able to do so: neither in the past nor in the present could they foretell what was to happen. This *Weissagungsbeweis* is another typical trait of the exilic prophet (cf. Is. xli 22-26; xliii 9; xliv 7; xlv 21; xlviii 14). It is missing in only one pericope of this group, namely xli 1-5, where the divine claim is founded on the fact that only Yahwe has stirred up Cyrus and conducted him to victory. If the gods are unable to foresee the future, they do not dominate history, they cannot perform anything (cf. xli 23b, 24, 29). Hence the prophet infers that these gods do not exist. The theological point thus consists in a demonstration of the strictest monotheism, i.e. excluding even the existence of any other deity (cf. the repeated *'ayin*). With our prophet the monotheistic belief assumes a somewhat more speculative air, as is common to all apologetics directed to pagans. We should notice, however, that the speculation does not become abstract. The argument is drawn from the history of salvation and the God for whom the prophet enters the lists is the God of Israel, the God who saves (*yš'*, *ṣdq*), the only Rock (xliv 8) in whom one can trust.

Dt.-Isaiah's trial speeches thus fall into two clearly distinct groups. Therefore, the general characterisation of this dt.-Isaian genre by WÜRTHWEIN, as well as by WESTERMANN in a former work, is one-sided. The latter asserts that a characteristic of the trial speeches is that the accusation always embraces the whole behaviour of the people

---

[1] Cf. p. 187; J. HARVEY, *Le plaidoyer prophétique contre Israël après la rupture de l'alliance*, Bruges 1967; also *Bib.* XLIII 1962, pp. 172-196.

[2] W. ZIMMERLI, "Der Wahrheitserweis Jahwes", *Fs. A. Weiser*, Göttingen 1963, p. 139. There is only an indirect appeal to it in Is. xlv 18 (the messenger's formula).

with regard to God. For this reason the professor of Heidelberg believes this genre becomes fully elaborated only with Dt.-Is., where the very lawsuit between God and his people concerns the whole history. It is obvious that this only applies to the trial speeches against Israel. WÜRTHWEIN, on the other hand, underlines that Dt.-Isaiah's trial speech is situated on a different level to the *rîbôt* of the former prophets. Our prophet would not be concerned with accusing Israel but with establishing a matter of fact (*Tatbestand*), in other words, he wants to prove something. This is true also, but only with respect to the trial speeches against the nations.[1]

My subdivision of the trial speeches coincides materially with the one proposed by VON WALDOW, namely in a secularized and a cultic type (*profanisierter Typ* and *kultischer Typ*). For he lists Is. xliii 22-28 and l 1-3 with the first type and xli 1-5, 21-29; xliii 8-13 and xliv 6-8 with the second. Let us remark that he adopts WÜRTHWEIN's position, viz. that the trial speech, as an accusation of Yahwe against the breach of the covenant, has its original *Sitz im Leben* in cult. But in the first group a *Profanisierung* would appear from the inverted situation—the accuser, Yahwe, has to defend himself—, and also from the challenge to retort, as is usual in profane action.[2] In view of WÜRHTWEIN's position, this typification is exact. In contrast with a merely cultic trial speech, wherein Yahwe accuses and condemns his people because of a rupture of the covenant, both elements show a more profane character. But, as I have already noted, H. J. BOECKER has demonstrated that the origin of the trial speech is not simply cultic, so that the term *Profanisierung* is not very apt.

About the second group VON WALDOW says that the original cultic setting, viz. the accusation with threat or condemnation, is still recognizable.[3] This is absolutely wrong, since we have seen that in those trial speeches there is neither accusation nor condemnation, but that the contest turns on claims.

2. In the first paragraph of this chapter, I mentioned the discussion about the question whether the trial speeches are rooted in a profane or a cultic *Sitz im Leben*. H. E. VON WALDOW exposes his thesis as

---

[1] C. WESTERMANN, *Grundformen prophetischer Rede*, p. 144; E. WÜRTHWEIN, "Der Ursprung der prophetischen Gerichtsrede", *ZTK*. XLIX 1952, pp. 6-7.

[2] Cf. p. 183-184.

[3] H. E. VON WALDOW, *o.c.*, p. 42: "... bei denen die ursprüngliche kultische Situation — Anklage mit Strafandrohung oder Urteil — noch zu erkennen ist".

follows: the fact that Yahwe is a judge and a plaintiff at the same time points to a close connection of the dt.-Isaian trial speeches with cult. But it is very questionable whether Yahwe acts as a judge and a plaintiff. As plaintiff he defends his claims. When in the conclusion of a pericope it is stated that the gods are nothing, such can be regarded as the sentence pronounced by a judge (e.g. xli 21-29). But nothing is more normal than that the pleader himself ends his speech concluding that his claim is valid and that of the opponents worthless. To distinguish within one trial speech between judge and plaintiff is an unfounded subtlety of von Waldow. Moreover, Boecker has made clear that the coincidence of both roles in one person is quite conceivable in the profane lawsuit: the identity of accuser and judge was possible in the person of the king in the framework of royal law (cf. 1 Sam. xxii 6-16).[1]

The cultic background, postulated by von Waldow, is not the Covenant Festival, he says, since there Israel is the accused and Yahwe is the accuser/judge. In Dt.-Is. the nations are accused and Yahwe acts mainly as a judge. Therefore the cultic background consists in a cosmic, eschatological Festival of Yahwe's Enthronement, which, still in von Waldow's opinion, plays an important part in the expectations of Dt.-Is. In the framework of such a liturgy there is room for a universal trial. But von Waldow does not conceive this as an actual cult. In the whole salvific event, which he announces, the prophet sees a great cosmic enthronement of Yahwe as king of the universe. The Babylonian Enthronement Festival would have been the model to this. Thus, Dt.-Is. has enlarged in a universalist sense the prophetic trial speech, which was originally situated in the liturgy of the Covenant Festival, and transposed it into the framework of the Enthronement Festival he expected. In this connection, Yahwe is twice called "king" in the trial speeches (xli 21; xliv 6).[2]

Let us admit that Is. lii 7-10 seems to favour von Waldow's thesis that the prophet expects an enthronement of Yahwe. We cannot go into the analysis of this pericope. In my opinion, it is a song of victory.[3]

---

[1] H. J. Boecker, *Redeformen des Rechtslebens*, pp. 87-89.

[2] H. E. von Waldow, *o.c.*, pp. 45-46: "Dtjes. hat also die prophetische Gerichtsrede, die ursprünglich ihren 'Sitz im Leben' im Bundesfestkult hatte, universalistisch erweitert und auf die Situation des von ihm erwarteten Festes der Thronbesteigung Jahve's übertragen". Cf. Id., "... *denn ich erlöse dich*", pp. 62-64.

[3] Cf. A. Schoors, *Recherches bibliques*, VIII, p. 122; H. Gressmann, *ZAW*. XXXIV 1914, p. 281.

The cry "Your God became king", which is borrowed from the famous psalms of divine kingship, is not the motto of the song. It is only the cry of the messenger who comes to announce the good tidings. But the aim of the whole song is to announce the same salvation, which we have already seen proclaimed in the salvation words. Still, it is clear that the prophet thinks of this salvation as a new enthronement of Yahwe at Zion. But this is not sufficient to project the trial speeches on such a background. I repeat that the nations are not accused, but that the trial speeches are about a claim. Moreover, in Is. xli 21, Yahwe is called the king of Jacob. in xliv 6 the king of Israel. This does not sound very cosmic. In Dt.-Is., Yahwe's kingship concerns Israel and it is to be understood on the background of the idea of covenant and election (cf. also xliii 15).

Elsewhere VON WALDOW asserts, in the footsteps of H. J. KRAUS, that the idea of Yahwe as judge of the nations is rooted in the traditions of the Jerusalem temple.[1] This idea certainly has a Canaanite background. Already in the Late Bronze Age (1500-1200 B.C.), Baal was thought to rule over the whole earth and all mankind.[2] In the Ugaritic texts El is called father of men, king and judge.[3] In an excursus on Ps. xxiv, KRAUS expounds the same idea but he goes a step further: the epithets of Yahwe: *'ēl 'elyôn, 'ădôn kol-hā'āreṣ, melek* and *šôpēṭ* are very probably adopted from the cultic traditions of the old Jebusite city.[4] But whether Dt.-Is. joins this cultic traditions is very dubious. Firstly, it should be noticed that the prophet never calls Yahwe *šôpēṭ*. In the trial speeches he does not clearly appear as a judge, but he joins issue with the nations about the claims on divinity.

The trial speeches against Israel are connected with the similar utterings of the former prophets. They state that the condemnation, announced by the prophets, has been realized and they justify that condemnation. Thus also this group of dt.-Isaian trial speeches have

---

[1] H. E. VON WALDOW, "... *denn ich erlöse dich*", pp. 63-64.

[2] Cf. *UT* 49 I: 27, 34, 37 (*wymlk barṣ*); III: 8-9, 20-21; 51 VII: 49-50; etc. Cf. M. DAHOOD, *Psalms II*, Garden City 1968, p. 120; W. F. ALBRIGHT, *From the Stone Age to Christianity*, Baltimore 1967, pp. 213-217.

[3] E.g. *ab adm* in *UT*, Krt: 36-37, 135-136, 150-151, 278, 296-297; *il mlk* in 51 IV-V: 20-24; 38-39, 48; 'nt V: 43-44; the personal name *dnil* in 314 I: 12 and frequently in the Danel legend; e.g. in 121 II: 7. Cf. H. BAUER, *ZAW*. LI 1933, pp. 82-83; O. EISSFELDT, *El im ugaritischen Pantheon*, Berlin 1951; W. SCHMIDT, *Das Königtum Gottes in Ugarit und Israel*, Berlin 1960.

[4] H. J. KRAUS, *Psalmen*, I, pp. 197-201.

a more polemic character and it is hard to situate them in a directly cultic setting. In this sense VON WALDOW rightly speaks of a *profanisierter Typ*. But the answer to the question of whether they descend from a cultic tradition of the Covenant Festival, depends on the answer to the question whether the pre-exilic trial speeches must be situated in such a tradition. E. WÜRTHWEIN solved the last question positively with a high degree of probability.[1] We thus come to the paradoxical result, that it is easier to ascribe a cultic background to the group, which VON WALDOW calls *profanisiert* than to the one he calls *kultisch*. That cultic background still appears from some details. In Is. l 2-3 the prophet alludes to the plagues of Egypt in a form that reminds of the cultic psalms. And in xlii 22 he quotes a psalm of lament. But there are no positive indications that either of them was really pronounced in an actual liturgy.

3. It is easier to present an historical background than a concrete *Sitz im Leben*. It is clear that the trial speeches against Israel suppose a condition of doubt of Yahwe's fidelity to the covenant. The Israelites think that Yahwe has broken the covenant, by delivering them into the hands of the enemy. They are convinced that they themselves were faithful, since they continually offered sacrifices (xliii 22-24). Here the prophet is confronted with the same cultic formalism as his great predecessors (Is. i 10-16; xxix 13-14; Hos. vi 6; Am. v 21-27; Mic. vi 5-8; Jer. vi 20). Some even doubt if Yahwe is able to keep his promises. Such is the background of Is. l 2-3. In chapter II we have seen that some salvation words, too, presuppose a complaint against Yahwe, who would be seen to have forsaken his people (cf. xlix 14; liv 7).

In the trial speeches against the nations, Yahwe's exclusive divinity is defended. This presupposes a dispute with pagan religion. The religious persecution under Nabonidus, with which J. M. WILKIE has dealt, could be the background of it.[2] But in xliii 8-13 and xliv 6-8, the trial speech, though directed against the pagan gods, is nevertheless clearly meant for Israel. One must thus accept that the prophet had to fight idolatry in his own community. Of course many an exiled Jew could conclude from the events of 587 that Yahwe was not better than the other gods, he is no *môšîa'*. They expect help from other gods.

---

[1] E. WÜRTHWEIN, *a.c.*, *ZTK*. XLIX 1952, pp. 1-16.

[2] J. M. WILKIE, "Nabonidus and the Later Jewish Exiles", *JTS*. n.s. II 1950-1951, p. 42. Cf. A. SCHOORS, *Orientalia Lovaniensia Periodica*, II 1971, pp. 114-115.

The same situation is the background of some disputations (cf. below) and other genres directed against the gods (e.g. the satire Is. xliv 9-20).

Among the trial speeches, xli 1-5 holds a special place: the point of the pericope is the assertion that Yahwe is the God who is behind Cyrus's activity. This is not the same as proving from Cyrus's activity that Yahwe is the only God, as in xli 21-29. With this peculiar position of xli 1-5, concentrated on Cyrus, the pericope is close to some disputations of the prophet, which I will study now.

§3. The Disputations in Is. xl-lv

1. *Is. xl 12-31*

12 Who has measured the *waters of the sea*[a] in the hollow of his hand
and marked off the heavens with a span,
enclosed the dust of the earth in a *seah*,[b]
and weighed the mountains in scales
and the hills in a balance?
13 Who has directed the spirit of Yahwe
or was his counsellor who instructed him?
14 Whom did he consult for his enlightenment
that he may instruct him in the path of justice
(*and teach him knowledge*)[c]
and show him the way of understanding?

15 Behold, the nations are like a drop from the bucket,
and are accounted as the dust on the scales;
behold, the islands *weigh*[d] only as fine dust.
16 Lebanon does not suffice for fuel,
nor are its beasts enough for a burnt offering.
17 All the nations are as nothing before him,
they are accounted by him as less than nothing and emptiness.

18 To whom will you liken God,
or what likeness compare with him?
19 The idol! a workman casts it,
and a goldsmith overlays it with gold,
and casts chains of silver.
20 *He who sets up an idol*[e]
chooses a wood that will not rot,

he seaks out a skilful craftsman
to set fast the image so that it does not totter.
xli 6 Every one helps his neighbour,
and says to his companion: "Take courage!"
7 The craftsman encourages the goldsmith,
and he who smooths with the hammer him who strikes the anvil,
saying[f] of the soldering: "It is good".
He fastens it with nails so that it cannot totter.

xl 21 Do you not know? Do you not hear?
Has it not been told you from the beginning?
Have you not understood *from*[g] the foundation of the earth?
22 He who sits above the circle of the earth,
and its inhabitants are like grasshoppers;
who stretches out the heavens like a veil,
and spreads them like a tent to dwell in;
23 he brings princes to nought,
and makes the rulers of the earth as nothing.
24 Scarcely are they planted, scarcely sown,
scarcely has their stem taken root in the earth,
when he blows upon them, and they wither,
the storm carries them off like stubble.
25 "To whom will you liken me,
that I should be his equal?" says the Holy One.
26 Lift up your eyes on high,
and see: who created these?
He who brings out their host by number,
calling them all by name;
by the greatness of his might and the strength of his power,
not one is missing.

27 Why do you say, O Jacob,
and speak, O Israel:
"My way is hid from Yahwe,
and my right is disregarded by my God"?
28 Do you not know? Have you not heard?
Yahwe is an everlasting God,
the Creator of the ends of the earth.
He does not faint or grow weary,

his mind is inscrutable.
29 He gives power to the faint,
and strength in plenty to him who has no might.
30 Youths shall faint and grow weary,
and young men shall stumble and fall.
31 But those who hope in Yahwe shall renew their strength,
they shall lift their wings like eagles,
they shall run and not be weary,
they shall walk and not faint.

[a] Lg מי ים c IQIa.
[b] Seah = 1/3 ephah. See comment.
[c] > LXX. Del. because of parallelism.
[d] Lg יטלון c LXX, Pesh, Aq, Sym, Th.
[e] See comment.
f IQIa: יואמר; LXX: *ἐρεῖ*.
[g] See comment.

Although form critics are unanimous in regarding Is. xl 12-31 as a disputation, there is no agreement among them concerning the division of the pericope. Those who opt for several sub-units within the pericope do not advance specific arguments to substantiate their position. In the text itself there are none of the standard formulas which indicate the beginning of a new unit. Hence, the discussion of the structure of the pericope must begin with an analysis of the text itself.

Vss. 12-17 consist of a series of rhetorical questions and assertions. The text offers a few minor difficulties but the general meaning is clear. Instead of *mayim* (12a), IQIa has *my ym*. M. Dahood finds here an enclitic *mem*: the original reading would have been *bš'lw-m ym*. *Yām* fits the enumeration better, and it is easier to understand that *mayim* appeared as a correction of *mê yām* than conversely. The reading of IQIa is a *lectio difficilior*, but we cannot be completely sure whether it is original or whether it stems from an enclitic *mem*.[1]

Most interpreters render *tikkēn* (vss. 12a; 13a) as "to measure". G. R. Driver thinks that this is wrong: the basic meaning of the root *tkn* is "to adjust"; there is no place in the Hebrew Bible where the word means "to measure", and modern translators have uncritically followed the ancient versions.[2] But it should be remarked that the parallelism in vs. 12 suggests the meaning "to measure". Besides "to

---

[1] M. Dahood, *Bib.* XLVII 1966, p. 412; cf. already *BHK*: *yammîm*.
[2] G. R. Driver, "Hebrew Notes", *VT.* I 1951, p. 243.

measure" is a derived meaning of "to adjust" (cf. Job xxviii 25). The ancient versions mostly distinguished between vs. 12a and 13a.[1] I am convinced that the meaning "to measure" is preferable in vs. 12a and "to adjust, to fix", i.e. "to enlighten correctly" in vs. 13a. So we have again a word-play such as we have met in other contexts.[2] In vs. 12b *šālîš* means a measure which is 1/3 of another measure. The *seah* may be meant, which according to the Septuagint (Ex. xvi 36; Is. v 10) and rabbinical literature, is one third of the *ephah*.[3] M. DAHOOD relates *šālîš* to Ug. *ṯlṯ*, "bronze, copper" and he understands it to mean here a bronze container, a bowl.[4] But this suggestion is scarcely an improvement on the traditional interpretation.

B. COUROYER thinks that the questions of vs. 12: "Who has measured etc ..?" do not suggest the answer "Yahwe". The answer anticipated by the author is "nobody", as is the case in vss. 13-14. This remark is rather subtle, for it is clear that Yahwe is in the center of interest. In vss. 13-14 as well as in vs. 12, God's sovereign and independent creative power is illustrated. The sense of vss. 12-14 thus is: Yahwe has done or is doing all this without anybody's help or advice.[5]

M. DAHOOD has proposed a completely new explanation of vs. 15a. He translates *mdl* (MT: *midd^{e}lî*) as "cloud", parallel to *šaḥaq*, which means the same. In this respect he refers to Ug. *mdl*, parallel to *ʿrpt* and *rḥ*. His translation is:

> Behold the nations are like a drop from a cloud
> Like a pan-sized cloud are they considered.[6]

This interpretation is ingenious but hard to accept. Firstly, the traditional interpretation is perfect as regards parallelism and context.

---

[1] LXX renders the first three verbs of vs. 12 by one word, *ἐμέτρησεν*, and *tikkēn* in vs. 13 as *ἔγνω*; Vg has *ponderavit* and *adiuvit*; Targ has twice תקן, which nowhere means "to measure"; Pesh renders ܡܫܚ, "to measure" and ܬܩܢ, "to establish, to create". The Greek versions of Aq, Th, and Sym have *ἡτοίμασεν* (to prepare) for *tikkēn* in vs. 12; in vs. 13, Aq has *ἐσταθμήσατο* (to measure), Sym *paravit* (Jerome).

[2] Cf. p. 133.

[3] ZORELL, p. 542; *BW*[3], col. 1651-1652.

[4] M. DAHOOD, *Psalms II*, p. 257.

[5] B. COUROYER, "Isaïe, XL, 12", *RB*. LXXIII 1966, pp. 186-196. Cf. already H. A. BRONGERS, *De scheppingstradities bij de profeten*, Amsterdam 1945, pp. 96-97; further J. L. MCKENZIE, *Second Isaiah*, p. 23; K. ELLIGER, *Jesaja II*, Neukirchen 1970, p. 47; C. STUHLMUELLER, *Creative Redemption in Deutero-Isaiah*, p. 146.

[6] M. DAHOOD, *Bib.* XLVII 1966, pp. 414-416; ID., "Ugaritic Lexicography", *Mélanges E. Tisserant*, I, Città del Vaticano 1964, p. 87.

Besides, DAHOOD has no satisfactory explanation of *mō'znayim*. He wrongly rejects "dust" as the meaning of *šaḥaq*, overlooking the verb *šḥq*, which means "to beat fine, to pulverize", in Hebrew as well as in Imperial Aramaic, Jewish Aramaic, Syriac and Arabic. He gives no weight to the fact that the expression *šḥq m'znym* occurs also in Sir. xlii 4, where *šḥq* certainly means "dust", not "cloud". R. SMEND's translation (*Prüfung*) is purely conjectural.[1] The connection between a particle of dust and the precision of a balance needs no comment.

D. W. THOMAS goes further in this line and claims that verse 15 has the same metaphor three times. In 15c, *nṭl* would mean "to weigh", and reading *yiṭṭôlû*, with the *waw* of *ûlᵉbānôn*, a change supported by LXX, Peshitta, Aquila, Symmachus and Theodotion, the verse runs: "the islands weigh only as fine dust".[2] This is a perfect parallel to 15b, and the suggestion is undoubtedly correct. As to 15a, *mar* and *dᵉlî* are *hapax legomena* (in Num. xxiv 7, *dᵉlî* is doubtful). Consonantal *mdly* would be connected with Ethiopic *dalawa*, "to weigh", *madlôt*, "weight, scales" and South Arabic *mdlw*, "weight", whereas *mar* can be related to Arab. *mâra*, "to move to and fro", and *mûr*, "dust moving to and fro in the air". Thus the whole verse would run:

> Behold, nations are like the dust of the balances,
> and like the fine dust of the scales are reckoned,
> behold, the isles weigh only as fine dust.[3]

This suggestion is more doubtful, since the traditional interpretation fits the context, the word *dᵉlî*, "bucket" is very well attested in Middle Hebrew, and the etymological parallels alleged by THOMAS are rather poor, especially for *mar*. J. KOENIG gives a plausible explanation of the parallelism between the bucket and the balance, by relating the former to the *shaduf*, the instrument used for drawing water from rivers and which looks like a large balance.[4]

In vs. 17, *mē'epes* is usually emended to *kᵉ'epes*. MT can be explained

---

[1] R. SMEND, *Die Weisheit des Jesus Sirach. Hebräisch und Deutsch*, Berlin 1906, p. 80; cf. D. W. THOMAS, "A Drop of a Bucket? Some Observations on the Hebrew Text of Isaiah 40, 15", *In Memoriam P. Kahle* (*BZAW*. 103), Berlin 1968, p. 216.

[2] D. W. THOMAS, *BZAW*. 103, p. 218; cf. *BHS*; KB. p. 612; C. WESTERMANN, *Jesaja 40-66*, p. 41; J. L. MCKENZIE, *o.c.*, p. 20. Cf. Syr. ܢܛܠ, "to incline the scale, outweigh", נֵטֶל, "weight, burden" (Prov. xxvii 3), and נְטִיל, "weighing" (Zeph. i 11).

[3] D. W. THOMAS, *BZAW*. 103, pp. 219-221.

[4] J. KOENIG, "Tradition iahviste et influence babylonienne à l'aurore du Judaïsme", *RHR*. CLXXIII 1968, p. 150.

with a comparative *min*: "they are counted as less than nothing" (*RSV*). Then, 17b is a good climax after the first hemistich. But the reading *ke'epes* is well attested (IQIa, LXX, Syh, Vg). Besides, in vs. 15 also, the verb *ḥšb* is constructed with *ke*. I prefer MT as *lectio difficilior* and for its poetic value. It is superfluous to see here an enclytic *mem*.[1]

The aim of vss. 12-17 is clearly to contrast Yahwe's immensity and absolute sovereignty with the nothingness of the nations. As such, vss. 12-17 do not necessarily involve a dispute. To be sure, one could suppose a sort of unbelief in Yahwe's omnipotence or a fear in the face of foreign nations. Alternatively, it could be the retort of the prophet to the misplaced questions of his hearers, such as we see in Job xxxviii. But 12-17 may also be a hymn. Already H. Gressmann termed Is. xl 12-17 a hymn introducing a word of comfort. P. Volz and H. Gunkel also stress the hymnic character of the pericope.[2] In his study on the hymns, Westermann distinguishes between the narrative and the descriptive hymn. The former is about a concrete act of God, the latter deals with a permanent attitude of God toward men (e.g. Pss. cxiii; cxvii; xxxiii; etc.). The descriptive hymn shows a polarity between Yahwe's eminence and his graciousness to men (e.g. Ps. xxxiii 6-12 and 13-19). The theme of God's eminence is developed along a double line: Yahwe is the creator and he is the Lord of history (e.g. Ps. xxxiii 6-9 and 10-12).[3] This motif is clearly present in the verses under consideration: vs. 12 refers to creation and the other verses are of the same type. But when comparing them to Ps. xxxiii, it appears that vss. 13-17 may correspond to vss. 10-12 of the psalm (*'ēṣâ, gôyim*), i.e. they are referring to history. Also *'ōraḥ mišpāṭ* points to this sense. Thus, the structure is not very clear. Besides, an invitation or any other typical formula introducing a hymn is lacking. Vss. 12-17 contain a hymnic motif, but certainly do not constitute a complete hymn. The rhetorical questions also are typical of a hymnic style.[4]

According to R. F. Melugin, Is. xl 12-17 is cast in the form of a Wisdom disputation rather than the form of a hymn. But out of the two parallels he quotes, only Job xl 25-xli 4 is valid, since Prov. xxx

---

[1] M. Dahood, *Bib.* XLVII 1966, p. 412.

[2] H. Gressmann, *ZAW.* XXXIV 1914, pp. 293-294; P. Volz, *Jesaia II*, p. 8; H. Gunkel - J. Begrich, *Einleitung in die Psalmen*, p. 33.

[3] C. Westermann, *Das Loben Gottes in den Psalmen*, Göttingen 1961, pp. 91-97.

[4] H. Gunkel - J. Begrich, *o.c.*, pp. 54-55.

1-4 is not a clearly outlined disputation. He admits himself that the similarity with the rhetorical questions of hymn-style is not to be overlooked. He also points out that vss. 18-31 are apparently examples of Deutero-Isaiah's incorporation of hymn-style into his own disputation framework. If so, why not vss. 12-17? These may be a disputation—with this I agree—but they are cast in a hymnic style.[1]

To the distinction between the interrogative and the affirmative clauses in the vss. 12-17 corresponds a difference in content. The rhetorical questions illustrate Yahwe's greatness as Creator and Ruler. Vss. 15-17 on the contrary, underline the nothingness of the nations. The former idea will occur more than once in the following pericopes, and in this connection, I would recall that the themes of creation of the universe and lordship of history are interwoven. F. STUMMER has pointed to a possible Babylonian inspiration of these verses. In a Babylonian hymn, Marduk is called "measurer of the waters of the sea" (*mâdidi mê tamtim*).[2] J. KOENIG has shown that probably the image of Yahwe's balance has been borrowed from the idea that Shamash holds the earth like a balance suspended from the midst of heaven.[3] With his specifications "in the hollow of his hand, with a span, etc.", the prophet would have illustrated Yahwe's superiority to Marduk. The idea of the nothingness of the nations in contrast with Yahwe's omnipotence is traditional in prophetism. Isaiah and Jeremiah developed it to encourage the leaders not to trust in foreign powers but to expect salvation from Yahwe alone. The nations are nothing, says the prophet. This absolute, substantivated "nothing" occurs only in Dt.-Is. (xl 17, 23; xli 11, 12, 24) and in texts that are certainly later (Hag. ii 3; Pss. xxxix 6; lxxiii 2).[4] WESTERMANN thinks that Dt.-Is. was the first to use the term in this way, so that his sentences would be very vigorous,[5] but such a conclusion is difficult to verify.

---

1 R. F. MELUGIN, "Deutero-Isaiah and Form Criticism", *VT*. XXI 1971, pp. 326-337. The terminological parallels he alleges (*'śh, byn, yd'*) are rather weak; the one with *'śh* is even non-existent.

2 F. THUREAU-DANGIN, *Rituels accadiens*, Paris 1921, p. 134, line 241; *ANET*, p. 332. Cf. F. STUMMER, *JBL*. XLV 1926, pp. 173-174; J. KOENIG, RHR. CLXXIII 1968, pp. 140-145.

3 *ANET*, p. 387. Cf. W. G. LAMBERT, *Babylonian Wisdom Literature*, Oxford 1960, pp. 126-127, 319; J. KOENIG, *a.c.*, pp. 153-164.

4 GB, p. 31; cf. P. VOLZ, *o.c.*, p. 10

5 C. WESTERMANN, *Jesaia 40-66*, p. 46.

Among the assertions about the nothingness of the nations, vs. 16 seems to be out of place. It bears on Yahwe's eminence, for it points out that it is impossible to bring him a suitable offering. Perhaps it has been added afterwards. H. KOSMALA even deletes vss. 14b-16: 14b is a superfluous elaboration of 14a; the idea of vs. 15 is readily expressed in vs. 17, and vs. 16 does not fit the context at all. He draws an argument from IQIa, where these verses have been added by a later hand.[1] The import of this fact, however, is not clear, since the first copyist did leave room for these verses. He thus knew of their existence. It may be they were illegible in his *Vorlage*. KOSMALA's other arguments are not conclusive. We can delete only *way^{e}lamm^e-dēhû da'at* in vs. 14b, since these words are missing in LXX and they are an evident gloss.

Verse 18 is again a question and it also deals with Yahwe's greatness. VOLZ eliminates vss. 19-20. So does WESTERMANN, but with a detailed justification. He thinks that Is. xl 19-20; xli 6-7 and xliv 9-20 belong to the same stratum and interrupt the movement of their present context. It is unquestionable that these texts are related: they all deal with the fabrication of idols. But exactly what is their literary relationship? It is not obvious that xli 6-7 disrupts the movement of its context. According to my analysis, this section is located between two independent units, viz. the trial speech xli 1-5 and the salvation oracle xli 8-13. I have already shown that xliv 6-8 and 21-22 do not belong together. So WESTERMANN's argument is not convincing. Also in the present context, vss. 19-20 can be kept. There is no direct answer to the question of vs. 18. In the formulation of his question the prophet alludes to idols as the work of men, whereas Yahwe is infinitely higher than such human artefacts. It is striking that the prophet uses the name El. This is already a monotheistic profession in itself. So the prophet expresses that Yahwe is the God κατ' ἐξοχήν, the only One who can be called El (cf. xliii 12; xlv 22).[2] True, the name is borrowed from the Canaanite pantheon, where El was the supreme god,[3] but the polytheistic connotation has completely faded

---

[1] H. KOSMALA, "Form and Structure in Ancient Hebrew Poetry", *VT*. XVI 1966, pp. 155-156.

[2] Cf. G. QUELL, "El und Elohim im AT", *TWNT*. III, p. 82: "Wird *'ēl* ohne Zusatz oder *hā'ēl* im Sinne von Jahve gebraucht ... so hat auch das keinen anderen Sinn als den einer emphatischen Aussage, dass für den Redenden die Gattung *'ēl* in Jahwe sich erschöpft".

[3] O. EISSFELDT, "El and Jahweh", *JSS*. I 1956, pp. 25-37.

in Dt.-Is. Instead of deleting vss. 19-20, I would couple them with xli 6-7. This text, as I have already pointed out, is isolated from its context and does not make much sense on its own. But when it is joined to xl 19-20, it makes a balanced whole. On this point, I agree with Duhm, von Waldow and Westermann.[1] But how did these verses get out of place? I propose this solution. Omitted by *homoeoteleuton* (*lō' yimmôṭ*), they were later added in the margin by a corrector, without a clear indication of where they were to be inserted. We have examples of such marginal and interlinear insertions in IQIa. This explanation by *homoeoteleuton* involves the placing of xli 6-7 after xl 19-20 and not between 19 and 20 (against Duhm and Van Hoonacker).

The meaning of vs. 19c, which is missing in LXX, is unclear. Perhaps *retuqôt* should not be understood as "chains", but as means to fix the image, akin to the *masmerîm* of vs. xli 7.[2] The second *ṣôrēp* makes a dt.-Isaian word play with the first: the same word has two distinct meanings in the same context, namely that of a substantive, designating an artisan, and that of a verb. Therefore it is superfluous to replace *ṣrp* by *rṣp*, which would mean "to join". This verb is *hapax* in the O.T. (Cant. iii 10) and it and its derivatives refer to marquetry or mosaic work. Nevertheless, the general meaning "to join" is well attested in Semitic languages, and it fits the context well.[3] That an inversion of consonants should not be excluded, appears from the next verse, where IQIa has *yrbq* instead of MT *yrqb*.

The beginning of vs. 20 is more difficult. I am dispensed from listing all the proposed interpretations of *hamesukkān terûma*; since it has been done by P. Trudinger some time ago.[4] The first word is commonly translated as "poor". Then it is vocalized *miskēn*, but some suggest that *mesukkān*, as a pual may have the same meaning.[5] The

---

1 B. Duhm, *Das Buch Jesaia*, p. 264; H. E. von Waldow, *o.c.*, p. 194, note 7; C. Westermann, *o.c.*, pp. 56-57; G. Fohrer, *Jesaja III*, pp. 26-27, joins xli 7 to xl 18-20 and regards the whole as inauthentic.

2 Cf. S. Smith, *Isaiah chs. XL-LV*, p. 171.

3 Akk. *raṣāpu*; J. Aram. רְצַף; Imp. Aram רצף (?); Syr ܪܨܦ; Arab. *raṣapa*. Cf. G. R. Driver, "Linguistics and Textual Problems: Isaiah XL-LXVI", *JTS*. XXXVI 1935, p. 398.

4 P. Trudinger, "To Whom then Will You Liken God?", *VT*. XVII 1967, pp. 220-225. Add the proposal made by J. L. McKenzie, *Second Isaiah*, p. 21, note f: "Heb. *mesukkān* is probably a kind of tree; literally 'a tree of consecration'".

5 G. R. Driver, *a.c.*, p. 397.

noun *t^{e}rûmâ* means "contribution (for sacred uses)". It is parsed as an accusative of specification and rendered: "a poor man as to the contribution", i.e. "somebody who is too poor for a high contribution". In this perspective, vs. 20 would have in mind an image of inferior value to the cast image of vs. 19.[1] G. R. DRIVER supposes that *t^{e}rûmâ* is related to Akk. *tarimtu,* which would designate "some kind of dedicatory offering of great value, possibly an effigy of some divine or semi-divine being". In view of the Babylonian background of Dt.-Is., such is quite possible. The texts brought forward by DRIVER are convincing. His translation is:

> The poor man (as) a costly idol
> was choosing a wood (that) would not rot.[2]

This translation is philologically better than "the man who is too poor for a costly idol". If this were meant, we would probably have a comparative *min.* But we should go further in the line of Akkadian in order to explain the strange *m^{e}sukkān.* I would connect this word with Akk. *šiknu,* "construction, image", also attested in Ugarit. In Ugaritic, one even has a verb *skn,* meaning "to form, to make an image".[3] So my interpretation comes closer to the LXX and it is satisfactory from every point: "He who sets up an idol, chooses a wood that will not rot".[4] TRUDINGER's suggestion is rather farfetched. He starts from *skn,* "to stay with", which in a derived sense would mean "to be familiar with" an in an even more derived sense "to be prosperous" (e.g. Job xxxiv 9). The piel participle *ham^{e}sakkēn t^{e}rûmâ* then would mean "the 'connoisseur' of idols, the man who is prosperous enough to be able to afford the very best".[5] TRUDINGER also notes that the comparison between Yahwe and the idols bears on the un-

---

[1] So ZORELL, sub מְסֻכָּן. Already H. GROTIUS, *Annotationes ad Esaiam,* in *Opera Theologica,* I, Londini 1679, p. 309.

[2] G. R. DRIVER, *l.c.* Same construction in ZORELL, sub תרומה. Remark the emendation suggested by A. VAN HOONACKER, תמורה, "exchange"; thus: "Who is too poor, chooses in exchange ..." Cf. *Het boek Isaias,* p. 194.

[3] Ug. *skn,* "stela, image": 2 Aqht i: 27; ii: 16; 69: 1; *skn,* verb: 51 i: 21, 43. Cf. J. AISTLEITNER, *Wörterbuch,* nr 1908. The solution has been proposed previously by J. GRAY, *The Legacy of Canaan,* Leiden 1957, p. 192. But he only cites the substantive *skn.* Cf. A. SCHOORS, "Two Notes on Is., xl-lv", *VT.* XXI 1971, pp. 501-503. After I finished the manuscript of this note, I received K. ELLIGER, *Jesaja II,* who does not accept any of the proposed emendations or explanations (cf. pp. 60-62).

[4] LXX: *ὁμοίωμα κατεσκεύασεν.* Cf. G. FOHRER, *o.c.,* p. 26.

[5] P. TRUDINGER, *VT.* XVII 1967, p. 224.

shakableness. Undoubtedly, the prophet pays a special attention to the fact that the idols are fastened by men (vss. 19-20 and xli 7).[1] This stress on securing the idol betrays a certain derision.[2] The fabrication of idols is simply described without any remark or criticism. In the prophet's opinion, the description speaks for itself. From an eloquent parallel in the ritual of the Babylonian New Year's Festival, it appears that the prophet visualizes the fabrication of idols in his Babylonian milieu:

> When it is three hours after sunrise, [he shall call] a metalworker and give him precious stones and gold [from] the treasury of the god Marduk to make two images for (the ceremonies of) the sixth day (of Nisannu). He shall call a woodworker and give him (some) cedar and tamarisk (pieces). He shall call a goldsmith and give him (some) gold.[3]

In *môs^{e}dôt* (vs. 21) one must accept either an haplography of the *mem* or a double duty prefix (*mērō'š*). The questions of vs. 21 refer to a revelation, to a certain understanding presupposed in the hearers. The object of that revelation is expressed in the following verses. The questions are intended only to draw attention to the following verses in the participial style, used in hymns. Again there is an affinity with the hymn of praise. We find the double theme of the descriptive hymn: in vs. 22, Yahwe is enthroned as the Creator of the universe, whereas in vss. 23-24, he appears as the Lord of history. We find verbal and thematic parallels to the first theme, in hymnic literature (Pss. xlvi 5: *yhwh šāmayim ʿāśâ*; civ 2: *nôṭeh šāmayim kay^{e}rîʿâ*). In the O.T., the term *ḥûg* is used only in connection with creation (cf. Prov. viii 27; Job xxii 14; xxvi 10). Also the idea that the great ones of the earth sink into nothingness beside Yahwe occurs elsewhere in a hymnic context (Job xii 13-25; xxxiv 19-20; ± Ps. xxxiii 16-17). Perhaps vss. 23-24 have been inspired concretely by the rapid Persian conquests (cf. xli 2-3; xlv 1).[4] At any rate, the point of 21-24 is the assertion of Yahwe's dominion over the princes rather than his work of creation, which is mentioned only to illustrate this dominion.

---

1 In ויחזקהו (xli 7), the suffix refers to the idol or to דבק. Cf. A. Bentzen, *Jesaja II*, p. 22.

2 Cf. also Jerome, *Commentar. in Isaiam prophetam*, *PL.* 24, col. 422: "Simulque irridet stultitiam nationum, quod artifex sive faber aerarius, aut aurifex aut argentarius deum sibi faciant, et laminis clavisque compingant ac fortiter statuant, ne ventorum flatibus detrudatur".

3 *ANET*, p. 331.

4 Cf. *Bible de la Pléiade*, II, p. 137; C. Stuhlmueller, *Creative Redemption*, p. 151.

In vss. 25-26 the hymnic style of the former verses is continued. The question is the same as in vs. 18, though, here, God himself is speaking, as appears from the first person suffixes. The title *qādôš* is most suitable for the one who is incomparable. The comparison now is not with idols, but with stars. The representation of the stars as a host is proper to the hymnic theme of creation (cf. xlv 12; Ps. xxxiii 6). There is a direct literary contact with Ps. cxlvii 4-5: "Yahwe determines the number of the stars, he gives to all of them their names" (cf. also *rab-kōaḥ* in vs. 5). According to F. DELITZSCH, the psalm is the *Lehnstelle*, whereas H. J. KRAUS regards it as secondary to Dt.-Is.[1] It is hard to date the psalm. Verse 2 points to a post-exilic condition, but several parts of the psalm stem from older hymns. So one cannot preclude the possibility that Ps. cxlvii 4-5 is earlier than Dt.-Is. The representation of the stars as a host is continued in vs. 26bc. The words *môṣîʾ* (cf. 2 Sam. v 2; x 16; Is. xliii 7) and *b^emispār* (2 Sam. ii 15; Num. i 2 and *passim*) are military terms.[2] Also *qārāʾ l^e* can be used for a mobilization (e.g. Jud. viii 1).

The whole of section 25-26 is clearly directed against the astral cult, which together with the worship of idols (vss. 18-19) was an important part of Babylonian religion. Yet, Yahwe has created the stars: the prophet uses the technical term *bārāʾ*. The fact that Yahwe calls this innumerable army by name, illustrates his absolute sovereignty over these so-called gods.

GRESSMANN and ELLIGER understand vss. 27-31 as a word of comfort, in which vs. 27 reflects the complaint of the people.[3] The meaning of the text is clear. In vs. 27, a complaint of the people is indeed cited. WESTERMANN notices that the verb "to hide" belongs to the fixed terminology of the lament. But all the instances he cites have the expression *histîr pānîm*, "to hide one's face", with God as subject (Pss. xiii 2; xxii 25; xxvii 9; xxx 8; xliv 25; lxix 18; lxxxviii 15; cii 3; civ 29; cxliii 7; Job xiii 24). In the present context, it is the condition of Israel which is hidden from God, i.e. God does not know what happens to Israel, he does not care about it. Moreover, DAHOOD has rightly suggested that *histîr* in the cited psalm texts is a form of *sûr* with infixed *t*, meaning "to turn away".[4] In Is. xl 27, however, we

---

[1] F. DELITZSCH, *Commentar*, p. 424; H. J. KRAUS, *Psalmen*, pp. 955-956.

[2] Cf. C. R. NORTH, *The Second Isaiah*, p. 88.

[3] H. GRESSMANN, *ZAW*. XXXIV 1914, p. 276; K. ELLIGER, *Deuterojesaja*, pp. 228-229.

[4] M. DAHOOD, *Psalms I*, p. 64.

have a niphal of the root *str*. In any case, it cannot be contested that a complaint of Israel is quoted here, and that in Ps. xxxviii 10, the verb *str* is used in the same sense but with a different subject: "my sighing is not hidden from thee".[1] In the psalms of lament, the psalmist more than once prays for *mišpāṭ*, "(right) judgment" (e.g. Pss. xxvi 1; xxxv 23; xxxvii 6; cxl 13; cxlvi 7). The parallelism in vs. 27b expresses the idea that Yahwe, by not paying attention to Israel's distress, is failing to do justice to his people. As in xlix 14, the complaint is a straight accusation against God.

In vss. 28-31, the refutation follows. In hymnic style the prophet reminds Israel of something that it is supposed to know (vs. 28a), viz. that Yahwe is an eternal God, who creates everything and never faints and whose mind is inscrutable (28bc). The unity of the verse consists in developing the first assertion: "Yahwe is an eternal God". The prophet does not have in mind an abstract or static quality. In this title is expressed Yahwe's sovereignty over temporality, the permanence and absoluteness of his operations, and his fidelity to himself and to his engagements.[2] As an eternal God he is eternally creating (cf. the participle *bôrē'*), he does not grow weary like men. And his mind is not human. The present distress is a token not of his powerlessness but of the fact that his intentions do not correspond with human plans (cf. lv 8-11). A comparison illustrates this conclusion: youths can grow weary, but he who hopes in Yahwe will not lack strength (vss. 30-31). For the theme of hope, I refer to the comment on Is. xlix 23. The reference to hope involves an admonition: Yahwe gives strength to his people, only if they continue to hope in him. In the picture of vs. 31b (run, walk), there may be an allusion to the Return.

What can we conclude about the connection between structure and content in Is. xl 12-31? Repeatedly, I pointed to the hymnic style of most of the verses in this pericope (12-17, 22-24, 26, 28-29). Taken on their own vss. 12-17 do not necessarily constitute a disputation. In 18-20 + xli 6-7, there is a disputation, in which the prophet rejects the idea that Yahwe is the equal of idols. In xl 21-24 also, there is a

[1] Against M. DAHOOD, *o.c.*, p. 235. DAHOOD's suggestion cannot rule out the existence of the root סתר (cf. the substantive סֵתֶר). In Pss. xxxviii 10 and Is. xl 27, it is preferable to accept the niphal of this root, because of a different semantic situation.

[2] Cf. A. SCHOORS, *Recherches bibliques*, VIII, p. 126; E. JENNI, *Das Wort ʿôlām*, Berlin 1953, pp. 68-69; J. FISCHER, *o.c.*, pp. 128-130.

disputation. This appears in the question: "Do you not know ... ?" (vs. 21), but it is settled by a reference to a hymn. Also in a hymnic style vss. 25-26 defend Yahwe's rule over the stars. These verses reproach Israel for its unbelief in Yahwe's omnipotence and in his eternal fidelity. Here the disputation genre is unquestionable, but the style is, again, partly hymnic. What is the connection between these sections? WESTERMANN defends the unity of Is. xl 12-31 on the grounds that only in 27-31, is there true disputation. Vss. 12-26 are not really disputation, they are only rhetorical questions: there is no thesis contested here. WESTERMANN asks: "Do the addressed in vs. 12 really assert that one can measure the sea in one's hand or God's mind with human means?".[1] This looks like hair-splitting. Indeed, the rhetorical questions do not reflect the disputed point. The latter is to be found in vss. 15-17: the nations are of no significance *lipnê yhwh.* The rhetorical questions act as arguments, as *Disputationsbasis* in VON WALDOW's terminology. Thus vss. 12-17 have a particular point: they prove that before Yahwe's creative power the nations shrink into nothing. The disputed point is thus Israel's discouragement before the strength of its enemies. Indeed, in his commentary, WESTERMANN interprets these verses in the same sense. We can find a particular point in 18-20 + xli 6-7 too: Yahwe cannot be assimilated to idols. In vss. 21-24, the nothingness of princes and rulers is the point, while in vss. 25-26, Yahwe's superiority above the star-gods is asserted. The four units recognized by VON WALDOW and partly by BEGRICH each have their own particular point. True, their structure is not very pronounced, partly because of their brevity. But even so, in 12-17 and 21-24, one can distinguish a *Disputationsbasis* and a conclusion. In 18-20 + xli 6-7 and in 25-26, the conclusion is expressed in the initial question, whereas the arguments are only given afterwards.

According to WESTERMANN, there are, with the omission of vss. 19-20, three sections, which assert respectively Yahwe's superiority to the nations, the rulers and the astral gods. All this is only a preparation for vss. 27-31, where the point of the whole composition appears: "God will help you, for he is able to".[2] This connection has been noticed by J. FISCHER and K. ELLIGER.[3] In the present analysis, which keeps vss. 19-20, and includes in this pericope xli 6-7, the structural unity

[1] C. WESTERMANN, *Forschung*, p. 128.

[2] C. WESTERMANN, *Jesaja 40-55*, pp. 42-43; *Forschung*, pp. 128-130.

[3] J. FISCHER, *o.c.*, p. 39.

of vss. 12-26 can be shown without a great deal of difficulty. The composition is divided into four sections thus:

I. A. 12-17: Hymnic	a. The great creating God
	b. *Thus*, before him the NATIONS are nothing (Yahwe not active)
B. 18ff.:	b'. To whom liken God?
	a'. *For* the IDOLS are nothing (Yahwe not active)
II. A. 21-24: Hymnic	a. The great creating God
	b. *Thus* he makes PRINCES as nothing (Yahwe active)
B. 25-26:	b'. To whom liken God?
	a'. *For* he has created the STAR-GODS (Yahwe active)

This perfect chiastic parallelism cannot be fortuitous, and it is difficult to accept that this passage is a mere collection of originally separate pieces, *pace* R. F. MELUGIN.[1] Is. xl 12-26 forms a strong unity, in which Yahwe's superiority to every possible rival is inculcated. Whether this composition is intended by the prophet as a substructure for the vss. 27-31, is not sure. According to content this is quite possible. But even by themselves, these verses constitute a complete disputation, as this analysis has shown: the contested statement (vs. 27), the *Disputationsbasis* (28), the conclusion (29-31). Also the change from a plural address to the singular in vss. 27-31 points to a separate unit. The pericope ends in a proclamation of salvation, as GRESSMANN has very well remarked. The disputation is thus connected with the prophet's message of salvation as its defence against discouragement or unbelief.

2. *Is. xlv 9-13*

9 Woe to him who strives with his maker,
a potsherd among earthen potsherds.
Does the clay say to him who fashions it: "What are you doing"?
and (does) your work (say): "He has no hands"?
10 Woe to him who says to a father: "What are you begetting?"
and to a woman: "With what are you in travail?"
11 Thus says Yahwe,
the Holy One of Israel and his Maker:
"*Will you question me*[a] about my children,
or command me concerning the work of my hands?
12 I made the earth

---

[1] R. F. MELUGIN, *VT*. XXI 1971, p. 336.

and created man upon it;
it was my hands that stretched out the heavens,
and I command all their host.
13 I have aroused him for victory,
and I make straight all his ways.
He shall build my city
and set my exiles free,
not for price or reward",
says Yahwe of hosts.

[a] See comment.

The literary unity of this disputation is quite generally accepted, KÖHLER and CASPARI being exceptions.[1] The messenger's formula of vs. 11 is an articulation which divides the whole in two parts.[2]

The first two verses are woe-formulas. It is generally accepted that such formulas originally belong to the proclamation of judgment. This genre, however, seems to be absent from Dt.-Is., so that the verses sound out of place here. For this reason, ELLIGER ascribes the vss. 9-10 to Trito-Is. He also argues from the vocabulary, but in this respect, there is no definite conclusion. WESTERMANN joins him.[3] In his opinion the woe-formulas are properly an announcement of condemnation but in the *Gerichtswort,* they are mostly combined with the accusation, the transgression being expressed in a participle or adjective.[4] As an example I quote Is. v 8:

Woe to those who join house to house,
who add field to field,
until there is no more room,
and you are made to dwell alone in the midst of the land.

The same style can be found in Is. v 11, 18, 20, 21, 22; Am. v 18; vi 1; Mic. ii 1; Jer. xxii 13-17; Hab. ii 6, 9, 12, 15, 19.

E. GERSTENBERGER has systematically analyzed the woe-formulas and has arrived at completely different conclusions. The normal

[1] L. KÖHLER, *Deuterojesaja,* pp. 26-27; W. CASPARI, *Lieder und Gottessprüche* pp. 92-93.

[2] IQIa marks this articulation. Also J. BEGRICH underlines the twofold structure; cf. *o.c.*, p. 51. The complete division into two units, as proposed by L. KÖHLER, W. CASPARI and G. FOHRER, seems to me to be an exaggeration.

[3] K. ELLIGER, *o.c.*, pp. 179-182; C. WESTERMANN, *o.c.*, p. 135: "Diese Deutung wird dem schwierigen Tatbestand am besten gerecht".

[4] C. WESTERMANN, *Grundformen prophetischer Rede,* pp. 137-140.

prophetic woe-formula contains a general and unhistorical accusation against evildoers. He shows convincingly that the formula has its roots in the same stratum of popular ethos as the wisdom utterances. The woe oracle thus is not an originally prophetic but a borrowed type.[1] Vss. xlv 9-10 could thus be a later addition under sapiential influence. However, it is possible that Dt.-Is. himself might have used such formulas. To establish whether or not this is so, we shall have to examine their connection with the context.

P. VOLZ, followed by G. R. DRIVER and C. F. WHITLEY, eliminates the first woe-formula by changing it into a question, parallel to vs. 9b. He replaces *hôy rāb* by *hăyārîb* and translates: "Streitet der Ton mit dem Töpfer?" These three scholars, however, differ in their interpretation of vs. 9aβ. VOLZ reads *'et-ḥărāśô ḥereś 'ădāmâ*, "mit seinem Meister der Ton von Erde". DRIVER, relying on LXX and Theodotion suggests *wᵉḥereš 'et-ḥōrᵉšê 'ădāmâ*, "or the ploughland with the ploughers of the soil". WHITLEY emends to *'et-ḥōrēš 'ădāmâ*, "the land with the ploughman".[2] WHITLEY's (eventually DRIVER's) suggestion is preferable to VOLZ's. This reading now has a third witness in IQIa.[3] It does not touch the consonantal text and offers a perfect parallelism. Recently, DRIVER has changed his standpoint. He now reads: *ḥereś 'ēt-ḥōrēś* (ev. *ḥōrᵉśê*) *'ădāmâ*, "(or shall) the potsherd (contend) with the scraper(s) of the earth?"[4]. He appeals to the technique of the potters, who when finishing off their work scrape away any small unevennesses. But he does not offer any philological evidence, and I think it is hard to find it. I keep MT, which fully suffices. The Isaiah scroll of Qumran supports MT as for vs. 9aα, whereas LXX does not offer a clear picture. Even if the latter read *hăyārîb*, *hôy-rāb* remains preferable as *lectio difficilior*. The reading with *hă-* then would be an adaptation of vs. 9a to 9b.[5] Perhaps an elimination of *hôy* in vs. 9 would render the verse more dt.-Isaian. But then the problem persists in vs. 10. IQIa is different, having a woe formula in vs. 9b also: *hwy*

---

[1] E. GERSTENBERGER, "The Woe Oracles of the Prophets", *JBL.* LXXXI 1962, pp. 249-263.

[2] P. VOLZ, *Jesaja II*, pp. 65-66; G. R. DRIVER, *JTS.* XXXVI 1935, p. 399; C. F. WHITLEY, *VT.* XI 1961, p. 458.

[3] LXX: *μὴ ὁ ἀροτριῶν ἀροτριάσει τὴν γῆν ὅλην τὴν ἡμέραν*; Th: *ἀροτριῶν τοὺς ἀροτριῶντας τὴν γῆν*; IQIa: חרש את חורשי האדמה.

[4] G. R. DRIVER, "Isaianic Problems", *Fs. W. Eilers*, Wiesbaden 1967, pp. 50-51. The *ḥatef qameṣ* under the *alef* of אדמה is a misprint. One reads *ḥatef pataḥ* of course.

[5] LXX: *Ποῖον βέλτιον κατεσκεύασα ὡς πηλὸν κεραμέως*;

h'wmr, "woe to him who says". This is later adaptation, as appears from the article before the participle, since the article does not occur in vs. 9a and 10 and in most of the *hôy*-formulas in the other prophetic books. The reproving question stems from a sapiential milieu, as well as the woe formula. Thus vss. 9-10, as formulated in the MT, make a good literary unit. True, in vs. 9aβ there is a strong tradition in favour of *ḥrš* instead of *ḥrś* (MT: *ḥarśê*), as can be seen in LXX, Theodotion and IQIa. Whether one prefers the reading Driver-Whitley or the MT, it does not make much difference for the interpretation. But the reading *ḥrš* makes sense only when one accepts *hăyārîb*. Moreover, *ḥrś* better harmonizes with the metaphor of the context.

Whitley moves some objections against vs. 9bβ, which are too hypothetical to be considered.[1] The Hebrew text allows two translations:

> Does the clay say to the potter: "What are you doing?" and (does) your work (say): "He (it) has no hands"?

or:

> Does the clay say to the potter: "What are you doing? Your work has no hands".[2]

In the latter rendering, *yād* may mean "handle" as suggested by M. Buber and *RSV*, but it also may mean "skill, value", thus P. Volz, J. Koenig, G. R. Driver and D. N. Freedman.[3] But in the first case, one rather would use the plural *yādôt* (cf. 1 Kings vii 35-36). Examples of the second meaning can be found in Deut. xxxii 36; Jos. viii 20; 2 Kings xix 26; Ps. lxxvi 6. Driver combines this meaning with the first rendering of the verse, but he supposes that the suffix pronouns should be inverted: *ûpo'ŏlô 'ên-yādayim lāk*. The form *po'ŏlô* occurs in the *Soncino Bible*, whereas *lāk* corresponds to LXX and Peshitta.[4] He thinks that the suffixes would have been adapted when the verse was understood in the second sense mentioned above. Undoubtedly, the reading is smoother than MT. Nevertheless, the cited witnesses support only the emendation of *lô* to *lāk*. Besides,

---

1 C. F. Whitley, *a.c.*, pp. 458-459.

2 The first translation in C. Westermann, *o.c.*, p. 133; J. Bachmann, *Praeparation und Commentar zum Deutero-Jesaja*, p. 54. The other in Pesh, Vg and more or less in LXX; *RSV*; M. Buber, *Bücher der Kündung*, Köln 1966, p. 145.

3 M. Buber, *l.c.*; P. Volz, *o.c.*, p. 66; J. Koenig, *Pléiade*, II, p. 159; G. R. Driver, *Fs. W. Eilers*, p. 51; J. L. McKenzie, *Second Isaiah*, p. 76.

4 LXX: οὐδε ἔχεις χεῖρας; Pesh: ܘܠܐ ܗܘܬ ܥܒܕܐ ܕܐܝ̈ܕܝܟ; cf. already *BHK*.

this testimony is not very strong and therefore, I stick to the MT, as a *lectio difficilior* with a satisfactory sense.

Verse 9 evokes the well-known metaphor of the potter. This metaphor is used more than once to express God's absolute liberty in disposing of his material, which is wholly powerless in his hand (cf. Is. xxix 16; Jer. xviii 1-6; Sir. xxxiii 13; Rom. ix 20-21).[1] Does the clay question the potter? The second figure (vs. 10) is a climax in the sense that the question does not only censure the "how" of God's working, but almost the very fact of that working, not only the *Wie*, but even the *Dass*. Can one reproach a father or mother giving birth to a child? These verses are clearly directed against human criticism of Yahwe's work.

In vs. 11, the prophet expresses clearly what the metaphors mean. The messenger's formula indicates that now he is about to pronounce the kernel of his utterance, the properly divine word. From the verbal contact (*yōṣēr*; *pōʿal*), it appears that 9-10 and 11-13 belong together.

Verse 11b presents a textual problem to most of the commentators. The correction, suggested by A. B. Ehrlich, has been largely adopted. He changes *hā'ōtiyyôt šᵉ'ālûnî* into *ha'attem tiš'ālûnî*. The emendation is sustained in part by the Targum. Besides, it requires only a slight change of the consonantal text, to obtain a meaningful question: "Will you question me about my children or command me concerning the work of my hands?".[2] The argument from the Targum has little value, because we find there also the equivalent of *hā'ōtiyyôt*.[3] The emendation is proposed mainly because the authors do not know what to do with the word. But it is attested in the whole textual tradition. And, along with G. R. Driver, one may object that in ancient Hebrew script, a *mem* could not easily be changed into a *waw* or *yod-waw*. From a text-critical standpoint, his proposal is more acceptable: *ha'ōtî tiš'ālûnî*. A strong stress then is put on the object "me". Such a proleptic use of the accusative occurs e.g. in 1 Sam. xxv 29; Gen. xiii 15; xxi 13; xlvii 21.[4] The Isaiah scroll of Qumran

---

[1] For an Egyptian parallel cf. B. Couroyer, *RB*. LXXV 1968, pp. 549-561.

[2] A. B. Ehrlich, *Randglossen zur hebräischen Bibel*, IV, Leipzig 1912, p. 166; *BHK*; *RSV*; L. Köhler, *o.c.*, p. 27; C. C. Torrey, *The Second Isaiah*, pp. 359-360; C. R. North, "The 'Former Things' and the 'New Things' in Deutero-Isaiah", *Studies in Old Testament Prophecy*, Edinburgh 1950, p. 114; J. Steinmann, *Le livre de la consolation*, p. 150.

[3] Targ: דעתידן למיתי אתון שאלין.

[4] G. R. Driver, "Studies in the Vocabulary of the O.T.", *JTS*. XXXIV 1933, p. 39.

gives additional support to this suggestion with its reading *h'wtyt.*[1] The LXX contains an interesting reading, which is the more important as IQIa has it also: *hā'ōtiyyôt* here becomes the object of *yōṣēr*. VAN HOONACKER accepted this reading in his commentary, as did MOWINCKEL in his *Psalmenstudien.*[2] Against this one should object that the masoretic reading of vs. 11a is so dt.-Isaian, that it does not permit any doubt: *hā'ōtiyyôt* is not the object of *yōṣēr*. In several other formulas the prophet terms Yahwe the "former" of Israel (xliii 1; xliv 2, 24; cf. xliii 21; xliv 21). G. R. DRIVER's reading is preferable as the original one, lost already before the Greek translation. Finally we must notice that MT itself is not completely meaningless:

> Ask me the future concerning my children
> and leave to me the care about my work.[3]

In this case the stress is on the suffix "me", as noted already by LUTHER.[4] Still, I prefer the reading DRIVER-SKEHAN. It is based on the same consonantal complex as MT, it fits the style of the context better, and it links well with the train of thought of the preceding verses. So the discussion about what facts are meant by *'ōtiyyôt* becomes superfluous. Even if one keeps the masoretic reading, the word designates future in general: "Ask me the future ...".[5] This interpretation is better than M. HARAN's. In the framework of his opinion about Is. xl-xlviii, this scholar thinks that *hā'ōtiyyôt* designates facts already happened, viz. the capture of Babylon by Cyrus, which would precede these prophecies. He then paraphrases vs. 11b as

---

[1] M. BURROWS, *The Isaiah Manuscript and the Habakkuk commentary*, pl. XXXVIII, wrongly reads האותות. P. W. SKEHAN, "Some Textual Problems in Isaias", *CBQ.* XXII 1960, pp. 54-55; cf. also *BHS.*

[2] LXX: *ὁ ποιήσας τὰ ἐπερχόμενα*; IQIa: יוצר האותית. A. VAN HOONACKER, *Het boek Isaias*, pp. 215-216; S. MOWINCKEL, *Psalmenstudien*, II, p. 283.

[3] The verb צִוָּה used with acc. of the person and על for the thing, means "*commendare* (cf. ZORELL, p. 686), to appoint somebody for something, to leave the care about something to somebody"; cf. J. BACHMANN, *o.c.*, p. 52: "anheimstellen, überlassen".

[4] M. LUTHER, *In Esaiam Scholia, ad. loc.* (*Werke*, Weimar, XXV, 1902, p. 292): "Emphasis est in pronomine ME".

[5] For this discussion cf. A. VAN HOONACKER, *RB.* VI 1909, p. 513; VIII 1911, p. 110; J. FISCHER, *Isaias 40-55 und die Perikopen vom Gottesknecht*, Münster 1916, p. 23; F. GIESEBRECHT, *Beiträge zur Jesajakritik*, Göttingen 1890, pp. 119-120; A. KNOBEL, *Der Prophet Jesaia*, Leipzig 1843, p. 321.

follows: "order me to do whatever with my sons; I will do it, for my power in unlimited".[1]

The meaning of the figurative speech in vss. 9-10 becomes clear now: Is it for you to question me about my works? Then follows the answer in the form of a *Selbstprädikation* with the threefold *ego* (*'ānōkî* - *'ănî* - *'ānōkî*), stressed at the beginning of the verses. At once we see the central acting person: it is Yahwe. At the end of the series comes the third actor of the drama: *hû'* (vs. 13b). He is the instrument that acts in dependence on Yahwe. Such a stylistic form renders in an imposing way the movement of the oracle: "I myself made the earth and man upon it, the heavens and all their host. Now, it's also I who have aroused *him*." This manifestly concerns Cyrus. "If *he* is going to rebuild my city and set my exiles free, it is still *I*, who work through him". P. VOLZ suggests that *beṣedeq* here means "with a salvific intention, for a salvific purpose". A better comment was given by F. DELITZSCH: the reversal, brought about by Cyrus, is ascribed to Yahwe's righteousness, i.e. his loving action that aims at the salvation of his people.[2] But we saw in xli 2 that, in connection with Cyrus, *ṣedeq* designates the victories of this king inasmuch as they have been given by Yahwe and thus represent a salvific reality. The same meaning fits the present context very well. It is Yahwe who leads this Cyrus, of whom the prophet often speaks in other utterances. So, at the end, the disputation passes into a motif of salvation. Cyrus will rebuild "my city" and bring home the exiles. The promise is about the material restoration of the city as a part of the coming salvation. It may even be a symbol of the complete restoration of Israel. For the term "city of Yahwe" connects this verse with the pericope, in which Jerusalem is represented as the centre of Yahwe's salvific order (xlvi 13). But from a literary standpoint, the prophet announces primarily the rebuilding of the city.

ELLIGER rejects the last member of vs. 13 as inauthentic.[3] But his arguments are far from convincing. The analysis of the vocabulary is not conclusive. Also the use of the *Ausleitungsformel* is not unusual in Dt.-Is., as may appear from Is. liv. As to rhythm, vs. 13b with its 3+2 metre seems to conclude the pericope which has a 3+3 metre;

---

[1] M. HARAN, בין ראשונות לחדשות, p. 58.

[2] P. VOLZ, *l.c.*; cf. also C. R. NORTH, *The Second Isaiah*, p. 155; F. DELITZSCH, *Commentar*, p. 476.

[3] K. ELLIGER, *o.c.*, pp. 182-183.

13c would be superfluous. This remark is correct, but the precarious state of our knowledge about Hebrew verse metre should render us cautious on this point. The most valuable arguments concern the content. The only verse which expresses the same idea, viz. lii 3 is not authentic.[1] Besides, the idea expressed in the verse is in contradiction with xliii 3. In a form-critical approach, this remark loses much of its value, for in the various genres, the point can be completely different. Still, we must admit that vs. xlv 13c does not have a clearly distinct function in the disputation, as DUHM and MARTI have already noted.[2] The disputation is not about the reward Cyrus received for his work. When keeping this verse, we must be content with WESTERMANN's comment: Cyrus performs his task gratis; the only cause of the deliverance is still God's will.[3]

In summary, I may say that the pericope asserts the sovereignty of Yahwe, as is suggested already by the metaphor of the potter. This sovereignty is based on the fact that he has created everything. Hence he is free to restore his people at his own pleasure, even through the pagan king Cyrus. Beyond any doubt, the oracle is to be seen against the discontent experienced by the Israelites at the announcement that a pagan was to be their liberator (cf. Is. xli 1-5, 25-29; xlii 5-9; xlv 1-6; xlviii 12-15). This historical setting of our pericope has been recognized by several scholars.[4] Using VON WALDOW's terminology we could say that the absolute and universal creative power of Yahwe is the basis of the discussion (*Disputationsbasis*). The point to be established is the sovereign right of Yahwe to save his people through the pagan Cyrus. We shall find a quite identical progression in other disputations. Vss. 9-13 make a very good unit and I cannot agree to WESTERMANN's opinion that vss. 11-13 do not contain a disputation. It is too simple to assert that the so-called disputation here consists only in a vigourous repetition of the contested thesis.[5] It is the point of the pericope that makes the difference between

---

[1] Cf. p. 32.

[2] B. DUHM, *Das Buch Jesaia*, p. 309; K. MARTI, *Das Buch Jesaja*, p. 311.

[3] C. WESTERMANN, *o.c.*, p. 137.

[4] P. VOLZ, *o.c.*, p. 66; A. B. EHRLICH, *o.c.*, p. 166; H. GRESSMANN, *ZAW*. XXXIV 1914, p. 270; C. WESTERMANN, *o.c.*, p. 134: J. KOENIG, *l.c.*; C. R. NORTH, *o.c.*, p. 154. Against T. K. CHEYNE, *The Prophecies of Isaiah*, I, p. 295.

[5] C. WESTERMANN, *o.c.*, p. 136: "Eine Bestreitung, die nur in der lautstarken Wiederholung des Bestrittenen besteht, ist kaum anzunehmen. Damit ist erwiesen, dass V. 11-13 für sich einen anderen Sinn gehabt haben müssen".

vs. 13; "I have aroused him", and similar phrases in xli 2, 25. In the context of these trial speeches, the fact that Yahwe has aroused Cyrus and foretold his activity is an argument to prove Yahwe's unique divinity, whereas in xlv 13, that fact must be justified by the preceding verses.

3. *Is. xliv 24-28*

24 Thus says Yahwe, your redeemer,
who formed you from the womb:
"I am Yahwe, who makes all things,
who stretches out the heavens alone,
who spreads out the earth—*Who is with me*?[a]—
25 who frustrates the omens of liars,
and makes fools of diviners;
who turns wise men back,
and makes their knowledge *foolish*;[b]
26 who confirms the word of his *servants*,[c]
and performs the plans of his messengers.
It is me, who say of Jerusalem: 'She shall be inhabited,
(and of the cities of Judah: 'They shall be built')
and I will raise up her ruins',
27 who say to the deep: 'Be dry,
I will dry up your rivers';
28 who say of Cyrus: 'My shepherd,
he shall fulfil all my purpose,
saying of Jerusalem: She shall be built,
and the foundation of the *temple*[d] shall be laid!'"

[a] Lg מי אתי c K, 31 mss, LXX: τίς ἕτερος; IQIa: מיא אתי; Vg: nullus mecum.
[b] Lg יסכל c C; IQIa.
[c] Lg עבדו c LXXA; Targ.
[d] Here היכל is fem. as in Assyrian; IQIa has emended תוסד to יוסד with a superscribed *yod*.

This pericope has a train of thought that is strikingly parallel to the one we found in xlv 9-13. Nevertheless, its genre is disputed. Most form critics treat the unit as a disputation, but WESTERMANN claims that it acts as a hymnic introduction to the Cyrus oracle in xlv 1-7.[1] As usual, there is something to be said for the two opinions.

[1] Cf. E. JENNI, *Die politischen Voraussagen der Propheten*, Zürich 1956, pp. 100-101; B. J. VAN DER MERWE, *Pentateuchtradisies*, p. 5; C. WESTERMANN, *o.c.*, pp. 125-126; *Forschung*, pp. 144-148.

Undoubtedly, the pericope is very hymnic, as Gressmann noted.[1] It consists of a chain of participles, which goes on till the end. So the genre could be determined as a broadly elaborated self-praise (*Selbstprädikation*) of Yahwe, a genre in which the deity presents himself in terms of self-glorification.[2] Westermann cites a series of Eastern parallels. Probably the prophet borrowed the genre from his Babylonian milieu. One of these parallels recalls the dt.-Isaian trial speeches, viz. the self-laudatory hymn of Inanna:

> I, the queen of heaven am I!
> Is there one god who can vie with me? ...
> I, a warrior am I ...
> Is there one god who can vie with me?[3]

The goddess here glorifies herself in contrast with other gods. In Westermann's opinion, this background would make it clear that xliv 24-28 is not a disputation but is closer to the trial speeches.

Let us analyze the text. Beyond any doubt, Yahwe speaks to Israel as appears from the messenger's formula. This is a first difficulty for Westermann, since in xlv 1, a second messenger's formula follows, according to which the next verses are directed to Cyrus. It is no explanation to assert simply that this difference of address is intentional.[4]

The self-praise develops the great themes of the descriptive praise: Yahwe, creator of the universe and lord of history. The latter is included in the assertion that he frustrates the omens and predictions of diviners but performs the word of his prophets (vss. 25-26a).[5] Here the word *'ēṣâ* does not mean "counsel" but "plan, decision" and the expression *'ăṣat mal'ākāyw* is a brachylogy for "the plan, announced by his messengers."[6] The God who is described thus, is the same who

---

[1] H. Gressmann, *a.c.*, pp. 289-290.

[2] Cf. W. Zimmerli, "Ich bin Jahve", *Theologische Bücherei*, 19, p. 31, note 40.

[3] According to *ANET*, pp. 578-579; cf. A. Falkenstein - W. von Soden, *Sumerische und Akkadische Hymnen und Gebete*, p. 67; H. M. Dion, *RB*. LXXIV 1967, pp. 222-224.

[4] C. Westermann, *Jesaia 40-66*, p. 125: "Wenn nach der Einleitung in 44, 24 ... ein Wort an Israel erwartet werden kann, in 45, 1ff. aber nach der wiederholten Einleitung eine Anrede an Kyros folgt, so ist das Absicht".

[5] In vs. 26a, I read עֲבָדָיו along with LXXA and Targ; this word, as well as מלאכיו means the prophets (so Marti, Duhm, Fischer, Condamin, Van Hoonacker, Volz).

[6] Cf. Zorell, p. 619; KB, p. 726; C. R. North, *o.c.*, p. 147; J. Knabenbauer, *Commentarius in Is.*, II, p. 166.

has in his hand the present events. He has charged Cyrus with Zion's restoration. In MT, Jerusalem is mentioned in the same breath with the cities of Judah. But, seeing that the verse is too heavy and the suffix of *ḥoreboteyhā* refers to Jerusalem, as if there were no mention of the cities of Judah, it seems that the verse member 26bβ is an addition. So vs. 28b loses its repetitive character, which DUHM and ELLIGER invoke to eliminate this verse also. It deals with the rebuilding of Jerusalem, not with its re-peopling. True, in contrast with Trito-Is., where the temple is an important topic (Is. lx 7, 13, 17; lxiii 18; lxiv 10; lxvi 1-2, 6) the restoration of the temple is mentioned nowhere else in Dt.-Is. But this does not mean that our prophet could not have mentioned it once, and his interest in the restoration of Zion as centre of the nation, is hardly conceivable without any reference to the temple. So I do not find convincing reasons to omit vs. 28b.

The prophet is so precise in his utterance as to mention the name of Cyrus. He applies to him the epithet *rōʿī*, "my shepherd". There is no reason to delete the name Cyrus. The usage of regarding the king as a shepherd, appointed by the deity, was well known in the Near East. We find it in Sumerian, Assyro-Babylonian and Egyptian texts.[1] Of course, the king is considered the shepherd of the people, but the epithet is used also with reference to the deity, i.e. it is followed by a genitive or suffix designating the deity who appointed the king. So Nabuchadnezzar wishes to be *re-é-u*$_{16}$*-ka ki-i-num*, "your (= Marduk's) faithful shepherd", and Attapakshu of Susa is called *rēʾû* *ᵈŠušinak*, "shepherd of Shushinak".[2] In the O.T., the title is never given directly to the king reigning. But the anointing of David is clearly put in the framework of this common eastern ideology, when the tribes of Israel address him with the words: "Yahwe said to you: 'You shall be shepherd of my people Israel' " (2 Sam. v 2).The great prophets at the beginning of the exile reproached the kings of being bad shepherds (Jer. ii 8; x 21; xxiii 1-2; Ez. xxxiv 2). They also announce the rule of better shepherds (Jer. iii 15; xxiii 4). Ezekiel

---

1 Cf. M. J. SEUX, *Epithètes royales akkadiennes et sumériennes*, Paris 1967, pp. 244-250, 441-446; J. JEREMIAS, art. *ποιμήν κτλ.*, *TWNT*, VI, p. 485. For Egyptian instances cf. J. M. A. JANSSEN, "De Farao als goede herder", *Een bundel opstellen ... aangeboden aan F. L. R. Sassen*, Amsterdam 1954, pp. 71-79; D. MÜLLER, "Der gute Hirte. Ein Beitrag zur Geschichte ägyptischer Bildrede", *ZÄS*. LXXXVI 1961, pp. 126-144.

2 M. J. SEUX, *o.c.*, pp. 245, 250. Sumerian examples are to be found on p. 442: s i p a - g i š - t u k u - n i, "his (= An's) obedient shepherd", s i p a - g ú - t u k u - ᵈ e n - l í l - l á, "first class shepherd of Enlil", etc.

puts these words in Yahwe's mouth: "I will set up over them one shepherd, my servant David, and he shall feed them: he shall feed them and be their shepherd" (Ez. xxxiv 23). Hence it is manifest that, in prophetic tradition, the epithet has a salvific and even a messianic sense. To Ezekiel, the expected "good" shepherd is a *David redivivus*.[1] Thus the utterance of Dt.-Is. is the more shocking. He gives the epithet to a pagan king, who obtains a place, appointed by God, in his salvific order. The expected liberator will not be a scion of the Davidic house but the pagan Cyrus.

K. Marti supposes that *rō'î* should be emended to *rē'î*, "my friend", without giving any critical argument.[2] Now, however, this emendation is supported by the first Isaiah scroll from Qumran, which reads *r'y*, whereas it uses *scriptio plena* in all other instances (*rw'y*: xxxi 4 —*waw* added afterwards—; xl 11; lvi 11; lxiii 11). The LXX read a form of the root *yd'*. All later witnesses support the masoretic reading.[3] If the Qumran reading is original, we can find a striking parallel in Cyrus's proclamation on his own appointment to king:

> He (Marduk) made him (Cyrus) set out on the road to Babylon (DIN.TIR^{ki}), going at his side like a real friend.[4]

In this case the verse presents Cyrus rather as Yahwe's vizir, just as in 1 Kings iv 5, Zabud is called *rē'eh hammelek*.[5] Let us note that in Is. xlviii 14, Cyrus is presented as Yahwe's friend with a word derived from the root *'hb*. Although perhaps less shocking than the epithet "my shepherd", it still remains a bold expression.

The present self-praise is meant as a disputation. Firstly, Westermann's argument, that these verses are meaningless except in combination with xlv 1-7, is weak in view of the clearly distinct messenger's formulas. In addition, the line of thought of these verses is exactly the same as in the disputation xlv 9-13. In Is. xliv 24-28 there is a particular point, which characterizes the pericope as a distinct unit.

---

[1] Cf. J. Jeremias, *TWNT*. VI, pp. 485-487; W. Zimmerli, *Ezechiel*, pp. 841-844.

[2] K. Marti, *o.c.*, p. 307; cf. M. Haller, "Die Kyroslieder Deuterojesajas", *Fs. Gunkel*, I, Göttingen 1923, p. 267.

[3] The reading of IQIb is equivocal since it is very sober in using *matres lectionis*. LXX: φρονεῖν; Vg: pastor meus; Targ: למיתן ליה מלכו; Pesh: ܪܥܝ.

[4] *ANET*, p. 315; cf. M. Smith, "II Isaiah and the Persians", *JAOS*. LXXXIII 1963, p. 416.

[5] I do not see why C. R. North, *l.c.* simply excludes this possibility. Cf. G. E. Wright, *Isaiah*, London 1964; p. 114.

In another disputation, viz. xl 12-31, the prophet uses motifs from the descriptive praise and other devices of hymnic style also. He only goes one step further in composing a disputation completely in hymnic style. This fact is not surprising, when we take into account the fact that his arguments (God as creator and ruler of history) belong to the typical topics of the hymns. The hymnic motifs, being well-known formulas, offer him a good base to found the point under discussion.[1] According to BEGRICH, the present disputation shows a binary structure, in which the two parts (24-26 and 27-28) have a parallel structure. Their movement goes from the undisputed to the disputed point: vs. 24 is the common introduction to both sections, each of which stretches from creation to the days of the prophet in three articulations. The two sections are different in the sense that the former relates the acts of Yahwe and the latter his words. Therefore, vs. 26b is eliminated as a discordant element in this structure.[2] This operation argues against the proposed structure, as J. ZIEGLER has rightly noted in his recension of BEGRICH's book.[3] The only acceptable twofold structure is the one proposed by VON WALDOW: the *Disputationsbasis* (A member: 24-26a) and the conclusion (B member: 26b-28). It appears both from the content and from the form (contrast VON WALDOW): from vs. 26b the participles are used with an article.[4] This is not an accidental change without any meaning. The article expresses that God, who says (*hā' ōmēr*) all these things about Jerusalem and Cyrus is identical with the God presented in the former verses (compare Gen. ii 11; xlv 12).[5] It thus underlines the progression of the disputation. In the first verses the participles are appositions to Yahwe, from vs. 26b on they are predicates: "I, Yahwe, who made everything, etc... I am the one who says to Jerusalem: be inhabited". Most of the commentators pass over this distinction.[6] There are other differences of form. In vs. 24, the three participles are used in parallelism, in 25-26a the participle is continued with an imperfect third

---

1 H. M. DION, *RB.* LXXIV 1967, p. 232.

2 J. BEGRICH, *o.c.*, p. 52.

3 J. ZIEGLER, *TR.* XXXIX 1940, p. 51.

4 H. E. VON WALDOW, *o.c.*, p. 31: "... so ist der Übergang von A zu B formal nicht deutlich. Doch der Inhalt zeigt klar, dass Glied B mit V. 26b beginnt".

5 Cf. JOÜON, § 137 l 1.

6 Cf. however F. DELITZSCH, *o.c.*, p. 470: "Mit *hā' ōmer* 26b werden die Präd. zu speziellen Weiss., weshalb sie sich auch äusserlich determinieren". Further J. KOENIG, *Bible de la Pléiade*, II, p. 157.

person, whereas in 26b-28 the participle *hā'ōmēr* has no parallel but is repeated, introducing each time a quotation composed of two parallel phrases.

But in this perspective, vs. 27 offers a problem. It is placed in the middle of the conclusion, but according to content, it belongs rather to the first member of the disputation, in which Yahwe presents himself as creator and lord of the universe. VON WALDOW also has noted the problem and he declares that the movement of the conclusion is interrupted with a new point of agreement, in order to prepare the culminating-point of the speech which follows immediately.[1] This explanation seems rather forced. Following my explanation above, the verse should be about Yahwe's salvific intervention. The Targum has already explained it in this sense: "Who says of Babylon: It shall be laid waste, and I will dry up the rivers thereof".[2] We find the same tradition reflected in the commentary of CYRIL OF ALEXANDRIA.[3] Several modern exegetes have sought an interpretation in this sense. Either they accept that the deep and the rivers are metaphors for the dangers and risks of the return,[4] or they think that the verse speaks of the Euphrates, which, according to HERODOTUS, Cyrus diverted in view of the capture of Babylon.[5] This much is sure, that the verse is reminiscent of the Exodus, more particularly of the passage through the Reed Sea. This could be accepted *a priori*, since the verse alludes to something similar to the passage through the Reed Sea and the same reminiscence occurs elsewhere in Dt.-Is. (e.g. xliii 16; li 10; l 2; xlii 15). But there is a verbal connection with the Exodus tradition. The word *ṣûlâ* is a *hapax legomenon*, but we find the synonym *mᵉṣôlâ* in Ex. xv 5 and Neh. ix 11, where it designates the Reed Sea. Moreover, the drying up of this sea is described with the same verbs (*ḥrb* and *ybš*) in Ex. xiv 21-22. The reminiscence of the Exodus could be strengthened by the context, if we accept, along with R. BEAUDET, that vs. 25 alludes to the embarrassment of the Egyptian magicians (Ex. viii 14; ix 11).[6] We have already seen that Dt.-Is. more than

[1] H. E. VON WALDOW, p. 30.

[2] Targ: דאמר על בבל תחרוב ונהרהא אוביש; translation: J. F. STENNING, *The Targum of Isaiah*, p. 152.

[3] S. CYRIL OF ALEXANDRIA, *Commentarius in Isaiam Prophetam*, *PG*. LXX, col. 948.

[4] Cf. J. KNABENBAUER, *o.c.*, p. 167; K. MARTI, *l.c.*; B. DUHM, *o.c.*, p. 305; F. FELDMANN, *Das Buch Isaias*, II, p. 88; B. J. VAN DER MERWE, *o.c.*, p. 208.

[5] HERODOTUS, I, 189; cf. F. DELITZSCH, *l.c.*; T. K. CHEYNE, *l.c.*; F. FELDMANN, *l.c.*

[6] R. BEAUDET, "La typologie de l'Exode dans le Second Isaïe", *Laval TP*. XIX 1963, p. 14.

once announces the coming deliverance with allusions to the Exodus (e.g. xlii 15; lii 12; xliii 2, 20; xlviii 21). It is thus unquestionable that Is. xliv 27 also refers to the protection which Yahwe will grant his people in the near future. Whether his protection is meant in a general sense, or concretely in connection with the Euphrates, is hard to decide. HERODOTUS's story is false, but still the prophet may have thought of the Euphrates as a hindrance for Cyrus. An allusion to the Euphrates is the more acceptable, as Jeremiah had announced, in his threat against Babylon, that its water, its sea and its springs would be dried up (Jer. l 38; li 36). According to W. RUDOLPH, in Jer. li 36, *yām* refers to the Euphrates, as it refers to the Nile in Is. xix 5.[1] Finally, it should be noted that *lē'mōr* (without the *waw*) in vs. 28b, does not continue the series of *hā' ōmēr*, but rather introduces the words Cyrus speaks in the execution of his task, as may be seen in my translation.

We may thus conclude that Is. xliv 24-28 is a disputation, having the same content and structure as xlv 9-13. The later redactor placed both pieces around xlv 1-7, probably because of their reference to Cyrus.

4. *Is. xlvi 5-11*

5 To whom will you liken me and make me equal,
and compare me, that we may be alike?
6 Those who lavish gold from the purse,
and weigh out silver in the scales,
hire a goldsmith, that he should make it into a god;
then they worship and fall down.
7 They lift it upon their shoulders, they carry it,
they set it in its place, and it stands there;
it cannot move from its place.
If one cries to it, it does not answer
or save him from his trouble.
8 Remember this and be strong,
recall it to mind, you transgressors,
9 remember the former things of old,
for I am God and there is no other,
I am God and there is none like me.

---

[1] W. RUDOLPH, *Jeremia*, Tübingen 1958, p. 288; Cf. B. N. WAMBACQ, *Jeremias*, Roermond 1957, p. 302; B. J. VAN DER MERWE, *o.c.*, p. 209.

10 I declare the end from the beginning
and beforehand things not yet done,
I say: "My counsel shall stand,
and I will accomplish all that I will".
11 I call a bird of prey from the east,
the man of *my*[a] counsel from a far country.
I have spoken, I bring it to pass,
I have purposed, and I do it.

[a] Lg עצתי c Q; LXX: *βεβούλευμαι*.

The delimitation of this unit is a problem, as may appear from table I. WESTERMANN defends the unity of ch. xlvi, in which he deletes 5-8 as a later addition. His argumentation is rather weak and amounts to this: the chapter is one poem, the parts of which are introduced by imperatives which are related to one another (vss. 3, 9, 12) and this is a typical dt.-Isaian composition. As we are interested in the relationship between genre and message, it is important to see that WESTERMANN also recognizes that the parts of the poem he proposes, belong to different genres. He thinks that the vss. 9-11, which characterize the whole chapter, come close to a disputation.[1]

Let us now analyze the text. Vss. 5-8 could constitute a small unit. We have already met the question of vs. 5 in xl 18, 25, where it was part of a disputation. Here also the question may introduce a disputation. And exactly as in xl 18-20, the answer consists in mockery of the idols. There is no doubt that xlvi 5-7 and xl 18-20 + xli 6-7 must belong to the same genre. In my opinion, the authenticity of vss. 5-8 is beyond any doubt (cf. comment on xl 18-20 + xli 6-7).

Verse 8 offers a problem with *hit' ōšāšû*, which is a *hapax legomenon*. Some scholars change it into *hitbôšāšû*, "be ashamed". Thus, CHEYNE who invokes the Vulgate, Joseph KIMCHI and CALVIN.[2] But it is possible to give a good sense to MT. To this effect one should not parse it as a denominative of *'îš*, meaning "behave as men".[3] The root *'šš* is very well known in Semitic languages with the meaning "to establish, to found", so that we could translate the form in vs. 8:

---

[1] C. WESTERMANN, *Forschung*, pp. 152-153: "Aber was es eigentlich charakterisiert, ist in dem Mittelteil 9-11 gesagt. Und dieser Teil steht dem Disputationswort nahe".

[2] T. K. CHEYNE, *The Prophecies of Isaiah*, I, p. 303. So still C. WESTERMANN, *Jesaja 40-66*, p. 148; J. L. McKENZIE, *Second Isaiah*, p. 86.

[3] Against ZORELL, p. 89. Proposed by DAVID KIMCHI.

"be strong". This interpretation is supported by the Targum and also by the fact that the Vulgate reading *confundamini* is a corruption of *fundamini*, as appears from JEROME's commentary.[1] This interpretation is the most acceptable. G. R. DRIVER has pointed out that in a Sumero-Akkadian glossary, *aššišu* is assimilated to *šēmû*; "to listen", so that we might translate the hitpolel here as "show yourselves attentive or obedient".[2] DRIVER subsequently withdrew this suggestion, joining VOLZ, who accepts the meaning of *'šš*, mentioned above, but transfers the word to vs. 7: *wᵉhit'ōšaš wayyaʿămōd*.[3] This is an improvement in the sense that the meaning of *aššišu*, suggested by DRIVER, is by no means certain, but he should not have transposed the word to the following verse.[4] Further on, we return to the question whether vs. 8 is the conclusion of the preceding verses or the introduction to what follows.

In vs. 9, the concrete content of *ri'šōnôt* is the whole past of Israel.[5] There is no reason why only the exodus would be meant.[6] Just as in the trial speeches, xli 21-29 and xliv 6-8, the *ri'šōnôt* are supposed to be a proof of Yahwe's incomparable divinity. The prophet does not clearly say that the "former things" have been foretold before and fulfilled now. But in vs. 10, he invokes the prediction proof in terms which refer clearly to the trial speeches mentioned above. The "former things" appear in a similar context. The specification *mēʿôlam* precludes a concrete allusion to recent facts, including Cyrus's first successes.[7] Verse 10a must be understood in a general sense. It states that Yahwe foretells the events. This statement guarantees the salvation which Yahwe will bring about through Cyrus (vss. 10b-11: conclusion of the disputation). Such a reasoning is valuable only if the events, which Yahwe foretold in the past, have in fact been realized. The *ri'šōnôt* again are in general the past events, which

---

[1] Cf. Arab. *'asasa*; BA: אֹשׁ, "fundament"; MH. אשש; Targ: ואיתקפו; S. JEROME, *Comm. in Is.*, *PL.* XXIV, col. 468.

[2] G. R. DRIVER, "Studies in the Vocabulary of the O.T., III", *JTS.* XXXII 1931, p. 365; cf. C. R. NORTH, *l.c.*

[3] G. R. DRIVER, "Linguistic and Textual Problems: Isaiah xl-lxvi", *JTS.* XXXVI 1935, p. 400; cf. P. VOLZ, *Jesaia II*, pp. 77-78.

[4] Cf. *CAD*, I, 2, p. 465 and W. VON SODEN, *AHW*, I, p. 84, where the meaning "unruly" (adj) is suggested with a question mark.

[5] On the vss. 9-11, cf. A. SCHOORS, "Les choses antérieures et les choses nouvelles", *ETL.* XL 1964, pp. 32-34.

[6] Against C. R. NORTH, *The Second Isaiah*, p. 166.

[7] Against GIESEBRECHT, SELLIN, STAERK. Along with KNABENBAUER.

Yahwe has both predicted and fulfilled. In my article on the "former things", I have shown that, in all the texts relative to the question, the word designates events predicted and not the predictions themselves. M. HARAN, who thinks that *ri'šōnôt* means the predictions, nevertheless makes an exception for xlvi 19. His interpretation is the same as that of MORGENSTERN which is discussed below.[1] Cyrus's intervention, which is announced in vs. 11, is not expressly called "new" as against the "former things".[2] The certainty of this intervention is founded on Yahwe's power to foretell the future, a power to which the *ri'šōnôt* bear witness and which, in its turn, testifies to Yahwe's dominion over history.

According to J. MORGENSTERN, "*ri'šōnôt mē'ôlām* can refer only to the successive stages of Yahwe's creation of the universe, Deutero-Isaiah's oft-cited proof that Yahwe is the one and only world-God, positively affirmed here in the second and third stichoi of this tristich".[3] He refers to a series of texts: xlviii 12b-13a, 3; xlv 7, 12, 18; xlii 5, 8-9; xliii 9, 18; xli 22.

Indeed, Dt.-Is. often bases his monotheism on the fact that Yahwe created the universe. But the prediction proof is no less important to him. It suffices to look at the texts cited by MORGENSTERN himself. Only xlv 7, 12, 18 and xlii 5 refer explicitly and exclusively to Yahwe's creative power. Above I have demonstrated that xliii 18-19 concerns the old and new exodus, and MORGENSTERN agrees to this opinion.[4] The remaining texts also deal with the prediction proof, and xliii 9 and xli 22 even exclusively. Undoubtedly, both activities of creating and foretelling go together in Dt.-Isaiah's mind: they are two expressions of one divine sovereignty. It is the same unique God who created the universe and who rules history (cf. also the disputations already analyzed). But literarily speaking, the *ri'šōnôt* are always in a context of "prediction", never directly in a context of "creation". Such is true of xlvi 9-10 also. Therefore I cannot agree with MORGENSTERN.

In vss. 9-11a, the movement of the disputation is again couched

---

[1] M. HARAN, "The Literary Structure and Chronological Framework of the Prophecies in Is. xl-xlviii", *SVT*. IX 1963, pp. 137-140. In his Hebrew book, he asserts that these verses are directed to the nations; cf. בין ראשונות לחדשות, Jerusalem 1963, p. 61. Cf. also *ibid.*, p. 24.

[2] Against VAN HOONACKER, FELDMANN and FISCHER.

[3] J. MORGENSTERN, *The Message of Deutero-Isaiah*, p. 97.

[4] J. MORGENSTERN, *o.c.*, p. 141.

in the language of a hymnic self-presentation. The train of thought is identical to that in xliv 24-28, except that in vss. 9b-11, Yahwe does not mention his creative power but only his dominion over history. Even the terminological contact between the two pericopes is striking (*'ēṣâ, ḥēpeṣ, qûm*). Now Cyrus appears in the metaphor of a bird of prey. According to XENOPHON, the eagle, placed on a long spear, was the emblem that accompanied Cyrus on his campaigns.[1] This notice suffices to refute the objections of G. R. DRIVER against the epithet "bird of prey" applied to the humane and magnanimous Cyrus. He renders *'āyiṭ* as "massed army", referring to Arab. *ǵâṭu*, "host, column of men".[2] The "bird of prey" is obviously Cyrus, *pace* N. H. SNAITH, who thinks that this identification is not so obvious but due to an universalist interpretation of Dt.-Isaiah's message.[3] He is wrong, for the identification is based on the fact that form-critically the "bird of prey" in xliv 11 has exactly the same function as Cyrus in xliv 28, where he is explicitly named. Verse 11b underlines once again the certainty of the coming events: what Yahwe has said and projected, he will also execute.

There is no proof that vss. 5-7 (8) and 9-11 were originally one unit, but it is highly probable. In the first part it is stated that Yahwe cannot be compared to any idol, but there is no clear conclusion. Verse 8 could be the conclusion, giving the whole the character of an admonition. The demonstrative *zō't* refers to what has just been said. However, the verse seems also to be an introduction to the following verses. In other words: it links the two parts together, as is also suggested by the repeated *zikᵉrû*, although we should not overstress the importance of this repetition. The clear conclusion which was missing after vs. 7, follows in vs. 9b: Yahwe alone is God, there is no other like him. Is. xlvi 5-11 is thus a disputation with its point in vs. 11. The line of thought is this: Yahwe cannot be compared to anyone, he is the only God, who rules history and therefore can say: "My plan will be executed". Now, it is his concrete will that Cyrus will be the executer of his decrees. It does not make much sense to say that the conclusion begins in vs. 8, as VON WALDOW does, and

---

[1] XENOPHON, *Cyropaedia*, VII, 1, 4: ἦν δέ αὐτῷ τὸ σημεῖον ἀετὸς χρυσοῦς ἐπὶ δόρατος μακροῦ ἀνατεταμένος.

[2] G. R. DRIVER, "Hebrew Homonyms", *Hebräische Wortforschung. Fs. W. Baumgartner* (*SVT*. XVI), Leiden 1967, p. 60.

[3] N. H. SNAITH, *Studies on the Second Part of the Book of Isaiah*, (*SVT*. XIV) Leiden 1967, pp. 163-164.

then to assert that in vs. 10, it is interrupted by a new point of agreement.[1] Actually, vss. 8-9 are only a link in the chain of argument, leading to the point under discussion: viz. the question of whether Yahwe's chosen instrument can be a pagan (vs. 11).

Vss. 12-13 are a proclamation of salvation, which I have already analyzed in the former chapter. As noted there, WESTERMANN thinks that the preceding disputation ends in this short salvation word. He seems to be right. Firstly, the proclamation of salvation is very brief. In addition, it is not very concrete, but expressed in general terms, announcing that God's salvation is soon to come. This makes a good epilogue to the preceding disputation. Once he has defended the fact that he is able to execute his plans through Cyrus, Yahwe can conclude: "You suppose that salvation is still far away, but I have already irrevocably brought it near". Finally, the designation of the hearers as "stubborn" receives its full meaning when understood against this background. In a proclamation of salvation, it sounds somewhat strange, but it is completely at home after a disputation.

5. *Is. xlviii 12-15 (16)*

12 Hearken to me, O Jacob,
and Israel, whom I called.
I am he, I am the first,
and I am the last.
13 Surely, my hand laid the foundation of the earth,
my right hand spread out the heavens;
when I call to them,
they stand forth together.
14 Let all of *them*[a] assemble and hear!
Who among them has announced these things?
My friend performs my purpose against Babylon
and my mighty deeds against the Chaldeans.[b]
15 I, even I, have spoken and called him,
I have brought him,
and he will prosper in his way.

16 Draw near to me, hear this:
From the beginning I have not spoken in secret,

---

[1] H. E. VON WALDOW, *Anlass und Hintergrund*, p. 30.

from the time it came to be I have been there.
(and now, the Lord Yahwe has sent me and his spirit ...)

[a] Lg יקבצו כלם וישמעו c IQIa and LXX: *συναχθήσονται πάντες καὶ ἀκούσονται.*
[b] יהוה > LXX; Lg אוהבי, חפצי c IQIa. See comment.

Chapter xlviii is one of the most difficult of Is. xl-lv. In discussing this chapter, I first analyze vss. 12-15, because in genre and line of thought they are akin to xlv 9-13; xliv 24-28 and xlvi 5-11.

The summons to listen (vs. 12a) is developed into a self-presentation (vss. 12b-13). The utterance is directed to Jacob-Israel, the one whom God has called. It is doubtful if one should add *'abdî* after *ya'ăqōb*, as a parallel to *m^eqōrā'î*.[1] God presents himself as the first and the last, the eternally present one as in xli 4 and xliv 6. In vs. 13, he claims to have made heaven and earth by his word. Rightly, VON WALDOW considers the two verses the *Disputationsbasis*.[2] The summons in verse 14aα is reminiscent of the trial speeches, as is the question in vs. 14aβ. After the address of vs. 12, there is no indication in the MT that the summons of 14 should be directed to the foreign nations.[3] If we want to maintain this, then the summons should be read in the third person, as in IQIa and the Septuagint. Both witnesses together are a strong text-critical argument and, moreover, this reading fits in better with the context. As a matter of fact, the whole pericope is directed to Israel, but it is normal that also the Gentiles with their gods are summoned for the contest. The question: "Who among them has declared these things?" can refer only to the gods. Yahwe appeals not only to his creation but also to his dominion over history (prediction proof). The demonstrative *'ēlleh* refers to the next sentence, in which the capture of Babylon by Cyrus is announced, as we can read even in the *Glossa ordinaria*.[4] This interpretation is unquestionable in spite of the text-critical problems the verse poses. The MT makes sense: The one, whom Yahwe loves, will perform his purpose on Babylon. The phrase *yhwh 'ăhēbô* is an asyndetic relative

---

[1] R. LOWTH, *Isaiah*, London 1778, p. 220, accepts this reading and is followed by others as KÖHLER, LOISY and WESTERMANN.

[2] H. E. VON WALDOW, *o.c.*, pp. 29 and 194, note 5.

[3] Against T. K. CHEYNE, *The Prophecies of Isaiah*, II, p. 5; along with K. MARTI, *Jesaja*, p. 324; B. DUHM, *Jesaia*, pp. 327-328.

[4] W. STRABO, *Glossa ordinaria*, *PL.* 117, col. 1291: "*Annuntiavit haec.* Quod Cyrus Babylonem destrueret".

clause without antecedent.[1] One could render also "Yahwe's friend", *yhwh* being a *casus pendens* and *'ăhēbô* being emended to *'ōhăbô*, according to IQIa and LXX.[2] But then a problem remains with the next verse, where Yahwe is speaking in the first person. On the basis of LXX and IQIa, we can obtain a satisfactory reading. Here follow the two texts:

LXX: ἀγαπῶν σε ἐποίησα τὸ θέλημα σου ἐπὶ Βαβυλῶνα τοῦ ἆραι σπέρμα Χαλδαίων.

IQIa: יהוה אוהבי וישה חפשי בבבל זרועו כשדיים

Yahwe is my friend and he will (cause to) forget my will (or: plan) against (or: on) Babylon, his arm (against) the Chaldeans.

Perhaps *yhwh* was originally missing, as appears from LXX. Later on, it has been added in the margin, to make clear that Yahwe is speaking here. The verse was in the first person, as still in IQIa: "My friend will perform (IQIa: forget; the *'ayin* is missing) my purpose on Babylon". This reading has already been proposed by M. Haller.[3] The last member of vs. 14b is no less difficult. We could translate it as "and (he will perform) my arm against the Chaldeans", emending *zᵉrōʿô* to *zᵉrōʿî*, in keeping with the first member in IQIa. Some scholars, inspired by the LXX, emend *zᵉrōʿô* to *zeraʿ*, ev. *bᵉzeraʿ* and render: "... and against the seed of the Chaldeans". But the reading *zᵉrōʿô* is well attested and meaningful, whereas the LXX has a paraphrastic translation, so that it is difficult to make out which Hebrew text is behind it. The word "arm" often designates the power or mighty deeds of Yahwe.[4]

Yahwe's friend who will perform all this is the Persian king Cyrus, just as in the related pericopes.[5] And the question is who among the gods has foretold the action of this king against Babylon. Yahwe gives the answer in vs. 15. Yahwe alone (double *'ănî*) has foretold it; it is he who has given Cyrus his mission, he who is the cause of his

---

[1] Cf. Joüon, § 158 d. So already R. Lowth, *l.c.*

[2] IQIa: אוהבי; LXX: ἀγαπῶν.

[3] M. Haller, "Die Kyroslieder Deuterojesajas", *Fs. Gunkel*, p. 270.

[4] Cf. Zorell, p. 216; H. Schlier, *βραχίων*, *TWNT*. I, p. 638.

[5] Cf. Theodoret of Cyrrhus, *Explanatio in Isaiam*, *PG*. 81, col. 428; W. Strabo, *Glossa ordinaria*, *l.c.*; H. Grotius, *Annot. ad Esaiam*, *Opera theologica*, I, Londini 1679, .p 319; G. E. Wright, *o.c.*, p. 120; K. Marti, *l.c.*; P. Auvray - J. Steinmann, *Isaïe*, p. 202.

success. The ancient translations illustrate this last point by using the first person,[1] but also in the third person *hiṣlîaḥ*, the prophet states that the succes follows the call by Yahwe: the one is clearly the result of the other.

The line of thought is thus clearly akin to that of the disputations analyzed before. It is the same Yahwe, who has created the universe and dominates history, and who now calls Cyrus for his mission. Moreover, Yahwe's dominion on history is again connected with the prediction proof (cf. Is. xlvi 10).[2]

The commentaries are divided over the question of whether vs. 16 belongs to the same unit.[3] The summons in vs. 16a is more suitable for the beginning than for the end of a pericope. But we could take it for a new articulation of the pericope: Yahwe is about to say something important. Nevertheless, it is clear that with vs. 15, the point of the disputation is past, so that this important statement has lost its thrust. On the other hand, since the verse does not seem to go with the following pericope, we have to understand it with vss. 12-15, if we do not want to eliminate it as a gloss or the remainder of a lost oracle. The meaning of vs. 16b is not very clear either. Yahwe has never spoken in secret. With this affirmation he falls back on vss. 14-15. The prophet expresses the same idea in xlv 19, where also the idea of prediction is present in the context. Verse 16b: "From the time it came into being I have been there", is close to vs. 12b in content and to the tenor of the whole pericope: Yahwe is the actively present to all that happens. The bearing of the feminine suffix in *heyôtāh* is not quite clear, but in the present context it can hardly refer to anything except the Cyrus episode. M. Haran thinks the suffix refers to the earth.[4] Indeed, vs. 13 speaks of the foundation of the earth, but it is incredible that the suffix in vs. 16 refers to *'ereṣ* in vs. 13.

Virtually no one accepts the authenticity of vs. 16c, although it is very well attested in textual tradition. The first person of the prophet

---

[1] LXX: *καὶ εὐόδωσα*; Targ: ואצלחית; Pesh: ܘܐܨܠܚܬ.

[2] Cf. A. Schoors, "The Rîb-Pattern in Isaiah xl-lv", *Bijdragen* XXX 1969, p. 36. J. Harvey, *Le plaidoyer prophétique contre Israël*, pp. 59-61, analyzes Is. xlviii 12-19 as a trial speech and is followed by C. Stuhlmueller, *Creative Redemption*, p. 159. Also C. Westermann, *Jesaja 40-66*, p. 162 remarks some *Nähe zu den Gerichtsreden.*

[3] A unit 12-16 is accepted by Delitzsch, Marti, Duhm, Gressmann, Fischer, Auvray-Steinmann.

[4] M. Haran, *o.c.*, p. 67: "ולי נראה : מאת היותה של הארץ ...".

is completely unexpected after the first person of Yahwe. According to TORREY, the glossator wanted to suggest that the one who speaks in vs. 16ab is the same as in l 4-9 and lxi 1. MOWINCKEL calls vs. 16c *völlig sinnlos*, because part of the text has been lost. VAN HOONACKER, on the contrary, suggests that the verse was originally placed in chapter xlix between vss. 2 and 3. In ELLIGER's book, the verse is reckoned with the trito-Isaian parts of Is. xl-lv. Even HARAN, who does not proceed according to a form-critical method and generally supposes large units, thinks the verse has been inserted in a mechanical way, because of the opposition *mērō'š* - *we'attâ*. FELDMANN keeps the verse, referring to xl 6 and lvii 21. CONDAMIN notes the lack of coherence but he needs the verse in his symmetric system. According to U. E. SIMON, the whole of vs. 16 is an autobiographic note, whereas STEINMANN emends the verse without deleting it.[1] J. A. BEWER also proposes a correction which is not based on any serious argument: *we'attâ 'ănî yhwh šōlēaḥ 'ănî 'ōhăbî* (or *beḥîrî*).[2] VAN HOONACKER's suggestion makes some sense, inasmuch as the verse is not out of place between vss. 2 and 3 of ch. xlix. But he does not explain what brought it from its original context to ch. xlviii. At any rate, it could have dropped out in ch. xlix, been added afterwards in the margin, and then been inserted again at the wrong place (cf. comments on xlix 7cd). An acceptable suggestion is that made by ELLIGER. We find all the elements of the verse again in Is. lxi 1 and also the idea is the same. The strange *rûḥô* should be a subject of a sentence that possibly ran like this: *werûḥô 'ālay lē'mōr*, "and his spirit was on me, saying". A trito-Isaian glossator, who made or knew lxi 1, has inserted vs. 16c, probably because he had a damaged text and thought, in vs. 16b the prophet is saying about himself: "I have not spoken in secret ..." Some scholars, such as VAN HOONACKER, have pointed to some connection with the Servant prophecies. Now, Is. lxi 1-3 certainly shows such a connection. Several critics have claimed that these verses belong to the Servant cycle. Nevertheless, I think it more probable that the author here imitates those prophecies. Indeed, Is. lxi 1-3 does

---

[1] C. C. TORREY, *The Second Isaiah*, p. 378; S. MOWINCKEL, *a.c.*, p. 103; A. VAN HOONACKER, *Het boek Isaias*, pp. 227 and 236; K. ELLIGER, *Deuterojesaja*, pp. 213-215; M. HARAN, *o.c.*, p. 68; F. FELDMANN, *Das Buch Isaias*, II, pp. 121-122; A. CONDAMIN, *Le livre d'Isaïe*, pp. 293-294; U. E. SIMON, *A Theology of Salvation*, p. 160; J. STEINMANN, *Le livre de la consolation*, pp. 154-155.

[2] J. A. BEWER, "Tekstkritische Bemerkungen zum A.T.", *Fs. A. Bertholet*, Tübingen 1950, p. 66.

not add anything new to the image of the mysterious Servant. We are rather confronted with a more or less felicitous combination of traits, which have been borrowed from the different songs.[1] I suggest that this imitation was made only after the Servant pericopes were inserted in the book of Dt.-Is., since we find in lxi 1-3, traits that seem to be borrowed from the immediate context of the first and second Servant prophecy, viz. the parallel between the release of captives in vs. 1 and what we read in xlii 7 and xlix 9. According to Is. xlix 8, Yahwe speaks to Israel in a time of favour (*rāṣôn*), whereas in lxi 2, the prophet himself proclaims the year of Yahwe's favour (*rāṣōn*). Then the same *terminus post quem* would apply to the insertion of Is. xlviii 16c. Thus, if a glossator wanted to complete a damaged text, it is probable that 16ab does not belong to the preceding pericope, but is only the beginning of a lost pericope.

6. *Is. xlviii 1-11*

1 Hear this, O house of Jacob,
who are called by the name of Israel,
(and who came forth from *the body*[a] of Judah),
who swear by the name of Yahwe,
and confess the God of Israel,
(but not in truth or righteousness;
2 for they call themselves after the holy city
and stay themselves on the God of Israel,
Yahwe of hosts is his name).
3 The former things I declared beforehand,
they went forth from my mouth, I *made*[b] them known,
suddenly I did them and they came to pass.
4 (Because I knew that you are obstinate,
and your neck is an iron sinew,
and your forehead brass).
5 Beforehand I declared them to you,
before they came to pass, I announced them to you,
lest you should say: "My idol did them,
my graven image and my molten image commanded them".
6 You have heard; now see all this;

[1] I presented my arguments in "שבי and גלות in Isa., 40-55; Historical Background", *Proceedings of the 5th World Congress of Jewish Studies*, Jerusalem 1969, pp. 97-99.

and will you not declare it?
From this time forth I make you hear new things,
hidden things which you have not known.
7 They are created now, not long ago,
before today you have *never*[c] heard of them,
(lest you should say: "Behold, I knew them").
8 No, you have not heard, you have not known them,
hitherto *you*[d] did not open your ear.
(For I knew that you are utterly faithless,
and that from birth you are called a rebel.
9 For my name's sake I defer my anger,
for the sake of my praise I spare you,
that I may not cut you off.
10 Behold, I have refined you, but not like silver,
I have tried you in the furnace of affliction).
11 For my sake, for my own sake, I will act,
(for how *it would be profaned*!)[e]
and I give my glory to no other.

[a] LXX: *ἐξ Ιουδα*; Targ: ומזרעית. Perhaps Lg וּמִמְּעֵי pro וּמִמֵּי.
[b] Lg וָ c LXX, Targ, Pesh, Vg, Var. Cairo Genizah.
[c] Lg לא pro ולא c IQIa.
[d] Lg פָּתַחְתָּ c IQIa, Targ; cf. LXX: *ἤνοιξα*. See comment.
[e] See comment, also for each of the glosses.

The motifs of Is. xlviii 1-11 have a familiar sound after all we have read, but the literary structure offers a lot of problems. K. ELLIGER calls the pericope a source of anxiety for the interpreters.[1] It is generally accepted that the pericope has been enriched with some glosses. Everybody deletes somewhat at will, because it is hard to distinguish accurately between the authentic and the inauthentic, and because, after emendation, no completely satisfactory result is obtained. Apart from the two introductory verses, there is a high degree of agreement between MARTI, KÖHLER, ELLIGER and WESTERMANN, as may appear from table VI, indicating the verses which they consider to be later additions.[2]

---

[1] K. ELLIGER, *o.c.*, p. 185: "Dies Stück ist schon immer ein Schmerzenskind der Auslegung gewesen".

[2] Cf. K. MARTI, *o.c.*, pp. 321-323; L. KÖHLER, *Deuterojesaja*, p. 34; S. MOWINCKEL, *l.c.*; P. VOLZ, *Jesaia II*, p. 86; K. ELLIGER, *o.c.*, pp. 187-196; J. BEGRICH, *o.c.*, pp. 169-170: "Beilage III. Zur Interpretation von Kap. 48, 1-11". C. WESTERMANN, *Forschung*,

Begrich also comes close to the cited authors. But it is striking that he considers the verses which the others regard as the practically complete basic text, as the fragmentary remainder of a second text. Besides, we see that the division between the scholars over the vss. 1-2 is much greater, which is in keeping with Begrich's remark that it is a hopeless task to disentangle these verses.

Table VI

Chapter xlviii

Marti	Köhler	Mowinckel	Volz	Elliger	Begrich	Westermann
1aβ.b	1aγ					
		Ibβ				
	1bγ			1bγ		Ibγ
2	2a		2	2		
4	4			4	4	4
5b	5b			5b	5	5b
	6aα				6b	
7b	7b			7b	7	7b
8b	8b			8b	8	8b
9-10	9-10	9b		9-10	9-10	9-10
11aβ	11aβ	11aβ				11aβ

In the present text, vs. 2 belongs to the development of the address (vss. 1-2). It is striking that this address is overloaded, without any parallel in Dt.-Is. The very first words are clearly dt.-Isaian. Not only does the prophet often use the imperative of *šmʿ* at the beginning of an oracle or a motif (xlii 18; xliv 1; xlvi 3, 12; xlvii 8; xlviii 12, 16; xlix 1; li 1, 7, 21), but the combination with *zō't* is also well attested in his prophecies (xlvii 8; xlviii 16; li 21). Is. xlvi 3 is practically parallel to vs. 1. The second colon is reminiscent of xliv 5: "another will be called by the name of Jacob". The word pair Jacob/Israel is as dt.-Isaian as possible (xl 27; xli 1, 14; xlii 24; xliii 1, 22, 28; xliv 1, 5, 23; xlv 4; xlvi 3; xlviii 12). But the third colon is strange in this context. Not only does it interrupt the 3 + 3 rhythm, but the Israelites are mentioned in the third person just as in vs. 1bβ and the whole of vs. 2. But the shift from second to third person is no valuable argument,

p. 154; *Jesaja 40-66*, p. 159; "Jesaja 48 und die 'Bezeugung gegen Israel'", *Fs. Vriezen*, Wageningen 1966, pp. 356-366.

as it is well attested in relative clauses (Is. liv 1; Ez. xxvi 3-4; xxviii 22; xxix 3; xxxii 12).[1] And at any rate, we must keep vs. 1bβ, where the same shift is in evidence. But besides the argument from rhythm, we should notice that nowhere else does the prophet remind his hearers of their descent from Judah. He does not even mention Judah, except in xli 9 and xliv 26, where he speaks of the cities of Judah, which is a completely different motif. So both laγ, and 1bγ may be omitted. The word *'ĕmet* does not occur in Dt.-Is., nor does *ṣᵉdāqâ*, in the sense of a human attitude (contrast Is. lvi 1; lvii 1, 12; lviii 2; lx 21; lxiv 4-5). Moreover, in Dt.-Is., the appositions in the address are positive (e.g. xlvi 3-4) and a negative interruption sounds very strange in the present context. Finally, by omitting these words, vs. 1b is in rhythmic harmony with 1a. In vs. 2, there are annoying repetitions of elements from vs. 1, which, moreover, have a slightly different meaning: *niqrā'* is repeated, no longer with the adjoint *bᵉšēm yiśrā'ēl*, but with *mē'îr haqqōdeš*. In these expressions, the preposition *min* is quite unusual, though not impossible. The epithet "holy city" for Jerusalem occurs again only in lii 1. P. Volz and K. Elliger justly pointed out that in lii 1, it fits the context very well, whereas here it appears as a *fester Begriff*.[2] "God of Israel" also is a superfluous repetition of 1bβ and at once vs. 2aβ lapses. The whole of vs. 2 is connected with the preceding sentence with a *kî*. If this *kî* has an explicative function, then the explanation "for they call themselves after the holy city and stay themselves on the God of Israel", cannot apply to vs. 1bγ: "not in truth or right". But when it is connected with the preceding epithets (1baβ) or when *kî* serves only to strengthen the assertion of vs. 2,[3] then the redundancy of vs. 2b becomes still more evident. To parse *kî* as a concessive particle, as E. Rosenmüller does, would suppose that 1bγ is conserved.[4] Verse 2b: "Yahwe of hosts is his name", can belong to the original text as well as to the gloss. Our prophet uses the title *yhwh ṣᵉbā'ōt* in xliv 6 and xlv 13 and the phrase *yhwh ṣᵉbā'ōt šᵉmô* occurs in xlvii 4 and liv 5. But we find it also in the unauthentic li 15. When emended, our text looks as follows:

---

[1] Cf. Joüon, § 158 m.

[2] Cf. P. Volz, *o.c.*, p. 86, note 1; K. Elliger, *o.c.*, p. 191, note 1.

[3] Cf. Joüon, § 164 b; GB, p. 341; KB, p. 431.

[4] E. Rosenmüller, *Scholia in Vetus Testamentum*, III, 3, Lipsiae 1834, p. 219. Cf. GB, p. 342; KB, p. 432.

Hear this, O house of Jacob,
who are called by the name of Israel,
who swear by the name of Yahwe,
and confess the God of Israel.[1]

The main problem associated with vss. 4, 5b, 7b and 8b-10 is whether they derive from Dt.-Is. KÖHLER notes that the verses pose no problem regarding translation or metre; their difficulty, as DUHM has shown, consists in novelty of expression and content.[2] In a way which will be specified further on, the prophet uses the prediction proof. Yahwe has announced the "former things" beforehand and they took place. Yahwe's intention was clear, the stubborn people must not ascribe these events to the idols (vss. 4-5), but it must be manifest to all that Yahwe alone brought them about. This is the normal intention of every prediction proof, and reflects a perfectly dt.-Isaian train of thought. With regard to the problematic verses, we thus arrive at the following result. Verse 5b reflects well the prophet's intention. It is not sure that it contains an accusation against idolatry and, if it does, such an accusation is not incompatible with the dt.-Isaian authenticity (against DUHM, WESTERMANN). Therefore, ELLIGER hesitates to delete the verse: probably the verse does not deal with real idolatry; in his rhetorical flight, the prophet wants to express in a negative phrase the idea that Yahwe has brought about everything: "lest you should say: another god did it".[3] Reading such trial speeches as xli 21-29; xliii 8-13; xliv 6-8; xlv 18-25 or a disputation like xl 12-31, one can hardly believe that the prophet did not know of any idolatry among his own people.[4] The authenticity of vs. 4 is harder to defend. Here also ELLIGER hit the mark. The verse is not in the exact place since it should not justify the realisation of the former things but the fact of their having been foretold. It thus should be inserted after vs. 3a. Furthermore, its language is not very dt.-Isaian, since the verse contains no less than four *hapax legomena* in Is. xl-lv: *qāšeh*, *gîd*, *ʿōrep*, *mēṣaḥ*. These words, as well as the whole

---

[1] I did not find this correction in any of the authors I examined.

[2] L. KÖHLER, *l.c.*: "Obwohl der überlieferte Text weder für die Übersetzung noch auch für die Metrisierung nennenswerte Schwierigkeiten bietet, macht er doch, wie namentlich DUHM zeigt, durch Wendungen und Anschauungen vielfach stutzig".

[3] K. ELLIGER, *o.c.*, p. 192.

[4] So also J. MUILENBURG, *Isaiah chs. 40-66*, p. 555; cf. A. SCHOORS, *ETL.* XL 1964, p. 47.

tenor of the verse, are deuteronomic, as DUHM has justly remarked (cf. Deut. xxxi 27; ix 6, 13; x 16; 2 Kings xvii 14; Jer. vii 26; xvii 23; xix 15).[1] Perhaps vs. 4b has been inspired by 5b, as a deuteronomic explicative reflection on the implicit accusation of the latter.

That vs. 7b is secondary, appears clearly from the feminine suffix in *yᵉdaʿtîn*, which contrasts with the masculine suffixes of the preceding verses (cf. 5b, 6b, 7a). This contrast confirms also my opinion concerning the authenticity of vs. 5b. The formula *pen-tōʾmar* in vs. 7b has been inserted afterwards to make a pendant to vs. 5b. The idea cannot come from Dt.-Is., who nowhere reacts against those who know God's working, but against those who cannot believe that something so unexpected could come from God.

It is clear also that vss. 8b-10 make a coherent whole. They are connected with 8a as its justification. Such a justification is unusual in Dt.-Is. According to this prophet, Israel has heard nothing about the coming things, because they are completely new. Even if vs. 8b could act as a justification, vss. 9-10 have little to do with that. We have here a loosely added accusation, which has its own significance. This accusation is reminiscent of Ez. xvi and xxiii. True, in Is. xliii 27, our prophet also asserts that Israel has sinned from its beginning. But with this assertion, he wanted to justify the condemnation which his people has already undergone. Since then, God has blotted out their sins (xliii 25). In xlviii 8-10, however, Yahwe says that Israel deserves destruction but that he defers his anger for his name's sake and subjects Israel only to a process of refining.[2] These arguments are impressive but not decisive. Nevertheless, it is true that the verses fit Trito-Is. better. A strong stylistic argument confirms this: i.e. the expression with *qrʾ* in vs. 8b. K. ELLIGER justly noticed that Trito-Is. likes to use the verb *qrʾ* with a typical name, a kind of title: repairer of the breach (lviii 12), city of Yahwe and Zion of the Holy One of Israel (lx 14), salvation and praise (lx 18), oaks of righteousness (lxi 3), priests of Yahwe (lxi 6), "my delight is in her" and married (lxii 4), holy people, redeemed of Yahwe, sought out, a city not forsaken (lxii 12). Related to these phrases are lxii 2 and lxv 15. Moreover, the use of the pual *qōrāʾ*, except for Ez. x 13, occurs only in Trito-Is. (Is. lviii 12; lxi 3; lxii 2).[3] This goes together with the fact that Dt.-Is.

---

[1] B. DUHM, *o.c.*, p. 325.

[2] C. WESTERMANN, "Jesaia 48", *Fs. T.C. Vriezen*, p. 360; *Jesaja 40-66*, p. 161.

[3] K. ELLIGER, *o.c.*, pp, 107 and 195.

nowhere uses the expression "for my name's sake", which we do find in lxvi 5. All these data considered together, allow us to eliminate 8b-10. The original oracle of Dt.-Is. runs thus:

1 Hear this, O house of Jacob,
who are called by the name of Israel,
who swear by the name of Yahwe,
and confess the God of Israel.
3 The former things I declared beforehand,
they went forth from my mouth, I made them known,
suddenly I did them and they came to pass.
5 Beforehand I declared them to you,
before they came to pass, I announced them to you,
lest you should say: "My idol did them,
my graven image and my molten image commanded them".
6 You have heard; now see all this;
and will you not declare it?
From this time forth I make you hear new things,
hidden things which you have not known.
7 They are created new, not long ago,
before today you have never heard of them.
8 No, you have not heard, you have not known them,
hitherto you did not open your ear.
11 For my sake, for my own sake, I will act,
and I give my glory to no other.

The following remarks remain to be made about this emended text. Although the substantive *ʿōṣeb* (vs. 5) is *hapax legomenon* in the whole Bible, its meaning "idol" is clear, since the root *ʿṣb* means "to intertwine, to shape". The vocalization may be emended to *ʿăṣabbî*, since *ʿāṣāb* is more usual.[1] In vs. 6, the imperative *ḥăzê* creates a slight problem in the context. To drop 6aα completely is the solution of Köhler, but it is one for which he gives no argument.[2] In the LXX, the verb is missing, which makes the text smoother. An infinitive absolute is also possible, but there are no parallels of it in Dt.-Is. The correction, suggested by Morgenstern, has a certain value: he reads *š^{e}maʿ teḥĕzeh*, "hear and see", but critically, there is no reason

[1] So C. C. Torrey, *The Second Isaiah*, p. 375; J. Morgenstern, *The Message of Deutero-Isaiah*, pp. 76-77; D. W. Thomas, in *BHS*.

[2] L. Köhler, *l.c.*

to change the MT. The piel *pitteḥâ* in vs. 8 is unintelligible. The passive reading of Vulgate and Peshitta is well attested in the Hebrew manuscripts also, where it occurs in the *Codex Babylonicus Petropolitanus* and in fragments from the Cairo genizah. It could be a qal passive.[1] G. R. Driver thinks one should read *pātaḥtā*, in which case, the hemistich is perfectly parallel with 8aα. Moreover, this reading is supported by the Targum, and indirectly by the Septuagint, where the first person can be explained as a misreading of a second person, due to defective writing. It is also possible that the form *ptḥt* has been understood at some point as an ancient form of third person feminine and emended to *ptḥh*. Driver's correction was confirmed by IQIa and is undoubtedly the best.[2]

In vs. 11, the words *kî 'ēk yēḥāl* are eliminated by several scholars. The main argument is that these words represent a complaint against the impious Jews, and are thus connected with 4b and 8b.[3] In the present context, the third person offers some difficulty. According to M. Haran, the subject is *šemî*, mentioned in vs. 9.[4] In the light of what I have written above about vs. 9, this is a fresh argument in favour of the elimination. Haran's interpretation is the best, since it conserves the MT, which contains the *lectio difficilior*. The various other readings can be explained as a correction of MT. So LXX smooths the text by adding "my name", which is an explicitation of MT. IQIa and Vulgate have the first person, although IQIa might be a conflation with MT. The MT has been explained in the same sense by Jewish medieval commentators and by Jerome.[5] It should be noted that according to lii 5, another secondary text, God's name is despised. There is no need to replace the second *lemaʿanî* by *šemî*. The repetition of a word at the beginning of an important verse is characteristic of Dt.-Is. (xl 1; xliii 11, 25; xlviii 15; li 9, 12, 17; lii 1,

---

[1] Vg: aperta est; Pesh: ܐܬܦܬܚܬ. Cf. M. Dahood, *Proverbs and Northwest Semitic Philology*, Rome 1963, p. 8, note 4.

[2] G. R. Driver, "Hebrew Notes", *JBL*. LXVIII 1949, p. 59. Targ: ארכינתא; LXX: *ἤνοιξα*; IQIa: פתחת.

[3] K. Marti, *Das Buch Jesaja*, p. 323; B. Duhm, *Das Buch Jesaja*, p. 327; C. Westermann, *l.c.*

[4] M. Haran, בין ראשונות לחדשות, p. 66.

[5] Kimchi: איך יהיה מחולל שמי; Rashi: איך יהולל שמי; Jerome: "Propter me ergo faciam, ne blasphemetur nomen meum in gentibus". — Cf. B. Kedar-Kopfstein, "Divergent Hebrew Readings in Jerome's Isaiah", *Textus*, IV 1964, p. 192. LXX: *ὅτι τὸ ἐμὸν ὄνομα βεβηλοῦται*; IQIa: איחל; Vg: ut non blasphemer.

11).[1] It is true, the Targum has "for my name's sake", but this is a paraphrase of the MT, for it is followed by "for my word's sake".[2]

What does the original oracle of Dt.-Is. mean? The line of thought of the disputation is now clear. In the starting point of his disputation, the prophet uses the prediction proof. Yahwe has foretold the former events and his predictions have been fulfilled. So it is sure that those events were his work, that he rules history (3-6a). In 6b-11 follows the conclusion: now Yahwe announces something new, a thing unheard-of. It is clear that he will fulfil this prediction too and so his glory will stand firm (vs. 11).

In the pericope, the prophet again uses the binome "former things —new things".[3] The context does not permit specification of the content of the "former things". At any rate, nothing points to Cyrus's first successes as being the *ri'šōnôt*.[4] Nor can it be deduced from the context that the fall of Babylon is meant.[5] According to E. Reuss and W. Staerk, the expression refers to the fall of Jerusalem.[6] Such cannot be proven and is very unlikely. In this respect, the article before *ri'šōnôt* is no conclusive argument.[7]

Can we specify the "new things"? It is impossible to follow P. Volz [8] in giving them the general meaning of the whole future, for they are realized now (*'attâ nibrᵉ'û*). Their newness is strongly stressed: they are hitherto unknown, they are unheard of, something revealed only now. From the pericope xliii 16-21, we know that they refer to the deliverance from Babylon by Cyrus. The same interpretation must be maintained with regard to xlii 9.[9] The deliverance, and more precisely Cyrus's role in it, is also the point of the disputations which I analyzed above. But are these events so unheard of? The former prophets since Amos (ix 11-15) spoke about the future restoration of the chosen

---

1 Against B. Duhm, *l.c.*

2 Targ: בדיל שמי בדיל מימרי.

3 Cf. A. Schoors, *a.c.*, pp. 41-42.

4 Against Ewald, Knobel, Condamin, S. R. Driver, Ley, Marti, Skinner, König, North. Along with Muilenburg.

5 Against M. Haran, *o.c.*, p. 65: "בבל נפלה והנבואות נתקיימו".

6 E. Reuss, *Les prophètes*, II, Paris 1876, p. 258, note 3; W. Staerk, *Die Ebed-Jahwe-Lieder in Jes. 40 ff.*, p. 83.

7 Cf. Joüon, § 137 f, note 3; L. Köhler, *Deuterojesaja*, p. 57: "Dtjes. setzt bestimmten Artikel nur aus Gründen des Wohlklanges ..." — L. Glahn, *Die Einheit von Kap. 40-66 des Buches Jesaja*, Giessen 1934, p. 170.

8 Cf. *Jesaia II*, pp. 89-90.

9 Cf. A. Schoors, *ETL.* XL 1964, pp. 35-40.

people (esp. Jer. xxx-xxxi; xxxiii; Ez. xi 14-21; xxxvii 40-48). The really "new" thing is the fact that the salvific events for Israel are brought about by a pagan, Cyrus.[1] Such is one of the main themes of Dt.-Is. (xli 1-5, 25-29; xlii 5-9; xlv 1-6; xlviii 12-16). Such an announcement is really unheard of in Israel. It was bound to provoke a reaction of resistance among the Israelites. We found traces of this reaction in xlv 9-13. Is. xlviii 1-11 also is a reply to such a resistance. Yahwe addresses Israel reproachfully in order to assert emphatically that he is the only and sovereign ruler of history. Some authors explain the "new things" as the prophetic mission of Israel (E. REUSS, E. KISSANE) or the Servant (C. C. TORREY, A. CONDAMIN) to the Gentiles. From the context one cannot even surmise this.

7. *Is. lv 8-13*

8 For your thoughts are not my thoughts,
neither are my ways your ways,
—oracle of Yahwe.
9 But as the heavens are higher than the earth,
so are my ways higher than your ways,
and my thoughts than your thoughts.
10 For as the rain and the snow come down from heaven
and return not thither
without watering the earth,
making it bring forth and sprout,
giving seed to the sower
and bread to the eater,
11 so is my word that goes forth from my mouth;
it does not return to me empty,
but it accomplishes that which I purpose,
and achieves the thing for which I sent it.
12 For you shall go out in joy
and be led forth in peace;
mountains and hills before you shall break forth into singing,
and all the trees of the fields shall clap their hands.

---

[1] So H. EWALD, *Die Propheten des Alten Bundes*, pp. 436-437; W. STAERK, *l.c.*; F. GIESEBRECHT, *Beiträge zur Jesajakritik*, Göttingen 1890, p. 119; J. MORGENSTERN, *o.c.*, p. 74; H. E. VON WALDOW, *Anlass und Hintergrund*, p. 243. — Contrast M. HALLER, *Fs. Gunkel*, I, p. 266; E. SELLIN, *Serubbabel*, Leipzig 1898, p. 121; C. STUHLMUELLER, *Creative Redemption*, p. 139.

13 Instead of the thorn shall come up the cypress,
instead of the brier shall come up the myrtle;
it shall be to Yahwe for a memorial,
for an everlasting sign, which shall not be cut down.

In the final verses of Dt.-Is., we find so many occurrences of *kî*, that the interconnection of the various elements is not always clear. Nevertheless, I think we may find in Is. lv 8-13 a disputation, which ends in a salvation word. J. BEGRICH, who numbers the pericope among the salvation oracles, admits at least a contact with the genre of disputation. GRESSMANN takes a similar stand, terming the unit a *Wort der Gewissheit,* which ends in a promise.[1] Such a combination is possible since, as we noted in the passages already analyzed, the disputations are intended to refute some objections against a particular promise of salvation.

In this disputation, the thesis under discussion (vss. 8-9) is the superiority of Yahwe's salvific design to any human thinking. As appears from vss. 10-11, this superiority has its roots in the absolute fidelity of Yahwe's word, i.e. in the reliability of a promise of salvation, such as expressed in the A motif of a salvation oracle or in the motif of God's turning to Israel in a proclamation of salvation. Just as in xl 6-8, the prophet opposes God's word to human weakness. His word stands for ever (*yāqûm*). The effects of this word are firm and reliable. The prophet connects the effectiveness of God's word with the meteorological phenomena, which are also accomplished by God's word (Ps. cxlvii 15-20).[2] God's word is active and creative. This conviction that God's word is reliable is closely connected with our prophet's theology of creation. He was "the first to emphasize that creation was effected by the might of God who speaks" (xl 26; xlviii 13).[3] This idea has been adopted in an impressive way by the author of Gen. i, in the solemnly repeated phrases: *wayyō'mer 'ĕlōhîm* ... *wayehî kēn.*

Once this certainty is established, the prophet passes on to the salvation word with the motif of outcome (vss. 12-13a) and the motif of final goal (C motif; vs. 13b). The motif of outcome contains the

---

[1] J. BEGRICH, *Studien*, p. 22. H. GRESSMANN, *ZAW*. XXXIV 1914, p. 280.

[2] Cf. G. VON RAD, *Theologie des A.T.*, II, München 1965, pp. 101-103.

[3] C. STUHLMUELLER, "The Theology of Creation in Second Isaias", *CBQ*. XXI 1959, pp. 451-457; esp. 454. Cf. his *Creative Redemption*, pp. 188-191.

theme of the *Naturwandlung*. As in xli 17-20, one might relate it here also to the march back (cf. Jer. xxxi 9, 12),[1] although the reminiscences of the journey through the desert are rather weak. At most, one could refer to the poetic description of Ps. cxiv 3-4. But the transformation of the desert belongs to the scenery of the return in the salvation words of our prophet (xli 18-19; xliii 19-20; xlix 9-10). The prophet might also mean the restoration of the homeland. In the oracles of doom, the destruction was more than once announced with the metaphor of thistles and thorns (Is. v 6: vii 23, 25; Jer. xii 13; cf. also Is. xxxiv 13; Hos. x 8). Both, return and restoration, can be taken together as one mighty deed of Yahwe, as in Is. xlv 13; xlix 8-9, 15-21).

In the final verse (13b), *šēm* means the lasting renown, and in parallel with *'ôt*, it could designate a monument. This salvific event will be a lasting monument, by which Yahwe's glory is preserved, just as the glorious deeds of kings are kept in view through their great constructions and inscriptions.

Conclusion

Finally, from the preceding analysis we have to see whether the disputations do have a particular point or function in the whole of the dt.-Isaian texts. They do indeed. All the disputations analyzed above, start either from Yahwe's creative power (xl 26, 28; xlv 12) or from his dominion over history (xlvi 9-10; xlviii 3), or from both together (xl 12-14, 22-23; xliv 24-26a; xlviii 12-14a). The theme of dominion over history is connected with the prediction proof (*ri'šōnôt, higgîd*).[2] The corollary of God's sovereignty is that the other gods (xl 19-20 + xli 6-7; xl 26; xlviii 5b, 14a) and the nations and princes who trust in them (xl 15-17, 21-24) are powerless. From this statement of Yahwe's sovereignty follows the conclusion that he is able to help his people (xl 27-31; xlviii 1-11; lv 8-13) and that he does so in the manner which pleases him. More particularly, it is often underlined in the conclusion of the disputation that the restoration will be realized

---

[1] Cf. P. Volz, *Jesaia II*, p. 148; J. Fischer, "Das Problem des neuen Exodus in Jes. 40-55", *TQ*. CX 1929, p. 116; G. E. Wright, *Isaiah*, p. 136; B. W. Anderson, "Exodus Typology in Second Isaiah", *Israel's Prophetic Heritage. Essays ... J. Muilenburg*, New York 1962, p. 183.

[2] Cf. A. Schoors, "Les choses antérieures et les choses nouvelles", *ETL*. XL 1964, p. 43.

by Cyrus, the anointed one and friend of Yahwe (xlv 9-13; xliv 24-28; xlvi 5-11; xlviii 1-11, 12-15). Dt.-Isaiah's disputations have thus an outlined function in the whole of his message: they are for the defence of his salvific message, as it is expressed in the salvific words. This appears formally, when the prophet himself connects his disputation with a salvation word or with elements from it (xlvi 5-13; lv 8-13). Hence we are able to recognize clearly the function of this genre in the prophet's speech. His salvific message meets with a double resistance on the part of his hearers. On the one hand, they are discouraged and they no longer believe in Yahwe's power to redeem them. On the other hand, they are indignant at the fact that the prophet gives such a unique place to the pagan king Cyrus, whose salvific function he underlines twice with an oracle of election (xlv 1-7; xlii 5-9).[1]

As discouragement is the background of the dt.-Isaian disputation, we should admit that in a certain sense WESTERMANN was right in designating Is. xlix 14-26 as a disputation.[2] Nevertheless, we should notice two important points which ultimately argue against his thesis. Firstly, I showed in the preceding chapter that in form as well as in content the pericope is an artistically constructed proclamation of salvation. Moreover, it lacks the typical startingpoint of the disputations, viz. the theme of Yahwe's sovereignty in nature and history. WESTERMANN's judgment is connected with his opinion that the forms of the disputation are so varying, that we do not have a real genre. But the analysis given above points to a genre that is clearly characterized in form and content and whose structure has been exactly grasped by H. E. VON WALDOW.[3] We thus cannot call Is. xlix 14-26 a disputation, but the pericope is an illustration of the connection between salvific message and disputation, which I alluded to above.

---

[1] I have defended this interpretation of Is. xlii 5-9 in my article in *ETL.* XL 1964, pp. 35-39.

[2] Cf. p. 120.

[3] Cf. p. 189.

GENERAL CONCLUSION

The results of an analysis of this kind cannot be spectacular. At the end of each chapter, I have summarized the findings concerning the genre under consideration. In the present section will be presented some general conclusions about the connection between genre and message in Is. xl-lv.

1. The studies of BEGRICH, VON WALDOW and WESTERMANN, with which I basically agree, were the starting point of the present work. When trying to understand the texts of the most important genres used by our prophet, according to the rules and structures laid down by these form critics, it appeared that these rules offer a valuable tool for a sound interpretation of the text. As a matter of fact, in spite of all that has been said about blending or loosening of the genres or lack of *Formenstrenge*,[1] the different genres show a clear structure. It remains, however, difficult to decide whether Dt.-Is. was a prophet who pronounced his utterances orally or a writer. But at the level of the primary units, as analyzed in this work, he is no less an oral prophet than e.g. Isaiah or Jeremiah.[2]

The genres have also their particular point. Hence, this method is useful for making commentaries. It is possible to abandon a purely "formal" approach to the genres and to penetrate into their specific message. Commentaries on Dt.-Is. should proceed along the lines followed, say by WESTERMANN.

The study of the genres does not split up the message of the prophet into a number of isolated topics. Even without any investigation of the redaction of the book as a whole, i.e. of an eventual structure in

---

[1] Cf. H. GRESSMANN, *ZAW*. XXXIV 1914, pp. 295-296; H. GUNKEL, *Die Propheten als Schriftsteller*, p. XLVIII; L. KÖHLER, *Deuterojesaja*, p. 121; C. WESTERMANN, *Grundformen prophetischer Rede*, p. 65.

[2] Dt.-Is. is often regarded as a "writer": e.g. K. MARTI, *Jesaja*, p. 268; E. GRAF, *De l'unité des chapitres xl-lxvi d'Esaïe*, Paris 1895, p. 24; H. GUNKEL, *o.c.*, p. XXXIX; L. KÖHLER, *o.c.*, p. 80; B. DUHM, *Israels Propheten*, p. 293; A. VON GALL, *Βασιλεία τοῦ θεοῦ*, Heidelberg 1926, p. 178; J. E. STEINMUELLER, *A Companion to Scripture Studies*, II, New York 1943, p. 227; S. HERRMANN, *Die prophetischen Heilserwartungen im AT*, Stuttgart 1965, p. 292. Contrast A. H. GUNNEWEG, *Mündliche und schriftliche Tradition der vorexilischen Prophetenbücher*, Göttingen 1959, pp. 47-48; E. NIELSEN, *VT*. XX 1970, p. 193.

the collection of the pericopes, we obtain a coherent message.[1] On the contrary, former works on the redaction of the whole of Dt.-Is. show no clear overall structure.[2] The message we obtain is not only coherent, but an analysis of the matter, according to the genres of the units, reveals the particular function of the main themes of that message.

2. The great quantity of salvation words makes it clear that the central point of the prophet's message is salvation. Basically, salvation consists in a divine intervention, as appears from the verbal substantiation of the oracle and the motif II, 1 of the proclamation. According to the nominal substantiation (I am God, etc.), this intervention is even based on an already-existing relation between God and Israel. The same idea appears in the addresses or messenger's formulas, where Yahwe is presented as Israel's maker and *gō'ēl* and Israel as his servant. Concretely, Yahwe's intervention will bring about especially the return of the exiles and a complete restoration, as can be seen in the motifs of outcome (B motifs and II, 2).[3]

As we saw at the end of chapter II, the message of Dt.-Is. is theocentric, which is most clearly expressed in the final motif of the proclamation of salvation. This motif is connected with the point of the trial speeches against the nations. Here the prophet defends Yahwe's unique divinity against the pagan claims. Hence the importance of the strict monotheism as one of the main themes of his message, being the point of an important genre among his prophecies. His monotheism is based on history, since the prediction proof is the main argument in his trial speeches. This is another point of contact

---

[1] Contrast J. van der Ploeg, "De literaire genres van het OT in het algemeen", *De wereld van de Bijbel,* Utrecht 1964, pp. 344-345.

[2] I am convinced that the collection of the pericopes in Dt.-Is. is secondary, and does not show any structure. The units have been collected according to purely external standards (Catchwords, similarity of subject); cf. S. Mowinckel, "Die Struktur des deuterojesajanischen Buches", *ZAW.* XLIX 1931, pp. 87-112, 242-260; J. Lindblom, *Prophecy in Ancient Israel,* Oxford 1962, pp. 267-270. For different ideas about the structure of the book, cf. G. E. Wright, *Isaiah,* p. 134 (an inner logic in the arrangement of the materials); A. Weiser, *Einleitung,* p. 178 (no "innerlich fortschreitender Gedankenzusammenhang", but "eine gewisse zeitliche und sachliche Ordnung"); C. Westermann, *Forschung,* pp. 164-165 (a deliberate, orderly arrangement); K. Elliger, *Deuterojesaja,* p. 232 and G. Fohrer, *TRu.* XIX 1951, pp. 299-300 (small orderly compositions of units within a large, loose collection); H. Gunkel, *Die Propheten als Schriftsteller,* p. XLIV and V. de Leeuw, *De Ebed Jahweh-profetieën,* pp. 115-116 (no arrangement).

[3] Cf. Ch. II, § 4,2.

between the genre and the proclamation of salvation: the final motif of the latter expresses the idea that Yahwe's glory will appear from his present and future intervention, just as his divinity was shown formerly in the historical fulfilment of his predictions: to foretell is to control history.[1]

As we have seen in the third paragraph of the third chapter, the disputations are the means employed by the prophet to counteract the incredulity that his salvific message would encounter. They show that Yahwe is able to deliver his people and that he is sovereign in disposing of the means to do so. They suppose the thesis which is defended in the trial speeches against the nations. Their arguments, too, are mainly historical (Yahwe rules history, the prediction proof), but they betray a substantial interest in Yahwe's creative power also. Both creation and history reveal Yahwe's divine sovereignty and they are intimately connected.[2]

Another defence of the salvific message is to be found in the trial speeches against Israel. In these pericopes, Yahwe rejects the accusation of having abandoned his people with the argument that Israel's sins obliged him to punish them. Here the prophet is in the line of the classical *rîb* of pre-exilic prophecy.

3. More than once I have insisted on the hymnic character of Dt.-Isaiah's oracles. He even has some short hymns distributed among his prophecies (Is. xliii 10-13; xliv 23; xlv 8 (?); xlix 13; lii 9-10; liv 1-3).[3] I did not analyze these passages in detail, but it suffices to read them to realize that all of them are connected with the message as treated above. The prophet invites his hearers to render praise or to exult, because Yahwe attacks his enemies (xlii 10-13), because he delivers and comforts his people (*g'l*, *nḥm*, *rḥm*, *yᵉšûʿâ*: xliv 23; xlix 13; lii 9-10), because the city of Jerusalem will be inhabited again (liv 1-3).

In the other genres, the hymnic style appears especially in the

---

[1] Cf. J. Ridderbos, *Het Godswoord der Profeten*, II, Kampen 1932, p. 278; S. Herrmann, *o.c.*, pp. 299-300; contrast S. Mowinckel, *Psalmenstudien*, II, pp. 259-260.

[2] Such is also the thesis of C. Stuhlmueller, *Creative Redemption in Deutero-Isaiah.* On this point his argumentation is conclusive, although, in the analysis of individual texts, he sometimes overdoes the historical import of the idea of creation present in them. I discuss some other objections to this work below.

[3] Cf. already H. Gunkel, *Die Propheten als Schriftsteller*, pp. LX-LXI; H. Gressmann, *ZAW.* XXXIV 1914, p. 292.

expansions of the messenger's formula and in the disputations. In the former context, the divine epithets underline the fact that Yahwe is the creator and redeemer of his people, the aim being to strengthen the prophet's message which is contained in the salvation word, viz. that Yahwe is about to deliver them from exile.[1] The hymnic style of his disputations is due to the importance of the prophet's faith in Yahwe as the only God creating his people and the whole world and ruling history in favour of Israel. The hymnic style is very apt to express this enthusiastic faith and hymnic tradition is a source of well-known formulas and concepts expressing this basic belief.

4. The form-critical analysis of Dt.-Isaiah's message offers us precious information about some very important theological themes, which have often been connected with that message, such as monotheism, creation, Exodus-typology, universalism and eschatology.

It has always been stressed that the strictest monotheism is one of the main themes of our prophet. "Nevertheless", as N. H. SNAITH rightly remarks, "this theme also is subservient to the declaration of the coming return".[2] This is clear when we consider the fact that the theme occurs in the disputations, where it provides an argument against those who suppose Yahwe incapable of doing anything on behalf of his chosen people. But in one genre, viz. the trial speech against the nations, monotheism is the point of the pericopes. We thus should not overstress the subordination of it to the message of return. The prophet expounds his monotheistic faith *ex professo*. In this sense, S. HERRMANN is right to some extant in mentioning two main points of Dt.-Isaiah's message: the people returns and Yahwe alone is God.[3] I think that the only way to explain the vigorous and often satirical attacks against the gods is to suppose that the prophet wants to combat apostasy, which must have existed among the exiles, in some degree at least.

According to Dt.-Is., creation is connected with monotheism, since Yahwe is the only creating God. Creation faith has a subordinate role, as the prophet argues from it in order to establish a foundation for faith in redemption. Such is certainly true with respect to the

---

[1] Cf. pp. 68-69.

[2] N. H. SNAITH, *Isaiah 40-66* (*SVT.* XIV), Leiden 1967, p. 149.

[3] P. AUVRAY - J. STEINMANN, *Isaïe*, p. 15; S. HERRMANN, *Die prophetischen Heilserwartungen*, p. 295: "Die heilsbotschaft Deuterojesajas konzentriert sich auf diese beiden Hauptpunkte: Das Volk kehrt heim, und Jahweh allein ist Gott".

disputations.[1] C. STUHLMUELLER, who has written the most recent study on the subject of creation in Dt.-Is., asserts in the conclusion of his sixth chapter that "Dt.-Is. never argued from the basis of Yahwe Creator".[2] Such a statement would not have been made if the form-critical approach to the text (esp. of the disputations) had been followed more closely. STUHLMUELLER is right in stressing the close connection between creation and salvation or salvation history. That the coming salvation is a new creation according to our prophet, may be true, but this idea is only very implicit. It is not enough to note that our prophet often uses *br'*.[3] All the occurrences of this verb act as substantiations of the salvific message. The only place where the prophet says explicitly that the salvation he announces is a "creation", is Is. xli 17-20. Even in the introduction to the oracles, the idea of creation does not anticipate what the prophet is announcing, as STUHLMUELLER maintains,[4] but it is the foundation of the salvific message of the oracle (cf. what I have written about *bōrē'*, *yōṣēr*, *'ōśeh*, as divine epithets in the expanded messenger's formulas). In general, his argumentation is based too much on an arbitrary arrangement of the texts. In my opinion, R. RENDTORFF is closer to the mark in noting that the idea of creation occurs mainly in two genres: the oracles of salvation and the disputations. He presents the prophet's thought as follows: Yahwe is the creator of the universe and thus he is able to do with this world as he likes (disputation); that he is particularly the creator of Israel, explains why he uses his power to carry out his will to redeem his people (salvation oracle).[5]

The vast majority of scholars have pointed out that to our prophet the return from Babylon is a new exodus.[6] We have already dealt

---

[1] Cf. G. VON RAD, "Das theologische Problem des alttestamentlichen Schöpfungsglaubens", *BZAW*. 66, 1936, pp. 138-147 = *Theologische Bücherei*, 8, München 1958, pp. 136-147, esp. p. 139.

[2] C. STUHLMUELLER, *Creative Redemption in Deutero-Isaiah*, p. 168. Cf. my review in *Tijdschrift voor Theologie*, XI 1971, pp. 310-311.

[3] Contrast T. C. VRIEZEN, "Prophecy and Eschatology", *SVT*. I 1953, p. 217, according to whom this frequency of ברא "proves that for him the salvation of Israel was no less than a new creation".

[4] C. STUHLMUELLER, *o.c.*, p. 233.

[5] R. RENDTORFF, "Die theologische Stellung des Schöpgungsglaubens bei Deuterojesaja", *ZTK*. LI 1954, p. 8. A somewhat intermediate stand is taken by P. B. HARNER, "Creation Faith in Deutero-Isaiah", *VT*. XVII 1967, pp. 298-306.

[6] Cf. especially A. ZILLESEN, "Der alte und der neue Exodus", *Archiv für Religionswissenschaft*, VI 1903, pp. 289-304; J. FISCHER, "Das Problem des neuen Exodus in

with the subject in the conclusion of chapter II. The interest of our prophet in the exodus is due to his connection with hymnic literature and with the lamentations. The episodes of the Reed Sea, and the exodus in general, are a frequent hymnic motif (cf. Ex. xv; Pss. lxvi 5-6; lxxviii 12-13; lxxxix 10; cvi 7-11; cxiv 3, 5). In a lamentation, the exodus can be presented to Yahwe as a motive for a new intervention (Is. lxiii 12-13; Ps. lxxiv 13-14). Our prophet does it also in the lamentation, li 9-10, with which he introduces a proclamation of salvation. In Dt.-Is., the exodus motif occurs mainly in the proclamations of salvation which reply precisely to a lamentation (xli 17-20; xlii 16; xliii 16-21; xlix 9-13) and once in a salvation oracle (xliii 2). In lv 8-13, it may occur in the short salvation word at the end (vss. 12-13). In xlviii 20-21, the exodus theme is put in a hymnic context, where the reason for joy and jubilation is, beyond any doubt, the deliverance from Babylon. All this means that it is an important feature of our prophet's salvific message. It gives an historical depth to that message: "it is an expression of the unity and continuity of history in Yahwe's purposive and dynamic will".[1] The theme appears either as a reference to the first exodus, in order to give a strong foundation to the expectation of the deliverance, or as the idea of a new or second exodus which is about to come. The new exodus supposes a kind of typology, which the prophet made possible by avoiding any direct reference to concrete persons (Moses, Aaron, Pharao) or places (the Reed Sea, Meriba, etc.).[2] However, the superiority of the new Exodus to the first one is clearly expressed in a text which I did not analyze, lii 11-13: "For you shall not go out in haste, and you shall not go in flight". Here, *lō' beḥippāzôn* is apparently in contrast with the haste of the departure from Egypt (*beḥippāzôn*: Ex. xii 11; cf. also vss. 31-34, 39).[3] Also in other contexts, the quite abundant descriptions of the miraculous changes in nature might

---

Jes. 40-55", *TQ.* CX 1929, pp. 111-130; W. ZIMMERLI, "Le nouvel 'exode' dans le message des deux grands prophètes de l'Exil (Ez. et Dt.-Is.)", *Maqqêl shâqêdh. Hommage W. Vischer,* Montpellier 1960, pp. 216-227; B.W. ANDERSON, "Exodus Typology in Second Isaiah", *Israel's Prophetic Heritage. Essays J. Muilenburg,* New York 1962, pp. 177-195; R. BEAUDET, "La typologie de l'Exode dans le Second-Isaïe", *LavalTPh.* XIX 1963, pp. 11-21.

[1] B. W. ANDERSON, *a.c.*, p. 182.

[2] B. VAN DER MERWE, *Pentateuchtradisies*, pp. 186-187 and 244.

[3] Cf. J. KNABENBAUER, *Commentarius*, p. 285; J. FISCHER, *Das Buch Isaias*, II, p. 130; J. KOENIG, *Bible de la Pléiade*, p. 186; W. ZIMMERLI, *a.c.*, p. 221.

suggest that the new exodus will surpass the first one in quality and importance. We should, however, take into account the fact of poetic exaggeration on this point. At any rate, it is clear that a statement like this: "the movement of the delivered Jews from Babylon to Judah is not described as a second exodus ..."[1] makes little sense.

"It is usually stated that the Second Isaiah is the great universalist: that is, his message and his promises extend to all mankind on a fully liberal scale, and he looks forward to the spread of Israel's faith throughout all the word".[2] According to N. H. SNAITH, there are but three exceptions to this general opinion, namely himself, P. A. H. DE BOER and R. MARTIN-ACHARD. We could add to them now H. M. ORLINSKY, D. E. HOLLENBERG and C. STUHLMUELLER.[3] In an article, I have already expressed some reserves concerning the universalism of our prophet.[4] The form-critical analysis of his prophecies has convinced me that they are not universalist at all. There is some universalism in them, in this sense that Yahwe is considered the creator of the universe, of all nations and kings, of the ends of the earth. But there is no expectation of salvation on behalf of the Gentiles. The salvation announced in the genre of salvation words is meant only for Israel. The fact that the nations will "see" or "know" that Yahwe delivers his people, does not involve their own salvation or conversion (xlix 7). On the contrary, Israel's enemies will be destroyed (xli 11-12, 15-16 ; li 13, 23), the nations will be given as ransom for Israel (xliii 3-4), the idol worshippers will be confused (xlii 17), the

---

[1] J. MAUCHLINE, "Implicit Signs of a Persistent Belief in the Davidic Empire", *VT.* XX 1970, p. 301.

[2] N. H. SNAITH, *SVT.* XIV, p. 154. Cf. e.g. K. MARTI, *Jesaja*, p. XXI; P. AUVRAY-J. STEINMANN, *o.c.*, p. 15; J. LINDBLOM, *Prophecy in Ancient Israel*, pp. 400-402; J. L. MCKENZIE, *Second Isaiah*, p. LXV; P. VOLZ, *Jesaia II*, p. 169; A. LODS, *Les prophètes d'Israël et le début du judaïsme*, Paris 1935, pp. 274-275; H. H. ROWLEY, *The Faith of Israel*, London 1956, p. 185; S. MOWINCKEL, *He that cometh*, Oxford 1956, pp. 148-149 (with some reserves).

[3] N. H. SNAITH, "The Servant of the Lord in Deutero-Isaiah", *Studies in Old Testament Prophecy*, pp. 187-200; esp. p. 191: "The so-called universalism of Deutero-Isaiah needs considerable qualification". — P. A. H. DE BOER, *Second-Isaiah's Message*, pp. 80-101: "The Limits of Second-Isaiah's Message"; R. MARTIN-ACHARD, *Israël et les nations: la perspective missionnaire de l'Ancien Testament*, Neuchâtel 1959, pp. 17-30; H. M. ORLINSKY, *Studies on the Second Part of the Book of Isaiah*, *SVT.* XIV, Leiden 1967, pp. 36-51; D. E. HOLLENBERG, "Nationalism and 'the Nations' in Is. xl-lv", *VT.* XIX 1969, pp. 23-36; C. STUHLMUELLER, *Creative Redemption*, pp. 129-131.

[4] A. SCHOORS, *Recherches bibliques*, VII, pp. 111-112: "En tout cas, il est abusif de faire de l'universalisme la notion-clé de tous les oracles de ce prophète".

nations with their kings will be in Zion's service (xlix 22-23). Even in lv 5, "a nation that knew you not shall run to you", does not involve a conversion; it only expresses Israel's authority over that nation. Is. li 4-5 is most probably not authentic[1].

In the polemical genres, the only text which could require a universalist interpretation is xlv 22-23, but the general trend of Dt.-Isaiah's prophecy and the immediate context of the phrase under consideration do not favour such an interpretation (cf. vs. 25: salvation is for Israel; vs. 24: the other nations will be ashamed).[2]

Of course, some crucial texts concerning this problem do not belong to the genres I have analyzed in the present work, the most important of which are xlv 14-17 and xlii 6 (*le' ôr gôyim*). But the former does not present a real problem, when we consider that the nations will come "in chains" and bow down, that they will be put to shame and confounded, whereas Israel will be saved by Yahwe. To accept that this pericope is in favour of the Gentiles, requires too much goodwill.[3] As to the second text, I dealt with it in my article on the former and the new things: Is. xlii 5-9 is directed to Cyrus, through whom Yahwe will show his glory, for he will be the liberator of the chosen people. This way he will be a light to the nations.[4]

---

[1] For a nationalist interpretation of these vss. cf. N. H. Snaith, *SVT.* XIV, pp. 191-192: קוה and יחל mean "to wait", but not necessarily "to hope", which is correct. According to P. E. Dion, *Bib.* LI 1970, p. 32, Is. li 4-6 is a secondary section imitating vss. 7-8.

[2] J. Koenig, "Tradition iahviste et influence babylonienne à l'aurore du judaïsme", *RHR.* 173, 1968, pp. 1-42, accepts that in Dt.-Is. universalism is only "un universalisme de décor, non un universalisme d'intégration dans la religion d'Israël" (p. 36) except for Is. xlv 22-24 and 14ff. (pp. 38-39). A good nationalist interpretation of Is. xlv 22-24 may be found in N. H. Snaith, *o.c.*, pp. 185-186. Cf. also R. Martin-Achard, *Israël et les nations*, pp. 20-21.

[3] Contrast *Recherches bibliques*, VIII, p. 124. Cf. N. H. Snaith, *o.c.*, p. 185; H. M. Orlinsky, *SVT.* XIV, pp. 33-34. Universalist explanations in J. Knabenbauer, *o.c.*, p. 184.

[4] Cf. A. Schoors, *ETL.* XL 1964, pp. 35-39. H. M. Orlinsky, *o.c.*, pp. 97-117, has an appendix on "A Light of Nations", with discussion of other interpretations. Applying the epithet to the prophet himself, he explains it in the same sense as I do; e.g. p. 100: "... the prophet's task in the service of the Lord is to lead exiled Israel to redemption and thereby cause the nations and their leaders to acknowledge abjectly the omnipotence of Israel's faithful God". Cf. also R. Martin-Achard, *o.c.*, pp. 27-28. According to S. Mowinckel, *He that cometh*, p. 245, note 5, Is. xlii 5-7 is a Cyrus oracle. P. E. Dion, "L'universalisme religieux dans les différentes couches rédactionnelles d'Isaïe 40-55", *Bib.* LI 1970, pp. 161-182, defends the universalist interpretation of some dt.-Isaian texts. In my opinion his argumentation is too rhetorical and not convincing.

Finally, "eschatological" is a term which is very often applied to the message of Dt.-Is.[1] I can be brief about this point, since I have devoted an article to it, in which I rejected the thesis that our prophet is an eschatologist.[2] My analysis of the main genres in Is. xl-lv confirms the soundness of this position. I did not find any eschatology in the genres analyzed in this work.[3] Of course, much depends on the definition of eschatology. In my opinion, it is of no use to call every expectation eschatological. If the prophet does not expect a new and definitive order, it is not an eschatological expectation, for eschatology must have something to do with τὰ ἔσχατα, otherwise it does not have any definite meaning at all. The *Nulpunktsituation*, which might be a constitutive element of eschatology, does not suffice to define it, *pace* G. von Rad.[4] According to Dt.-Is., Israel will still have to face enemies, and it is not said that the coming deliverance will be the last of history. The elements which have been explained in an eschatological sense, are only metaphors and figurative speech to describe a simple historical event. The return from Babylon, irrespective of how large it looms in the prophet's view, is not, strictly speaking, an eschatological event. Also the binome "former things—new things"

---

[1] J. Knabenbauer, *o.c.*, *passim*; B. Duhm, *Israels Propheten*, Tübingen 1922, p. 298; W. Rudolph, "Der exilische Messias", *ZAW*. XLIII 1925, p. 111; P. Volz, *o.c.*, p. 31: "Dtjes ist durch und durch eschatologisch gestimmt". L. Glahn, *Die Einheit von Kap. 40-66 des Buches Jesaja*, Giessen 1934, p. 122: "Alles ist bei Dtj. eschatologisch". J. Begrich, *Studien*, pp. 96-114: "Die eschatologische Periode in der Botschaft Deuterojesajas"; T. C. Vriezen, "Prophecy and eschatology", *SVT*. I 1953, pp. 217-227; E. Jenni, "Die Rolle des Kyros bei Deuterojesaja", *ThZ*. X 1954, pp. 245-247; C. R. North, "The Interpretation of Deutero-Isaiah", *Interpretationes ad VT ... S. Mowinckel*, Oslo 1955, p. 139; G. H. Box, "Isaiah", *Encyclopaedia Britannica*, 1957, vol. 12, p. 702; G. E. Wright, *Isaiah*, p. 92; G. Fohrer, *Das Buch Jesaja*, p. 7.

[2] A. Schoors, "L'eschatologie dans les prophéties du Deutéro-Isaïe", *Recherches bibliques*, VIII, pp. 107-128.

[3] In *a.c.*, p. 128, I wrote: "Il ne convient pas de refuser catégoriquement toute attente eschatologique au prophète". This was an undue concession to the *consensus* among the majority of the scholars. Others who oppose the thesis of the eschatological Dt.-Is.: S. Smith, *Isaiah chs. xl-lv*, p. 105; J. Lindblom, *The Servant Songs in Deutero-Isaiah*, Lund 1951, pp. 94-102; Id., "Gibt es eine Eschatologie bei den alttestamentlichen Propheten?" *ST*. VI 1953, pp. 79-114; S. Mowinckel, *He that cometh*, pp. 153-154: "Any sober historical consideration which avoids the confusion of different ideas will recognize that Deutero-Isaiah himself does not yet present a true eschatology". S. Herrmann, *Die prophetischen Heilserwartungen*, pp. 298-304. Cf. already A. von Gall, *Βασιλεία τοῦ θεοῦ*, p. 188.

[4] G. von Rad, *Theologie des AT*, II, p. 125.

has nothing to do with eschatology, when we place it within the framework of the genres in which it occurs.[1]

The same is to be said about messianism. There is no messianism at all in Is. xl-lv. The only text which can reasonably be alleged in favour of a messianic expectation is lv 1-5, but this text must be explained in a different sense (see comment).[2] Of course, I have not studied here the so-called Servant Songs. But I am convinced that they have nothing to do with messianism: all of them are prophecies about the prophet himself.[3]

The main theme of Dt.-Is. is not eschatology but "consolation", i.e. the announcement of instant deliverance. The frequent use of the root *nḥm* (xl 1 (bis); xlix 13; li 3 (bis), 12, 19; lii 9) is an indication in that direction. Wanting to comfort his people, the prophet insists with all his force that the exile did not abolish Yahwe's faithfulness to his people. This faithfulness is shown again in their deliverance and restoration. This idea binds together salvation words and polemic sections. So we meet again the very traditional title of Is. xl-lv: "The Book of Consolation",[4] and we are in agreement with the final redactor of the book, who put at the head of the book the verse: "Comfort, comfort my people".

---

1 Cf. my article in *ETL.* XL 1964, pp. 19-47; further S. HERRMANN, *o.c.*, pp. 298-300.

2 Already F. DELITZSCH, *Commentar*, p. 405: "Wir finden in diesen Reden nirgends eine eig. messianische Weiss".

3 Cf. S. MOWINCKEL, *Der Knecht Jahwäs*, Giessen 1921 (contrast *He that cometh*, p. 248); H. GUNKEL, "Knecht Jahwes", *RGG.* III 1929, col. 1100-1103; E. BALLA, "Das Problem des Leidens in der israelitisch-jüdischen Religion", *ΕΥΧΑΡΙΣΤΗΡΙΟΝ. Fs. Gunkel*, Göttingen 1925, pp. 214-261; M. HALLER, "Die Kyros-lieder Deuterojesajas", *ibid.*, pp. 261-277; H. SCHMIDT, *Gott und das Leid im Alten Testament*, Giessen 1926; J. BEGRICH, *Studien*, pp. 133-136; A. WEISER, *Einleitung*, pp. 179-180; S. SMITH, *o.c.*, p. 20; H. M. ORLINSKY, *o.c.*, pp. 74-96.

4 Cf. Sir. xlviii 24. The midrash calls Is. xl-lxvi ספר נחמות, "Book of Consolation"; Cf. J. FÜRST, *Der Kanon des Alten Testaments*, Leipzig 1868, p. 15.

LIST OF ABBREVIATIONS

ActOr	*Acta Orientalia.*
AHW	W. von Soden, *Akkadisches Handwörterbuch*, Wiesbaden 1965ff.
ANET	J. B. Pritchard, *Ancient Near Eastern Texts Relating to the OT*, Princeton 1969.
AOT	H. Gressmann, *Altorientalische Texte zum Alten Testament*, Berlin 1926.
Aq	Aquila.
ATD	*Altes Testament Deutsch.*
BHK	R. Kittel - P. Kahle, *Biblia Hebraica*, 11th ed, Stuttgart.
BHS	*Biblia Hebraica Stuttgartensia* (D. W. Thomas, *Liber Jesaiae*, Stuttgart 1968).
Bib	*Biblica.*
BJ	*La Sainte Bible traduite en français sous la direction de l'École biblique de Jérusalem.*
BKAT	*Biblischer Kommentar. Altes Testament.*
BW	*Bijbels Woordenboek*, Roermond ²1954-1957, ³1966-1969.
BWANT	*Beiträge zur Wissenschaft vom Alten und Neuen Testament.*
BZAW	*Beihefte zur Zeitschrift für die alttestamentliche Wissenschaft.*
CAD	*The Assyrian Dictionary of the Oriental Institute of the University of Chicago*, Glückstadt 1956ff.
CBQ	*The Catholic Biblical Quarterly.*
CDC	Cairo Damascus Covenant.
CiTom	*Ciencia Tomista.*
DBS	*Dictionnaire de la Bible. Supplément.*
DISO	C. F. Jean - J. Hoftijzer, *Dictionnaire des inscriptions sémitiques de l'ouest*, Leiden 1965.
DLZ	*Deutsche Literaturzeitung.*
EsthR	Esther Rabba.
ETL	*Ephemerides Theologicae Lovanienses.*
EvTh	*Evangelische Theologie.*
ExpTim	*Expository Times.*
ExR	Exodus Rabba
FRLANT	*Forschungen zur Religion und Literatur des Alten und Neuen Testaments.*
GB	W. Gesenius - F. Buhl, *Hebräisches und aramäisches Handwörterbuch*, Leipzig 1921.
GK	W. Gesenius - E. Kautzsch, *Hebräische Grammatik*, Leipzig 1909 = Hildesheim 1962.
HarvTR	*Harvard Theological Review.*
HUCA	*Hebrew Union College Annual.*
JAOS	*Journal of the American Oriental Society.*
JBL	*Journal of Biblical Literature.*
JNES	*Journal of Near Eastern Studies.*
Joüon	P. Joüon, *Grammaire de l'hébreu biblique*, Rome 1947.
JQR	*Jewish Quarterly Review.*

JSS	*Journal of Semitic Studies.*
JTS	*Journal of Theological Studies.*
K	Ketib.
KAI	H. DONNER - W. RÖLLIG, *Kanaanäische und aramäische Inschriften*, Wiesbaden 1962-1964.
KB	L. KÖHLER - W. BAUMGARTNER, *Lexicon in Veteris Testamenti Libros*, Leiden 1958.
KB^3	ID., *Hebräisches und aramäisches Lexikon zum AT*, 3d ed, Leiden 1967.
KÖNIG	E. KÖNIG, *Hebräisches und aramäisches Wörterbuch*, Leipzig 1936.
LavalTPh	*Laval Théologique et Philosophique.*
LTK	*Lexikon für Theologie und Kirche*, Freiburg 1957-1964.
LXX	Septuagint, according to J. ZIEGLER, *Isaias* (*Septuaginta. Vetus Testamentum Graecum auctoritate Societatis Litterarum Gottingensis editum*, XIV), Göttingen 1939.
ms(s)	manuscript(s).
MT	Masoretic text.
NedTTs	*Nederlands Theologisch Tijdschrift.*
NRT	*Nouvelle Revue Théologique.*
OLZ	*Orientalistische Literaturzeitung.*
OTS	*Oudtestamentische Studiën.*
Pesh	Peshitta, according to *Biblia Sacra juxta versionem simplicem quae dicitur Pschitta*, Beirut 1951.
PG	*Patrologia Graeca.*
PL	*Patrologia Latina.*
Pléiade	*Bible de la Pléiade*, Paris 1961-1962.
Q	Qere.
IQIa	Complete Isaiah scroll of Qumran, according to M. BURROWS, *The Isaiah Manuscript and the Habakkuk Commentary*, (*The Dead Sea Scrolls of St. Mark's Monastery*, I), New Haven 1950.
IQIb	Fragmentary Isaiah scroll of Qumran, according to E. L. SUKENIK, *The Dead Sea Scrolls of the Hebrew University*, Jerusalem 1955.
RB	*Revue biblique.*
REJ	*Revue des Études Juives.*
RES	*Répertoire d'épigraphie sémitique*, Paris 1905ff.
RGG	*Die Religion in Geschichte und Gegenwart.*
RHR	*Revue de l'histoire des religions.*
RScPhilThéol	*Revue des Sciences Philosophiques et Théologiques.*
RSV	*Revised Standard Version.*
ScotJT	*Scottisch Journal of Theology.*
Seb	Sebir.
SIEGFRIED-STADE	C. SIEGFRIED - B. STADE, *Hebräisches Wörterbuch zum AT*, Leipzig 1893.
ST	*Studia Theologica.*
SVT	*Supplements to Vetus Testamentum.*
SvTKv	*Svensk Teologisk Kvartalskrift.*
Sym	Symmachus.
Targ	Targum, according to A. SPERBER, *The Bible in Aramaic*, III, Leiden 1962.
TB	Babylonian Talmud.

TGegw	*Theologie der Gegenwart.*
TGl	*Theologie und Glaube.*
Th	Theodotion.
TLZ	*Theologische Literaturzeitung.*
TQ	*Theologische Quartalschrift.*
TR	*Theologische Revue.*
TRu	*Theologische Rundschau.*
TWNT	G. Kittel, *Theologisches Wörterbuch zum Neuen Testament*, Stuttgart 1933ff.
TZ	*Theologische Zeitschrift.*
UT	C. H. Gordon, *Ugaritic Textbook*, Rome 1965.
Vg	Vulgata, according to *Biblia Sacra iuxta Vulgatam Versionem*, Stuttgart 1969.
VT	*Vetus Testamentum.*
ZÄS	*Zeitschrift für ägyptische Sprache und Altertumskunde.*
ZAW	*Zeitschrift für die alttestamentliche Wissenschaft.*
ZDMG	*Zeitschrift der Deutschen Morgenländischen Gesellschaft.*
Zorell	F. Zorell, *Lexicon Hebraicum et Aramaicum Veteris Testamenti*, Roma 1962.
ZS	*Zeitschrift für Semitistik.*
ZTK	*Zeitschrift für Theologie und Kirche.*

BIBLIOGRAPHY

1. *Commentaries*

Augé R., *Isaïas II* (*La Biblia pels Monjos de Montserrat*, XIII), Montserrat 1936.

Auvray P.-Steinmann J., *Isaïe* (*BJ*), Paris 1957.

Bachmann J., *Praeparation und Commentar zum Deutero-Jesaja*, 3 vol., Berlin 1890-1891.

Bentzen A., *Jesaja*, II, København 1943.

Bratsiotis P. I., *'Ο προφήτης 'Ησαΐας*, I, Athens 1956.

Bredenkamp C. J., *Der Prophet Jesaia*, Erlangen 1887.

Bruno D. A., *Jesaja. Eine rhythmische und textkritische Untersuchung*, Stockholm 1953.

Budde K., *Das Buch Jesaia Kap. 40-66*, in E. Kautzsch, *Die heilige Schrift des Alten Testaments*, I, Tübingen 1922, pp. 653-692.

Calvin J., *Auslegung der Heiligen Schrift*. Bd. 7 *Jesaja* (trad. W. Boudriot), Neukirchen 1949.

Cheyne T. K., *The Book of the Prophet Isaiah* (*The Polychrome Bible in English*, 10) London 1988.

——, *The Prophecies of Isaiah*, 2 vol., London 1886-1889.

Condamin A., *Le livre d'Isaïe*, Paris 1905.

Cyril of Alexandria, *Commentarium in Isaiam Prophetam*, in *PG*. LXX, col. 8-1450.

Delitzsch Franz, *Commentar über das Buch Jesaia* (*Biblischer Commentar über das Alte Testament*, III, 1), Leipzig 1889.

Dennefeld L., *Isaïe - Jérémie - Lam. - Baruch - Ezéchiel - Daniel*, (Pirot, *La sainte bible*, VII), Paris 1946.

Dillmann A., *Der Prophet Jesaia*, Leipzig 1890.

Döderlein J. C., *Esaias ex recensione textus hebraei ad fidem Codicum Manuscriptorum et Versionum antiquarum latine vertit Notasque varii Argumenti subiecit*, Altdorf 1775, 2d ed., Neurenberg 1789.

Duhm B., *Das Buch Jesaia* (*Handkommentar zum Alten Testament*, III, 1), Göttingen 1902.

Elliger K., *Jesaja II* (*BKAT*. XI), Neukirchen 1970-1971.

Ewald H., *Die Propheten des Alten Bundes erklärt*, II, Stuttgart 1841.

Feldmann F., *Das Buch Isaias*, II, Münster 1926.

Fischer J., *Das Buch Isaias übersetzt und erklärt* (*Die Hl. Schrift des AT*, VII, 2), Bonn 1939.

Fohrer G., *Das Buch Jesaja. Bd. III, Kap. 40-66 ausgelegt*, Zürich 1964.

Frey H., *Das Buch der Weltpolitik Gottes. Kap. 40-55 des Buches Jesaja*, Stuttgart 1954.

Friedlaender M., *The Commentary of Ibn Ezra on Isaiah*, London 1873-1877; reprint: New York 1964.

Garcia Cordero M., *Libros Proféticos* (*Biblia Comentada*, III), Madrid 1961.

Grotius H., *Annotationes ad Esajam*, in *Opera Theologica*, t. I, Londini 1679, pp. 275-342.

Haymo of Halberstadt, *Commentaria in Isaiam*, in *PL*. CXVI.

Henne E., *Der Prophet Isaias*, in *Das Alte Testament aus dem Grundtext übersetzt und erklärt*, Paderborn 1936, II, pp. 519-666.

Hoonacker A. Van, *Het boek Isaias. Vertaald uit het Hebreeuwsch en in doorlopende aantekeningen verklaard*, Brugge 1932.

IBN EZRA, cf. FRIEDLAENDER M.

JEROME, *Commentariorum in Isaiam prophetam libri XVIII*, in *PL.* XXIV, col. 17-704.

KISSANE E. J., *The Book of Isaiah, Translated from a critically Revised Hebrew Text with Commentary*, II, Dublin 1943.

KNABENBAUER J., *Commentarius in Isaiam prophetam. Pars altera*, Parisiis 1887.

KNOBEL A., *Der Prophet Jesaia* (*Kurzgefasstes exegetisches Handbuch zum AT*, V), Leipzig 1843.

KÖNIG E., *Das Buch Jesaja, eingeleitet, übersetzt und erklärt*, Gütersloh 1926.

LESLIE E. A., *Isaiah. Chronologically arranged, translated and interpreted*, New York 1963.

LEVY R., *Deutero-Isaiah: A Commentary together with a Preliminary Essay on Deutero-Isaiah's Influence on Jewish Thought*, London 1925.

LOISY A., *La consolation d'Israël* (*Second Isaïe*). *Traduction nouvelle avec introduction et notes*, Paris 1927.

LOWTH R., *Isaiah. A new translation with a preliminary dissertation and notes critical, philological and explanatory*, London 1778.

LUTHER M., *In Esaiam Scholia ex praelectionibus collecta*, in ID., *Werke*, XXV, Weimar 1902.

LUZZATTO S. D., *Il Profeta Isaia volgarizzato e commentato ad uso degli Israeliti*, Padova 1867.

MCKENZIE J. L., *Second Isaiah. Introduction, Translation and Notes* (*Anchor Bible*, 20), Garden City 1968.

MARTI K., *Das Buch Jesaja*, Tübingen 1900.

MUILENBURG J., *The Book of Isaiah, Chapters 40-66* in *The Interpreter's Bible*, V, New York 1956, pp. 381-773.

NÄGELSBACH C. W. E., *Der Prophet Jesaia* (*Theologisch-homiletisches Bibelwerk*, 14), Bielefeld 1877.

NORTH C. R., *Isaiah 40-55*, London 1952.

——, *The Second Isaiah*, Oxford 1965.

PENNA A., *Isaia*, Torino 1958.

REUSS E., *Les Prophètes*, II, Paris 1876.

RIDDERBOS J., *Het Godswoord der Profeten. II. Jesaja*, Kampen 1932.

ROSENMÜLLER E. F. C., *Scholia in Vetus Testamentum. Partis tertiae Jesajae vaticinia continentis Volumen tertium*, Lipsiae 1834.

SIMON U. E., *A Theology of Salvation. A Commentary on Isaiah 40-55*, London 1953.

SMITH G. A., *The Book of Isaiah*, II, London 1890.

STEINMANN J., *Le Livre de la Consolation d'Israël et les prophètes de l'exil* (*Lectio divina*, 28), Paris 1960.

THEODORE OF HERACLEA, *Ex interpretatione in Isaiam*, in *PG.*, XVIII, col. 1307-1378.

THEXTON S. C., *Isaiah 40-66* (*Epworth Preacher's Commentaries*, 5) London 1959.

THOMAS AQUINAS, *In Isaiam Prophetam*, Romae 1880.

TORREY C. C., *The Second Isaiah. A New Interpretation*, New York 1928.

VITRINGA C., *Commentarium in librum Prophetiarum Jesaiae... cum prolegomenis*, Leovardiae 1724.

VOLZ P., *Jesaja II, übersetzt und erklärt* (*Komm. zum AT*, 9, 2), Leipzig 1932.

WESTERMANN C., *Das Buch Jesaia. Kapitel 40-66* (*ATD.* 19), Göttingen 1966.

WRIGHT G. E., *Isaiah* (*The Layman's Bible Commentaries*), London 1964.

ZIEGLER J., *Isaias* (*Echterbibel, AT*, 5), Würzburg 1948.

2. *Studies on Deutero-Isaiah*

Allegro J. M., "The Meaning of בין in Isaiah xliv 4", *ZAW*. LXIII 1951, pp. 154-156.
Allis O. T., *The Unity of Isaiah*, Philadelphia 1950.
Anderson B. W., "Exodus Typology in Second Isaiah", *Israel's Prophetic Heritage, Essays... J. Muilenburg*, New York 1962, pp. 177-195.
Balla E., "Jesaja und Jesajabuch", *RGG.*, III, Tübingen 1929, col. 93-103.
Banwell B. O., "A Suggested Analysis of Isaiah xl-lxvi", *ExpTim*. LXXVI 1965, p. 166.
Beaudet R., "La typologie de l'Exode dans le Second Isaïe", *LavalTPh*. XIX 1963, pp. 11-21.
Begrich J., *Studien zu Deuterojesaja* (*BWANT*. 77), Stuttgart 1938; reprint in *Theologische Bücherei*, 20, München 1963.
Bentzen A., "On the Idea of 'the Old' and 'the New' in Deutero-Isaiah", *ST*. I 1947, pp. 183-187.
Bewer J. A., "Textkritische Bemerkungen zum AT", *Festschrift Bertholet*, Tübingen 1950, pp. 65-76.
Blank S. H., "Studies in Deutero-Isaiah", *HUCA*. XV 1940-1941, pp. 1-46.
Blenkinsopp J., "The Unknown Prophet of the Exile", *Scripture*, XIV 1962, pp. 81-90, 109-118.
Boer P. A. H. de, *Second-Isaiah's Message* (*OTS*. XI), Leiden 1956.
Briggs C. A., "An Analysis of Isaiah 40-62", *Old Testament and Semitic Studies in Memory of W. R. Harper*, I, Chicago 1908, pp. 65-111.
Buttenwieser M., "Where did Deutero-Isaiah live ?" *JBL*. XXXVIII 1919, pp. 94-112.
Cannon W. W., "Isaiah c. 57, 14-21; cc. 60-62", *ZAW*. LII 1934, pp. 75-77.
Caspari W., *Lieder und Gottessprüche der Rückwanderer* (*Jes. 40-55*) (*BZAW*. 65), Giessen 1934.
Cheyne T. K., "Critical Problems of the Second Part of Isaiah", *JQR*. III 1891, pp. 587-603.
——, *Introduction to the Book of Isaiah*, London 1895.
Cobb W. C., "On integrating the Book of Isaiah", *JBL*. XX 1901, pp. 77-100.
Coppens J., "Nieuw licht over de Ebed-Jahweh-liederen", *Pro Regno. Pro Sanctuario*, Nijkerk 1950, pp. 115-123.
Couroyer B., "Is. 40, 12", *RB*. LXXIII 1966, pp. 186-196.
Cramer K., "Der Begriff צדקה bei Tritojesaja", *ZAW*. XXVII 1907, pp. 79-99.
Creager H. L., "The Grace of God in Second Isaiah", *Biblical Studies in Memory of H. C. Alleman*, New York 1960, pp. 123-136.
Cross F. M. Jr., "The Council of Yahweh in Second Isaiah", *JNES*. XII 1953, pp. 274-277.
Dahl G., "Some Recent Interpretations of Second Isaiah", *JBL*. XLVIII 1929, pp. 362-377.
Dahood M., "Some Ambiguous Texts in Isaias", *CBQ*. XX 1958, pp. 41-48.
——, "Textual Problems in Isaia", *CBQ*. XXII 1960, pp. 400-409.
Davidson R., "Universalism in Second Isaiah", *ScotJT*. XVI 1963, pp. 166-185.
Dion P. E., "Les chants du Serviteur de Yahweh et quelques passages apparentés d'Is. 40-55. Un essai sur leur limites précises et sur leurs origines respectives", *Bib*. LI 1970, pp. 17-38.
——, "Le genre littéraire sumérien de l''hymne à soi-même' et quelques passages du Dt.-Is.", *RB*. LXXIV 1967, pp. 215-234.

——, "L'universalisme religieux dans les différentes couches rédactionnelles d'Isaïe 40-55", *Bib.* LI 1970, pp. 161-182.

Driver G. R., "Hebrew Notes", *JBL.* LXVIII 1949, pp. 57-59.

——, "Hebrew Notes", *VT.* I 1951, pp. 241-250.

——, "Isaianic Problems", *Fs. W. Eilers*, Wiesbaden 1967, pp. 43-57.

——, "Linguistic and Textual Problems: Isaiah xl-lxvi", *JTS.* XXXVI 1935, pp. 396-406.

——, "Notes on Isaiah", *BZAW.* 77, 1958, pp. 42-48.

——, "Problems of the Hebrew Text and Language", *Alttestamentliche Studien, F. Nötscher Festschrift*, Bonn 1950, pp. 46-61.

——, "Studies in the Vocabulary of the OT", *JTS.* XXXII 1930-31, pp. 361-366; XXXIII 1931-32, pp. 38-47; XXXIV 1933, pp. 33-44; XXXVI 1935, pp. 293-301.

Eissfeldt O., *Der Gottesknecht bei Deuterojesaja im Lichte der israelitischen Anschauung von Gemeinschaft und Individuum*, Halle 1933.

——, "The Promises of Grace to David in Is. 55, 1-5", *Israel's Prophetic Heritage, Essays .. J. Muilenburg*, New York 1962, pp. 196-207.

Elliger K., "Der Begriff 'Geschichte' bei Deuterojesaja", *Verbum Dei manet in aeternum, O. Schmitz Festschrift*, Witten 1953, pp. 26-36.

——, *Deuterojesaja in seinem Verhältnis zu Tritojesaja* (*BWANT.* 63), Stuttgart 1933.

Feldmann F., "Das Frühere und das Neue", *Festschrift E. Sachau*, Berlin 1915, pp. 162-169.

Feuillet A., "Isaïe", *DBS.* IV, Paris 1949, col. 647-729.

Fischer J., *Isaias 40-55 und die Perikopen vom Gottesknecht* (*Alttestamentliche Abhandlungen*, VI, 4/5), Münster 1916.

——, "Das Problem des neuen Exodus in Jes. 40-55", *TQ.* CX 1929, pp. 111-130.

Fohrer G., "Zum Text von Jes. xli 8-13", *VT.* V 1955, pp. 239-249.

Francisco C. T., "The Great Redemption", *Review and Expositor*, LI 1954, pp. 155-167.

Gelston A., "Some Notes on Second Isaiah", *VT*, XXI 1971, pp. 517-527.

Giesebrecht F., *Beiträge zur Jesajakritik*, Göttingen 1890.

Ginsberg H. L., "The Arm of YHWH in Is. 51-63 and the Text of Is. 53, 10-11", *JBL.* LXXVII 1958, pp. 152-156.

——, "Some Emendations in Isaiah", *JBL.* LXIX 1950, pp. 51-60.

——, "The Ugaritic Texts and Textual Criticism", *JBL.* LXII 1943, pp. 109-115.

Glahn L. - Köhler L., *Der Prophet der Heimkehr* (*Jes 40-66*), Giessen 1934.

Gozzo S., "De catholicorum sententia circa authenticitatem Is 40-66 inde ab anno 1908", *Antonianum*, XXXII 1957, pp. 369-410.

——, *La dottrina teologica del libro di Isaia* (*Bibliotheca Pontificii Athenaei Antoniani*, 11), Roma 1962.

Graf E., *De l'unité des chapitres XL-LXVI d'Esaïe*, Paris 1895.

Gressmann H., "Die literarische Analyse Deuterojesajas (Kp. 40-55)", *ZAW.* XXXIV 1914, pp. 254-297.

Guillet J., "La polémique contre les idoles et le Serviteur de Yahvé", *Bib.* XL 1960, pp. 428-434.

Haller M., *Das Judentum, Geschichtsschreibung, Prophetie und Gesetzgebung nach dem Exil*, Göttingen 1914.

——, "Die Kyroslieder Deuterojesajas", *ΕΥΧΑΡΙΣΤΗΡΙΟΝ, Fs. H. Gunkel*, I, Göttingen 1923, pp. 261-277.

Hamlin E. J., "The Meaning of 'Mountains and Hills' in Isa 41, 14-16", *JNES.* XIII 1954, pp. 185-190.

Haran M., "The Literary Structure and Chronological Framework of the Prophecies in Is. xl-xlviii", *Congress Volume Bonn* (*SVT*. IX), Leiden 1963, pp. 127-155.

——, בין ראשונות לחדשות, Jerusalem 1963.

Harner P. B., "Creation Faith in Dt.-Is.", *VT*. XVII 1967, pp. 298-306.

——, "The Salvation Oracle in Second Isaiah", *JBL*. LXXXVIII 1969, pp. 418-434.

Herntrich V., "Gottes Knecht und Gottes Reich nach Is. 40-55", *Zeitschrift für systematische Theologie*, XVI 1939, pp. 132-170.

Hessler Eva, "Die Struktur der Bilder bei Deuterojesaja", *EvTh*. XXV 1965, pp. 349-369.

Hollenberg D. E., "Nationalism and 'the Nations' in Is. 40-55", *VT*. XIX 1969, pp. 23-36.

Holmgren F., "Chiastic Structure in Is. 51, 1-11", *VT*. XIX 1969, p. 196-201.

Hoonacker A. Van, "L'Ebed Jahvé et la composition littéraire des chapitres xl ss. d'Isaïe", *RB*. XVIII 1909, pp. 497-528.

——, "Questions de critique littéraire et d'exégèse touchant les ch. xl ss. d'Isaïe", *RB*. XIX 1910, pp. 557-572; XX 1911, pp. 107-114, 279-385.

Itkonen L., *Deuterojesaja metrisch untersucht*, Helsinki 1916.

Jackson R. G., "The Prophetic Vision. The Nature of the Utterance in Isaiah 40-55", *Interpretation*, XVI 1962, pp. 65-75.

Jenni E., "Die Rolle des Kyros bei Deuterojesaja", *TZ*. X 1954, p. 241-256.

Joüon P., "Notes philologiques sur le texte hébreu d'Isaïe 11, 13; 42, 14; 50, 11", *Bib*. X 1929, pp. 195-199.

Kahmann J., "Die Heilszukunft in ihrer Beziehung zur Heilsgeschichte nach Js. 40-55", *Bib*. XXXII 1951, pp. 65-69, 141-172.

Kaiser O., *Der königliche Knecht. Eine traditionsgeschichtlich-exegetische Studie über die Ebed-Jahwe-Lieder bei Deuterojesaja* (*FRLANT*. 70), Göttingen 1959.

Kaminka A., *Le prophète Isaïe*, Paris 1925.

Kedar-Kopfstein B., "Divergent Hebrew Readings in Jerome's Isaiah", *Textus*, IV 1964, pp. 176-210.

Kennett R. H., *The Composition of the Book of Isaiah in the Light of History and Archaeology*, London 1910.

Kissane E. J., "The Land of Sinim (Is 49, 12)", *The Irish Theological Quarterly*, XXI 1954, pp. 63-64.

Koenig J., "La revanche d'Amurru sur Babel", *Ugaritica, VI*, Paris 1969, pp. 333-347.

——, "Tradition iahviste et influence babylonienne à l'aurore du judaïsme", *RHR*. 178, 1968, pp. 1-42, 133-172.

Köhler L., *Deuterojesaja stilkritisch untersucht* (*BZAW*. 37), Giessen 1923.

——, cf. Glahn L.

König E., "Deuterojesajanisches", *Neue Kirchliche Zeitschrift*, IX 1898, pp. 895-935, 937-997.

Kosters W. H., "Deutero- en Trito-Jesaja", *Theol. Tijdschrift*, XXX 1896, pp. 577-623.

Lambert G., "Le livre d'Isaïe parle-t-il des Chinois?" *NRT*. LXXXV 1953, pp. 965-972.

Leeuw V. de, *De Ebed Jahwe-Profetieën; historisch-kritisch onderzoek naar hun ontstaan en hun betekenis*, Assen 1956.

Liebreich L. J., "The Compilation of the Book of Isajah", *JQR*. XLVI 1955-56, pp. 259-277; XLVII 1956-57, pp. 114-138.

Lindblom J., *The Servant Songs in Deutero-Isaiah. A New Attempt to solve an Old Problem*, Lund 1951.

Löhr M., *Zur Frage über die Echtheit von Jesaia 40-66*, Berlin 1878-1879.

McEleney N. J., "The Translation of Isaias 41, 27", *CBQ*. XIX 1957, pp. 441-443.

Margalioth Rachel, *The Indivisible Isaiah. Evidence for the Single Authorship of the Prophetic Book*, New York 1964.

Martini C., *Commentatio philologico-critica in locum Esaiae lii 13-liii 12*, Rostock 1791.

Melugin R. F., "Deutero-Isaiah and Form Criticism", *VT*. XXI 1971, pp. 326-337.

Merwe B. J. van der, *Pentateuchtradisies in die Prediking van Deutrojesaja*, Groningen 1955.

Morgenstern J., *The Message of Deutero-Isaiah in Its Sequential Unfolding*, Cincinnati 1961.

——, "'The Oppressor' of Isa. 51, 13. Who was he?" *JBL*. LXXXI 1962, pp. 25-34.

——, "Two Prophecies from 520-516 BC.", *HUCA*. XXII 1949, pp. 365-431.

Mowinckel S., *Der Knecht Jahwäs*, Giessen 1921.

——, "Die Komposition des deuterojesajanischen Buches", *ZAW*. XLIX 1931, pp. 87-112, 242-260.

——, "Neuere Forschungen zu Deuterojesaja, Tritojesaja und dem 'Äbäd-Jahwe-Problem", *ActOr*. XVI 1937, pp. 1-40.

Murphy R. T., "Second Isaias: the Literary Problem", *CBQ*., IX 1947, p. 170-178.

Nielsen E., "Deuterojesaja. Erwägungen zur Formkritik, Traditions- und Redaktionsgeschichte", *VT*. XX 1970, pp. 190-205.

North C. R., "The 'Former Things' and the 'New Things' in Deutero-Isaiah", *Studies in Old Testament Prophecy*, Edinburgh 1950, pp. 111-126.

——, "The Interpretation of Deutero-Isaiah", *Interpretationes ad VT...S. Mowinckel*, Oslo 1955, pp. 133-145.

——, *The Suffering Servant in Deutero-Isaiah. An Historical and Critical Study*, Oxford 1956.

Orlinsky H. M., "Studies in the St. Mark's Isaiah Scroll", *Tarbiz*, XXIV 1954, pp. 4-8.

—— - Snaith N. H., *Studies on the Second Part of the Book of Isaiah* (*SVT*. XIV), Leiden 1967.

Palache J. L., *The Ebed-Jahwe Enigma in Pseudo-Isaiah. A New Point of View*, Amsterdam 1934.

Ploeg J. S. van der, *Les chants du Serviteur de Jahvé dans la seconde partie du livre d'Isaïe* (*chap. 40-55*), Paris 1936.

Porúbčan Š., *Il Patto nuovo in Is. 40-66* (*Analecta Biblica*, 8) Roma 1958.

Reinwald G., *Cyrus im 2. Teil des Buches Is., Kap. 40-55*, Bamberg 1956.

Rendtorff R., "Die theologische Stellung des Schöpfungsglaubens bei Deuterojesaja", *ZTK*. LI 1954, pp. 3-13.

Rignell L. G., "Jesaja Kap. 50", *SvTKv*. XXIV 1953, pp. 108-119.

——, *A Study of Is. 40-55*, Lund 1956.

Rinaldi G., "Isaias 40, 28c", *Aegyptus*, XXXIV 1954, p. 55.

Rowley H. H., *The Servant of the Lord and Other Essays on the OT*, London 1952.

Rudolph W., "Der exilische Messias", *ZAW*. XLIII 1925, pp. 90-114.

Rüetschi R., "Versuch einer Nachweisung des Planes und Ganges der Prophetie B. Jesaja. Kap 40-66", *Theologische Studien und Kritiken* XXVII 1854, pp. 261-296.

Rutgers A., *De echtheid van het tweede gedeelte van Jesaia*, Leiden 1866.

Saydon P., "The Literary Structure of Isaias 40-55 and the Servant Songs", *Melita theologica* VI 1953, pp. 1-15.

Schelhaas J., *De lijdende knecht des Heeren* (*Het Ebed-Jahwe-probleem*), Groningen 1933.

SCHOORS A., "Arrière-fond historique et critique d'authenticité des textes deutéro-isaïens", *Orientalia Lovaniensia Periodica* II 1971, pp. 105-135.

——, "Les choses antérieures et les choses nouvelles dans les oracles deutéro-isaïens", *ETL.* XL 1964, pp. 19-47.

——, "L'Eschatologie dans les prophéties du Deutéro-Isaïe", *Recherches Bibliques,* VIII, Bruges 1967, pp. 107-128.

——, "Two Notes on Isaiah", *VT.* XXI 1971, pp. 501-505.

——, "The Rîb-Pattern in Is 40-55", *Bijdragen* XXX 1969, pp. 25-38.

——, "Het thema van het vroegere en het nieuwe in Deutero-Isaias", *Handelingen van het XXVe Vlaams Filologencongres,* Antwerpen 1963, pp. 129-133.

SCHROTEN E. N. P., "Het gerundium in Deutero-Jesaja", *NedTTs.* XVII 1962, pp. 54-58.

SEELIGMANN I. L., *The Septuagint Version of Isaiah,* Leiden 1948.

SELLIN E., "Die Lösung des deuterojesajanischen Gottesknechtsrätsels", *ZAW.* LV 1937, pp. 177-217.

SKEHAN P. W., "Some Textual Problems in Isaia", *CBQ.* XXII 1960, pp. 47-55.

SMITH M., "II Isaiah and the Persians", *JAOS.* LXXXIII 1963, pp. 415-421.

SMITH S., *Isaiah, chs. XL-LV. Literary Criticism and History* (*Schweich Lectures 1940*), London 1944.

SNAITH N. H., "The Servant of the Lord in Deutero-Isaiah", *Studies in Old Testament Prophecy,* Edinburgh 1950, pp. 187-200.

——, cf. ORLINSKY H. M.

SONIES K., "Gerechtigheid bij Deutero-Jesaja", *Nederlandse Theologische Studiën,* XXII 1939, pp. 167-171.

SPADAFORA E., "Gli esuli e la seconda parte d'Isaia", *Divinitas* III 1959, pp. 438-450.

STAERK W., *Die Ebed-Jahwe-Lieder in Jes. 40ff.: ein Beitrag zur Deuterojesaja-Kritik* (*BWAT.* XIV), Leipzig 1913.

STENNING J. F., *The Targum of Isaiah,* Oxford 1949.

STEVENSON W. B., "Successive Phases in the Career of the Babylonian Isaiah", *Werden und Wesen des A.T.* (*BZAW.* 66), Berlin 1936, pp. 89-96.

STUHLMUELLER C., *Creative Redemption in Deutero-Isaiah* (*Analecta Biblica,* 43), Rome 1970.

——, "The Theology of Creation in Second Isaias", *CBQ.* XXI 1959, pp. 429-467.

STUMMER F., "Einige keilschriftliche Parallelen zu Jes 40-66", *JBL.* XLV 1926, pp. 171-189.

——, "הַמְסֻכָּן תְּרוּמָה (Jes 40,20) in der Vulgata", *ZAW.* LIII 1935, pp. 283-285.

THOMAS D. W., "'A Drop of a Bucket'? Some Observations on the Hebrew Text of Is. 40,15", *BZAW.* 103, 1968, pp. 214-221.

TORREY C. C., "Isaiah 41", *HarvTR.* XLIV 1951, pp. 129-136.

TREVER J. C., "Isaiah 43:19 according to the first Isaiah Scroll (DSIa)", *BASOR.* 121, 1951, pp. 13-16.

TRUDINGER P., "'To Whom then Will You Liken God?' (A Note on the Interpretation of Is. 40, 18-20)", *VT.* XVII 1967, pp. 220-225.

VOGT E., "Einige hebräische Wortbedeutungen", *Bib.* XLVIII 1967, pp. 57-74.

WALDOW H. E. VON, *Anlass und Hintergrund der Verkündigung des Deuterojesaja,* Diss. Bonn 1953.

——, "*... denn ich erlöse dich*". *Eine Auslegung von Jesaja 43,* (*Biblische Studien,* 29), Neukirchen 1960.

WATERMAN L., *Forerunners of Jesus,* New York 1959.

WESTERMANN C., "Das Heilswort bei Deuterojesaja", *EvTh.* XXIV 1964, pp. 355-373.
——, "Jes 48 und die 'Bezeugung gegen Israel'", *Fs. T. C. Vriezen*, Wageningen 1966, pp. 356-366.
——, "Sprache und Struktur der Prophetie Deuterojesajas", *Forschung am Alten Testament. Gesammelte Studien* (*Theologische Bücherei*, 24), München 1964, pp. 72-170. (Quoted as *Forschung*).
WHITEHOUSE O. C., "The Historical Background of the Deutero-Isaiah", *The Expositor* XXV 1923, pp. 241-259, 321-344, 405-426; XXVI 1923, pp. 108-129.
WHITLEY C. F., "A Note on Isa. XLI, 27", *JSS.* II 1957, pp. 327-328.
——, "Textual Notes on Deutero-Isaiah", *VT.* XI 1961, pp. 457-461.
ZILLESEN A., "Der alte und der neue Exodus", *Archiv für Religionswissenschaft* VI 1903, pp. 289-304.
——, "Israel in Darstellung und Beurteilung Deuterojesajas", *ZAW.* XXIV 1904, pp. 251-295.
——, "Tritojesaja und Deuterojesaja", *ZAW.* XXVI 1906, pp. 231-276.
ZIMMERLI W., "Le nouvel 'exode' dans le message des deux grands prophètes de l'Exil (Ez. et Dt.-Is.)", *Maqqél shâqédh, Hommage W. Vischer*, Montpellier 1960, pp. 216-227.
——, "Der Wahrheitserweis Jahwes nach der Botschaft der beiden Exilspropheten", *Tradition und Situation* (*Fs. A. Weiser*), Göttingen 1963, pp. 133-151.

3. *Form-critical Studies*

BEGRICH J., "Das priesterliche Heilsorakel", *ZAW.* LII 1934, pp. 81-92.
——, cf. GUNKEL H.
BOECKER H. J., "Anklagereden und Verteidigungsreden im A.T.", *EvTh.* XX 1960, pp. 398-412.
——, *Redeformen des Rechtslebens im Alten Testament*, Neukirchen 1964.
CASTELLINO R. G., *Le lamentazioni individuali e gli inni in Babilonia e in Israele*, Torino 1939.
DION P. E., "The 'Fear not' Formula and Holy War", *CBQ.* XXXII 1970, pp. 565-570.
GEMSER B., "The Rîb- or Controversy-Pattern in Hebrew Mentality", *SVT.* III, Leiden 1955, pp. 120-137.
GERSTENBERGER E., "The Woe-Oracles of the Prophets", *JBL.* LXXXI 1962, pp. 249-263.
GUNKEL H., "Die Propheten als Schriftsteller und Dichter", in H. SCHMIDT, *Die grossen Propheten*, Göttingen 1915, pp. XXXVI-LXXII.
—— - BEGRICH J., *Einleitung in die Psalmen*, Göttingen 1933.
HARVEY J., *Le plaidoyer prophétique contre Israël après la rupture de l'alliance. Étude d'une formule littéraire de l'AT*, Bruges 1967.
——, "Le 'Rîb-Pattern", Réquisitoire prophétique sur la rupture de l'Alliance", *Bib.* XLIII 1962, pp. 172-196.
HESSE F., "Wurzelt die prophetische Gerichtsrede im israelitischen Kult?", *ZAW.* LXV 1953, pp. 45-53.
HILLERS D. R., *Treaty-Curses and the Old Testament Prophets* (*Biblica et Orientalia*, 16), Roma 1964.
KÖHLER L., "Der Botenspruch", *Kleine Lichter*, Zürich 1945, pp. 11-17.

——, "Die Offenbarungsformel 'Fürchte dich nicht!' im Alten Testament", *Schweizerische Theologische Zeitschrift* XXXVI 1919, pp. 33-39.

Küchler F., "Das priesterliche Orakel in Israel und Juda", *Baudissin-Festschrift* (*BZAW*. 33), Giessen 1918, pp. 285-301.

Mowinckel S., *Psalmenstudien*. III: *Die Kultprophetie und Prophetische Psalmen*, Kristiania 1922 (= Amsterdam 1961). V: *Segen und Fluch in Israels Kult und Psalmdichtung*, Kristiania 1924 (= Amsterdam 1961).

Rendtorff R., "Botenformel und Botenspruch", *ZAW*. LXXIV 1962, pp. 165-177.

Waldow H. E. von, *Der traditionsgeschichtliche Hintergrund der prophetischen Gerichtsreden* (*BZAW*. 85), Berlin 1963.

Westermann C., *Grundformen prophetischer Rede* (*Beiträge zur evangelischen Theologie*, 31), München 1960.

——, "Struktur und Geschichte der Klage im Alten Testament", *ZAW*. LXVI 1954, pp. 44-80 (= *Forschung*, pp. 266-305).

Widengren G., *The Accadian and Hebrew Psalms of Lamentation*, Uppsala 1936.

Wolff H. W., "Die Begründung der prophetischen Heils- und Unheilssprüche", *ZAW*. LII 1934, pp. 1-21.

——, *Das Zitat im Prophetenspruch*, München 1937.

Würthwein E., "Der Ursprung der prophetischen Gerichtsrede", *ZTK*. XLIX 1952, pp. 1-16.

Zimmerli W., "Ich bin Jahwe", *Fs. A. Alt*, Tübingen 1953, pp. 179-209 (= *Gottes Offenbarung* (*Theologische Bücherei*, 19), München 1963, pp. 11-40).

——, "Das Wort des göttlichen Selbsterweises (Erweiswort), eine prophetische Gattung", *Mélanges Robert*, Paris 1957, pp. 154-164 (= *Gottes Offenbarung*, pp. 120-132).

INDEX OF BIBLICAL REFERENCES

See also the Table of Contents and Table I

ix 11 204
xvi 2, 11 158
xvi 17 137
xxiv 5 196
xxix 2 141

2 Chronicles
i 5 158
vi 14 134, 136
vi 42 148
ix 7 49
xx 24
xx 3-17 34
xx 7 51
xx 22-23 65
xx 23 196
xxi 16 219
xxix 11 153
xxxii 31 195

Sirach
iv 27 21
viii 14 21
x 2 195
xxiv 19-22 146
xxxi 26 57

xxxiii 13 263
xxxvii 25 77
xlii 4 249
xlviii 24 305

2 Maccabees
vii 28 69

Tobias
xiii 16-17 140

Baruch
iv 9 - v 9 37

Matthew
iii 9 160

Luke
iii 8 160

Romans
ix 20-21 263

Apocalypse
xxi 18-21 140

INDEX OF AUTHORS

See also the Table of Contents and the Bibliography